AutoCAD 2006

(ENGINEERING AND ARCHITECTURAL DRAWING HAND BOOK)

AutoCAD 2006

ENGINEERING AND ARCHITECTURAL DRAWING HAND BOOK

P.B. SINHA

2007

Cyber Tech Publications
4264/3, ANSARI ROAD, DARYA GANJ, NEW DELHI-110 002
Phone: 011-23244078 Fax: 011-23280028
Email: cybertechpublications@yahoo.com

AutoCAD 2006: Engineering and Architectural Drawing Handbook

Published by
Gautam Rawat for
Cyber Tech Publications
4264/3 Ansari Road, Darya Ganj
Delhi - 110 002
Tel. 3244078

First Edition 2007

Typeset at

Printed at

Preface

These days everybody wants to learn computers. Not everyone has the time to go to the training institutes for learning. There are lots of people who prefer to buy the computer and try to learn the computer on their own. Either way you learn the computer from the basics. But, there is no book which can teach you from A to Z of computers. Some of them are those which will give you the text which will go above your head and the others would be very childish. So there has always been a demand for a complete book. This book has been written to fill this void.

This book would serve as an ideal tool for someone who is keen to learn about the various aspects of engineering drawing, architectural drawing and even drafting. This books would act as a stepping stone for learning these subjects. This book would provide the first hand knowledge of AutoCAD 2006.

I am indeed debited to the staff of Cyber Tech Publications for their suggestions and encouragement in producing this book in this form.

Suggestions for improvement are always welcomed.

Author

Contents

Introduction to AutoCAD 2006

1

What is AutoCAD?

AutoCAD is a powerful software from Autodesk and is used for creating drawings. We will not be wrong in saying that no Architecture can do his work without using one of the versions of the software. Through a high level of technical innovation and expertise, Autodesk has created a program with unequated features and capabilities, including 3D surface and solid modeling and visualization, access to external databases, intelligent dimensioning, importing and exporting of other file formats, internet support, and much more.

The major disciplines that use AutoCAD are:

- Architectural, Engineering and Construction
- Mechanical
- Geographical Information System
- Surveying and Civil Engineering
- Facilities management
- Electrical/electronic
- Multimedia

The drawing area

The blank area in the middle of the screen, the graphics window or drawing area, is where you draw. You can think of this as a sheet of drafting paper, except that this piece of paper can be any size. At the bottom of the drawing area is a tab labeled Model. You draw on this tab. You use the layout tabs to lay out your drawing for plotting. When you start to draw, you need to specify where to start drawing. One way is to use coordinates. To specify a coordinate, the universally accepted conventions is to put the X-coordinate first, followed by comma, and then the Y-coordinate.

Notice the symbol with two arrows at the bottom-left corner of the drawing area. This symbol is called the User Coordinate System (UCS) icon. The arrows point to the positive directions of the X and Y axes to help you keep your bearings.

In the drawing area, notice the two intersecting lines with a small box at thier intersection. The small box is called pickbox because it helps you to pick objects. The lines are called crosshairs. They show you the location of the mouse cursor in relation to other objects in your drawing.

Menu Commands

From the screen of the AutoCAD 2005, we had seen the various menus which are available in the software. Let us now see what each one of them contains under it.

File Menu

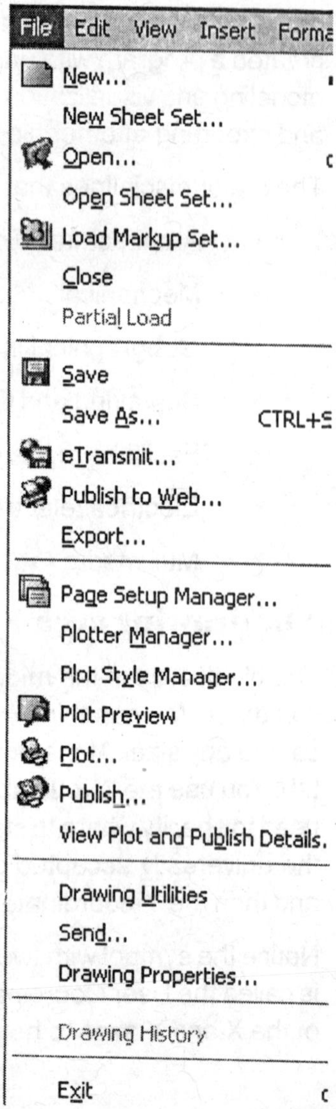

Various options under this menu are as follows:

New

Creates a new drawing file.

New Sheet Set

Creates a new sheet set using the Sheet Set wizard, which has 4 screens, which are shown on the next few pages. Just fill the details and you are ready to use.

Open

Opens an existing drawing file.

Open Sheet Set

Opens an existing sheet set.

Load Markup Set

Opens Markup Set dialog box.

Close

Closes the drawing file.

Partial Load

Displays the views and layers available for specifying additional geometry to load into a partially open drawing. You can select and load geometry from a view or a selected area and from layers. You cannot unload any information that is currently loaded

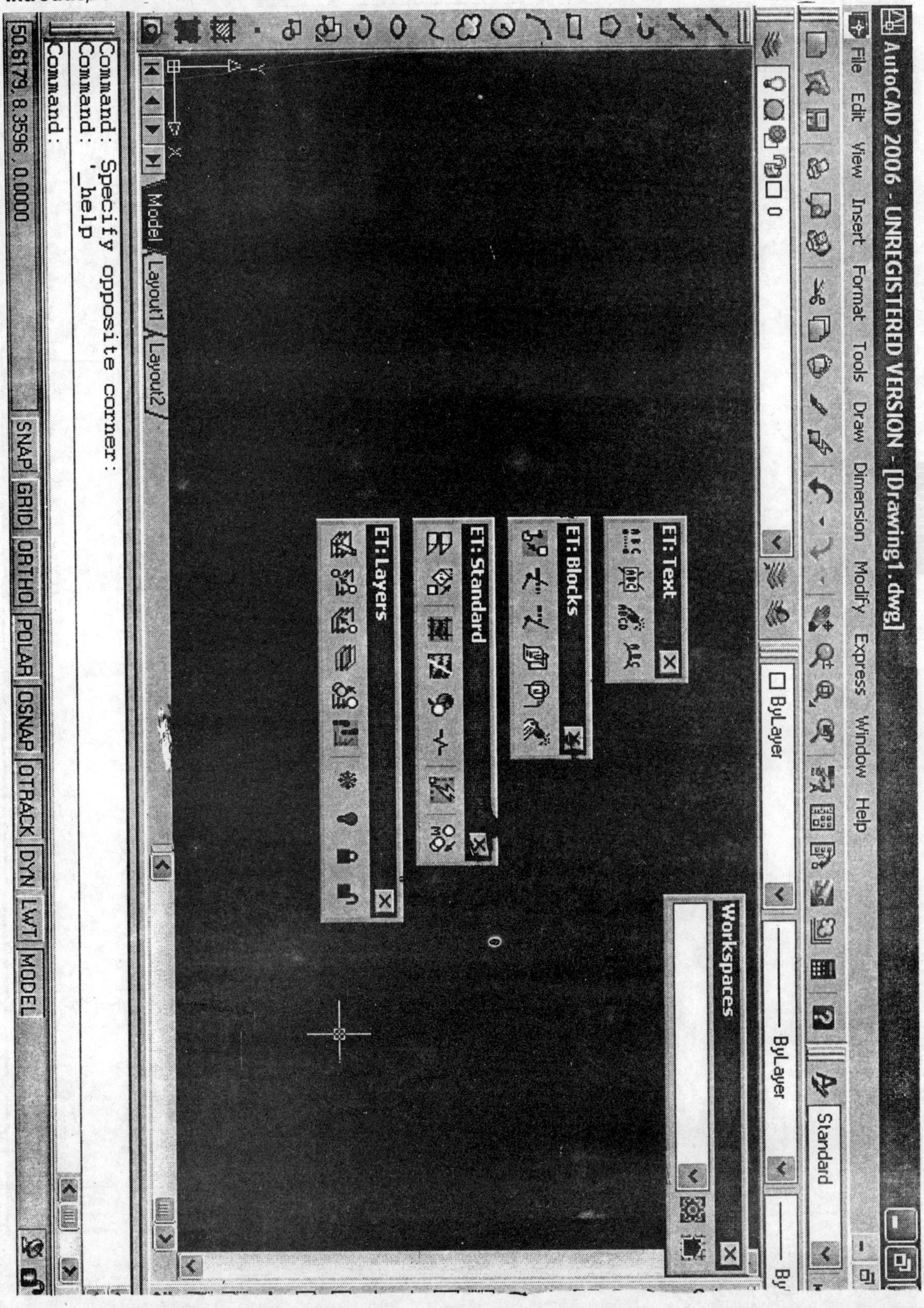
AutoCAD 2006 - UNREGISTERED VERSION - [Drawing1.dwg]
File Edit View Insert Format Tools Draw Dimension Modify Express Window Help
ByLayer
ByLayer
Standard
Workspaces
ET: Text
ET: Blocks
ET: Standard
ET: Layers
Model
Layout1
Layout2
Command: Specify opposite corner:
Command: '_help
Command:
50.6179, 8.3596 , 0.0000
SNAP GRID ORTHO POLAR OSNAP OTRACK DYN LWT MODEL

4

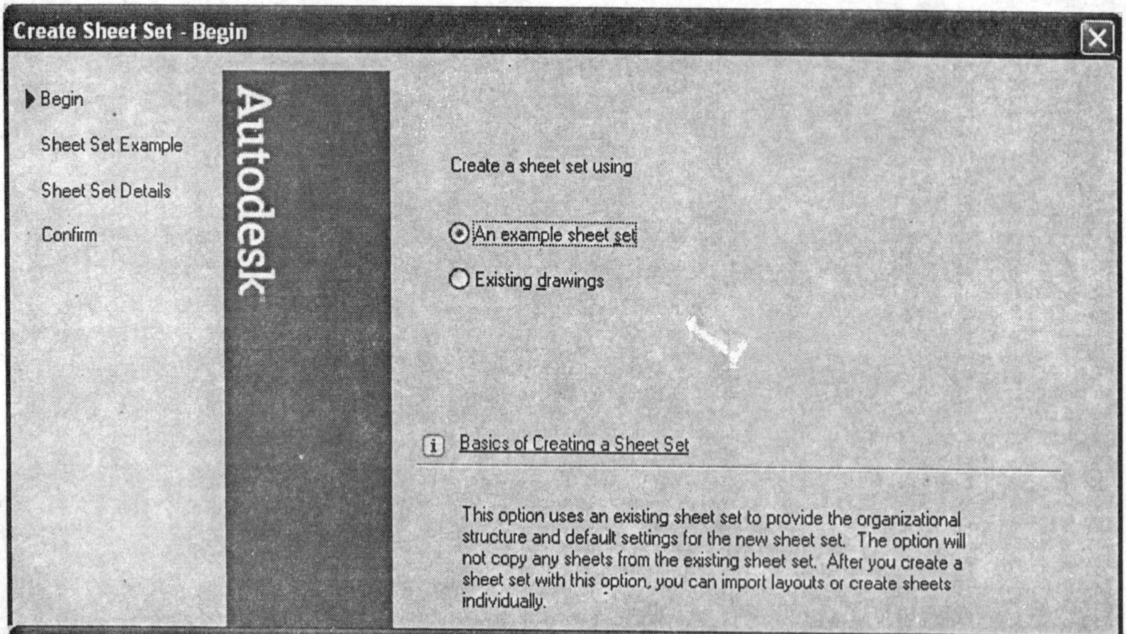
Create Sheet Set - Begin
Begin
Sheet Set Example
Sheet Set Details
Confirm
Autodesk
Create a sheet set using
An example sheet set
Existing drawings
Basics of Creating a Sheet Set
This option uses an existing sheet set to provide the organizational structure and default settings for the new sheet set. The option will not copy any sheets from the existing sheet set. After you create a sheet set with this option, you can import layouts or create sheets individually.

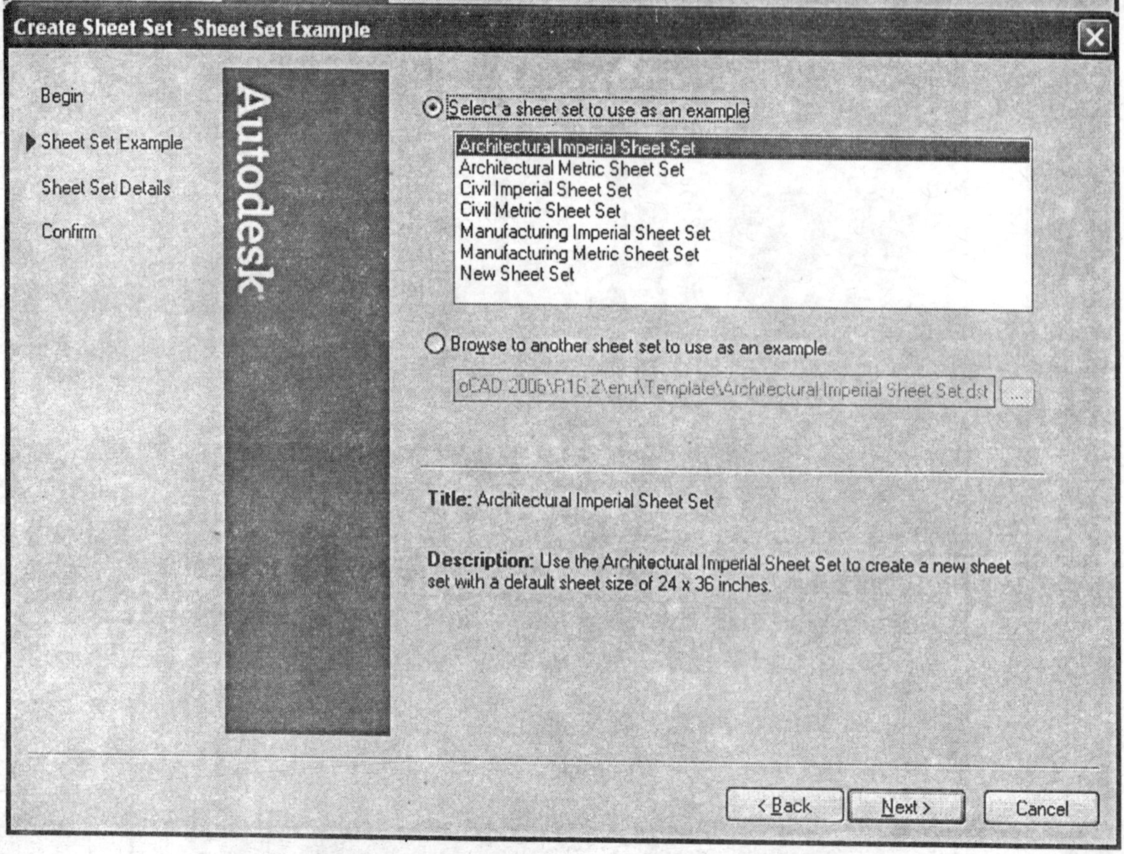
Create Sheet Set - Sheet Set Example
Begin
Sheet Set Example
Sheet Set Details
Confirm
Autodesk
Select a sheet set to use as an example
Architectural Imperial Sheet Set
Architectural Metric Sheet Set
Civil Imperial Sheet Set
Civil Metric Sheet Set
Manufacturing Imperial Sheet Set
Manufacturing Metric Sheet Set
New Sheet Set
Browse to another sheet set to use as an example
oCAD 2006\R16.2\enu\Template\Architectural Imperial Sheet Set.dst
Title: Architectural Imperial Sheet Set
Description: Use the Architectural Imperial Sheet Set to create a new sheet set with a default sheet size of 24 x 36 inches.
< Back
Next >
Cancel

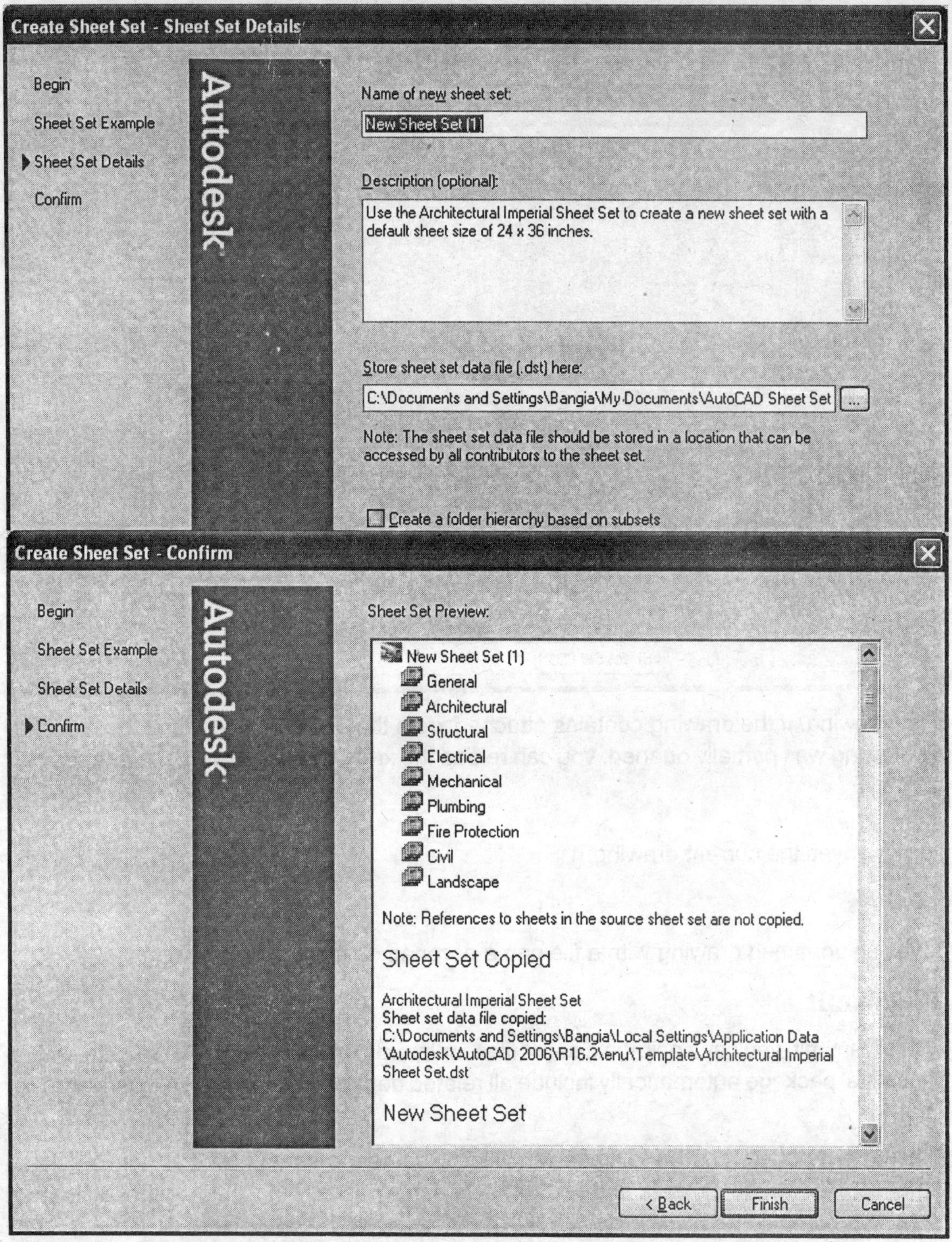
Create Sheet Set - Sheet Set Details
Begin
Sheet Set Example
Sheet Set Details
Confirm
Autodesk
Name of new sheet set:
New Sheet Set (1)
Description (optional):
Use the Architectural Imperial Sheet Set to create a new sheet set with a default sheet size of 24 x 36 inches.
Store sheet set data file (.dst) here:
C:\Documents and Settings\Bangia\My Documents\AutoCAD Sheet Set
Note: The sheet set data file should be stored in a location that can be accessed by all contributors to the sheet set.
Create a folder hierarchy based on subsets
Create Sheet Set - Confirm
Begin
Sheet Set Example
Sheet Set Details
Confirm
Autodesk
Sheet Set Preview:
New Sheet Set (1)
General
Architectural
Structural
Electrical
Mechanical
Plumbing
Fire Protection
Civil
Landscape
Note: References to sheets in the source sheet set are not copied.
Sheet Set Copied
Architectural Imperial Sheet Set
Sheet set data file copied:
C:\Documents and Settings\Bangia\Local Settings\Application Data \Autodesk\AutoCAD 2006\R16.2\enu\Template\Architectural Imperial Sheet Set.dst
New Sheet Set
< Back
Finish
Cancel

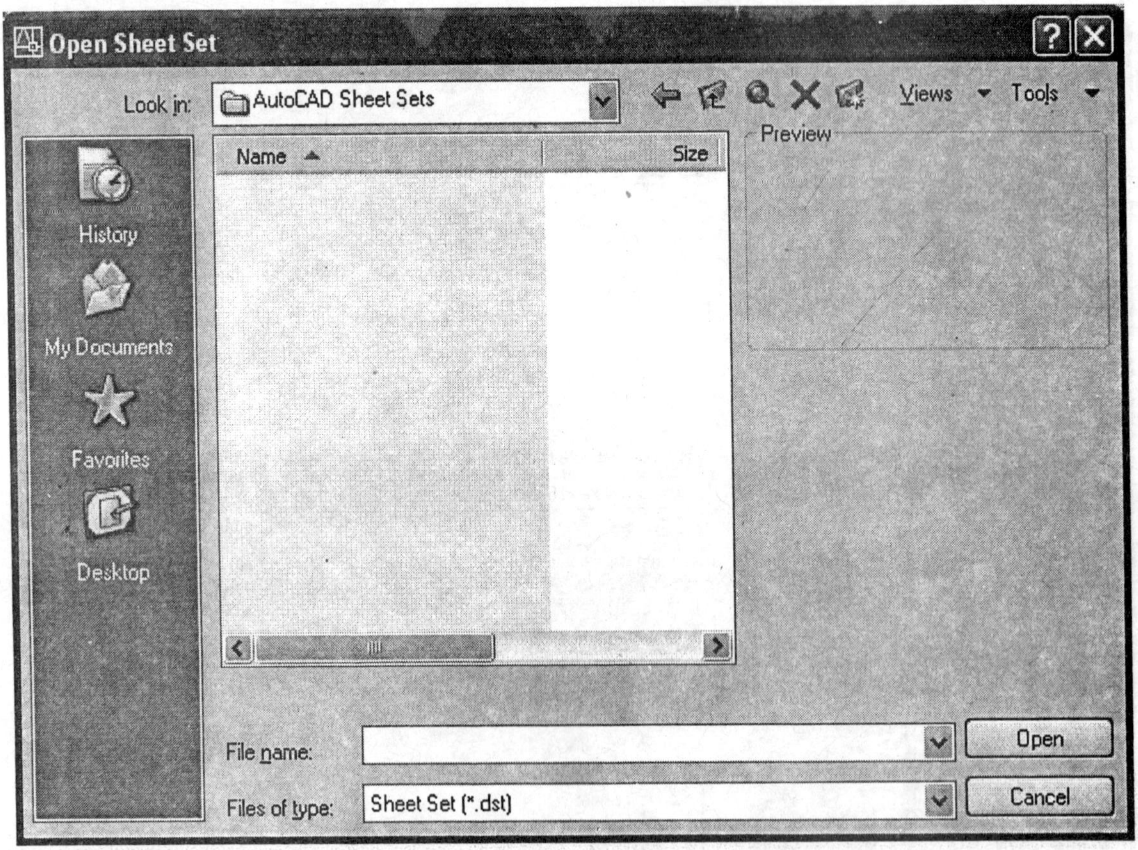

in the drawing. If the drawing contains attached xrefs that were not loaded at the time that the drawing was partially opened, you can reload the xrefs by using the Xref Manager.

Save

Quickly saves the current drawing.

Save As

Saves an unnamed drawing with a file name or renames the current drawing.

eTransmit

With eTransmit, you can package a set of files for Internet transmission. Drawing files in the transmittal package automatically include all related dependent files such as xrefs and font files.

A common problem when sending drawing files to someone is neglecting to include related dependent files such as xrefs and text fonts. In some cases, not including these files can

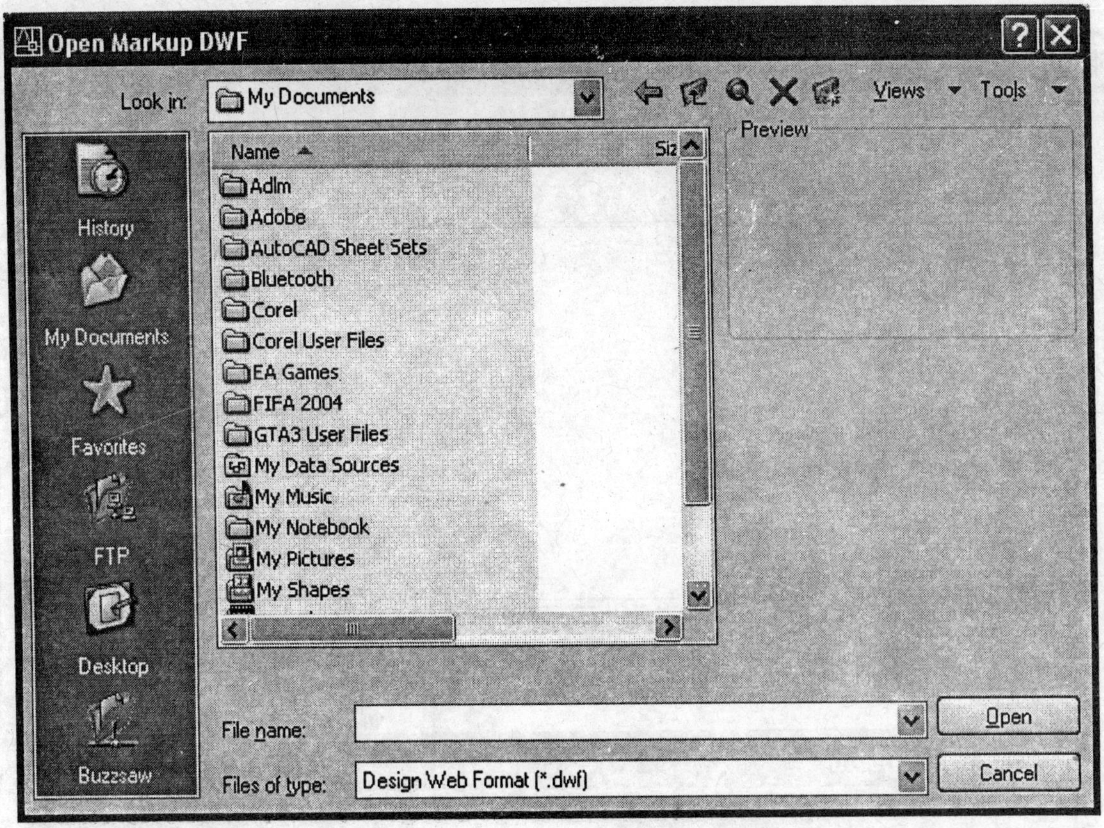

make the drawing files unusable by the recipient. With eTransmit, dependent files are included automatically in the transmittal package, reducing the possibility of error.

Publish to the Web

You can customize the Publish to Web templates provided with AutoCAD by modifying an existing Publish to Web template (PWT) file. You can use any HTML editor or text editor to customize a template. Some of the customizations you may want to make in a template include adding or modifying the following: Images, Text, Hyperlinks, Color, Title, Video, animation, and so on. AutoCAD provides four types of Publish to Web templates that you can customize:

Array of Thumbnails

Creates a Web page containing an array of thumbnail images.

Array Plus Summary

Creates a Web page containing an array of thumbnail images and summary information about an image.

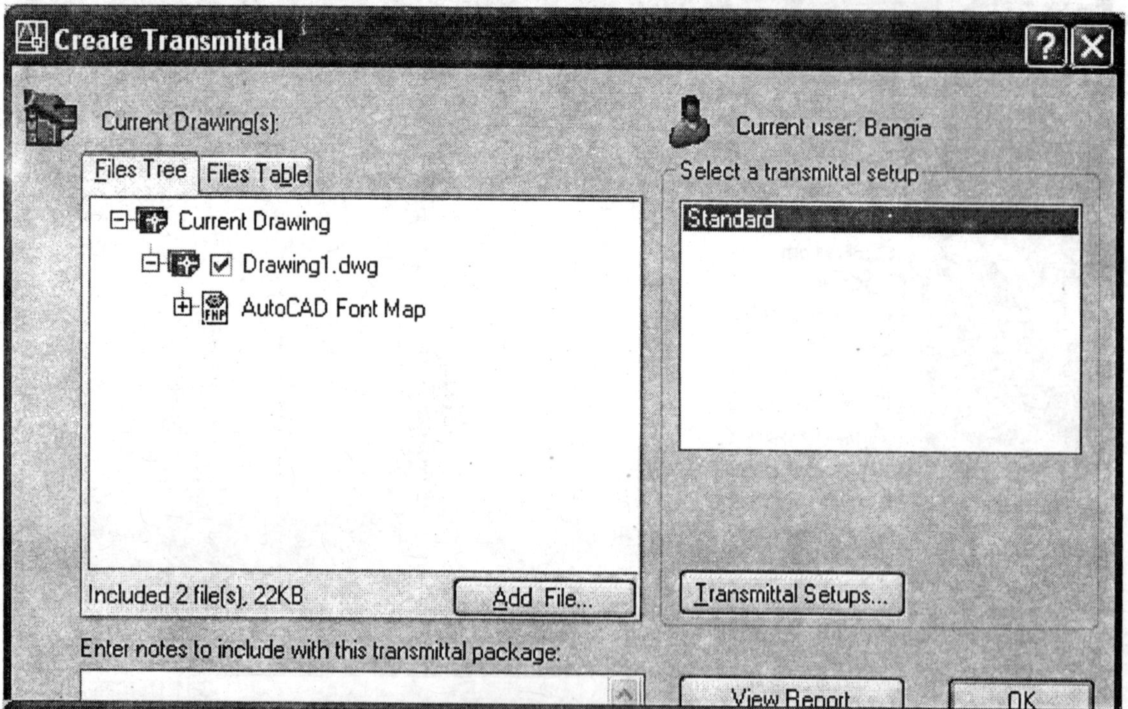
Create Transmittal
Current Drawing(s):
Current user: Bangia
Files Tree
Files Table
Select a transmittal setup
Current Drawing
Drawing1.dwg
AutoCAD Font Map
Standard
Included 2 file(s), 22KB
Add File...
Transmittal Setups...
Enter notes to include with this transmittal package:
View Report
OK

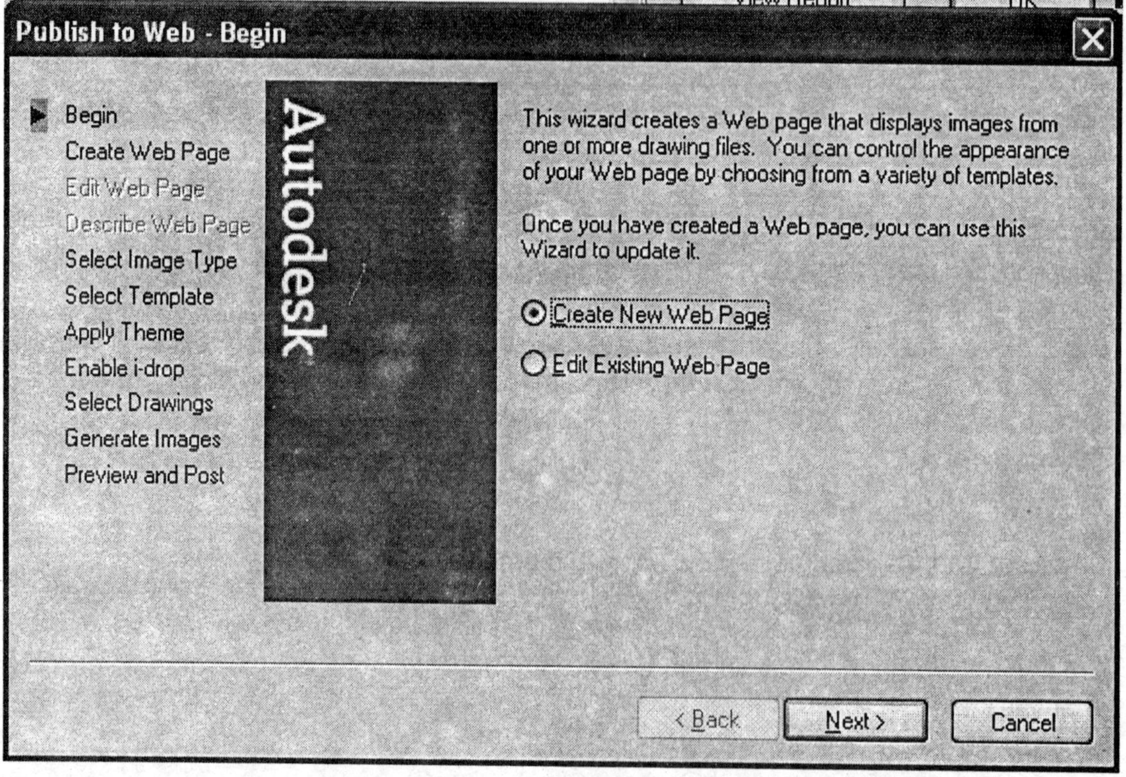
Publish to Web - Begin
Begin
Create Web Page
Edit Web Page
Describe Web Page
Select Image Type
Select Template
Apply Theme
Enable i-drop
Select Drawings
Generate Images
Preview and Post
Autodesk
This wizard creates a Web page that displays images from one or more drawing files. You can control the appearance of your Web page by choosing from a variety of templates.
Once you have created a Web page, you can use this Wizard to update it.
Create New Web Page
Edit Existing Web Page
< Back
Next >
Cancel

List of Drawings

Creates a Web page containing a list of drawings and an image frame.

List Plus Summary

Creates a Web page containing a list of drawings, an image frame, and summary information about a selected image.

Export

Saves objects to other file formats.

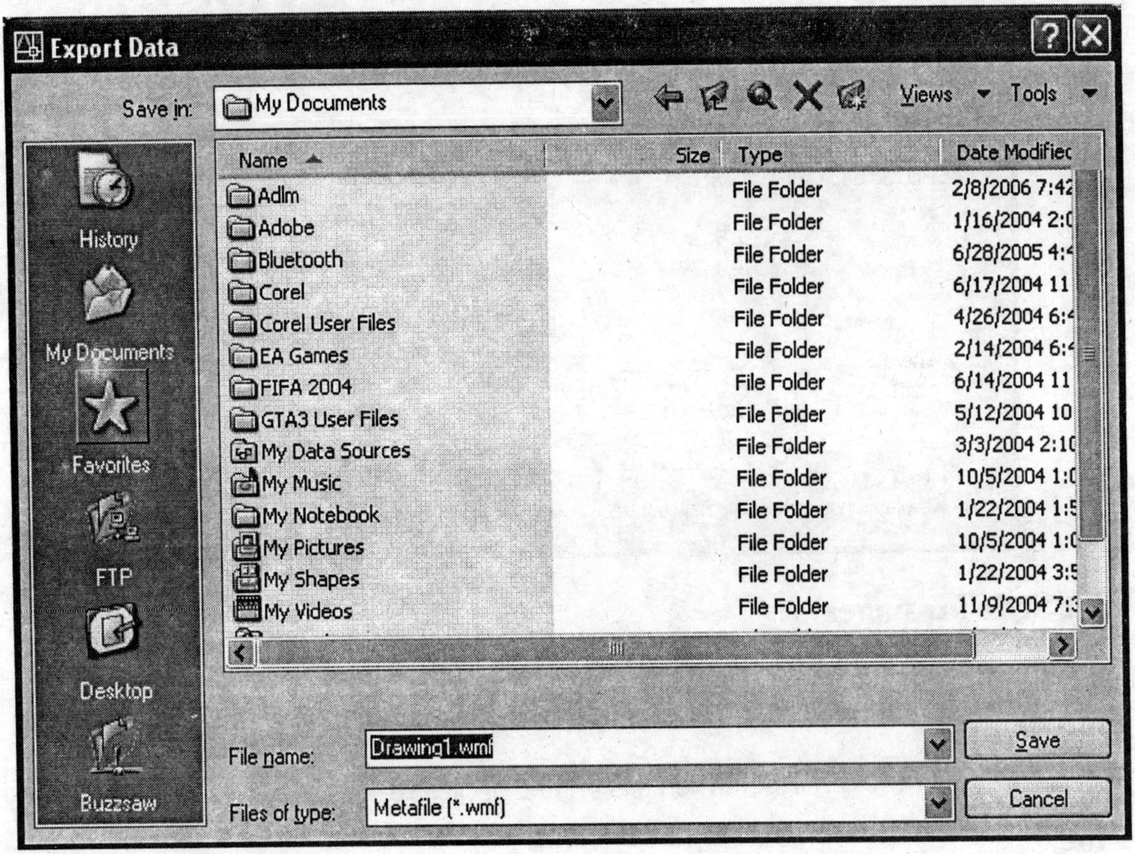

Page Setup Manager

Displays the Page Setup dialog box.

Plotter Manager

Provides access to the Add Plotter wizard and the Plotter Configuration Editor.

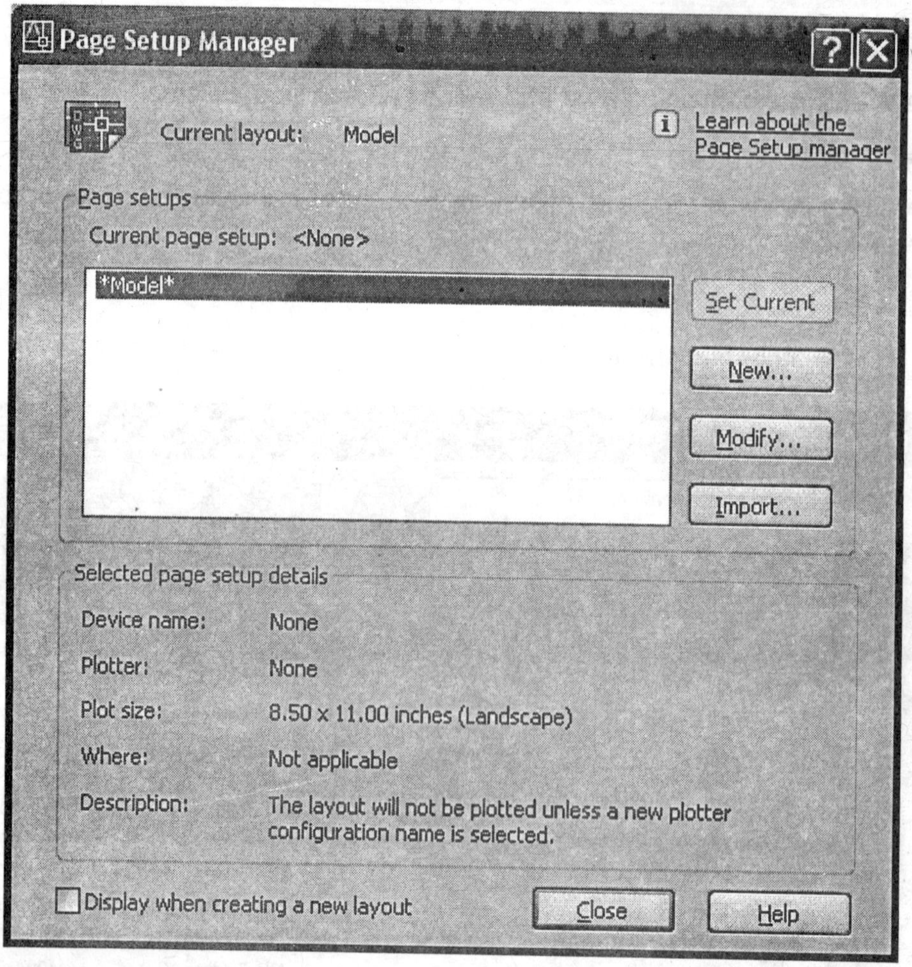

Plot Style Manager

Provides access to the Add Plot Style Table wizard and the Plot Style Table Editor.

Plot Preview

Shows how the drawing will look when it is printed or plotted.

Plot

Plots a drawing to a plotting device or file.

Publish

Creates a single sheet or multi sheet Design Web Format file.

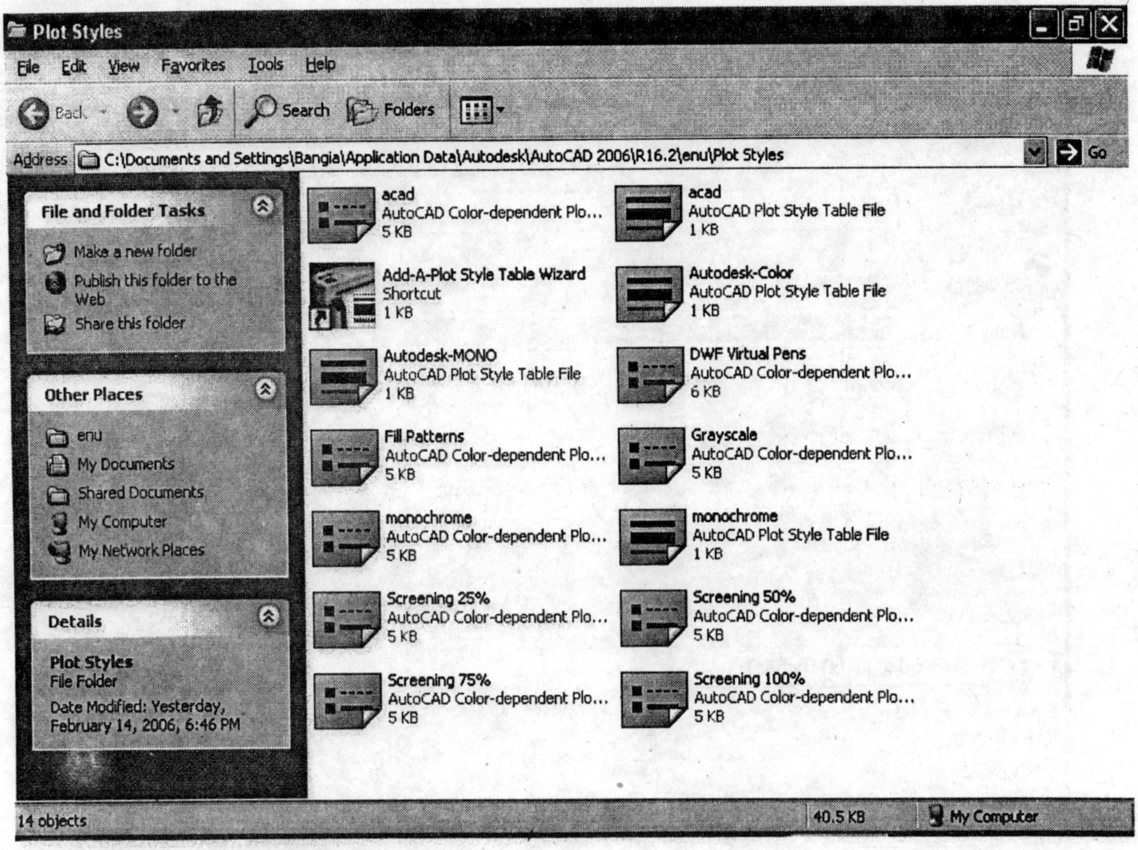

View Plot and Publish Details

You can see the plot and its details on the same page.

Drawing Utilities

This is further divided into the following 3 options as shown below:

Audit

Evaluates the integrity of a drawing.

Recover

Repairs a damaged drawing.

Drawing Recovery Manager..

Calls drawing recovery manager to recover drawing.

Update Block Icons

Generates preview images for blocks displayeـ in Design Center.

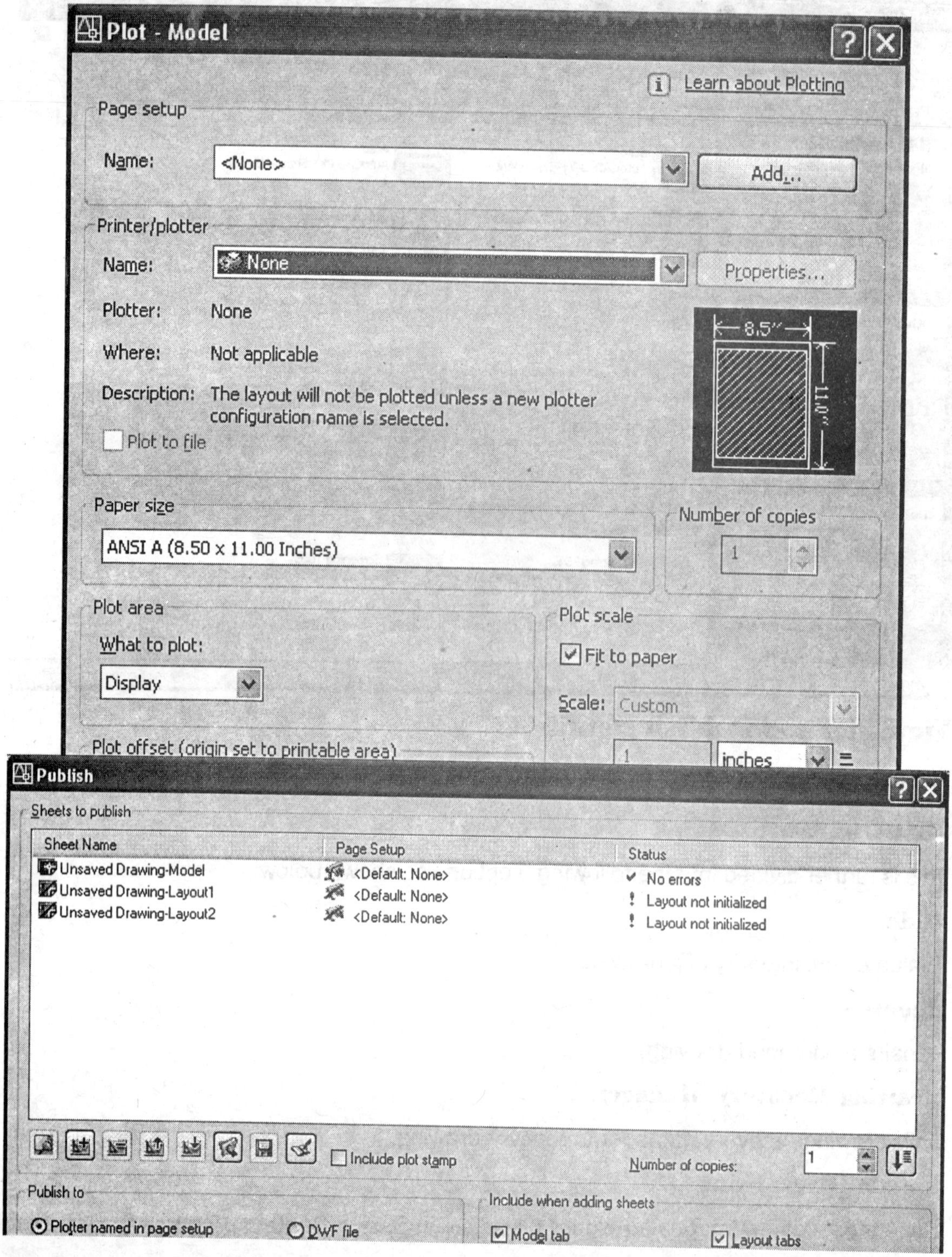
Plot - Model
Learn about Plotting
Page setup
Name: <None>
Add...
Printer/plotter
Name: None
Properties...
Plotter: None
Where: Not applicable
Description: The layout will not be plotted unless a new plotter configuration name is selected.
Plot to file
8.5″
11.0″
Paper size
ANSI A (8.50 x 11.00 Inches)
Number of copies
1
Plot area
What to plot:
Display
Plot scale
Fit to paper
Scale: Custom
1
inches
Plot offset (origin set to printable area)
Publish
Sheets to publish
Sheet Name
Page Setup
Status
Unsaved Drawing-Model
Unsaved Drawing-Layout1
Unsaved Drawing-Layout2
<Default: None>
<Default: None>
<Default: None>
No errors
Layout not initialized
Layout not initialized
Include plot stamp
Number of copies:
1
Publish to
Plotter named in page setup
DWF file
Include when adding sheets
Model tab
Layout tabs

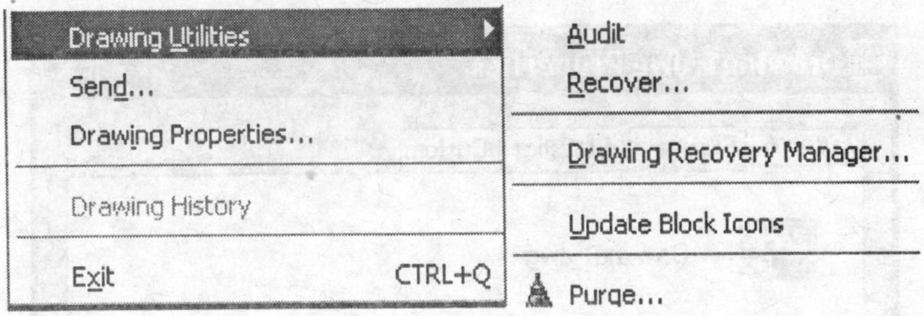

Purge

There are many options under it, they are shown here in the figure.

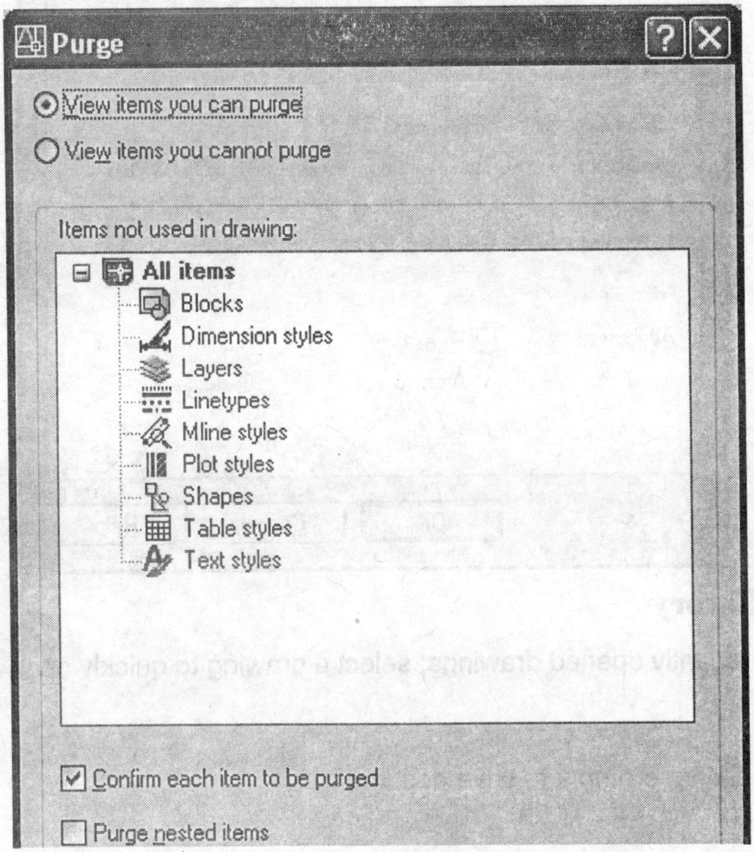

Send

Faxes or emails the current drawing file

Drawing Properties

Sets and displays the properties of the current drawing.

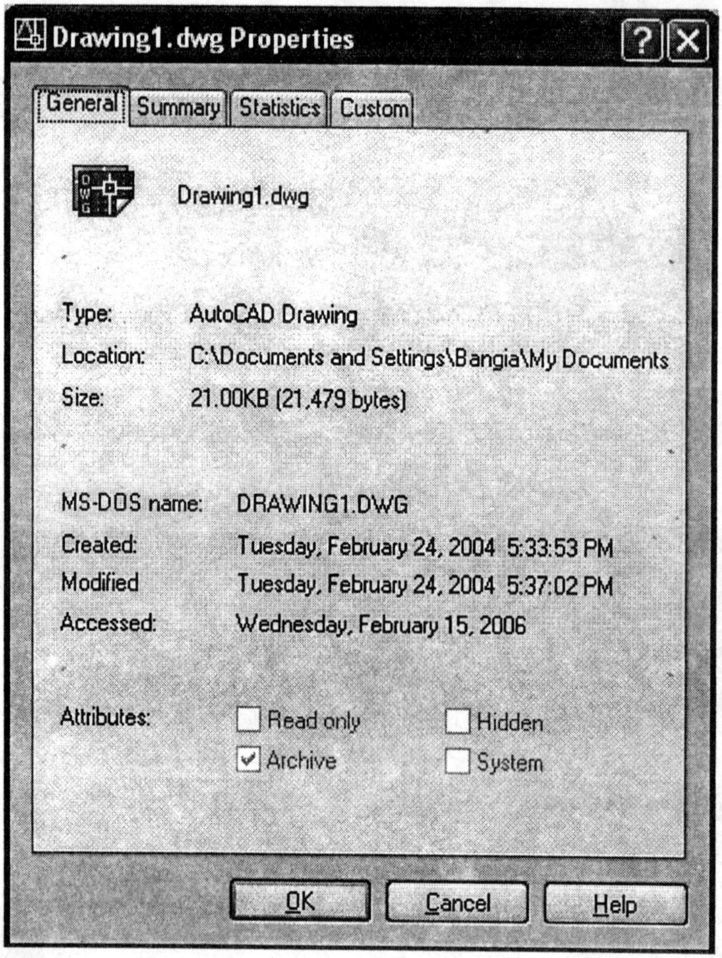

Drawing History

Lists the most recently opened drawings; select a drawing to quickly open it.

Exit

Quits the application; prompts to save documents

Edit Menu

Various options under this menu are:

Undo

Reverses the most recent operation.

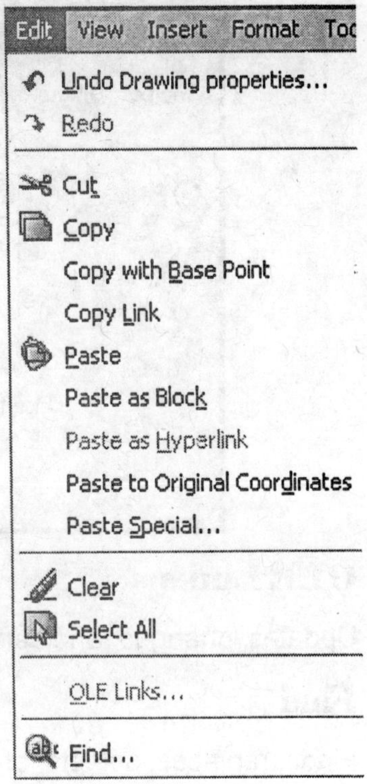

Redo

Reverses the effects of the previous UNDO or U command.

Cut

Copies objects to the Clipboard and erases the objects from the drawing.

Copy

Copies objects to the Clipboard.

Copy with Base Point

Copies objects to the Clipboard with a base point.

Copy Link

Copies the current view to the Clipboard for linking to other OLE applications.

Paste

Inserts data from the Clipboard.

Paste as Block

Pastes objects from the Clipboard as a block.

Paste as Hyperlink

Pastes a hyperlink to the selected object.

Paste to Original Coordinates

Pastes objects to the same coordinates as in the original drawing.

Paste Special

Inserts data from the Clipboard and controls the format of the data.

Clear

Removes objects from a drawing.

Select All

Selects all the items on the screen.

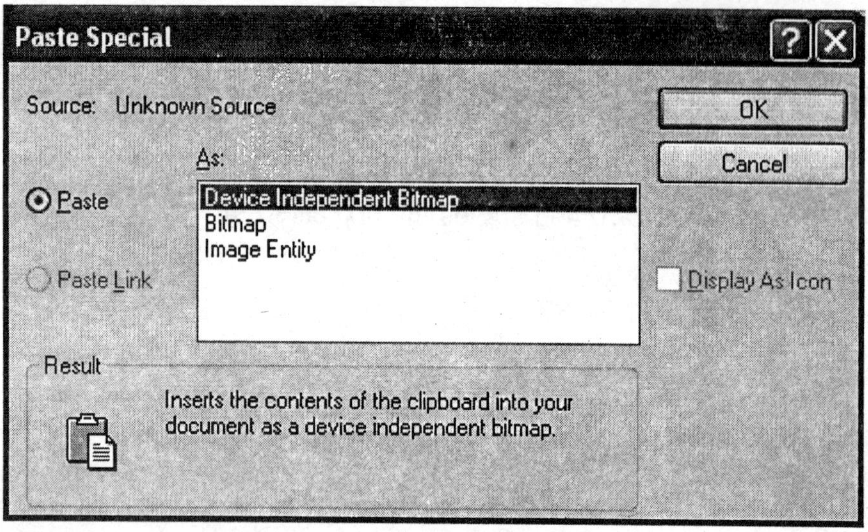

OLE Links

Updates, changes, and cancels existing OLE links.

Find

Finds, replaces, selects, or zooms to specified text.

View Menu

Various options under this menu are:

Redraw

Refreshes the display of all the viewports.

Regen

Regenerates the drawing and refreshes the current viewport.

Regen All

Regenerates the drawing and refreshes all viewports.

Zoom

Various options under Zoom are:

Realtime

Zooms in realtime.

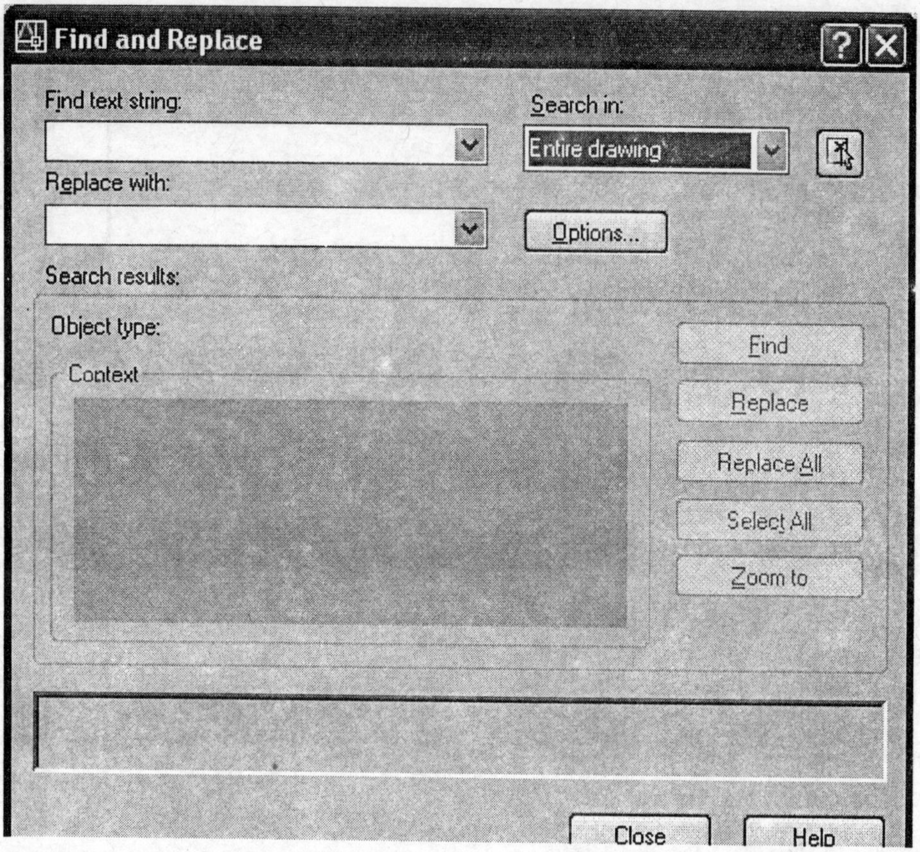

Previous

Zooms to display the previous view.

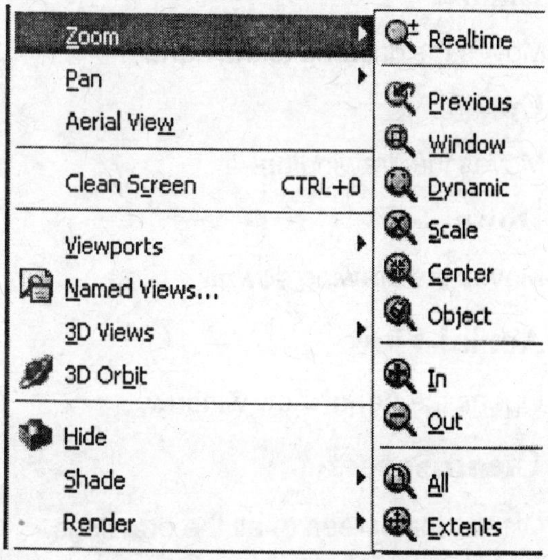

Window

Zooms to display an area specified by a rectangular window.

Dynamic

Zooms to display the generated portion of the drawing.

Scale

Zooms with a specified scale factor.

Center

Displays a window specified by a center point and height.

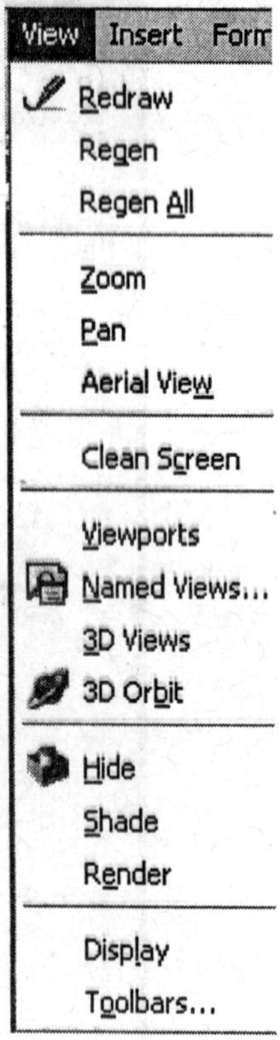

In

Increases the apparent size of objects in the current viewport.

Out

Decreases the apparent size of objects in the current viewport.

All

Zooms to display the entire drawing in the current viewport.

Extents

Zooms to display the drawing extents.

Pan

Various options under Pan are:

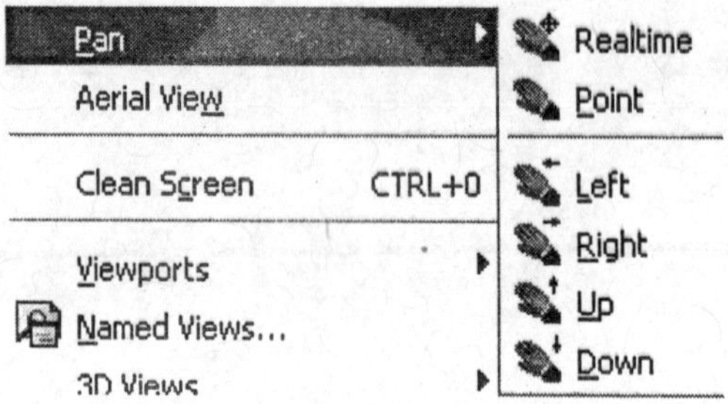

Real Time

Moves the drawing display in the current viewport.

Point

Moves the view of the drawing by the specified distance.

Left

Moves the drawing to the left.

Right

Moves the drawing to the right.

Up

Moves the drawing up.

Down

Moves the drawing down.

Aerial View

Opens the Aerial View window.

Clean Screen

Cleans the screen of all the drawings.

Viewports

Various options under Viewports are:

Named Viewports

Displays layout options for named viewports.

New Viewports

Opens a new viewport using a specified name.

1 Viewport

Returns the drawing to a single viewport view, using the view from the active viewport.

2 Viewports

Divides the current viewport in half.

3 Viewports

Divides the current viewport into three viewports.

4 Viewports

Divides the current viewport into four viewports of equal size.

Polygonal Viewport

The Polygonal option can be used to create a nonrectangular layout viewport by specifying points. The prompt sequence is the same as the prompt sequence for creating a polyline.

Object

With the Object option, you can select a closed object, such as a circle or closed polyline created in paper space, to convert into a layout viewport. The object

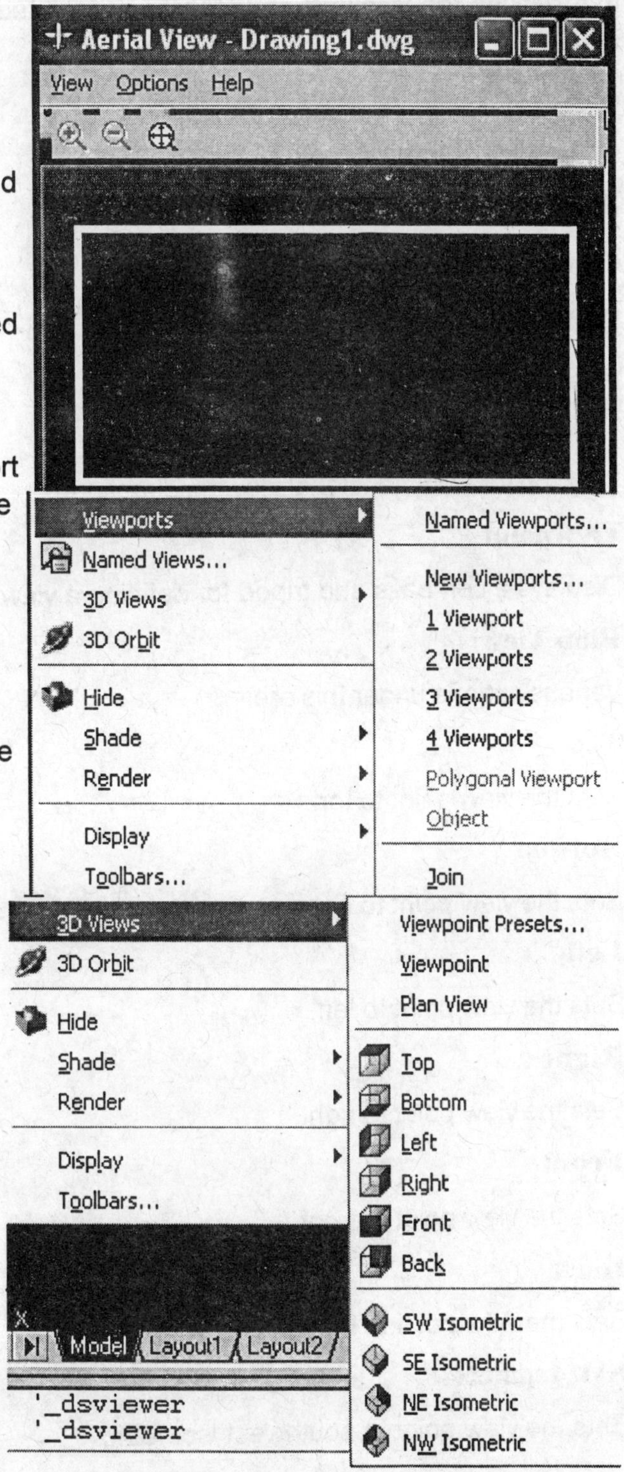

that defines the viewport boundary is associated with the viewport after the viewport is created.

Join

Joins two or more viewports.

Named Views

Creates and restores views.

3D Views

Various options are under 3D views are:

Viewpoint Presets

Sets the three-dimensional viewing direction.

Viewpoint

Displays a compass and tripod for defining a view direction in model space.

Plan View

Various options under this are:

Top

Sets the view point to top.

Bottom

Sets the view point to bottom.

Left

Sets the view point to left.

Right

Sets the view point to right.

Front

Sets the view point to front.

Back

Sets the view point to back.

SW Isometric

Sets the view point to southwest isometric.

SE Isometric

Sets the view point to southeast isometric.

NE Isometric

Sets the view point to northeast isometric.

NW Isometric

Sets the view point to northwest isometric.

3D Orbit

Defines parallel projection or prespective views.

Hide

Regenerates a three-dimensional model with hidden lines suppressed: HIDE

Shade

Various options under this are:

2D Wireframe

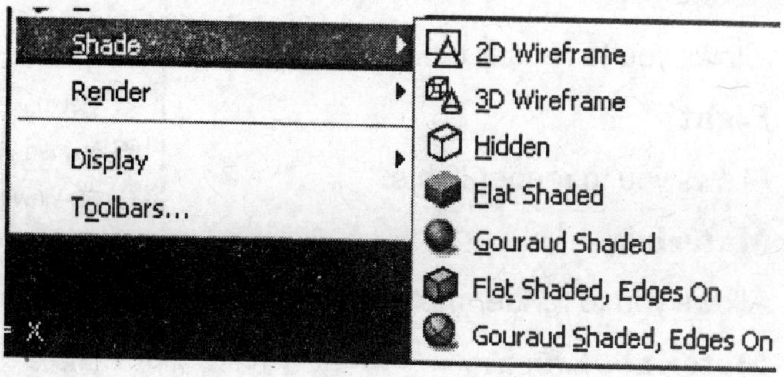

Displays the objects using lines and curves to represent the boundaries. Raster and OLE objects, linetypes, and lineweights are visible. Even if the COMPASS system variable is set to on, the compass is not visible in the 2D Wireframe view.

3D Wireframe

Displays the objects using lines and curves to represent the boundaries. Displays a shaded 3D user coordinate system (UCS) icon. You can set the COMPASS system variable to on to view the compass. Material colors that have been applied to objects are shown.

Hidden

Displays the objects using the 3D wireframe representation and hides the lines representing the back faces.

Flat Shaded

Shades the objects between the polygon faces. The objects appear flatter and less smooth than Gouraud Shaded objects. Materials that have been applied to objects are shown.

Gouraud Shaded

Shades the objects and smooths the edges between polygon faces, giving the objects a smooth, realistic appearance. Materials that have been applied to objects are shown.

Flat Shaded, Edges On

Combines the Flat Shaded and Wireframe options. The objects are flat shaded with the wireframe showing through.

Gouraud Shaded, Edges On

Combines the Gouraud Shaded and Wireframe options. The objects are Gouraud shaded with the wireframe showing through.

Render

Various options under this are:

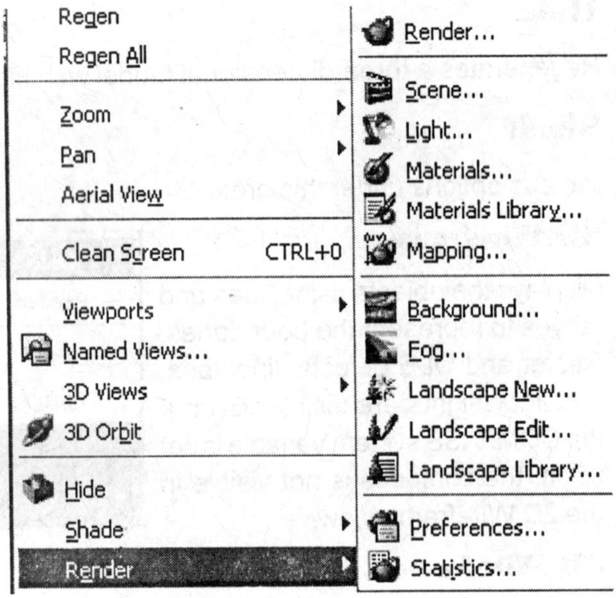

Render

Allows you to render the drawing.

Scene

Allows you to render the scene.

Light

Allows you to render lights.

Materials

Allows you to render materials.

Materials Library

Allows you to render the materials library.

Mapping

Allows you to render mapping.

Background

Allows you to render the background.

Fog

Allows you to render the fog.

Landscape New

Allows you to render the landscape.

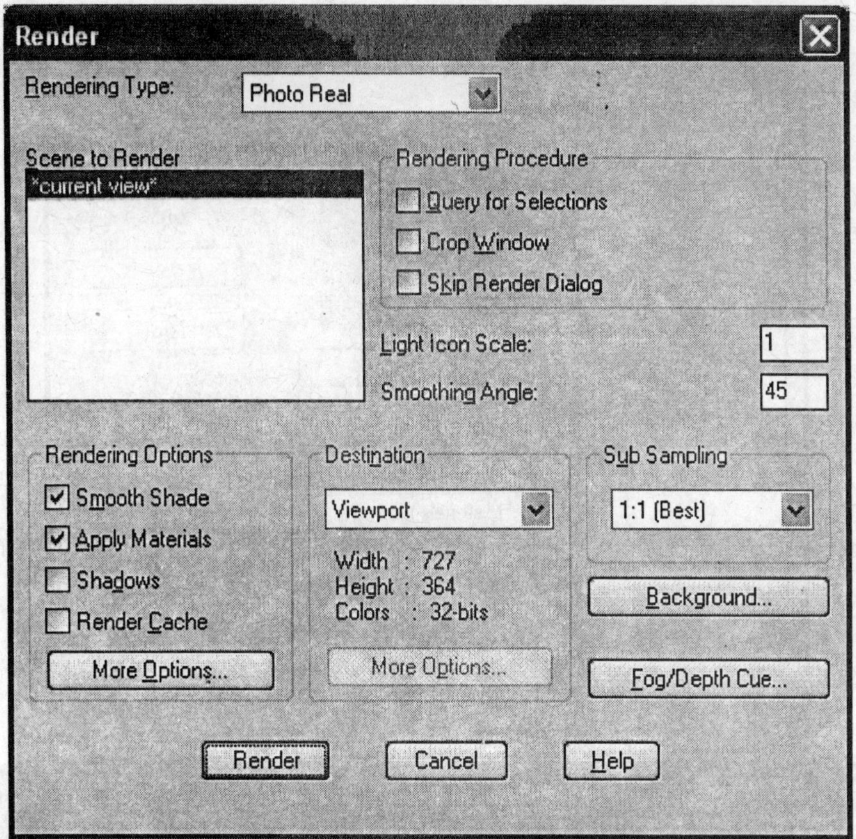
Render
Rendering Type:
Photo Real
Scene to Render
current view
Rendering Procedure
Query for Selections
Crop Window
Skip Render Dialog
Light Icon Scale:
1
Smoothing Angle:
45
Rendering Options
Smooth Shade
Apply Materials
Shadows
Render Cache
More Options...
Destination
Viewport
Width : 727
Height : 364
Colors : 32-bits
More Options...
Sub Sampling
1:1 (Best)
Background...
Fog/Depth Cue...
Render
Cancel
Help

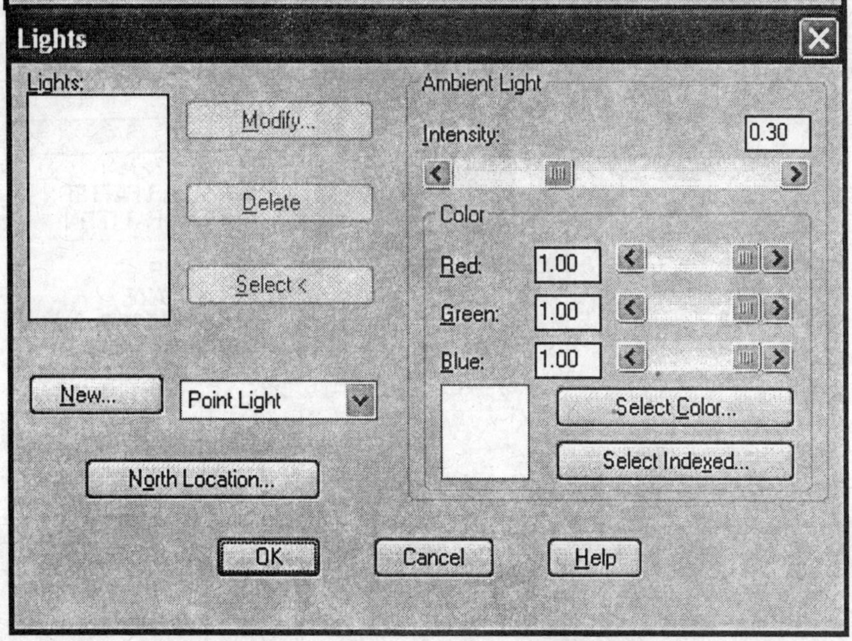
Lights
Lights:
Modify...
Delete
Select <
New...
Point Light
North Location...
Ambient Light
Intensity:
0.30
Color
Red:
1.00
Green:
1.00
Blue:
1.00
Select Color...
Select Indexed...
OK
Cancel
Help

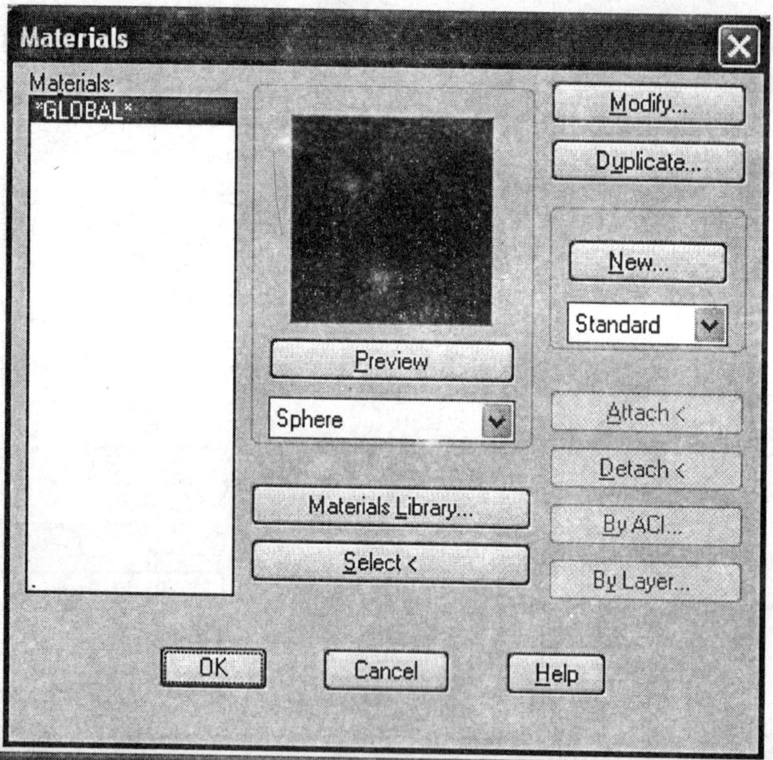
Materials
Materials:
GLOBAL
Modify...
Duplicate...
New...
Standard
Preview
Sphere
Attach <
Detach <
Materials Library...
By ACI...
Select <
By Layer...
OK
Cancel
Help

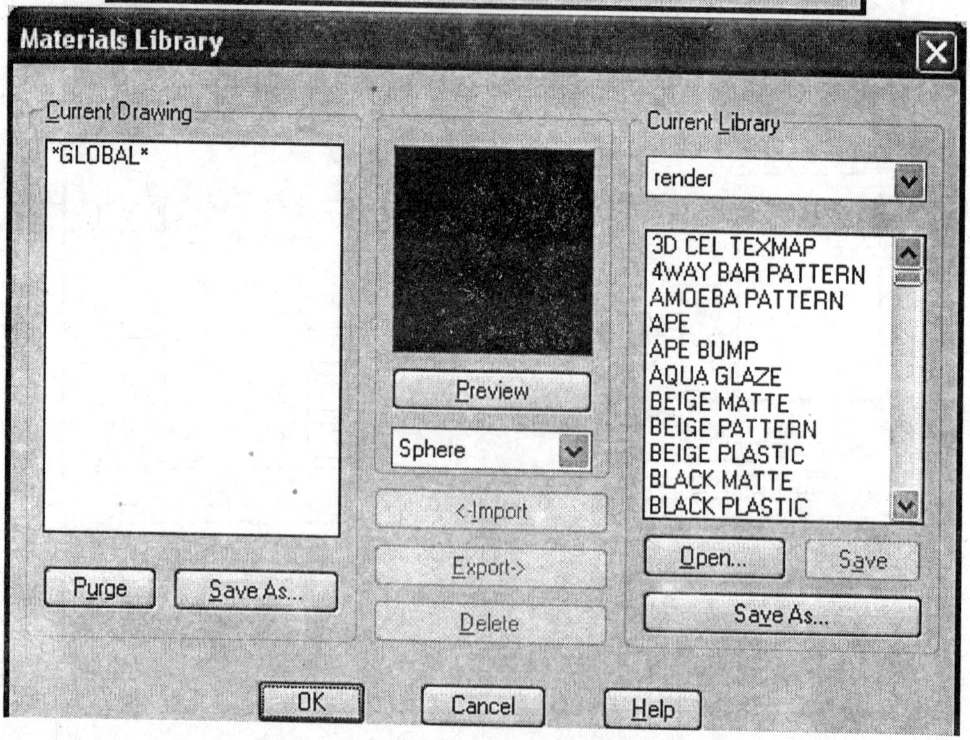
Materials Library
Current Drawing
GLOBAL
Current Library
render
3D CEL TEXMAP
4WAY BAR PATTERN
AMOEBA PATTERN
APE
APE BUMP
AQUA GLAZE
BEIGE MATTE
BEIGE PATTERN
BEIGE PLASTIC
BLACK MATTE
BLACK PLASTIC
Preview
Sphere
<-Import
Export->
Delete
Purge
Save As...
Open...
Save
Save As...
OK
Cancel
Help

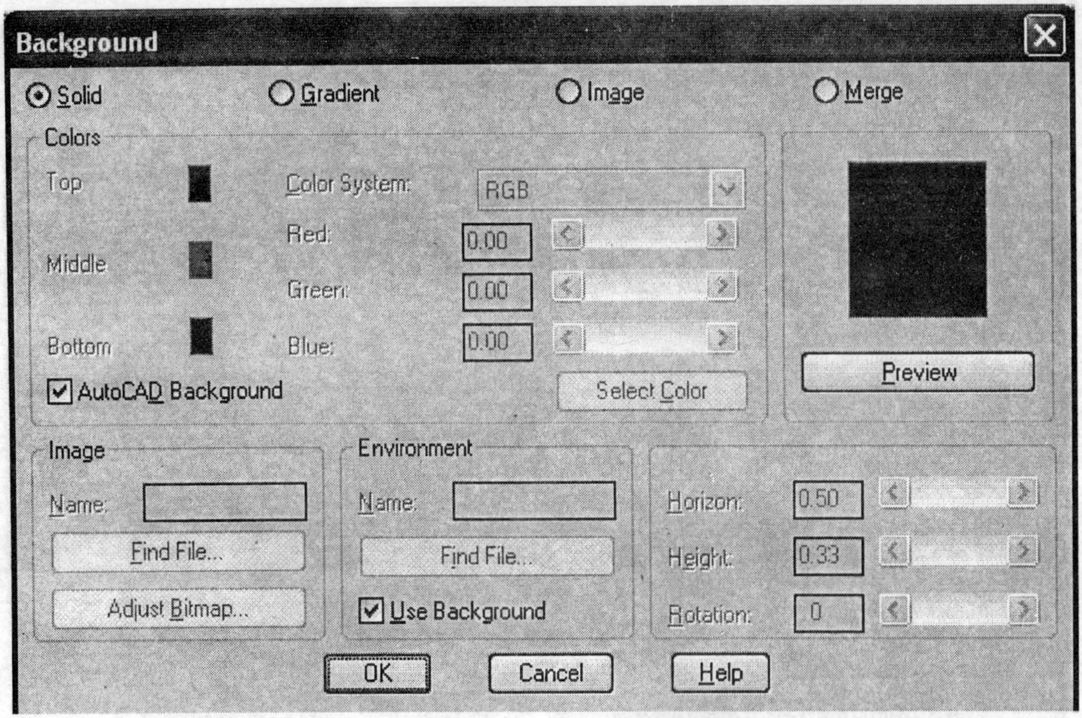

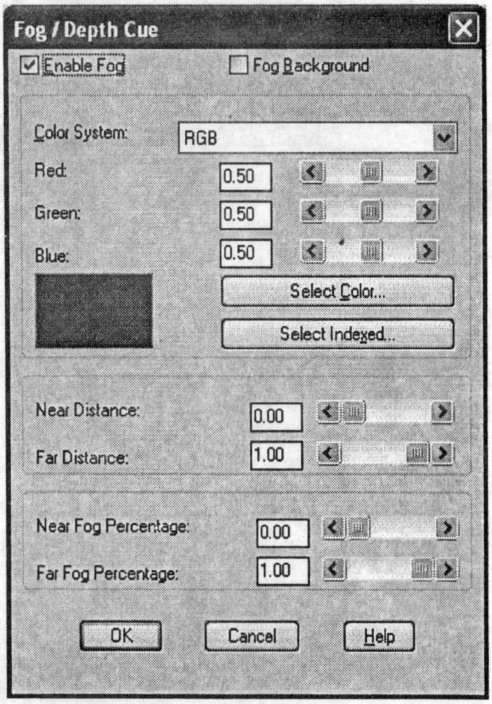

Landscape Edit

Allows you to edit the landscape.

Landscape Library

Allows you to access the landscape library.

Preferences

Allows you to select render preferences

Statistics

Gives you the render statistics.

Display

Various options under this are:

Ucs icon

Under this you would find the following:

On

Controls the visibility and placement of the UCS icon: UCSICON

Landscape New
Library: render.lli
Bush #1
Cactus
Dawn Redwood
Eastern Palm
Norway Maple, Fall
People #1
People #2
Quaking Aspen
Road Sign
Preview
Geometry
Single Face
Crossing Faces
View Aligned
Height:
20.0
Position <
OK
Cancel
Help

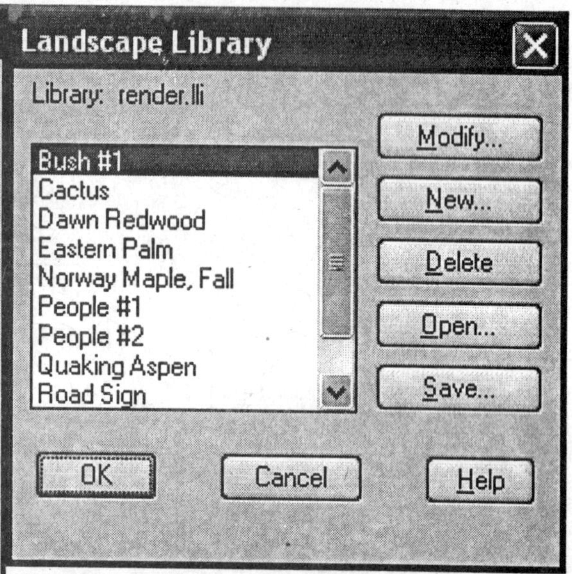
Landscape Library
Library: render.lli
Bush #1
Cactus
Dawn Redwood
Eastern Palm
Norway Maple, Fall
People #1
People #2
Quaking Aspen
Road Sign
Modify...
New...
Delete
Open...
Save...
OK
Cancel
Help

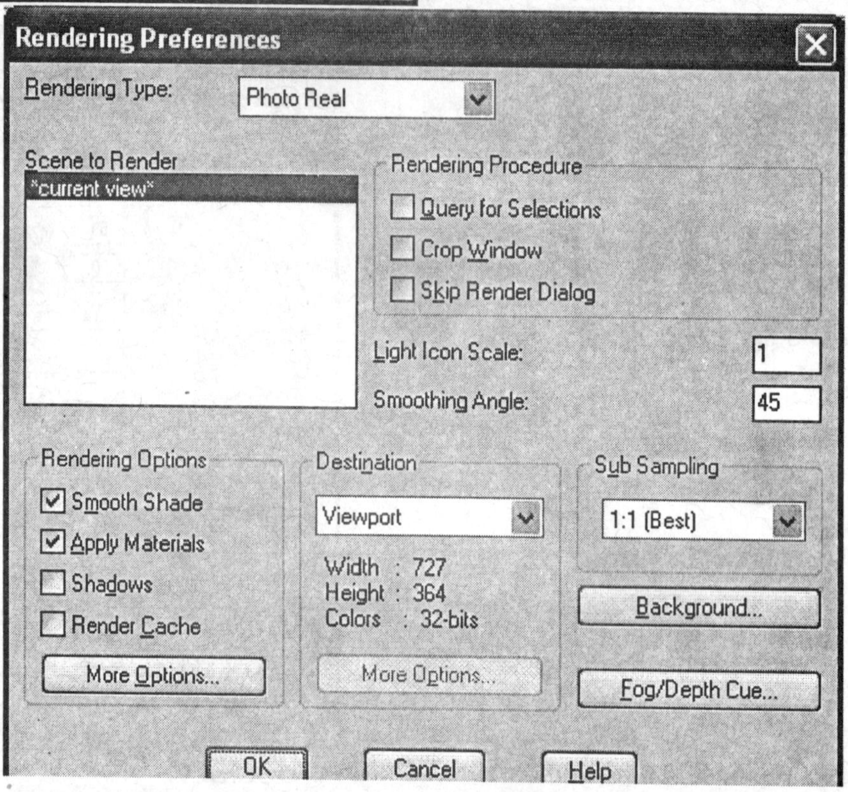
Rendering Preferences
Rendering Type:
Photo Real
Scene to Render
current view
Rendering Procedure
Query for Selections
Crop Window
Skip Render Dialog
Light Icon Scale:
1
Smoothing Angle:
45
Rendering Options
Smooth Shade
Apply Materials
Shadows
Render Cache
More Options...
Destination
Viewport
Width : 727
Height : 364
Colors : 32-bits
More Options...
Sub Sampling
1:1 (Best)
Background...
Fog/Depth Cue...
OK
Cancel
Help

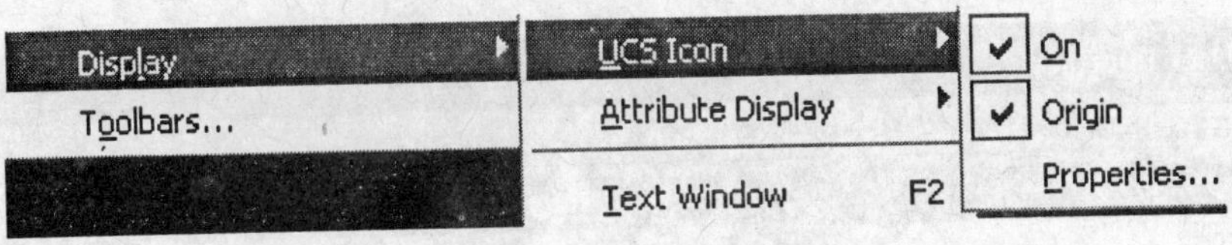

Origin

Forces the icon to appear at the origin of the current coordinate system: UCSICON

Properties

Displays the properties.

Attribute Display

Under this you would find the following:

Normal

Displays visible attributes; hides invisible attributes.

On

Makes all attributes visible.

Off

Makes all attributes invisible.

Text Window

Opens the AutoCAD text window: TEXTSCR

Toolbars

Displays, hides, and customizes toolbars.

Insert Menu

Various options under this menu are:

Block

Inserts a block or another drawing.

External Reference

Attaches an external reference to the current drawing.

Raster Image

Allows you to insert a Raster Image.

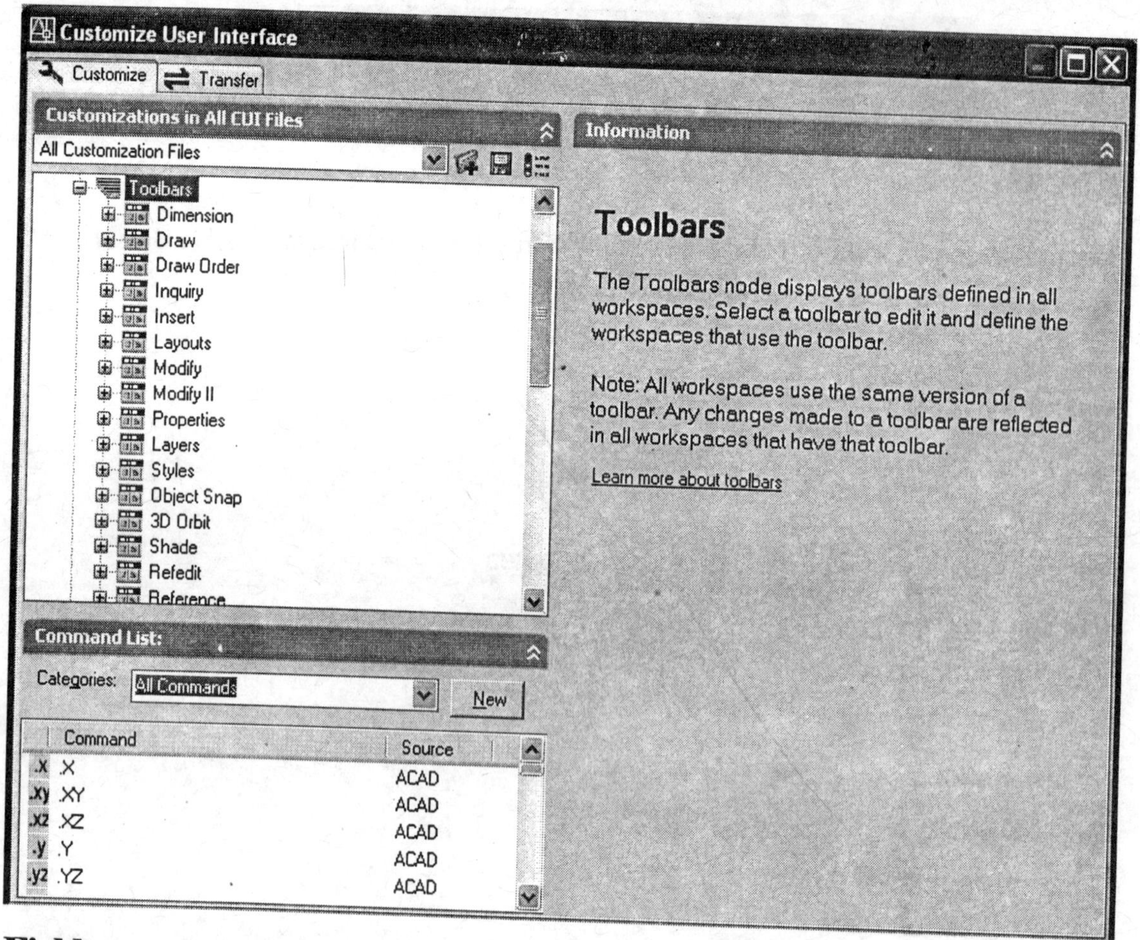

Field

Inserts a field.

Layout

Various options under this are:

New Layout

Creates a new layout with page settings and plotting device information.

Layout from Template

Inserts a new layout based on an existing layout template.

Create Layout Wizard

Starts the Layout wizard to designate page and plot settings for a new layout.

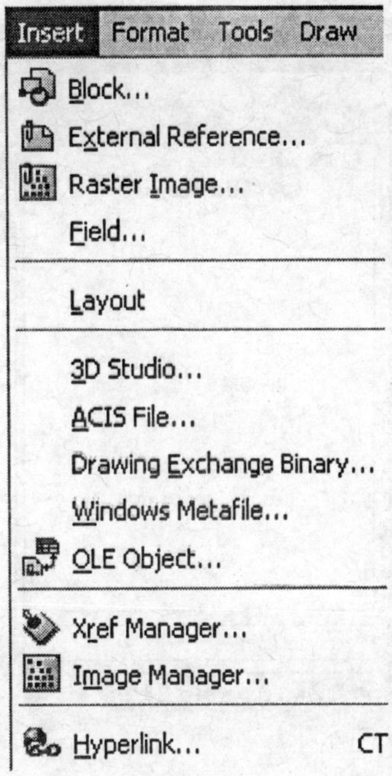

3D Studio

Imports a 3D studio file.

ACIS File

Imports a ACIS File.

Drawing Exchange Binary

Imports a drawing from the exchange in the binary format.

Windows Metafile

Imports a Windows metafile.

OLE Object

Inserts a linked or embedded object.

Xref Manager

Controls external references to drawing files.

Image Manager

Using this you can manage the image being inserted.

Hyperlink

Attaches a hyperlink to a graphical object or modifies an existing hyperlink.

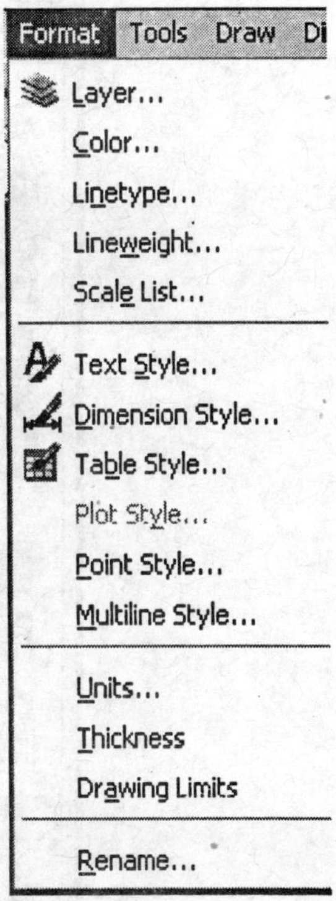

Format Menu

Various options under this menu are:

Layer

Manages layers and layer properties.

Color

Sets the color for new objects.

Linetype

Creates, loads, and sets linetypes.

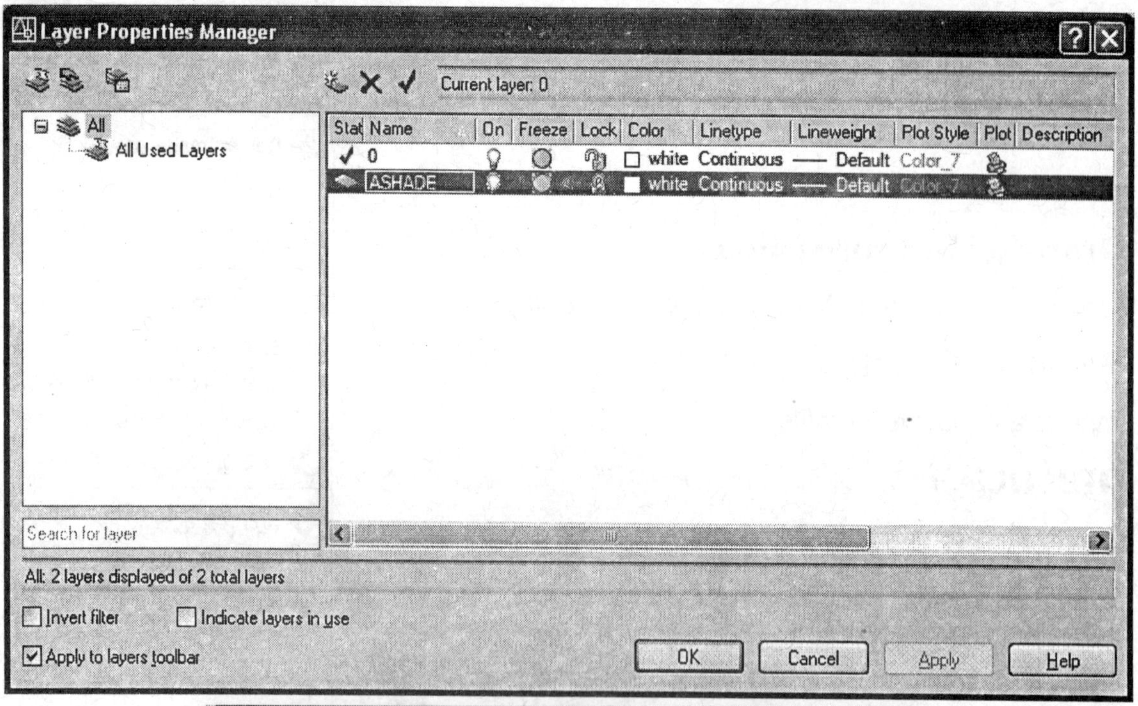
Layer Properties Manager
Current layer: 0
All
All Used Layers
Stat Name On Freeze Lock Color Linetype Lineweight Plot Style Plot Description
0 white Continuous Default Color_7
ASHADE white Continuous Default Color_7
Search for layer
All: 2 layers displayed of 2 total layers
Invert filter
Indicate layers in use
Apply to layers toolbar
OK
Cancel
Apply
Help

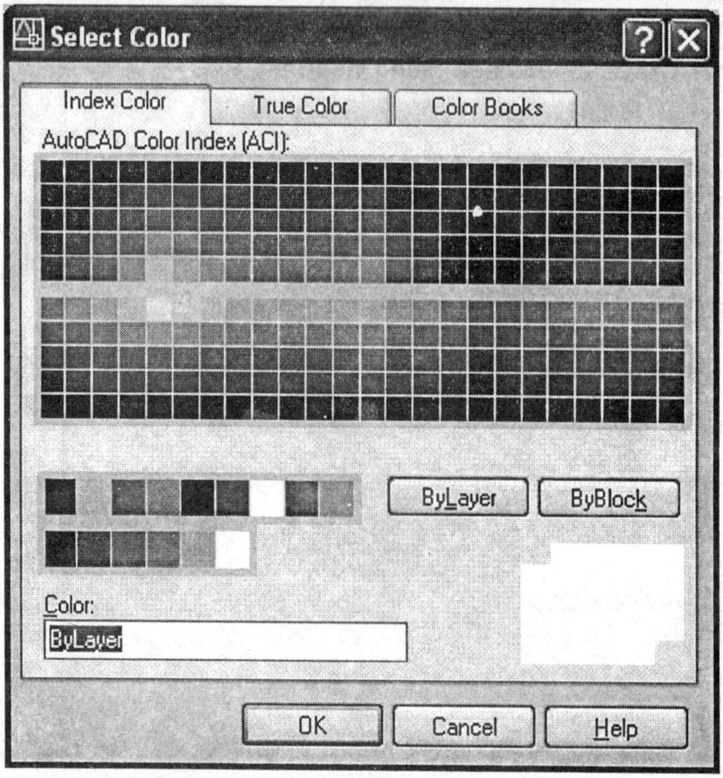
Select Color
Index Color
True Color
Color Books
AutoCAD Color Index (ACI):
ByLayer
ByBlock
Color:
ByLayer
OK
Cancel
Help

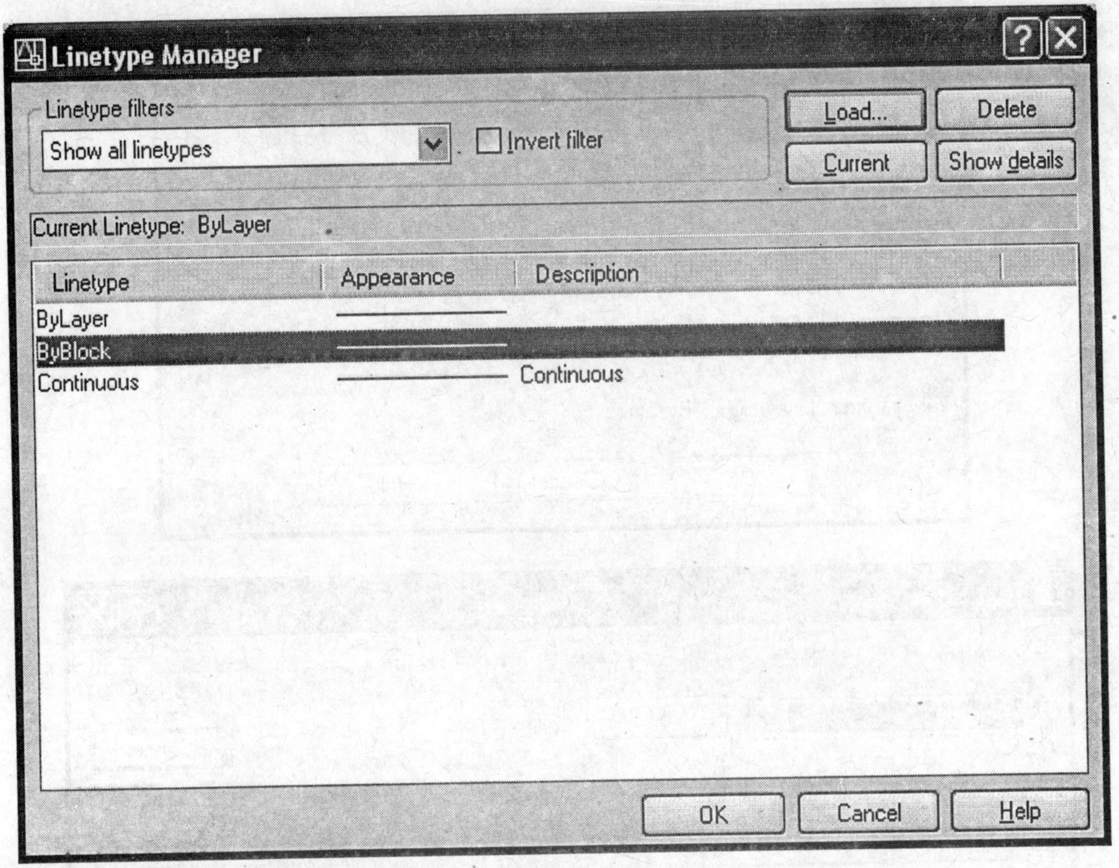

Lineweight

Sets the current lineweight, lineweight display options, and lineweight units.

Text Style

Creates or modifies named styles and sets the current style for text in your drawing.

Dimension Style

Creates and modifies dimension styles.

Table Style

Creates and modifies table styles.

Plot Style

Sets the current plot style for new objects, or the assigned plot style for selected objects.

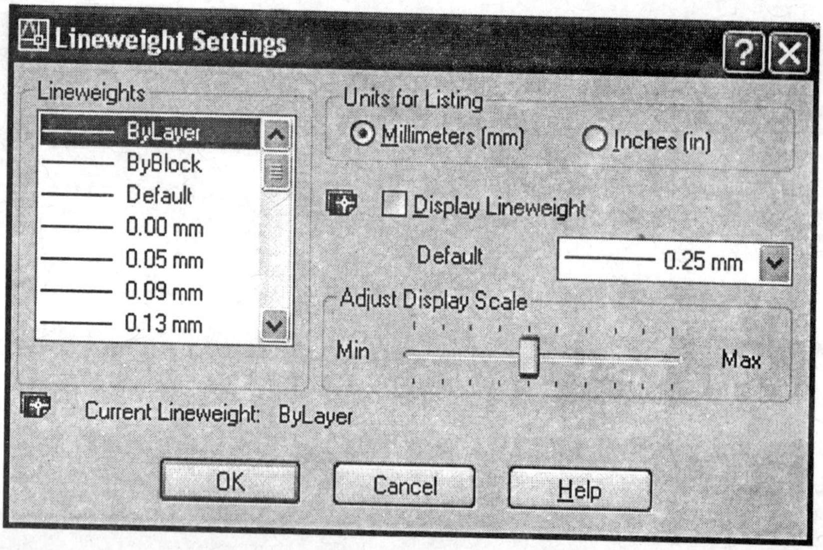

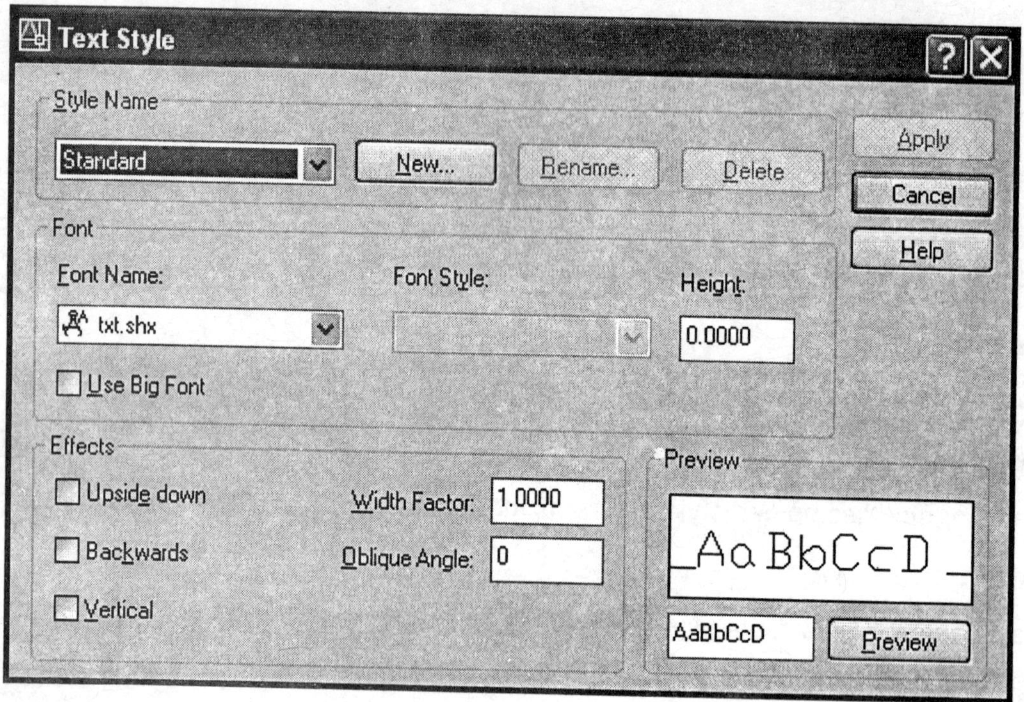

Point Style

Specifies the display style and size of point objects.

Multiline Style

Manages styles for multiple parallel lines.

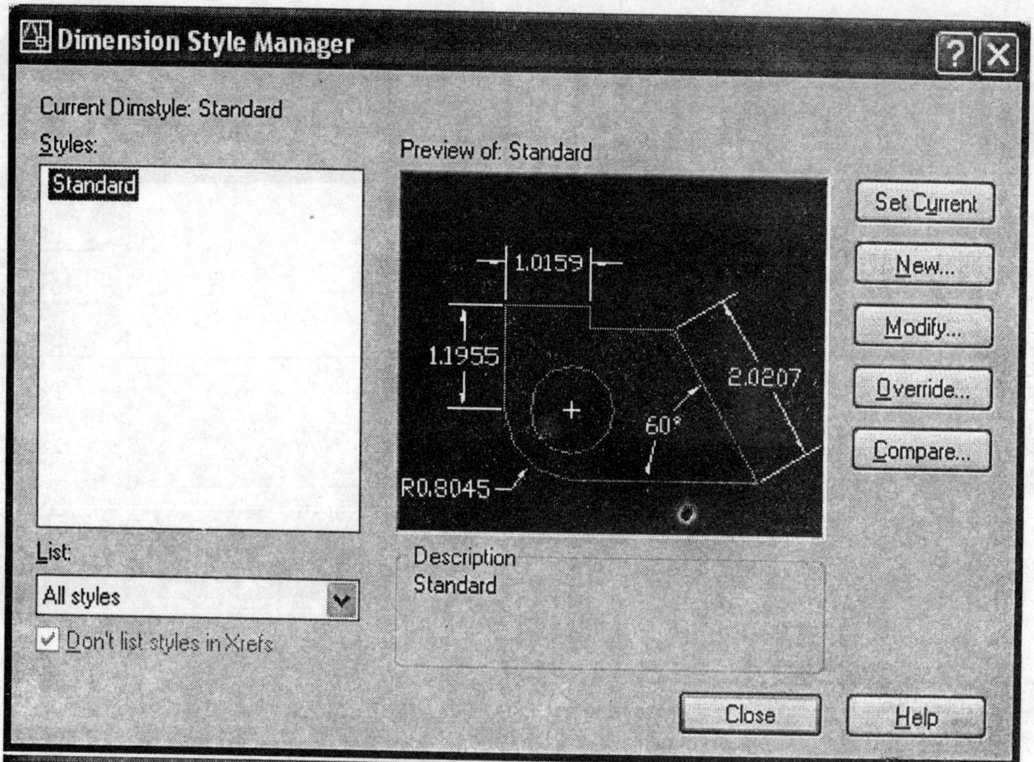
Dimension Style Manager
Current Dimstyle: Standard
Styles:
Standard
Preview of: Standard
1.0159
1.1955
2.0207
60°
R0.8045
Set Current
New...
Modify...
Override...
Compare...
List:
All styles
Don't list styles in Xrefs
Description
Standard
Close
Help

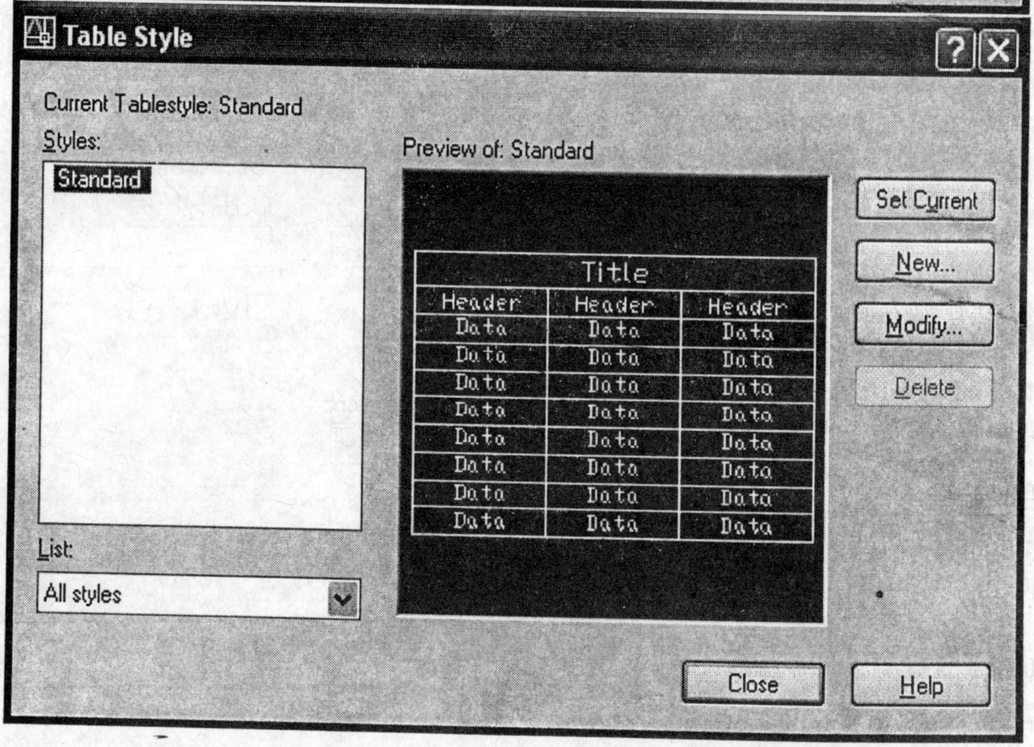
Table Style
Current Tablestyle: Standard
Styles:
Standard
Preview of: Standard
Title
Header
Data
Set Current
New...
Modify...
Delete
List:
All styles
Close
Help

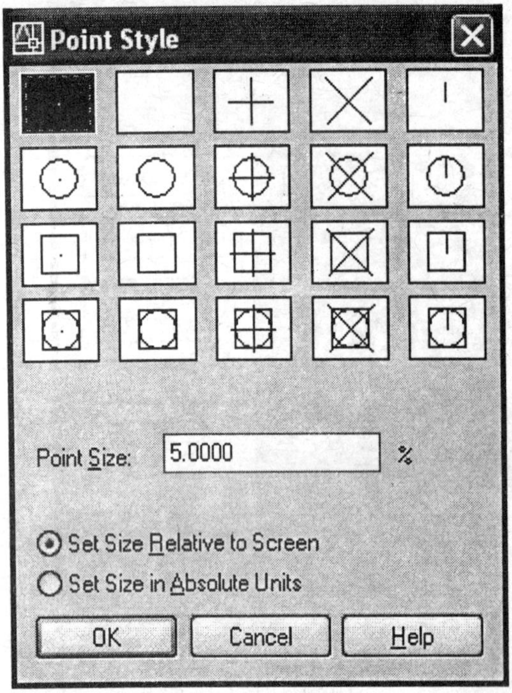

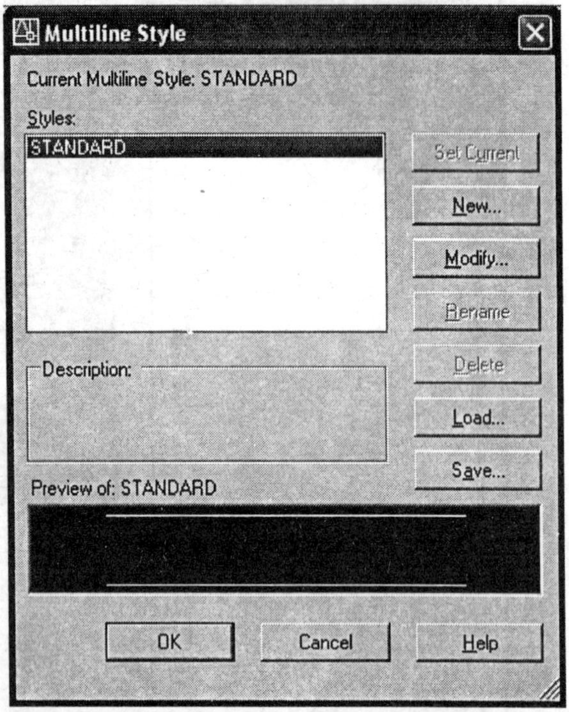

Units

Controls coordinate and angle display formats and determines precision.

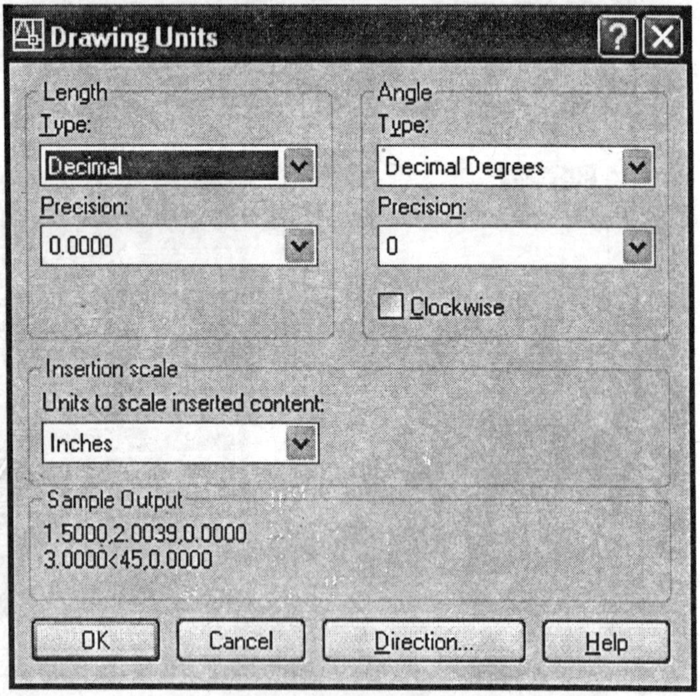

Thickness

Sets the current 3D thickness.

Drawing Limits

Sets and controls the drawing boundaries.

Rename

Changes the names of named objects.

Tools Menu

Various options under this menu are:

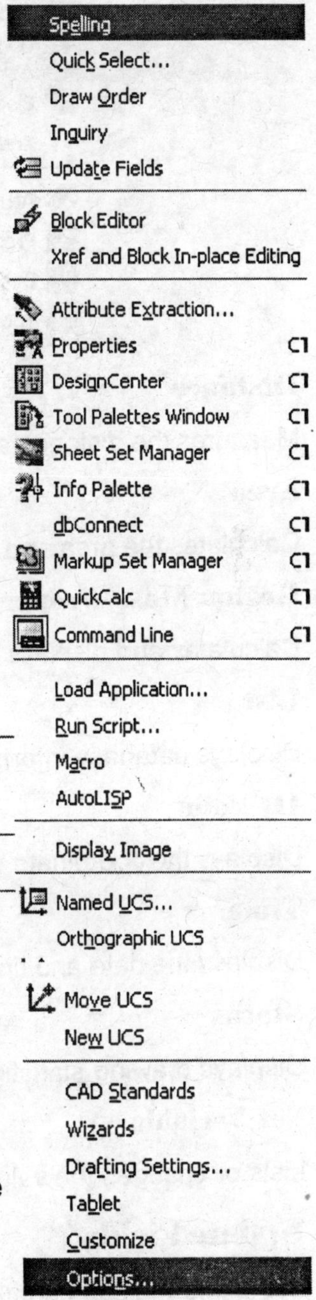

Autodesk Website

Launches the default web browser defined in your system's registery.

CAD Standards

Using this you can specify how the CAD standard feature functions to provide real-time notification and automatic repair.

Spelling

Checks spelling in a drawing.

Quick Select

Quickly creates selection sets based on filtering criteria.

Draw Order

Various options under this heading are:

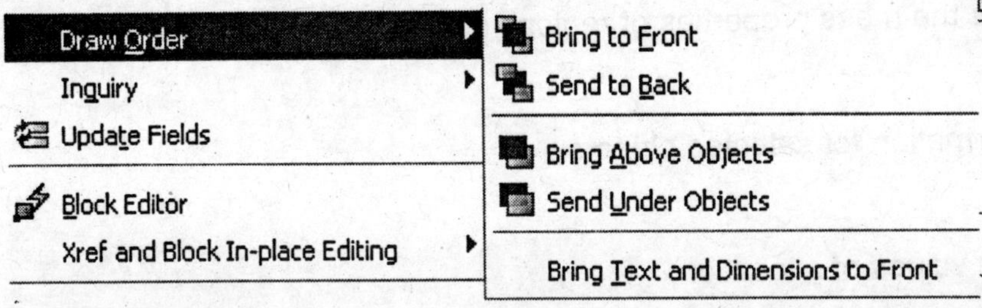

Bring to Front

Forces selected objects to be displayed in front of all other objects.

Send to Back

Forces selected objects to be displayed behind all other objects.

Bring Above Object

Forces selected objects to be displayed in front of a reference object.

Send Under Object

Forces selected objects to be displayed behind a reference object.

Inquiry

Various options under this are:

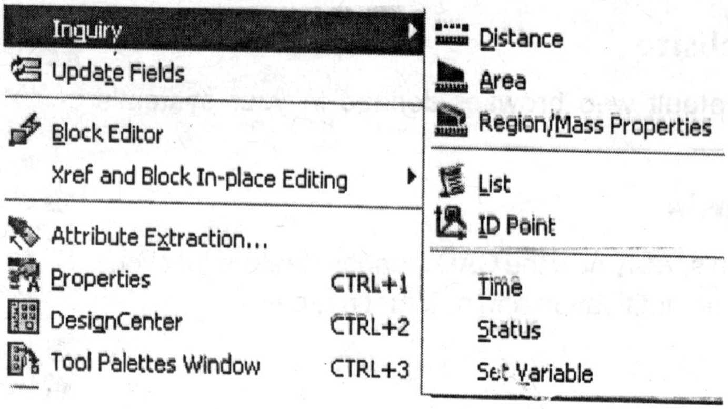

Distance

Measures the distance and angle between two points.

Area

Calculates the area and perimeter of objects or of defined areas.

Region/Mass Properties

Calculates and displays the mass properties of regions or solids.

List

Displays database information for selected objects.

ID Point

Displays the coordinate values of a location.

Time

Displays the date and time statistics of a drawing.

Status

Displays drawing statistics, modes, and extents.

Set Variable

Lists or changes the values of system variables.

Update Fields

Using this you can update various fields.

Block Editor

You use the Block Editor to define dynamic behavior for a block definition. In the Block

Editor, you add parameters and actions, which define custom properties and dynamic behavior. The Block Editor contains a special authoring area in which you can draw and edit geometry as you would in the drawing area.

Xref and Block In-place Editing

Converts xref definitions to standard local block definitions. If you bind an xref into the current drawing, the xref and all its dependent named objects become a part of the current drawing. Use XBIND to add individual xref-dependent named objects, such as blocks, text styles, dimension styles, layers, and linetypes, to the local definition table. The two methods of binding xrefs to the current drawing are Bind and Insert. Bind alters the definition table names of an xref when it is inserted. Insert does not alter the definition table names of an xref when it is inserted. To bind a nested xref, you must also select the parent xref.

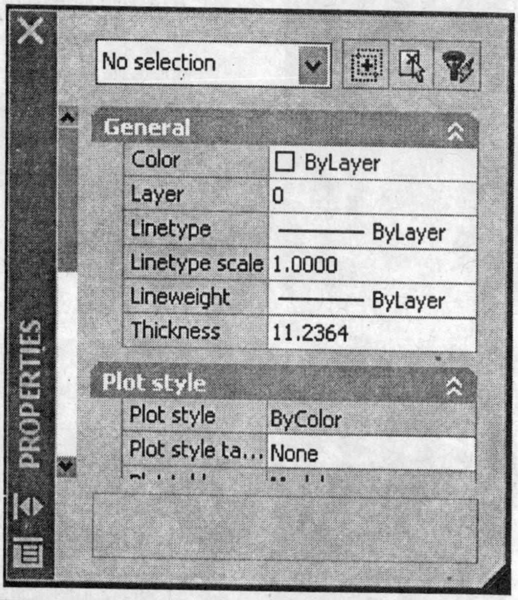

Attribute Extraction

Provides step-by-step instructions for extracting information from block attributes in the current drawing or other drawings. The information is used to create a table in the current drawing or is saved to an external file.

Properties

Controls properties of existing objects.

DesignCenter

Runs AutoCAD DesignCenter.

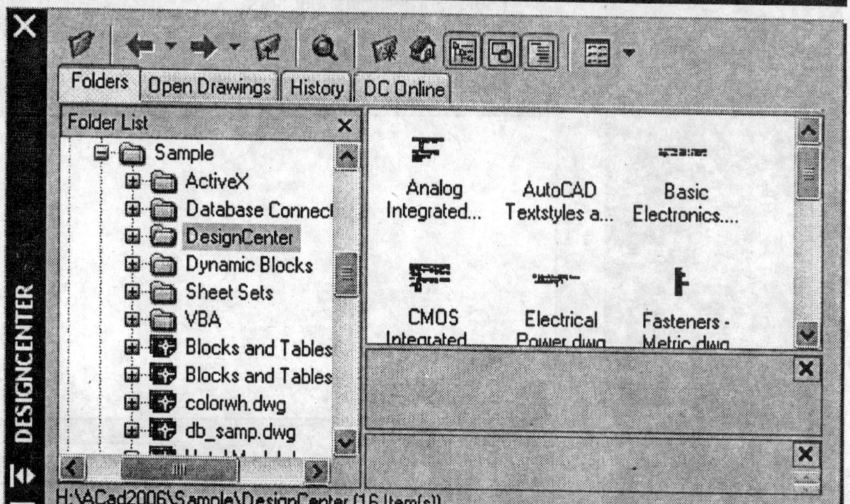

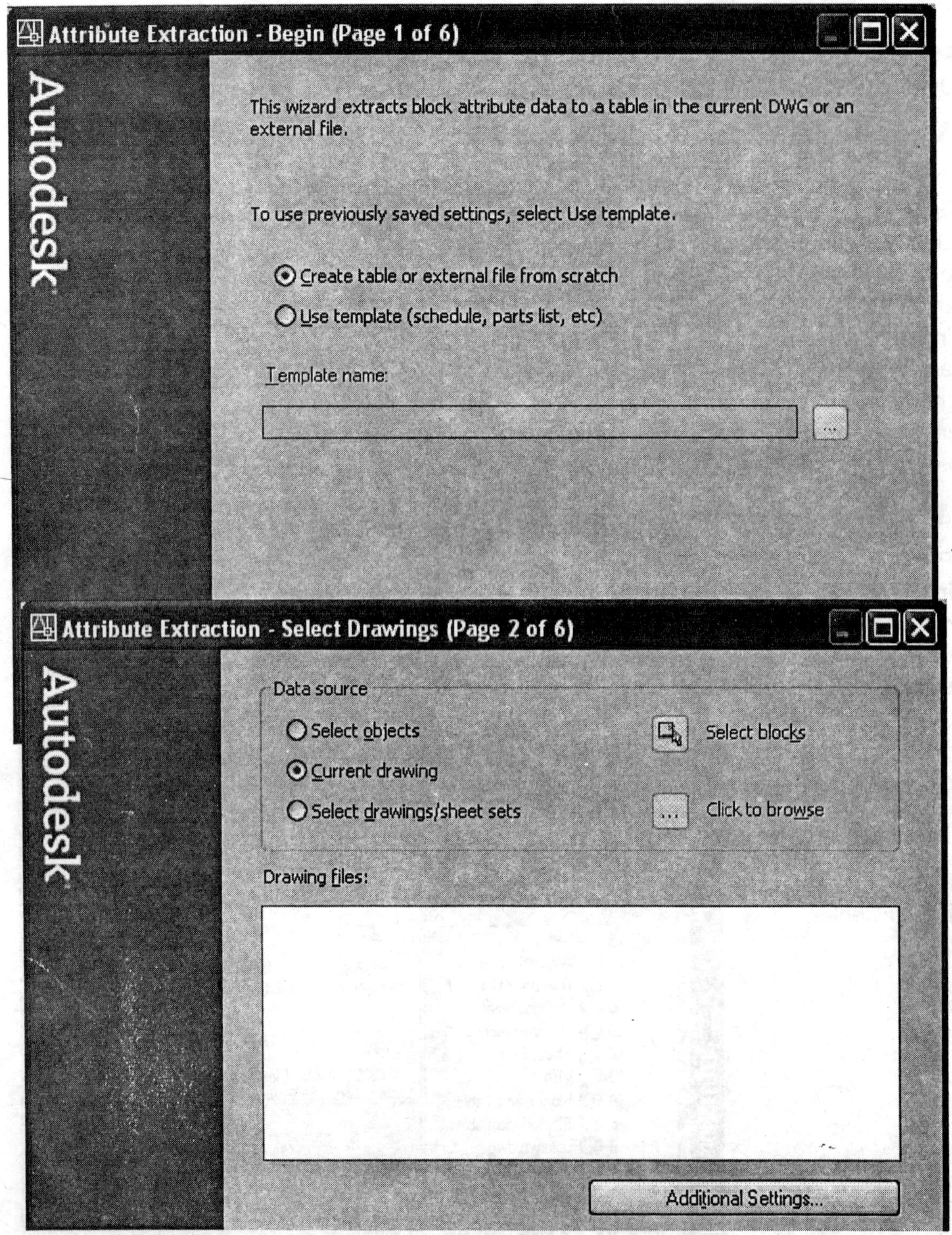
Attribute Extraction - Begin (Page 1 of 6)
Autodesk
This wizard extracts block attribute data to a table in the current DWG or an external file.
To use previously saved settings, select Use template.
Create table or external file from scratch
Use template (schedule, parts list, etc)
Template name:
Attribute Extraction - Select Drawings (Page 2 of 6)
Autodesk
Data source
Select objects
Select blocks
Current drawing
Select drawings/sheet sets
Click to browse
Drawing files:
Additional Settings...

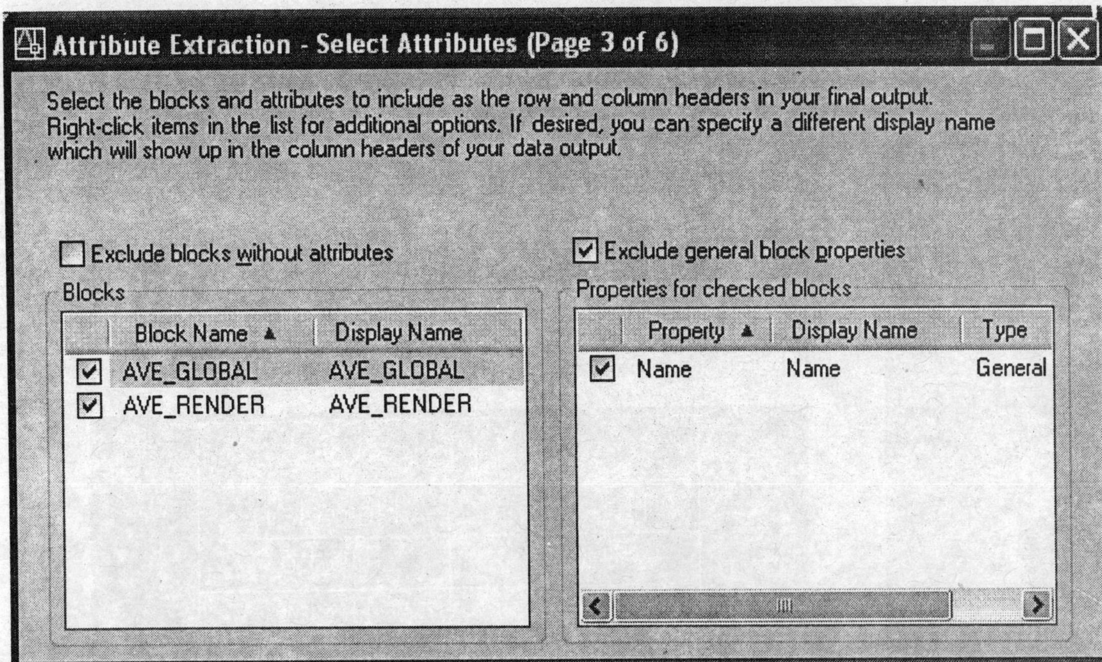
Attribute Extraction - Select Attributes (Page 3 of 6)
Select the blocks and attributes to include as the row and column headers in your final output. Right-click items in the list for additional options. If desired, you can specify a different display name which will show up in the column headers of your data output.
Exclude blocks without attributes
Exclude general block properties
Blocks
Block Name
Display Name
AVE_GLOBAL
AVE_GLOBAL
AVE_RENDER
AVE_RENDER
Properties for checked blocks
Property
Display Name
Type
Name
Name
General

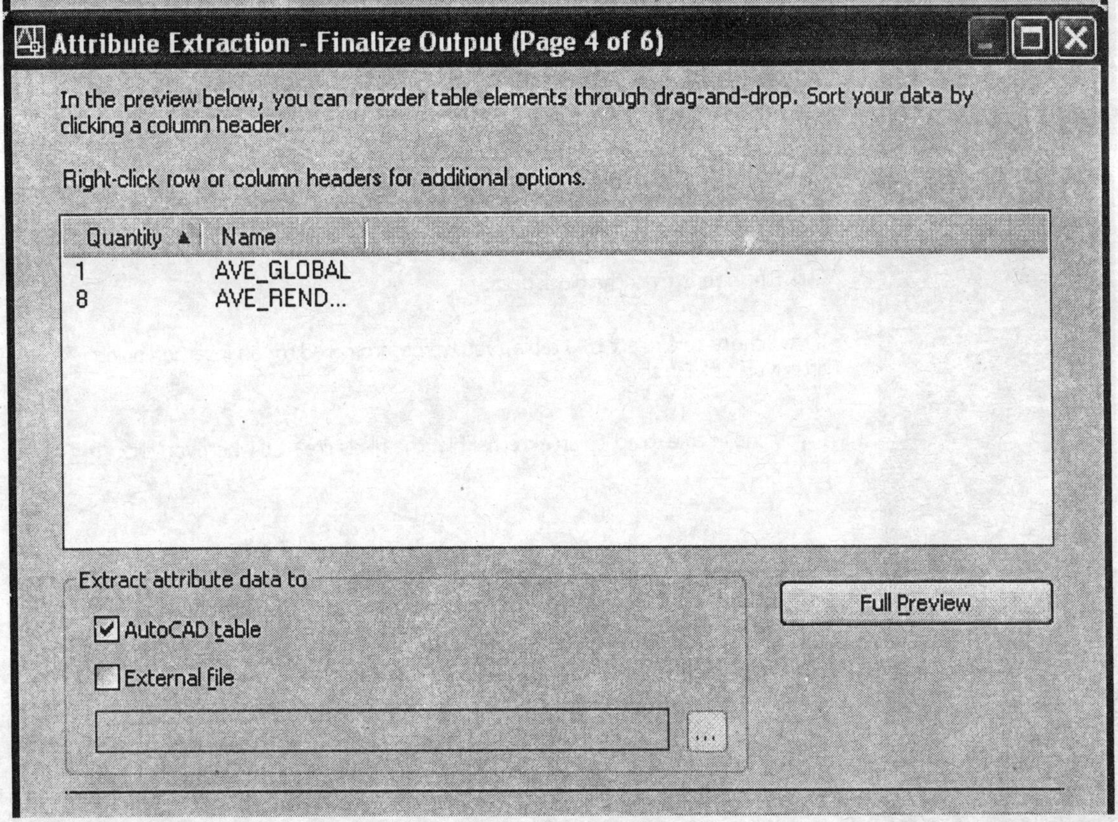
Attribute Extraction - Finalize Output (Page 4 of 6)
In the preview below, you can reorder table elements through drag-and-drop. Sort your data by clicking a column header.
Right-click row or column headers for additional options.
Quantity
Name
1
AVE_GLOBAL
8
AVE_REND...
Extract attribute data to
AutoCAD table
External file
Full Preview

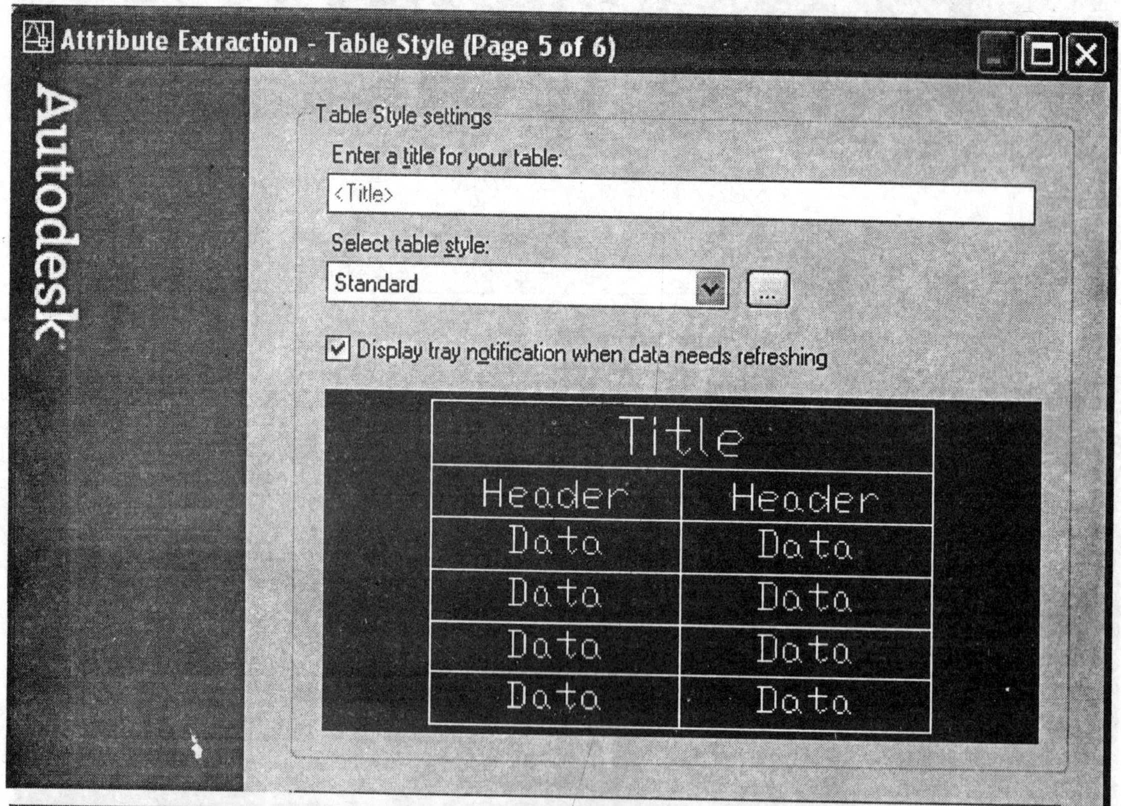
Attribute Extraction - Table Style (Page 5 of 6)
Autodesk
Table Style settings
Enter a title for your table:
<Title>
Select table style:
Standard
Display tray notification when data needs refreshing
Title
Header
Header
Data
Data
Data
Data
Data
Data
Data
Data

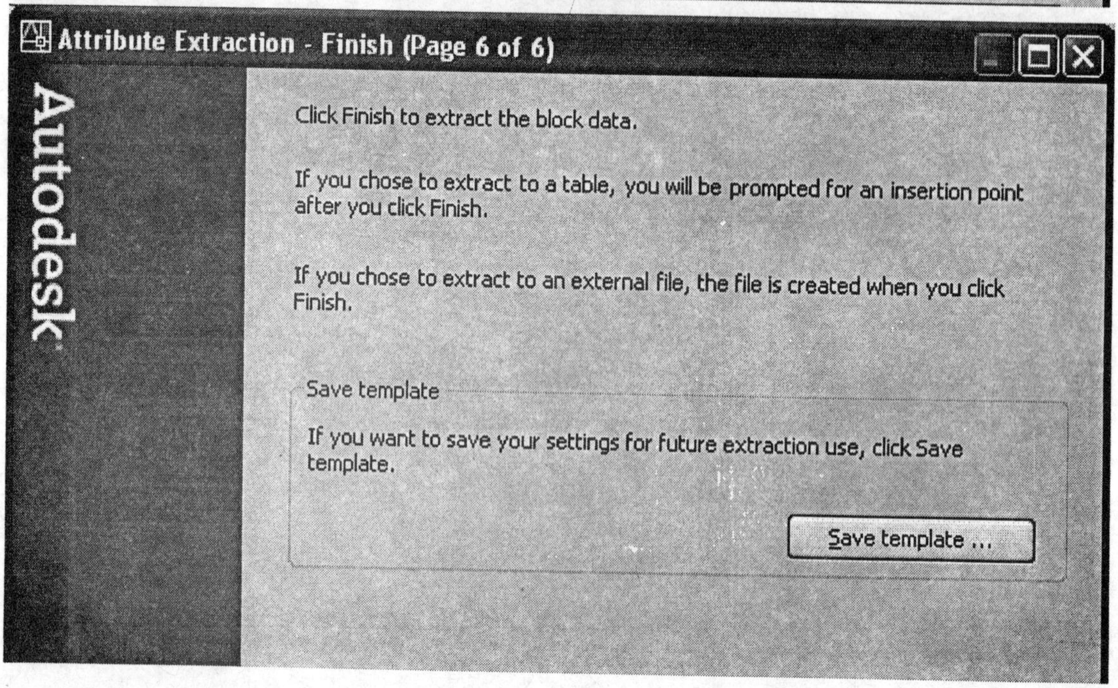
Attribute Extraction - Finish (Page 6 of 6)
Autodesk
Click Finish to extract the block data.
If you chose to extract to a table, you will be prompted for an insertion point after you click Finish.
If you chose to extract to an external file, the file is created when you click Finish.
Save template
If you want to save your settings for future extraction use, click Save template.
Save template ...

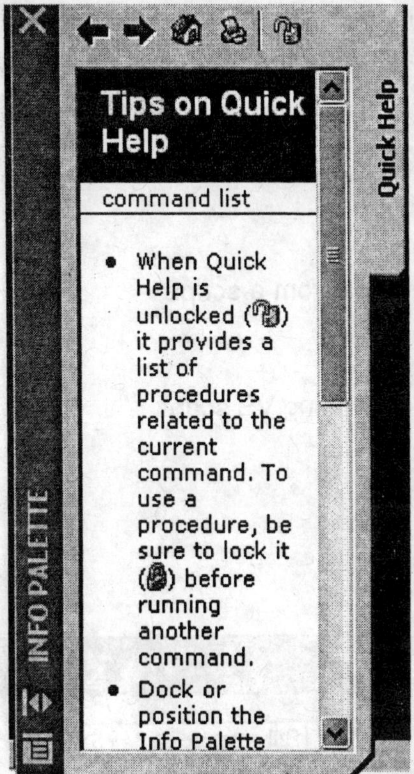

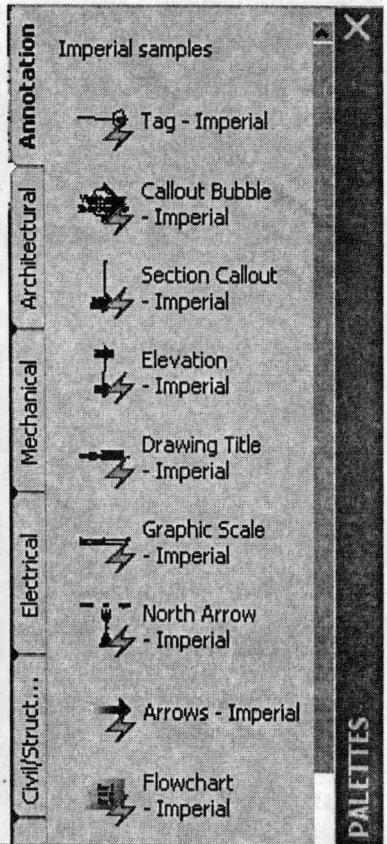

Tool Palettes Window

Displays/hides the tool palette window.

Sheet Set Manager

It allows you to manage sheet sets and their individual sheets.

Info Palette

It offers you context-sensitive Quick Help as you work.

dbConnect

It can be used to perform all the connectivity functions.

Markup Set Manager

You can use it to open DWF.

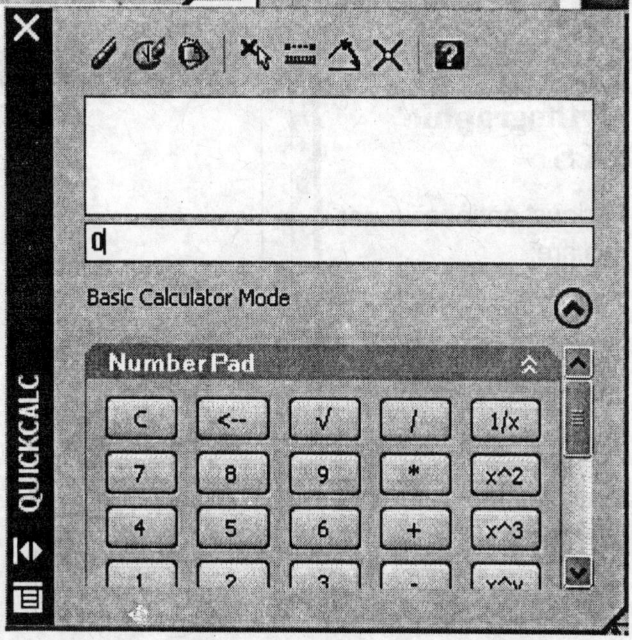

QuickCalc

With the QuickCalc calculator, an interface that looks and functions like a hand-held calculator, you can perform mathematical, scientific, and geometric calculations, convert units of measurement, manipulate the properties of objects, and evaluate expressions.

Command Line

To relocate and resize the command window for your convenience, drag it or use the splitter bar. To hide the command window, click Command Line on the Tools menu. By default, the command window is docked. The docked command window is the same width as the AutoCAD window. If text that is entered becomes longer than the width of the command line, the window pops up in front of the command line to show the full text of the line.

Load Application

You can use it to load various type of files.

Run Script

Executes a sequence of commands from a script.

Macro

Allows you to load and edit macros using VB script.

AutoLISP

Allows you to load LISP and its editor.

Display Image

You can view and save the display image.

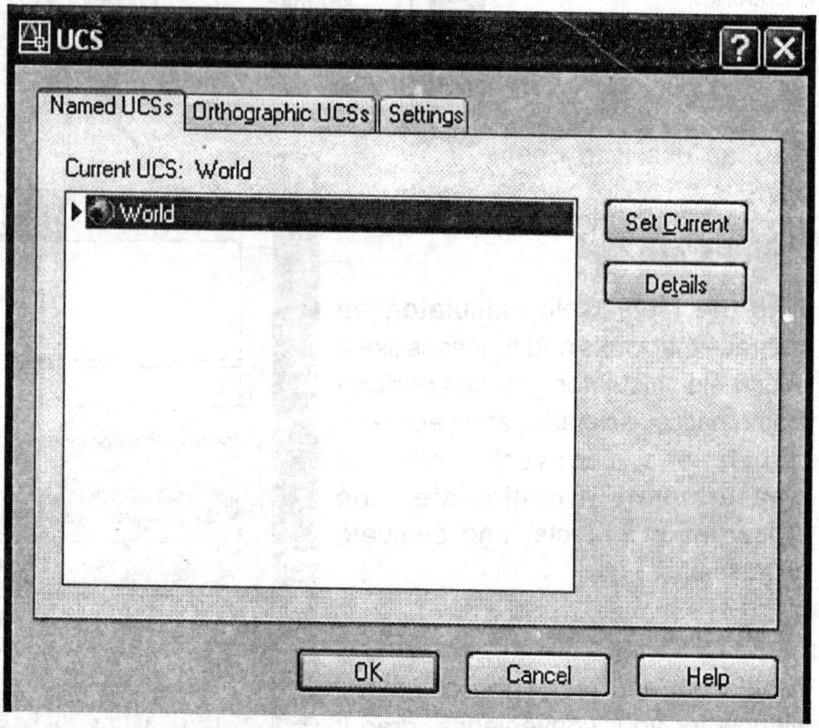

Named UCS

Manages defined user coordinate systems.

Orthographic UCS

Various options under this are:

Preset

Manages defined user coordinate systems.

Top

Specifies the Top UCS orientation.

Bottom

Specifies the Bottom UCS orientation.

Left

Specifies the Left UCS orientation.

Right

Specifies the Right UCS orientation.

Front

Specifies the Front UCS orientation.

Back

Specifies the Back UCS orientation.

Move UCS

Moves the defined UCS.

New UCS

Various options under this are:

World

Sets the UCS to the World Coordinate System.

Object

Defines a new coordinate system based on a selected object.

Face

Defines a new coordinate system based on a selected face.

View

Establishes a new coordinate system with the XY plane parallel to the screen.

Origin

Defines a new UCS by shifting the origin.

Z Axis Vector

Defines a UCS using a positive Z axis extrusion method.

3 Point

Specifies the new UCS origin and the direction of the X and Y axes.

X

Rotates the current UCS about the X axis.

Y

Rotates the current UCS about the Y axis.

Z

Rotates the current UCS about the Z axis.

Apply

Applies current UCS to a selected viewport.

CAD Standards

Drawings are easier to interpret if you set standards to enforce consistency. You can set standards for layer names, dimension styles, and other elements; check drawings against these standards; and then change any properties that do not conform.

Define Standards

To set standards, you create a file that defines properties for layers, dimension styles, linetypes, and text styles, and you save it as a standards file with the .dws file name extension.

Check Drawings for Standards Violations

You can audit a drawing file for violations of standards and then fix violations. The Batch Standards Checker audits more than one file at a time.

Translate Layer Names and Properties

With the Layer Translator, you can change a drawing's layers to match layer standards you set.

Wizards

Various options under this are:

Publish to Web..

Publishes your current drawing to the Web.

Add Plotter

Adds and configures plotters

Add Plot Style Table

Creates a plot style table.

Add Color-Dependent/Named Plot Style Table

Creates a color-dependent plot style table.

Create Layout

Creates a layout using the settings you apply to the wizard.

Import Plot Settings

Displays a wizard to import PCP and PC2 configuration file plot settings into the Model tab or current layout.

Drafting Settings

Specifies settings for Snap mode, grid, and polar and object snap tracking.

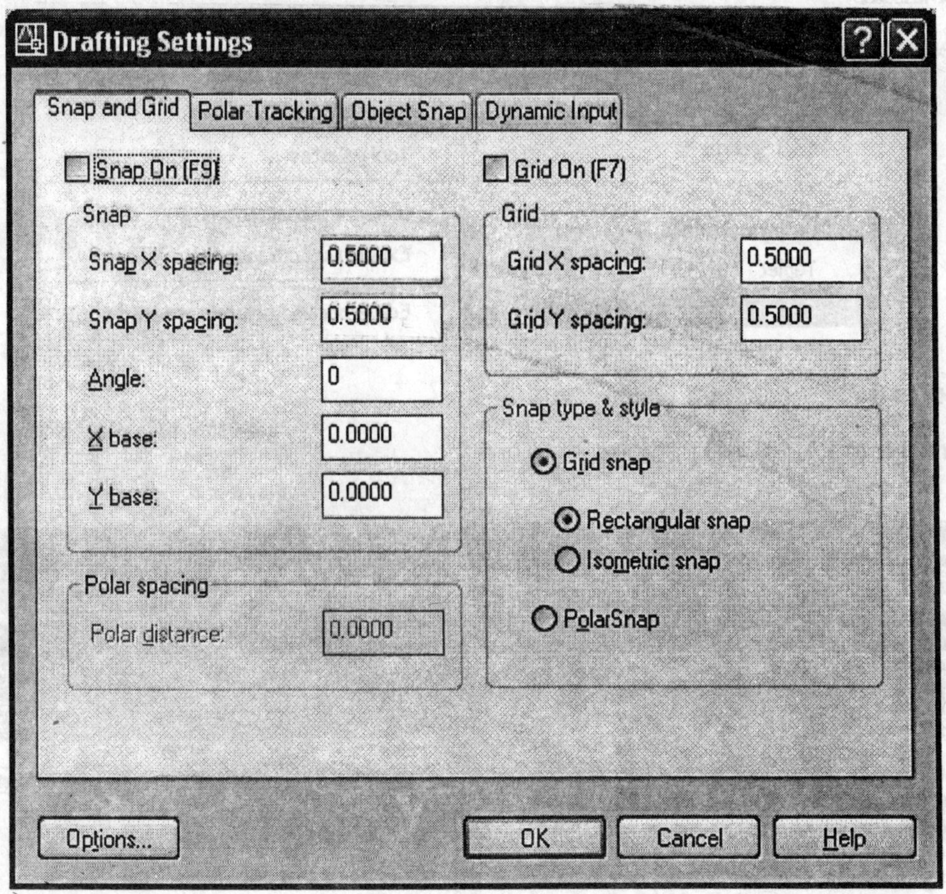

Tablet

Various options under this are:

On

Turns Tablet mode on.

Off

Turns Tablet mode off.

Calibrate

Calibrates the digitizer with the drawing's coordinate system.

Configure

Designates or realigns the tablet menu areas.

Customize

Different options available under this are:

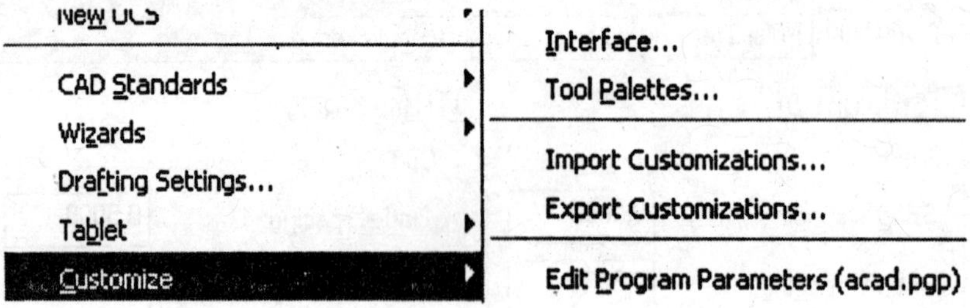

Options

Customizes the AutoCAD settings.

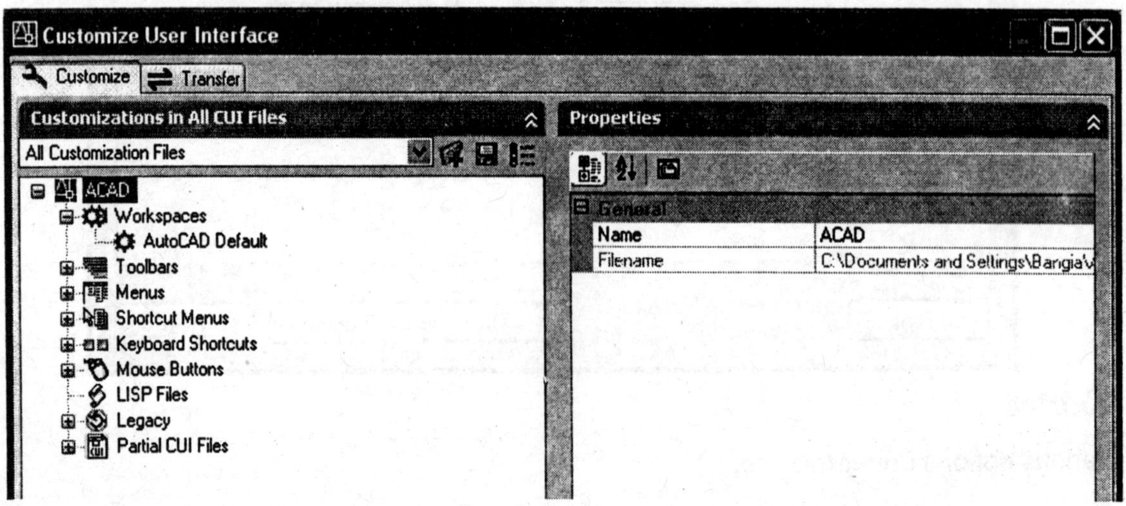

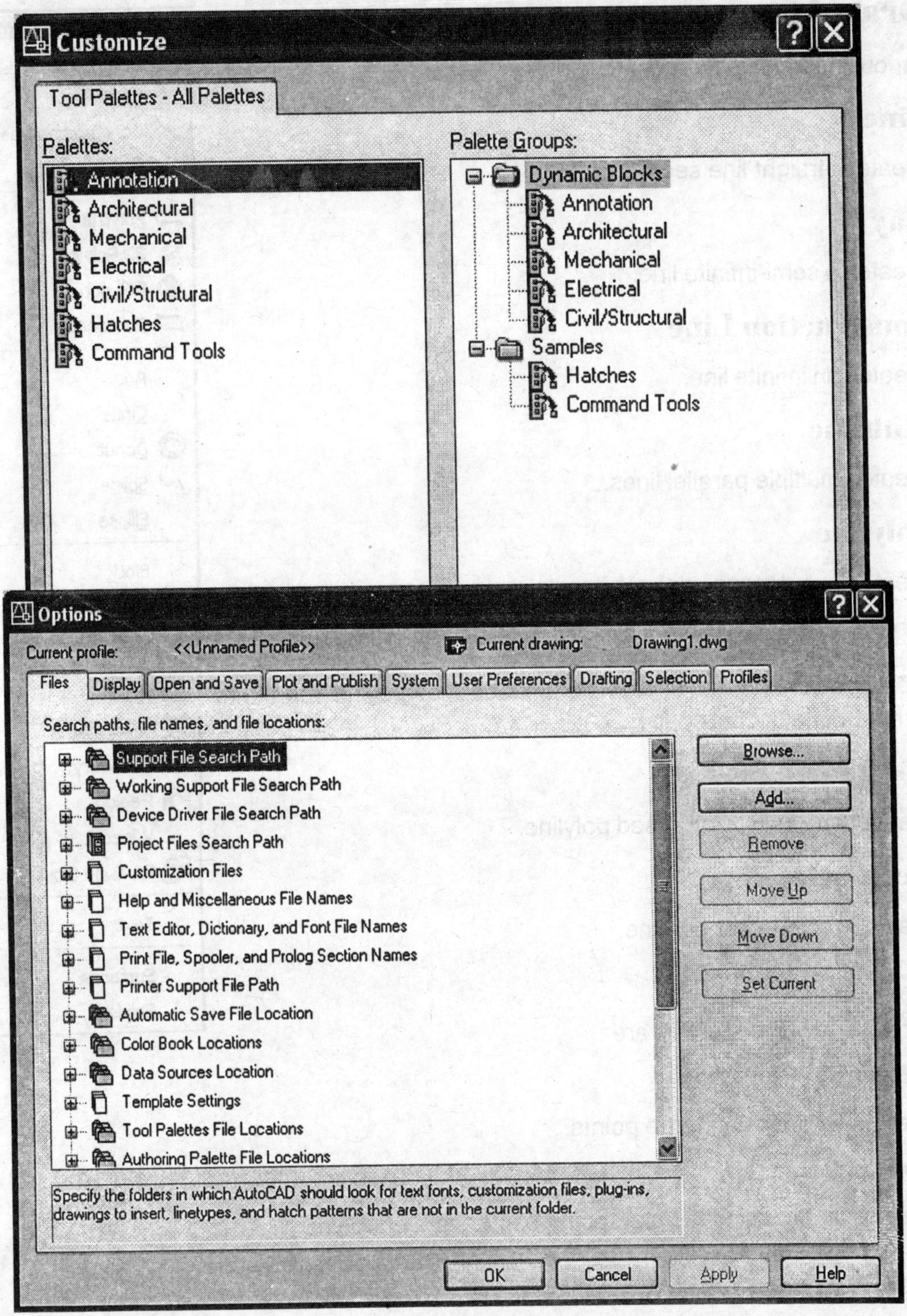
Customize
Tool Palettes - All Palettes
Palettes:
Annotation
Architectural
Mechanical
Electrical
Civil/Structural
Hatches
Command Tools
Palette Groups:
Dynamic Blocks
Annotation
Architectural
Mechanical
Electrical
Civil/Structural
Samples
Hatches
Command Tools
Options
Current profile: <<Unnamed Profile>>
Current drawing: Drawing1.dwg
Files
Display
Open and Save
Plot and Publish
System
User Preferences
Drafting
Selection
Profiles
Search paths, file names, and file locations:
Support File Search Path
Working Support File Search Path
Device Driver File Search Path
Project Files Search Path
Customization Files
Help and Miscellaneous File Names
Text Editor, Dictionary, and Font File Names
Print File, Spooler, and Prolog Section Names
Printer Support File Path
Automatic Save File Location
Color Book Locations
Data Sources Location
Template Settings
Tool Palettes File Locations
Authoring Palette File Locations
Browse...
Add...
Remove
Move Up
Move Down
Set Current
Specify the folders in which AutoCAD should look for text fonts, customization files, plug-ins, drawings to insert, linetypes, and hatch patterns that are not in the current folder.
OK
Cancel
Apply
Help

Draw Menu

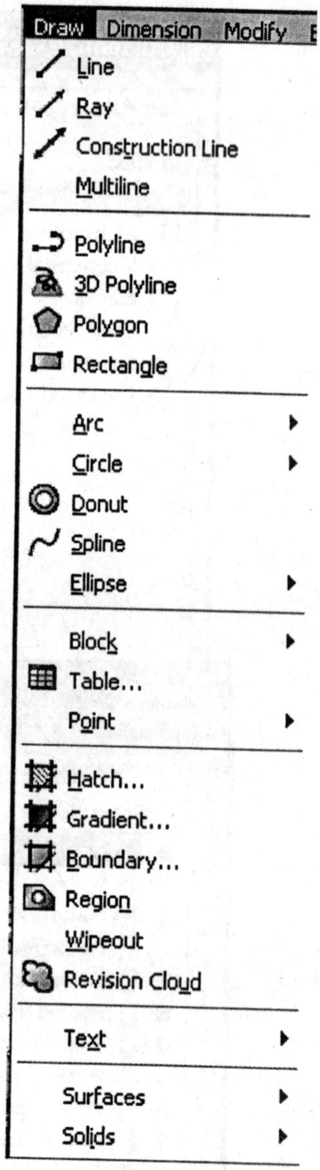

Various options under this are:

Line

Creates straight line segments:.

Ray

Creates a semi-infinite line.

Construction Line

Creates an infinite line.

Multline

Creates multiple parallel lines.

Polyline

Creates two-dimensional polylines.

3D Polyline

Creates a polyline with straight continuous linetype line segments in three-dimensional space.

Polygon

Creates an equilateral closed polyline.

Rectangle

Draws a rectangular polyline.

Arc

Various options under this are:

3 Points

Creates an arc using three points.

Start, Center, End

Creates an arc using the start point, center, and endpoint.

Start, Center, Angle

Creates an arc using the start point, center, and included angle.

Start, Center, Length

Creates an arc using the start point, center, and length of chord.

Start, End, Angle

Creates an arc using the start point, endpoint, and included angle.

Start, End, Direction

Creates an arc using the start point, endpoint, and starting direction.

Start, End, Radius

Creates an arc using the start point, endpoint, and radius.

Center, Start, End

Creates an arc using the center, start point, and endpoint.

Center, Start, Angle

Creates an arc using the center, start point, and included angle.

Center, Start, Length

Creates an arc using the center, start point, and length of chord.

Continue

Creates an arc tangent to the last line or arc drawn.

Circle

Various options under this are:

Center, Radius

Creates a circle using a specified radius.

Center, Diameter

Creates a circle using a specified diameter.

2 Points

Creates a circle using two endpoints of the diameter.

3 Points

Creates a circle using three points on the circumference.

Tan, Tan, Radius

Creates a circle tangent to two objects with a specified radius.

Tan, Tan, Tan

Creates a circle tangent to three objects.

Donut

Draws filled circles and rings.

Spline

Creates a quadratic or cubic spline (NURBS) curve.

Ellipse

Various options under this are:

Center

Creates an ellipse using a center point.

Axis, End

Creates an ellipse or an elliptical arc.

Arc

Creates an elliptical arc.

Block

Various options under this are:

Make

Creates a block definition from objects you select.

Base

Sets the insertion base point for the current drawing.

Define Attributes

Creates an attribute definition.

Table

Draws a table.

Point

Various options under this are:

Single Point

Creates a single point.

Multiple Point

Creates multiple points.

Divide

Places evenly spaced point objects or blocks along the length or perimeter of an object.

Measure

Places point objects or blocks at measured intervals on an object.

Hatch

Fills an enclosed area or selected objects with a hatch pattern.

Boundary

Creates a region or a polyline from an enclosed area.

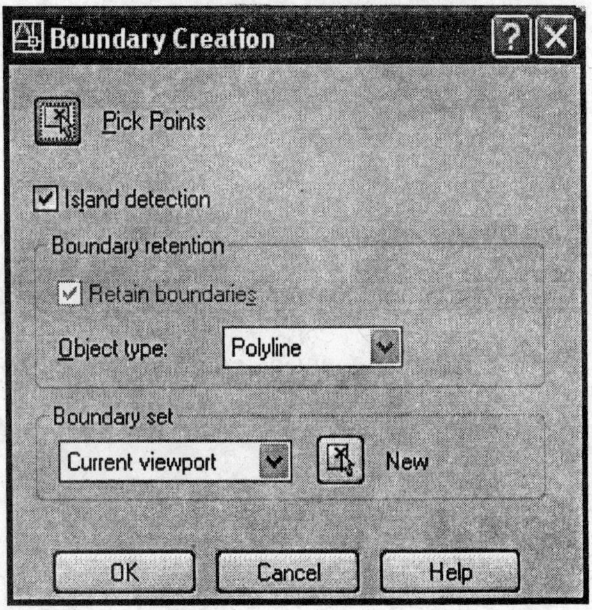

Region

Creates a region object from a selection set of existing objects.

Wipeout

Covers existing objects with a blank area.

Revision Cloud

You may need to mark areas of your drawings that contain revisions, to draw attention to these revisions. A common method is to draw a revision cloud around the revision objects. This command is used for the same.

Text

Various options under this are:

Multiline Text

Creates multiline text.

Single Line Text

Displays text on screen as it is entered.

Surfaces

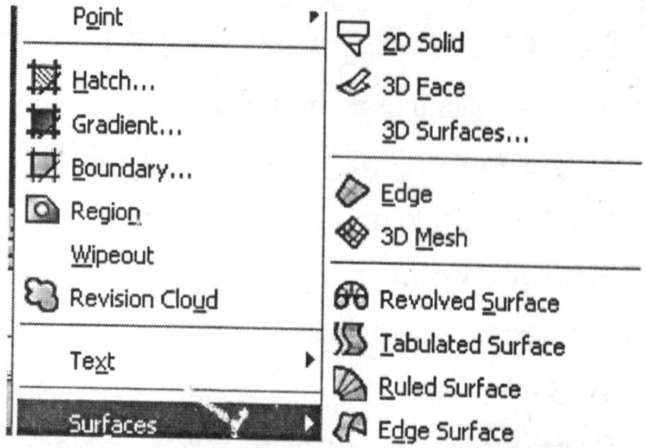

Various options under this are: 2D Solid, 3D Face, 3D Surfaces, Edge, 3D Mesh, Revolved Surface, Tabulated Surface, Ruled Surface and Edge Surface. Using them you draw these.

Solids

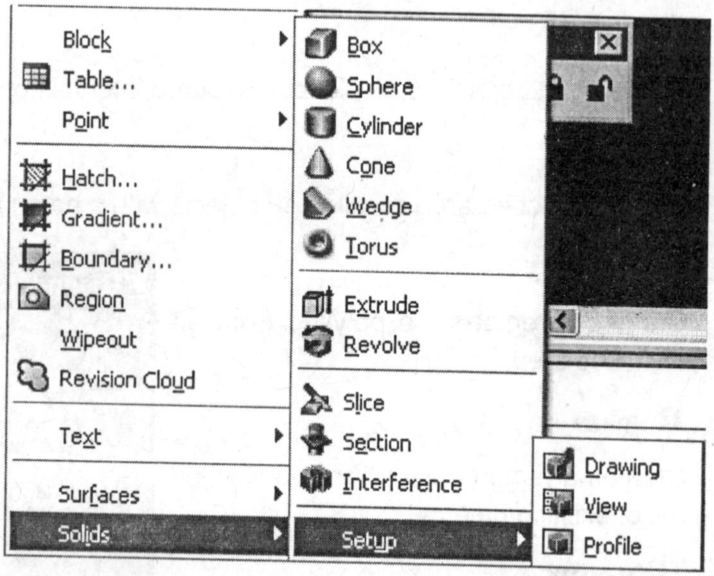

Various options under this are: Box, Sphere, Cylinder, Cone, Wedge, Torus, Extrude, Revolve, Slice, Section, Interference and Setup. Using these you can draw solids figures from them.

Dimension Menu

Various options under this menu are:

Quick Dimension

It allows you to dimension serveral objects at one time.

Linear

Creates linear dimensions.

Aligned

Creates an aligned linear dimension.

Ordinate

Creates ordinate dimensions.

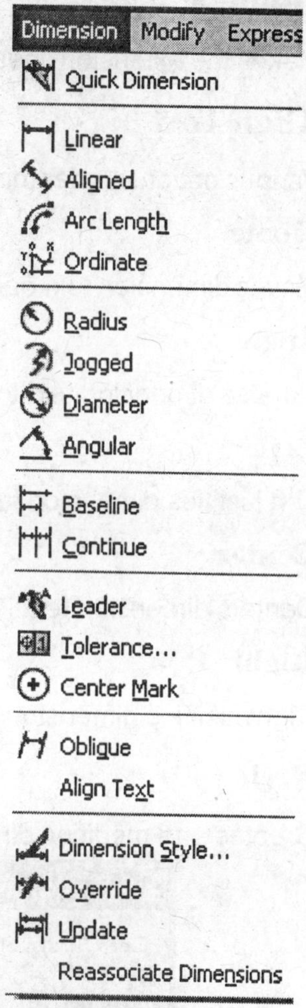

Radius

Creates radius dimensions for circles and arcs.

Diameter

Creates a diameter dimension for circles and arcs.

Angular

Creates an angular dimension.

Baseline

Creates a linear, angular, or ordinate dimension from the baseline of the previous dimension or a selected dimension.

Continue

Creates a linear, angular, or ordinate dimension from the second extension line of the previous dimension or a selected dimension.

Leader

Quickly creates a leader and leader annotation.

Tolerance

Creates geometric tolerances.

Center Mark

Creates a center mark for circles and arcs.

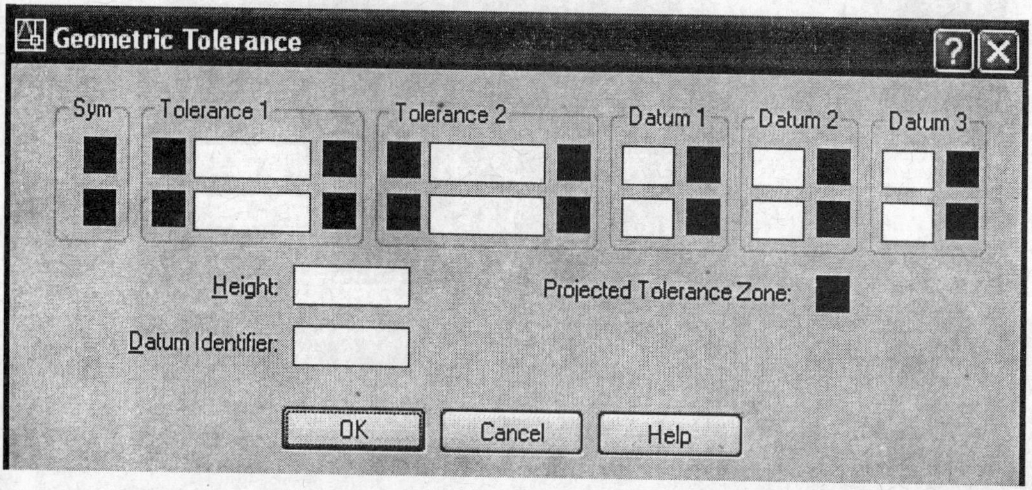

Oblique

Makes the extension lines of linear dimensions oblique.

Align Text

Various options under this are:

Home

Moves dimension text back to its default position.

Angle

Rotates dimension text to an angle.

Left

Left justifies dimension text.

Center

Centers dimension text:.

Right

Right justifies dimension text.

Style

Creates and modifies dimension styles.

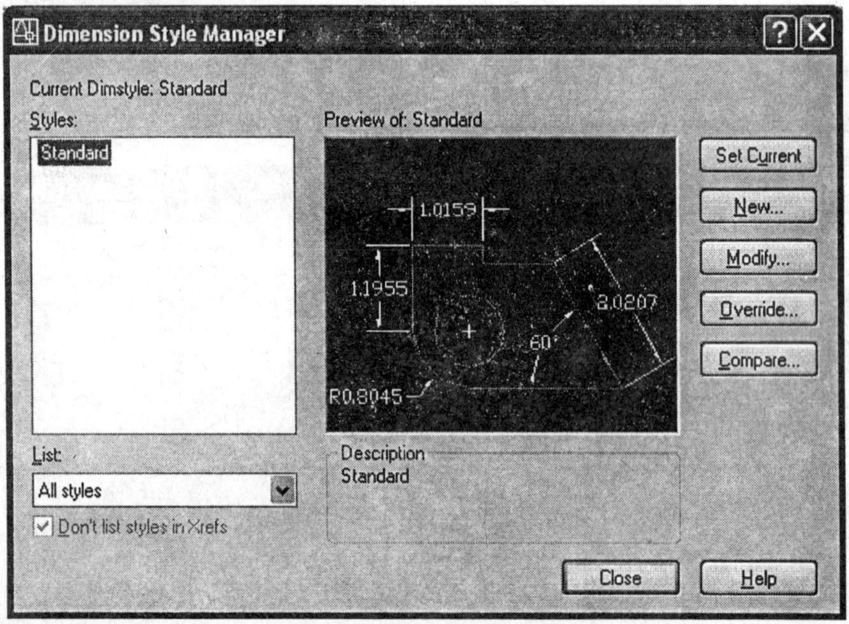

Override

Overrides dimension system variables.

Update

Updates dimensions so they use the most current dimension style settings.

Reassociate Dimensions

You may need to change the associativity of dimensions in several circumstances such as:

- Redefine the associativity of dimensions in drawings that have been edited significantly;
- Add associativity to dimensions that have been partially disassociated;
- Add associativity to dimensions in legacy drawings;
- Remove associativity from dimensions in drawings that will be used by people on releases prior to AutoCAD 2005, but who do not want any proxy objects in the drawings.

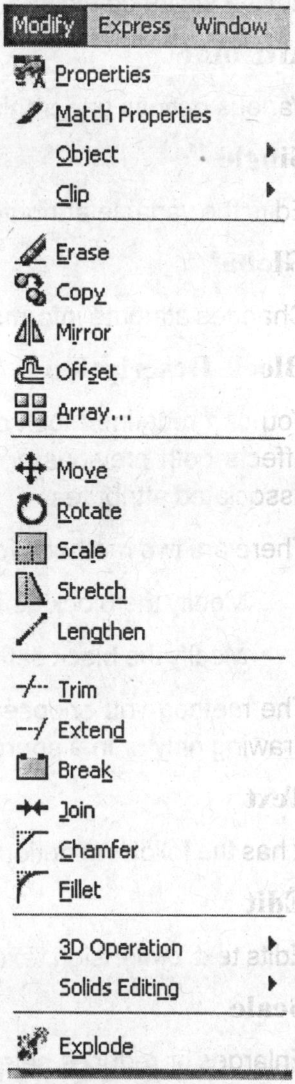

Modify Menu

Various options under this are:

Properties

Controls properties of existing objects.

Match Properties

Copies the properties from one object to one or more objects.

Object

Various options under this are:

External Reference

Various options under this are:

Bind

Binds individual dependent symbols of an xref to a drawing.

Image

Various options under this are:

Frame

Controls whether AutoCAD displays the image frame or hides it from view.

Hatch

Modifies an existing hatch object.

Polyline

Edits polylines and three-dimensional polygon meshes:.

Spline

Edits a spline object.

Attribute

Various options under this are:

Single

Edits the variable attributes of a block.

Global

Changes attribute information independent of its block definition.

Block Description

You can redefine block definitions in your current drawing. Redefining a block definition affects both previous and future insertions of the block in the current drawing and any associated attributes.

There are two methods for redefining a block definition:

- Modify the block definition in the current drawing.
- Modify the block definition in the source drawing and reinsert it into the current drawing.

The method you choose depends on whether you want to make changes in the current drawing only or in a source drawing also.

Text

It has the following options:

Edit

Edits text, dimension text, attribute definitions, and feature control frames.

Scale

Enlarges or reduces selected text objects without changing their locations.

Justify

Changes the justification point of selected text objects without changing their locations.

Clip

It has options to modify Image, Ref or Viewport .

Xref and Block Editing

Various types of references can be edited using this.

Erase

Removes objects from a drawing.

Copy

Duplicates the objects you select.

Mirror

Creates a mirror image copy of objects.

Offset

Creates concentric circles, parallel lines, and parallel curves.

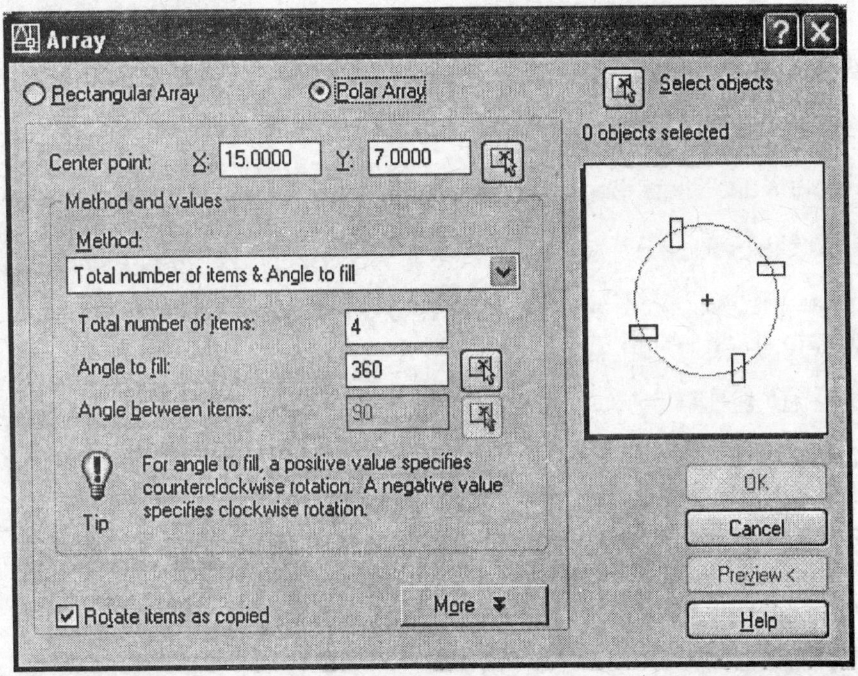

Array

Creates multiple copies of objects in a pattern.

Move

Displaces objects a specified distance in a specified direction.

Rotate

Moves objects about a base point.

Scale

Enlarges or reduces objects equally in the X, Y, and Z directions.

Stretch

Moves or stretches objects.

Lengthen

Lengthens an object.

Trim

Trims objects at a cutting edge defined by other objects.

Extend

Extends an object to meet another object.

Break

Erases parts of objects or splits an object in two.

Chamfer

Bevels the edges of objects.

Fillet

Rounds and fillets the edges of objects.

3D Operation

It has the options to modify 3D Array, Mirror 3D, Rotate 3D and Align.

Solids Editing

It has the options to modify solids such as Union, Subtract, Intersect, Extrude faces, Move faces, Offset faces, Delete faces, Rotate faces, Taper faces, Color faces, Copy faces, Color edges, Copy edges, Imprint, Clean, Separate, Shell and Check.

Explode

Breaks a compound object into its component objects.

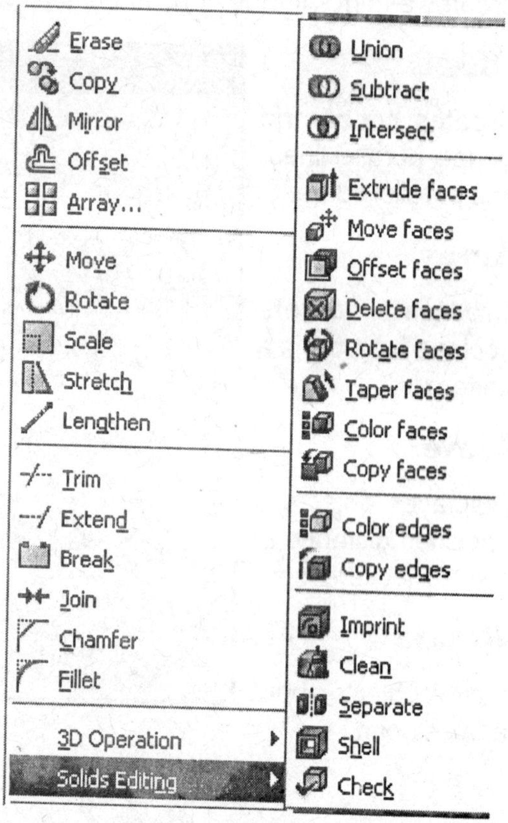

Express Menu

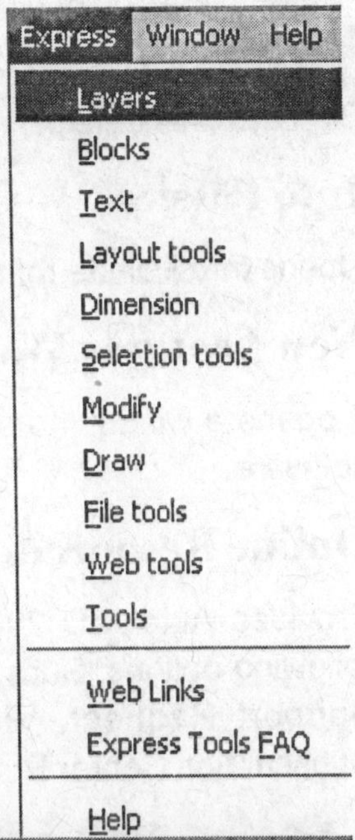

This is a new menu in AutoCAD 2006. Each of the command has a fly-out option with an option to quickly work through the various options. The commands are: Layers, Blocks, Text, Layout tools, Dimension, Selection tools, Modify, Draw, File tools, Web tools, Tools, Web Links, Express Tools FAQ and Help. Various options of Layer are shown next.

Window Menu

Various options under this menu are:

Close

Closes the current drawing.

Close All

Closes all the open drawings.

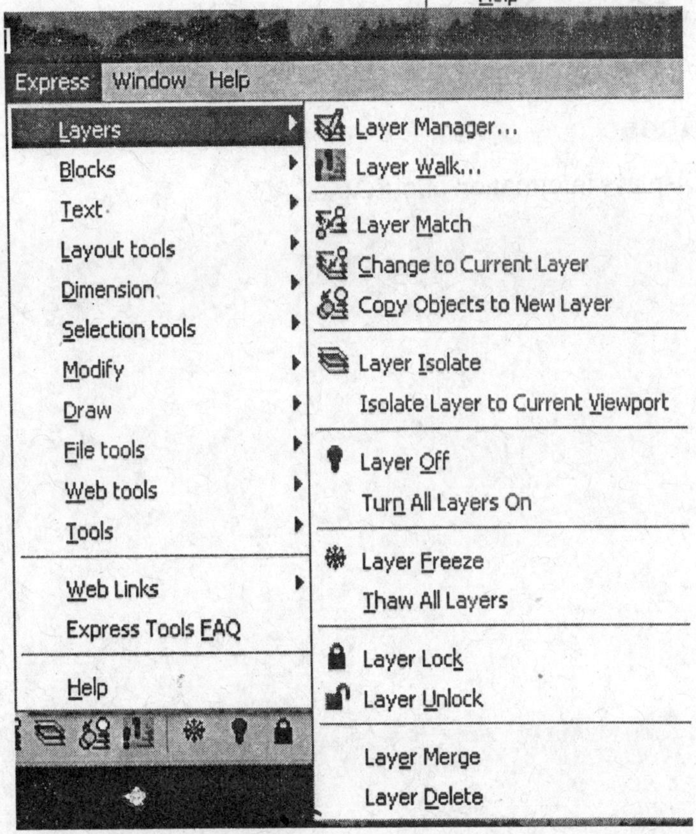

Cascade

Arrange windows so they overlap

Tile Horizontally

Arrange windows as non-overlapping tiles

Tile Vertically

Arrange windows as non-overlapping tiles

Arrange Icons

Arrange icons at the bottom of the window.

Help Menu

Various options under this menu are:

Help

Displays online help.

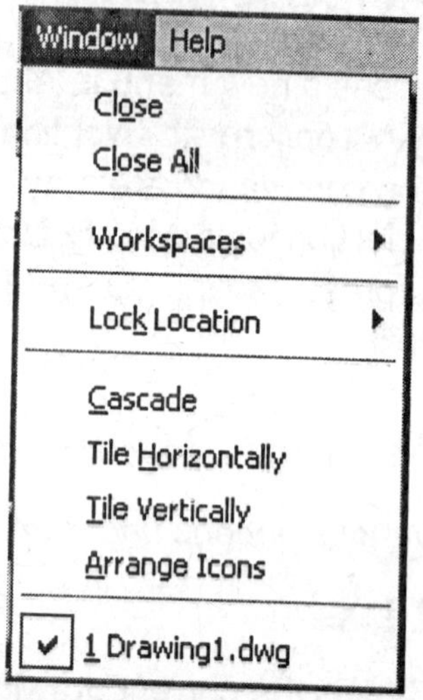

Info Palette

Opens Info Palette for assistance.

New Features Workshop

It opens a window to show you the various new features of the software.

Online Resources

Provides AutoCAD 2006 support from the website. It has the following options: Subscription e-Learning Catalog, Create Support Request, View Support Requests and Edit Subscription Center Profile.

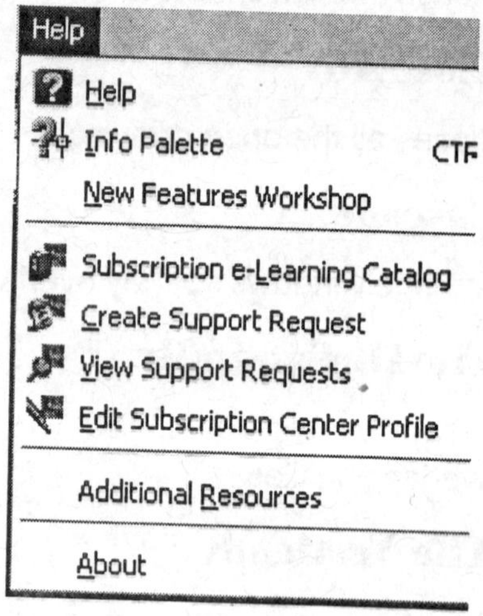

Additional Resources

Provides additional AutoCAD 2006 support from the website.

About

Displays information about AutoCAD.

Cutomizing AutoCAD 2006 | 2

Working with AutoCAD 2006

Before you start working with the software, it is better to set it according to your liking. For this we have commands like Options, Customize and options like setting limits, colours, etc. Once these are set, it becomes easy to work with the software.

Let us start with Customize.

Customizing

By customizing we mean here that you set the software according to your needs of working. Everybody has his own style of working, so you can set your own too. The command for this is available under Tools menu. There are options here: Workspaces, Toolbars, Menus, Shortcut Menus, Mouse Buttons, Legacy and Partial CUI Files. Of these the last 2 are for the advanced version. Let us discuss the other ones.

Workspace Customization

Workspaces are user interface configurations that you create. For each workspace, you can display toolbars, buttons, menus or menu items, and dockable windows such as the Properties palette and the Sheet Set Manager.

To edit the contents of a workspace, drag elements in the tree view. You can also use the Customize Workspace mode workspace to select groups of content to add to workspaces.

Toolbars Customization

The Toolbars node displays toolbars defined in all workspaces. Select a toolbar to edit it and define the workspaces that use the toolbar.

Menu Customization

The Menus node displays menus defined in all workspaces. Select a menu to edit it and define the workspaces that use it.

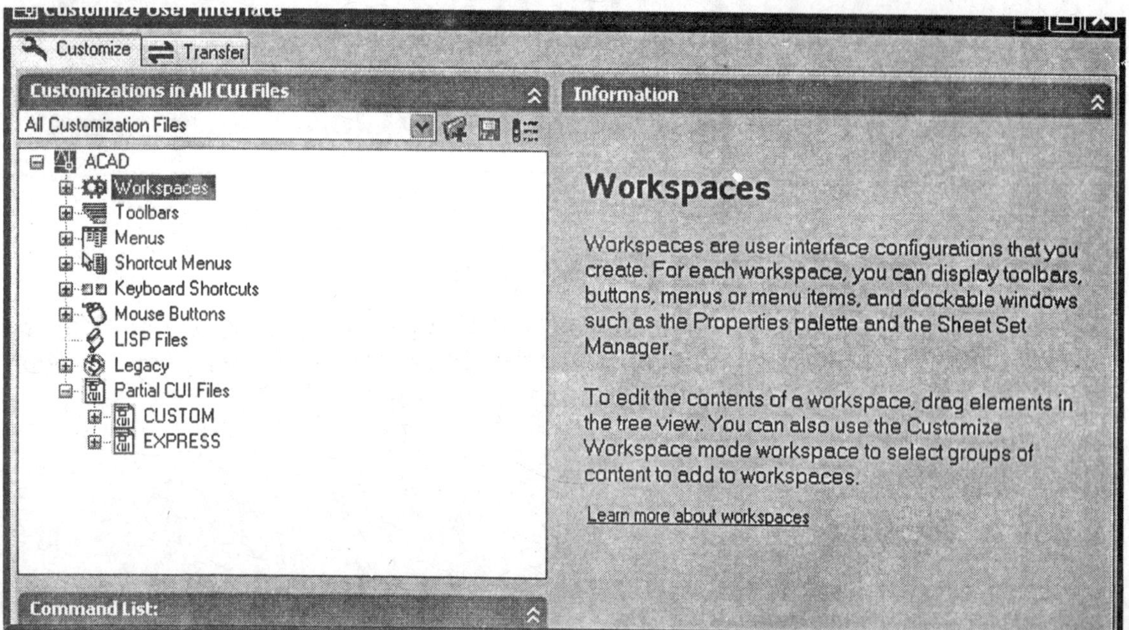
Customize User Interface
Customize
Transfer
Customizations in All CUI Files
All Customization Files
ACAD
Workspaces
Toolbars
Menus
Shortcut Menus
Keyboard Shortcuts
Mouse Buttons
LISP Files
Legacy
Partial CUI Files
CUSTOM
EXPRESS
Information
Workspaces
Workspaces are user interface configurations that you create. For each workspace, you can display toolbars, buttons, menus or menu items, and dockable windows such as the Properties palette and the Sheet Set Manager.
To edit the contents of a workspace, drag elements in the tree view. You can also use the Customize Workspace mode workspace to select groups of content to add to workspaces.
Learn more about workspaces
Command List:

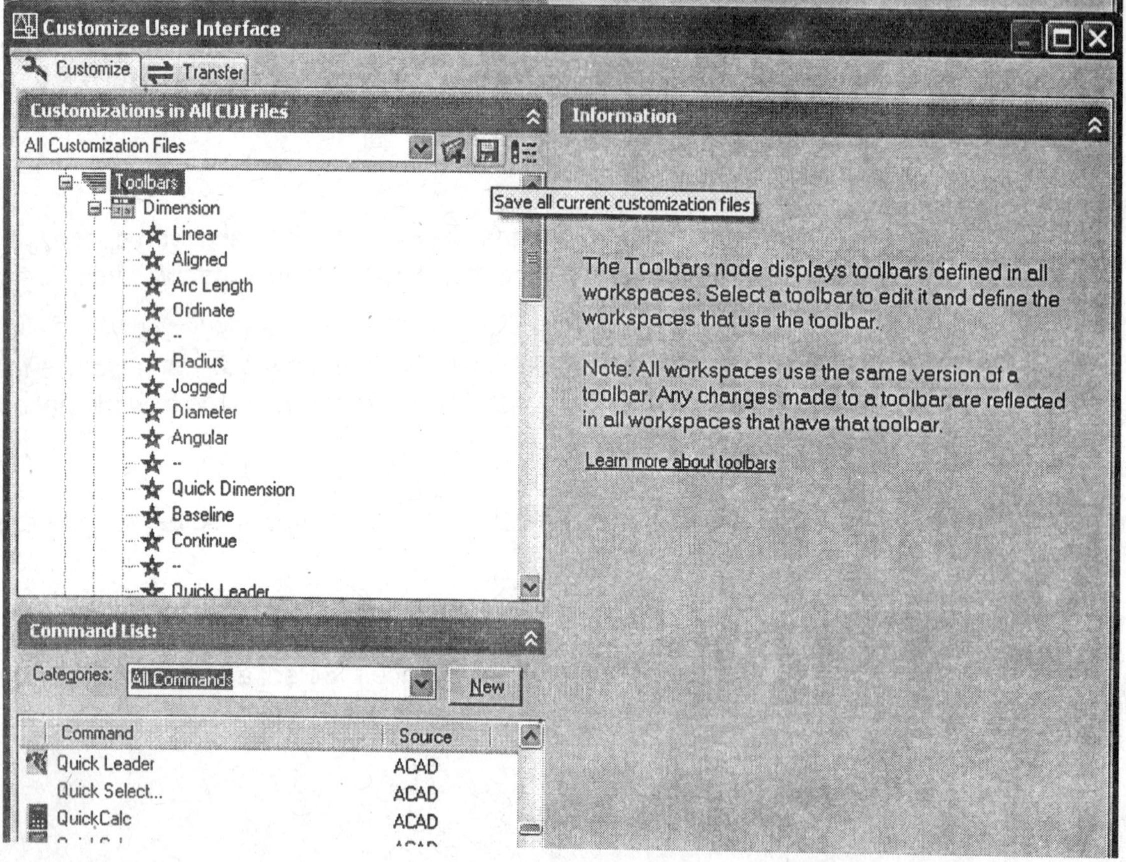
Customize User Interface
Customize
Transfer
Customizations in All CUI Files
All Customization Files
Toolbars
Dimension
Linear
Aligned
Arc Length
Ordinate
--
Radius
Jogged
Diameter
Angular
--
Quick Dimension
Baseline
Continue
--
Quick Leader
Save all current customization files
Information
The Toolbars node displays toolbars defined in all workspaces. Select a toolbar to edit it and define the workspaces that use the toolbar.
Note: All workspaces use the same version of a toolbar. Any changes made to a toolbar are reflected in all workspaces that have that toolbar.
Learn more about toolbars
Command List:
Categories:
All Commands
New
Command
Source
Quick Leader
ACAD
Quick Select...
ACAD
QuickCalc
ACAD

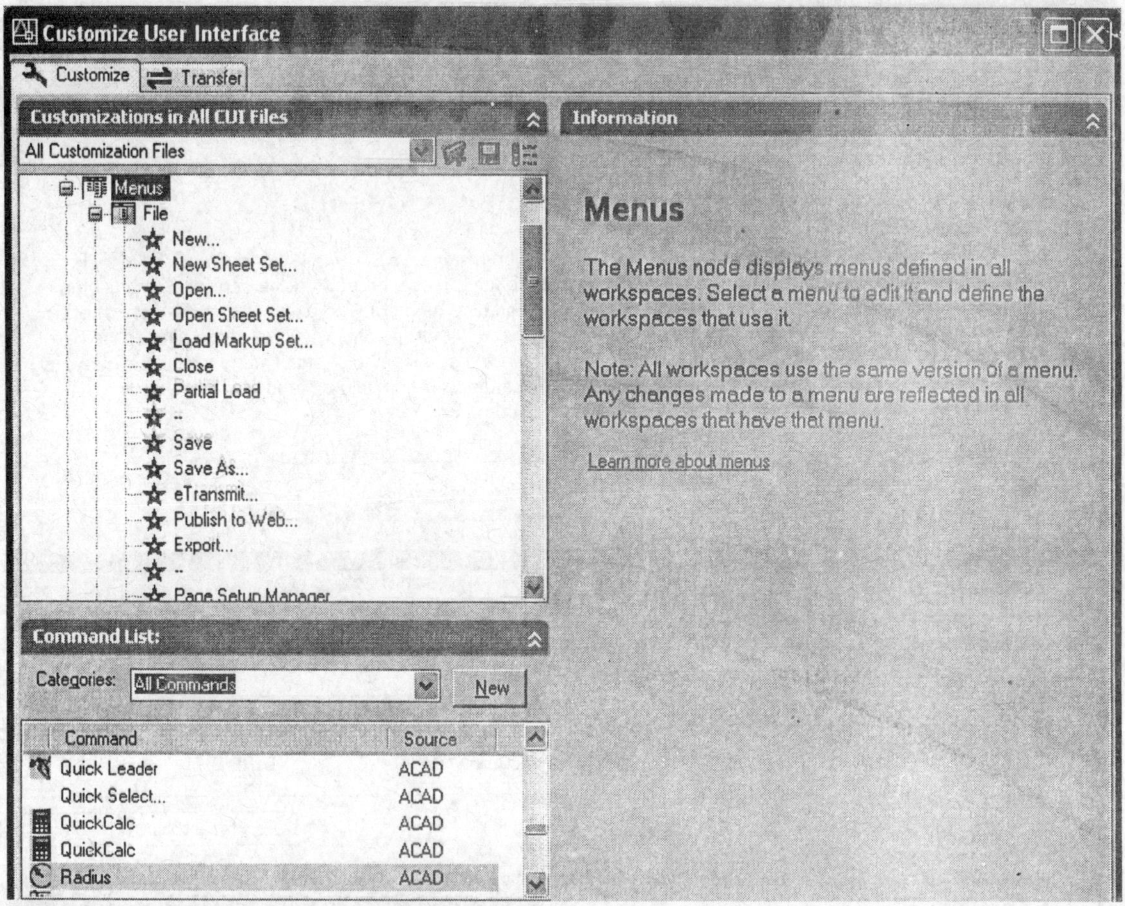

Shortcut Menus Customization

Shortcut menus are available when you right-click certain objects or areas of the screen. Shortcut menus can also be displayed using scripts. Select a shortcut menu to edit its contents. Drag commands to the tree view to add them to shortcut menus. You can also drag a shortcut menu onto a menu item to create a submenu.

Keyboard Shortcuts Customization

Keyboard shortcuts are used to assign commands to custom keystroke combinations. Temporary override keys execute a command or change a setting only when a key is pressed.

You can create and edit keyboard shortcuts for a selected command in the Properties pane. You can select a command for a keyboard shortcut from the Shortcuts view in this pane, the tree view in the Available Customizations In pane, or in the Command List pane.

To create a new temporary override key, right-click any of the keyboard-shortcut nodes in

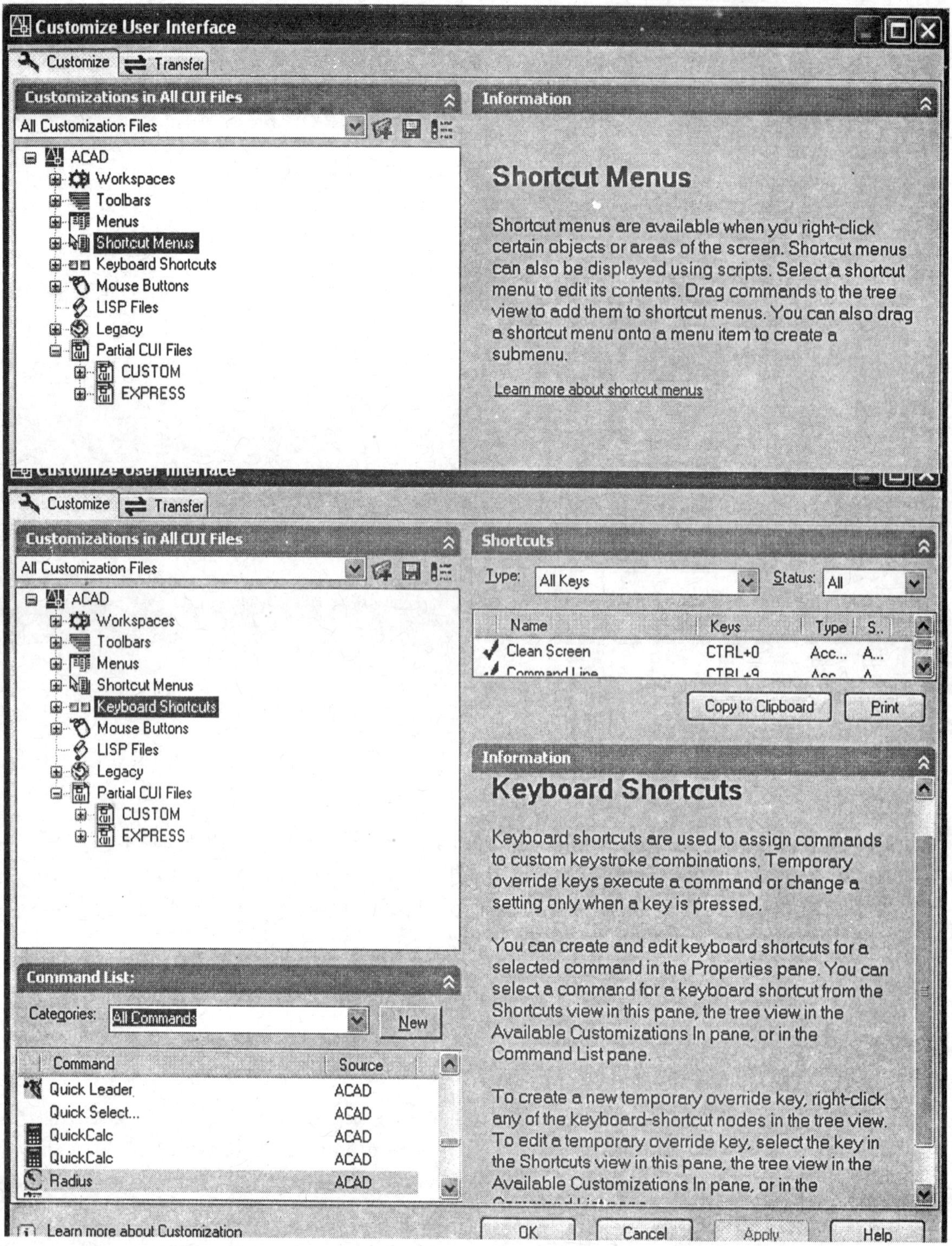
Customize User Interface
Customize
Transfer
Customizations in All CUI Files
All Customization Files
ACAD
Workspaces
Toolbars
Menus
Shortcut Menus
Keyboard Shortcuts
Mouse Buttons
LISP Files
Legacy
Partial CUI Files
CUSTOM
EXPRESS
Information
Shortcut Menus
Shortcut menus are available when you right-click certain objects or areas of the screen. Shortcut menus can also be displayed using scripts. Select a shortcut menu to edit its contents. Drag commands to the tree view to add them to shortcut menus. You can also drag a shortcut menu onto a menu item to create a submenu.
Learn more about shortcut menus
Customize
Transfer
Customizations in All CUI Files
All Customization Files
ACAD
Workspaces
Toolbars
Menus
Shortcut Menus
Keyboard Shortcuts
Mouse Buttons
LISP Files
Legacy
Partial CUI Files
CUSTOM
EXPRESS
Shortcuts
Type: All Keys
Status: All
Name
Keys
Type
S..
Clean Screen
CTRL+0
Acc...
A...
Copy to Clipboard
Print
Information
Keyboard Shortcuts
Keyboard shortcuts are used to assign commands to custom keystroke combinations. Temporary override keys execute a command or change a setting only when a key is pressed.
You can create and edit keyboard shortcuts for a selected command in the Properties pane. You can select a command for a keyboard shortcut from the Shortcuts view in this pane, the tree view in the Available Customizations In pane, or in the Command List pane.
To create a new temporary override key, right-click any of the keyboard-shortcut nodes in the tree view. To edit a temporary override key, select the key in the Shortcuts view in this pane, the tree view in the Available Customizations In pane, or in the
Command List:
Categories: All Commands
New
Command
Source
Quick Leader
ACAD
Quick Select...
ACAD
QuickCalc
ACAD
QuickCalc
ACAD
Radius
ACAD
Learn more about Customization
OK
Cancel
Apply
Help

the tree view. To edit a temporary override key, select the key in the Shortcuts view in this pane, the tree view in the Available Customizations In pane, or in the Command List pane.

Mouse Buttons Customization

The Mouse Buttons node is organized by keyboard/mouse-click combination and then by button. The first two buttons correspond to mouse buttons 2 and 3 and are named Right-Click and Middle-Click, respectively. Drag a command to assign the command to a mouse button. Create additional buttons by dragging commands to the Click node.

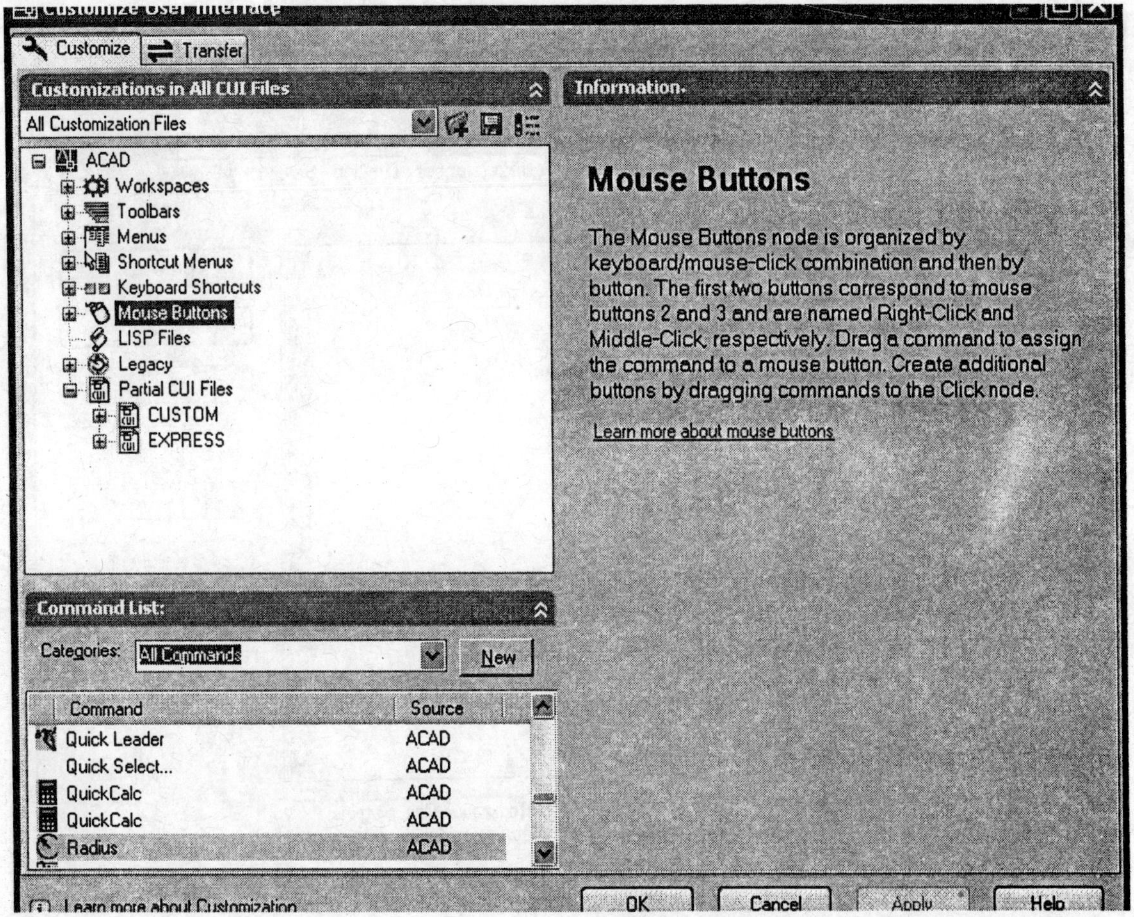

All these are shown on the next pages. What all you can change of the New command of the File menu, is also shown.

Next is Options

Setting the Options

Before starting with any software, I always suggest that you go through the various options available to you in that software. Here also the various options available under Options dialog box under Tools menu has the following tabs:

File

Here you can see where the various files of the AutoCAD are. You can alter them if the need be.

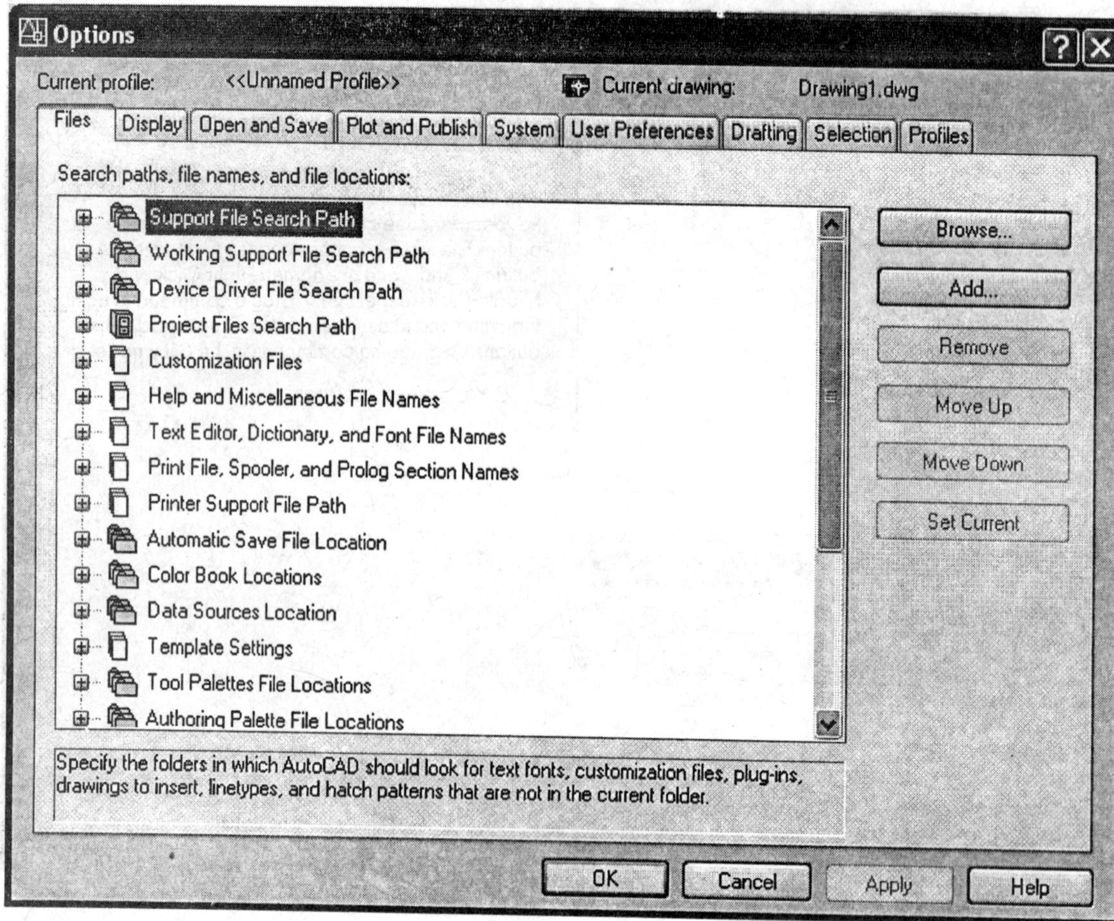

Display

From here you can set the settings of Window elements, Display resolutions, Layout elements, Display performance, Cross hair size and Reference edit fading intensity.

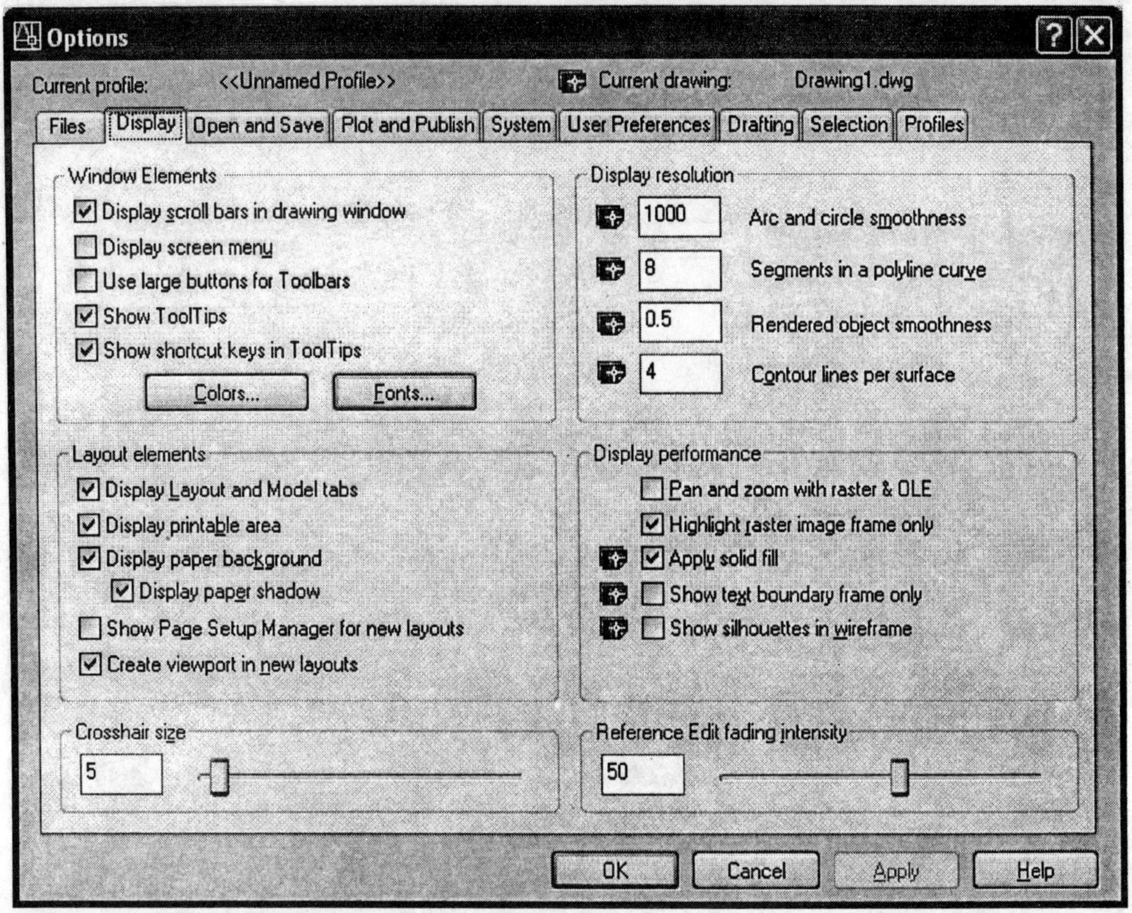

Open and Save

From here you can set the file extension of the drawing files, file protection precautions, external references and objectARX applications.

Plot and Publish

You can set the various options of plotter from here.

System

You can set from here the various options of the peripherals used in the system.

User Preferences

From here you can set the various options regarding the various types of dimensions you are going to use in your drawings. You can also set your priorities for entering the data.

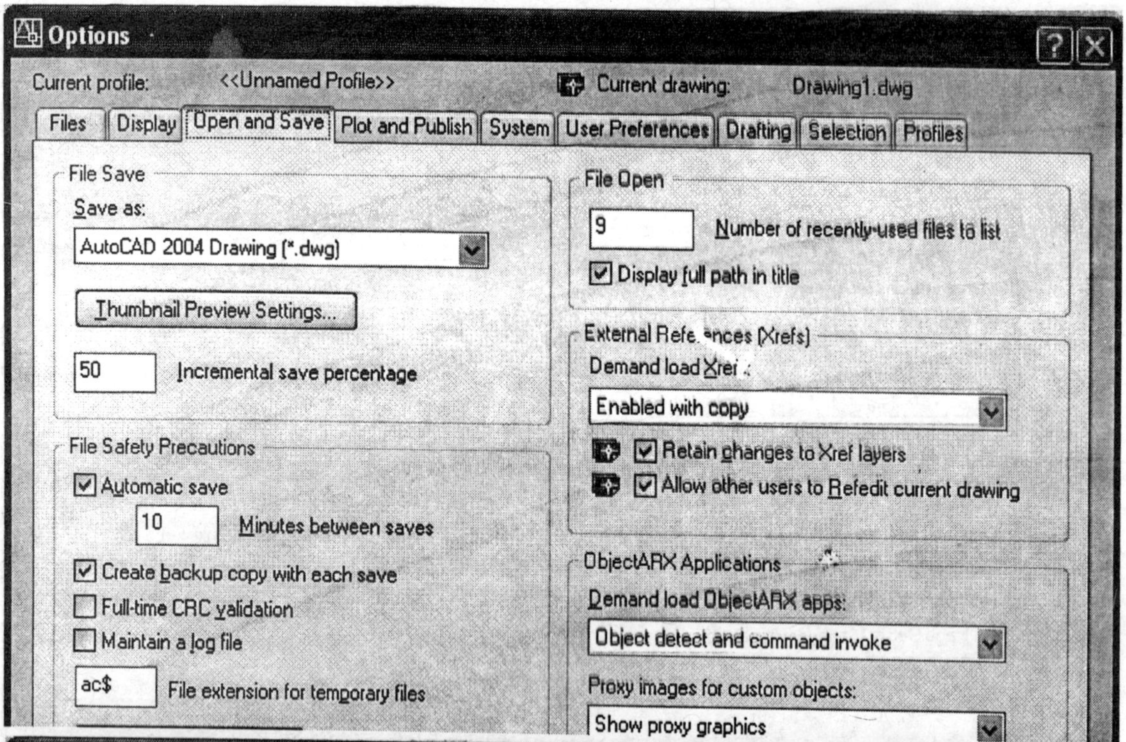
Options
Current profile: <<Unnamed Profile>>
Current drawing: Drawing1.dwg
Files
Display
Open and Save
Plot and Publish
System
User Preferences
Drafting
Selection
Profiles
File Save
Save as:
AutoCAD 2004 Drawing (*.dwg)
Thumbnail Preview Settings...
50
Incremental save percentage
File Safety Precautions
Automatic save
10
Minutes between saves
Create backup copy with each save
Full-time CRC validation
Maintain a log file
ac$
File extension for temporary files
File Open
9
Number of recently-used files to list
Display full path in title
Enabled with copy
Retain changes to Xref layers
Allow other users to Refedit current drawing
ObjectARX Applications
Demand load ObjectARX apps:
Object detect and command invoke
Proxy images for custom objects:
Show proxy graphics

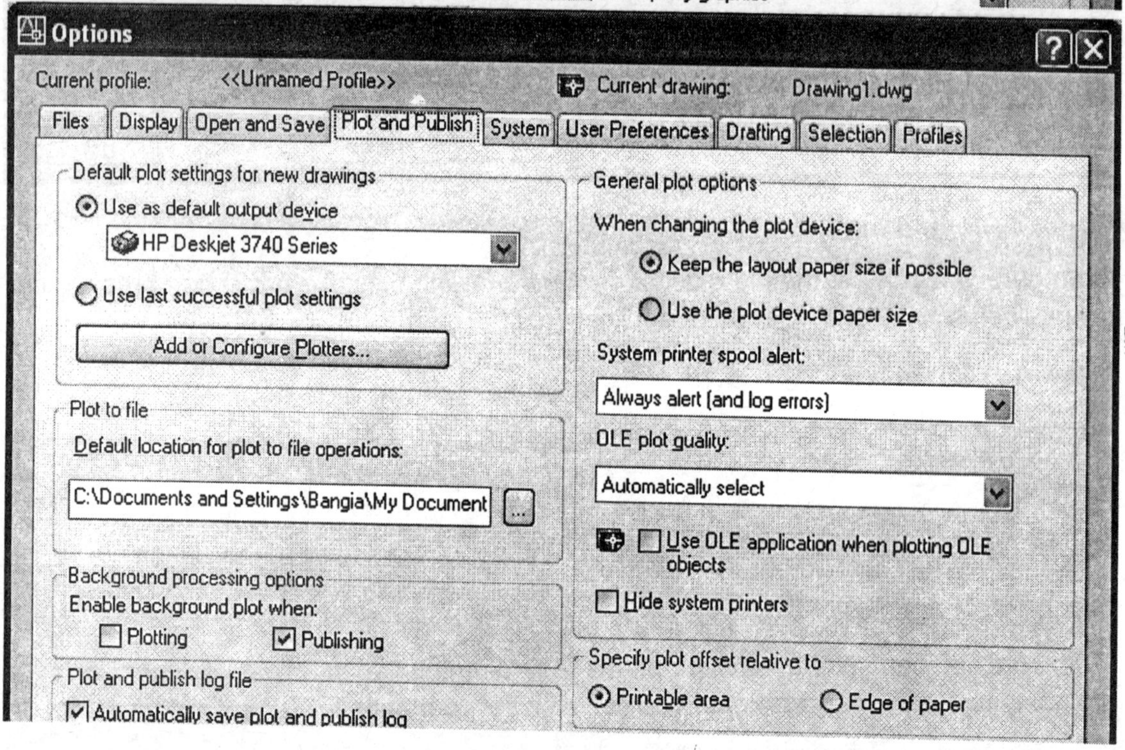
Options
Current profile: <<Unnamed Profile>>
Current drawing: Drawing1.dwg
Files
Display
Open and Save
Plot and Publish
System
User Preferences
Drafting
Selection
Profiles
Default plot settings for new drawings
Use as default output device
HP Deskjet 3740 Series
Use last successful plot settings
Add or Configure Plotters...
Plot to file
Default location for plot to file operations:
C:\Documents and Settings\Bangia\My Document
Background processing options
Enable background plot when:
Plotting
Publishing
Plot and publish log file
Automatically save plot and publish log
General plot options
When changing the plot device:
Keep the layout paper size if possible
Use the plot device paper size
System printer spool alert:
Always alert (and log errors)
OLE plot quality:
Automatically select
Use OLE application when plotting OLE objects
Hide system printers
Specify plot offset relative to
Printable area
Edge of paper

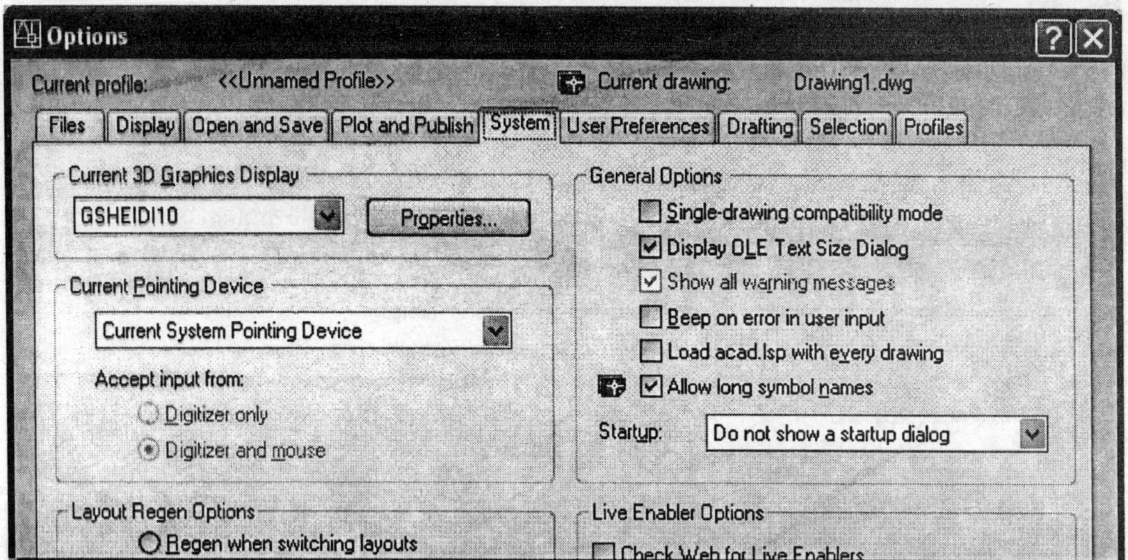
Options
Current profile: <<Unnamed Profile>>
Current drawing: Drawing1.dwg
Files
Display
Open and Save
Plot and Publish
System
User Preferences
Drafting
Selection
Profiles
Current 3D Graphics Display
GSHEIDI10
Properties...
Current Pointing Device
Current System Pointing Device
Accept input from:
Digitizer only
Digitizer and mouse
Layout Regen Options
Regen when switching layouts
General Options
Single-drawing compatibility mode
Display OLE Text Size Dialog
Show all warning messages
Beep on error in user input
Load acad.lsp with every drawing
Allow long symbol names
Startup:
Do not show a startup dialog
Live Enabler Options

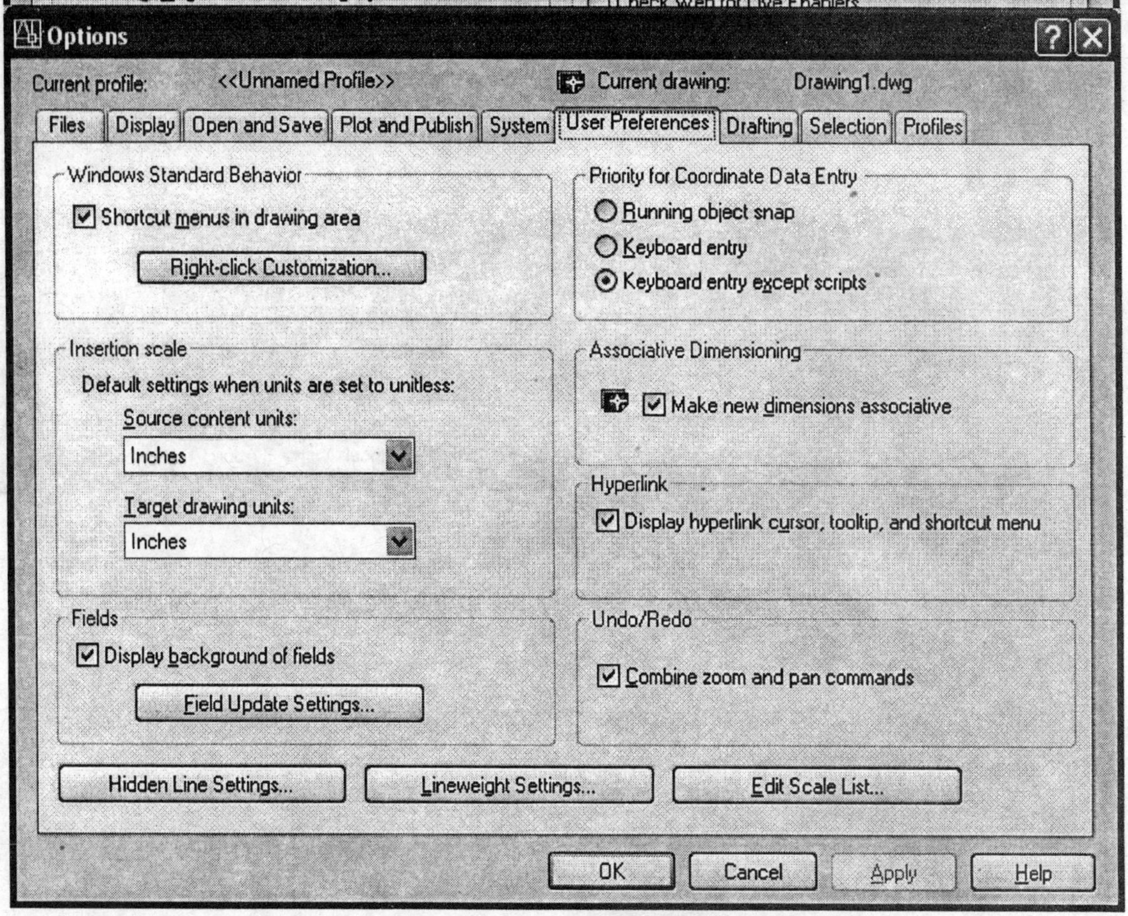
Options
Current profile: <<Unnamed Profile>>
Current drawing: Drawing1.dwg
Files
Display
Open and Save
Plot and Publish
System
User Preferences
Drafting
Selection
Profiles
Windows Standard Behavior
Shortcut menus in drawing area
Right-click Customization...
Insertion scale
Default settings when units are set to unitless:
Source content units:
Inches
Target drawing units:
Inches
Fields
Display background of fields
Field Update Settings...
Priority for Coordinate Data Entry
Running object snap
Keyboard entry
Keyboard entry except scripts
Associative Dimensioning
Make new dimensions associative
Hyperlink
Display hyperlink cursor, tooltip, and shortcut menu
Undo/Redo
Combine zoom and pan commands
Hidden Line Settings...
Lineweight Settings...
Edit Scale List...
OK
Cancel
Apply
Help

Drafting

From here you can set the AutoSnap settings and its size. AutoTrack settings, Alignment Point Acquisition and Aperture size.

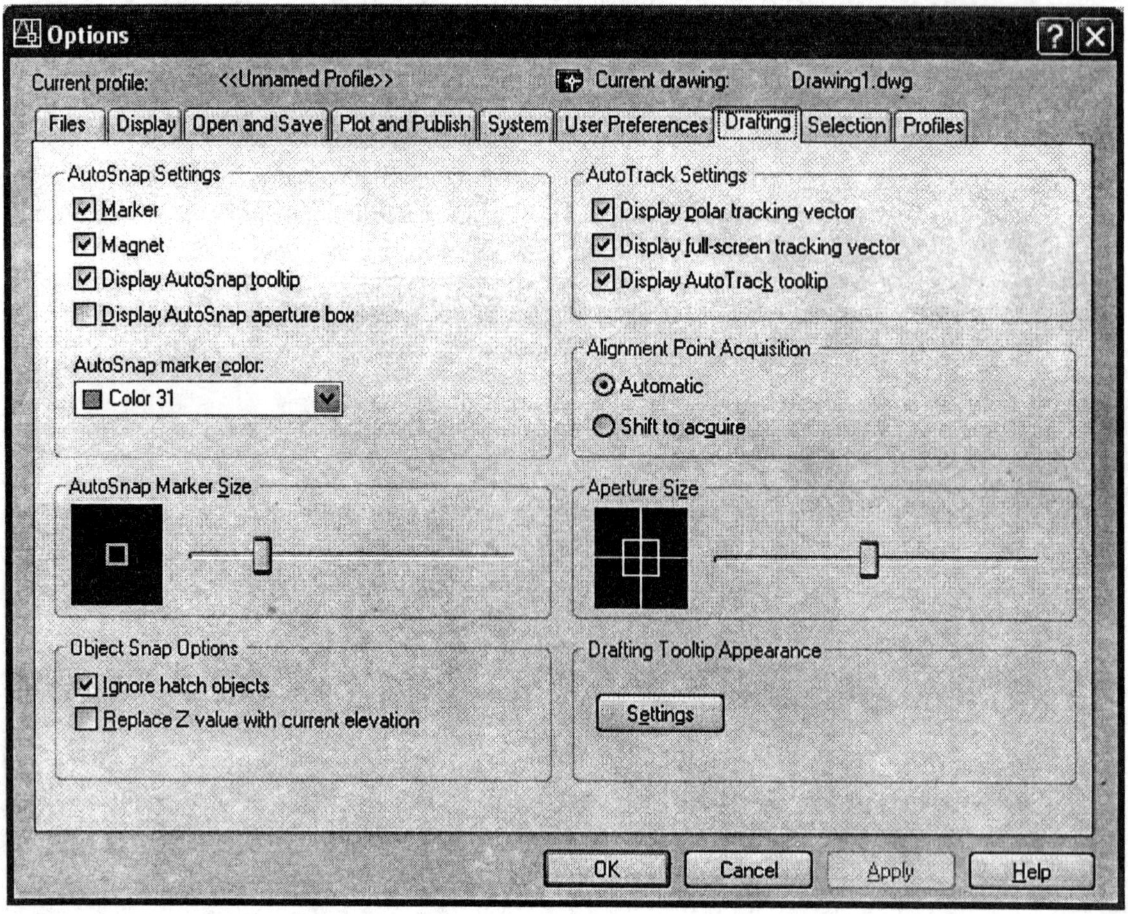

Selection

From here you can set the selection modes, Grips and grips size, pickbox size.

Profiles

From here you can set the current profiles or add them to the list, etc..

All these options are shown on the next few pages.

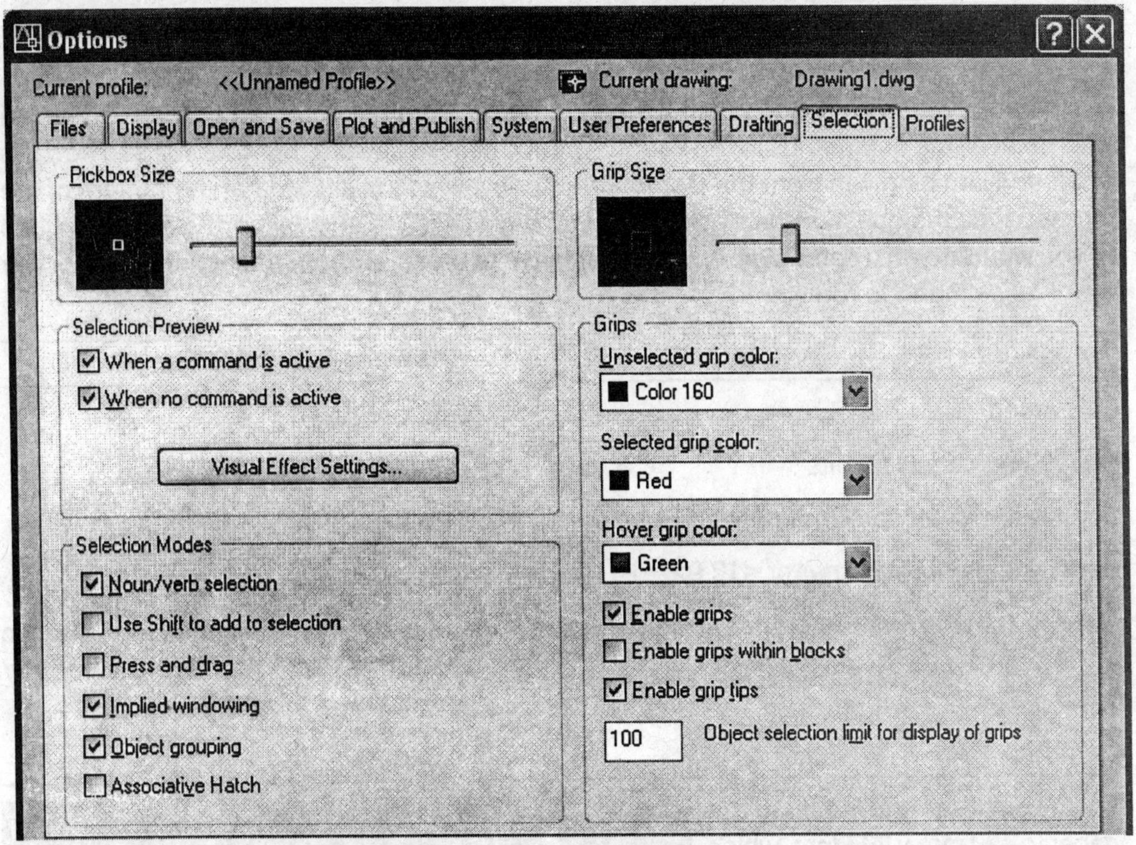
Options
Current profile: <<Unnamed Profile>>
Current drawing: Drawing1.dwg
Files
Display
Open and Save
Plot and Publish
System
User Preferences
Drafting
Selection
Profiles
Pickbox Size
Grip Size
Selection Preview
When a command is active
When no command is active
Visual Effect Settings...
Selection Modes
Noun/verb selection
Use Shift to add to selection
Press and drag
Implied windowing
Object grouping
Associative Hatch
Grips
Unselected grip color:
Color 160
Selected grip color:
Red
Hover grip color:
Green
Enable grips
Enable grips within blocks
Enable grip tips
100
Object selection limit for display of grips

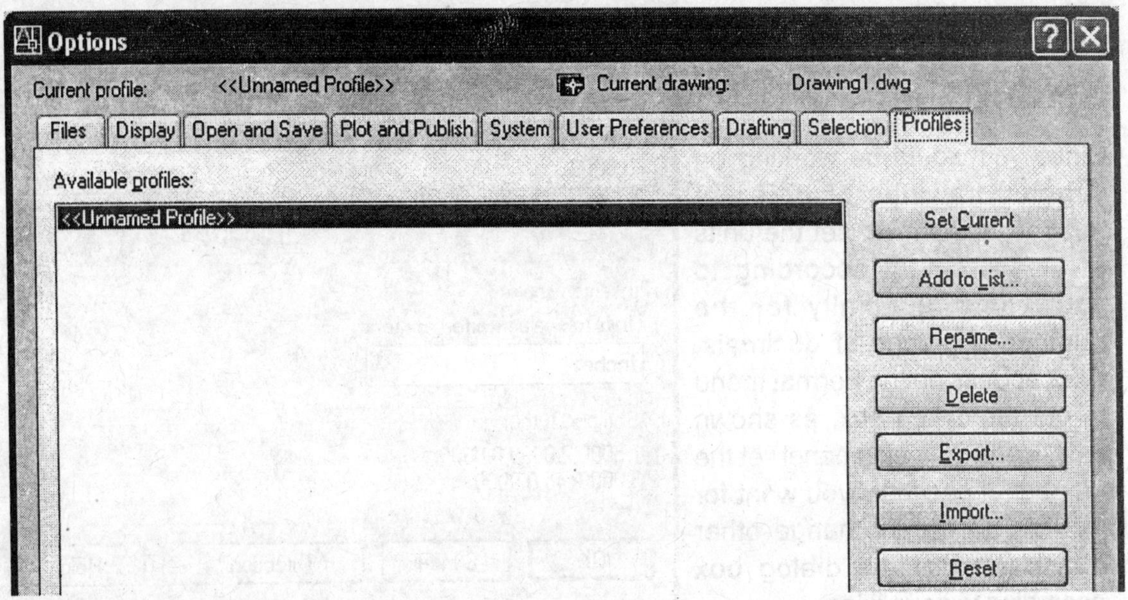
Options
Current profile: <<Unnamed Profile>>
Current drawing: Drawing1.dwg
Files
Display
Open and Save
Plot and Publish
System
User Preferences
Drafting
Selection
Profiles
Available profiles:
<<Unnamed Profile>>
Set Current
Add to List...
Rename...
Delete
Export...
Import...
Reset

Setting Limits

This command has no dialog box but it has to be set from the command menu. So far we have seen all the commands in the various menus of the software. Now we will see how the command can be given from the Command window which is situated at the bottom of the screen. Here the questions are asked and you have to fill the answers in the form of values as you would do on a computer terminal. You have to press <Enter> after typing the answer to each command to register it.

Command	*Answer*
Command	limits <Enter>
Reset Model space limits	<Enter>
Specify lower left corner or [ON/OFF] <0,0>	<Enter>
Specify upper right corner or <12,9>:	420,297
Specify corner of window, enter a scale fraction	(nX or nXP) or [All/Center/Left/Dynamic /Extents/Previous/Scale/Window/
VMax	/<real time> a [for All] <Enter>
Command	<Enter>

This would set the limit of the paper to 420 mm x 297 mm, which is the size of A3 paper.

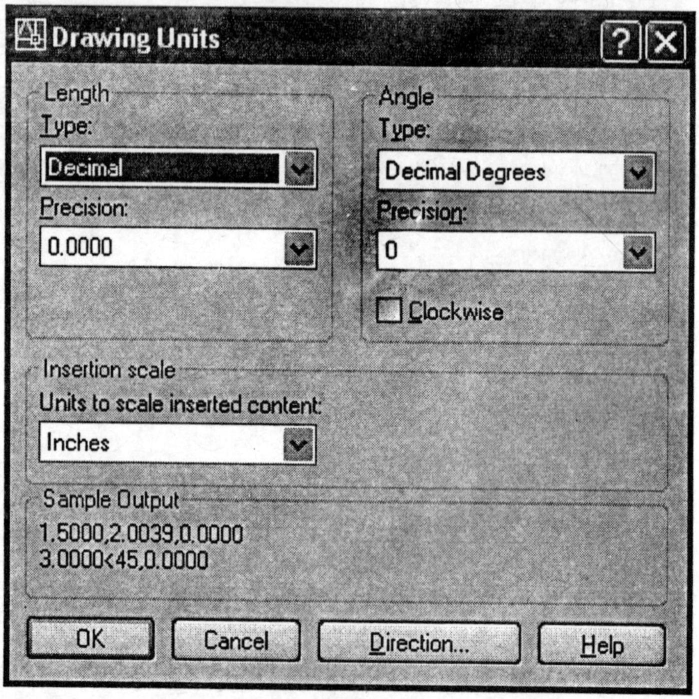

Setting Units

Since you would be working on various drawings of different natures, you should set the units of measurement according to your liking, specially for the number of places of decimals. Click at Units on the Format menu to get the dialog box, as shown next. In the Precision panel set the number of decimals you want for working. You can change other options too of the dialog box according to your liking.

Setting Grid and Snap

Click at Drafting Settings in the Tools menu to get a dialog box, as shown on the next page. Click at the Snap and Grid panel. In the Snap settings area enter .5 in both the X spacing and Y spacing boxes and the same in those of the Grid settings area of the dialog box. Press Ok to register them.

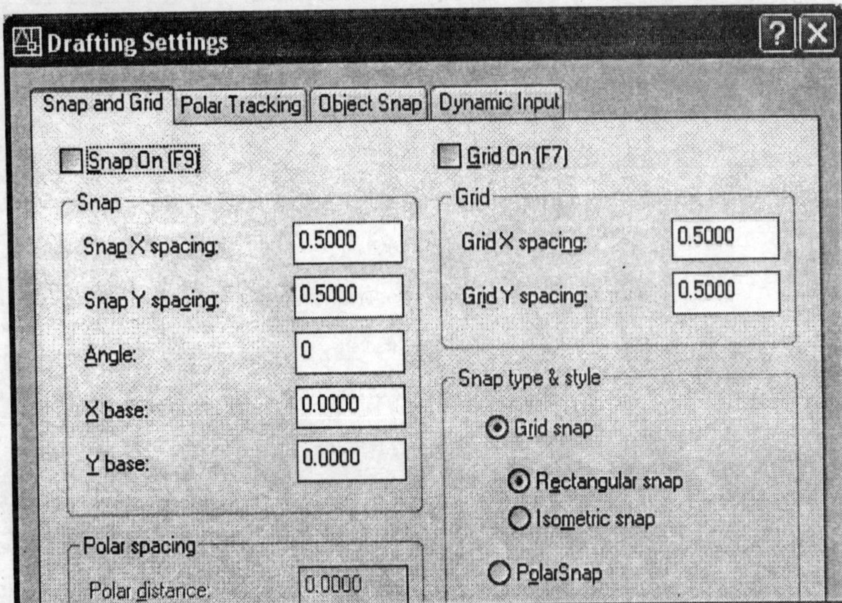

Other options like Polar Tracking, Object Snap and Dynamic Input are shown on the next page.

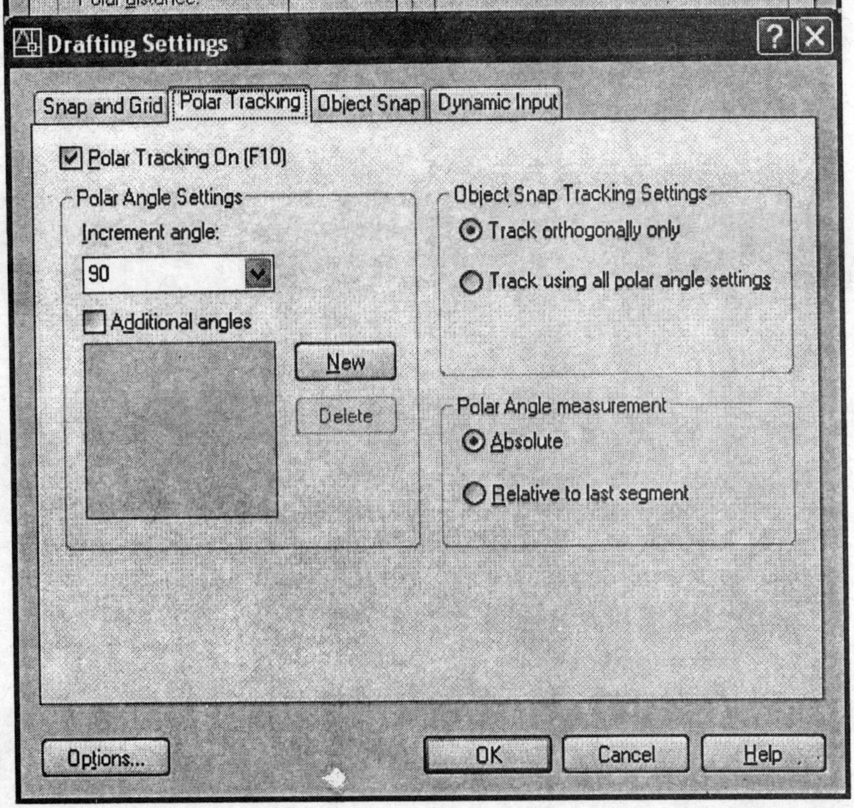

Setting Screen Colours

We had seen earlier in the case of Options that the background and other screen colours can be set using the Display panel. Click at the Colour in the Display panel of Options dialog box to get another dialog box, as shown on the next page. Here you can select the background colour for the layout tab as well for the model tab. Click at Apply & Close to register these options.

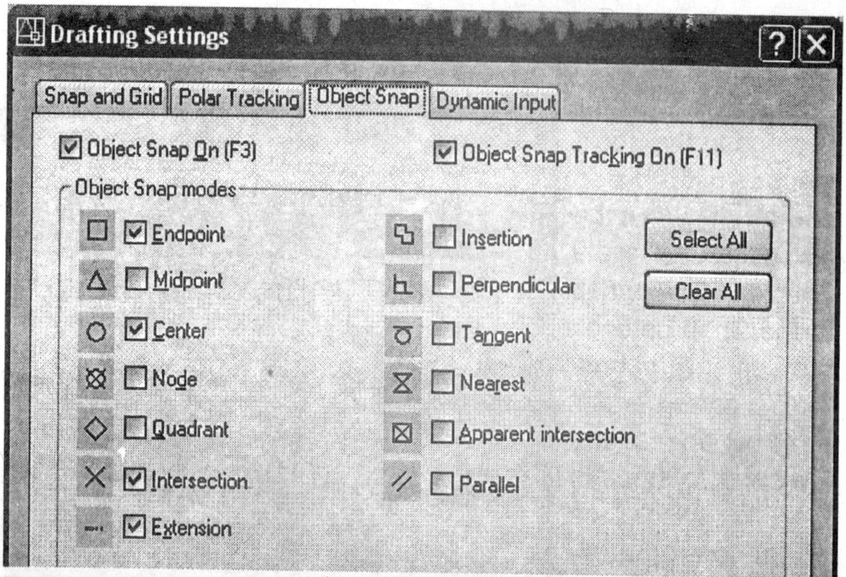

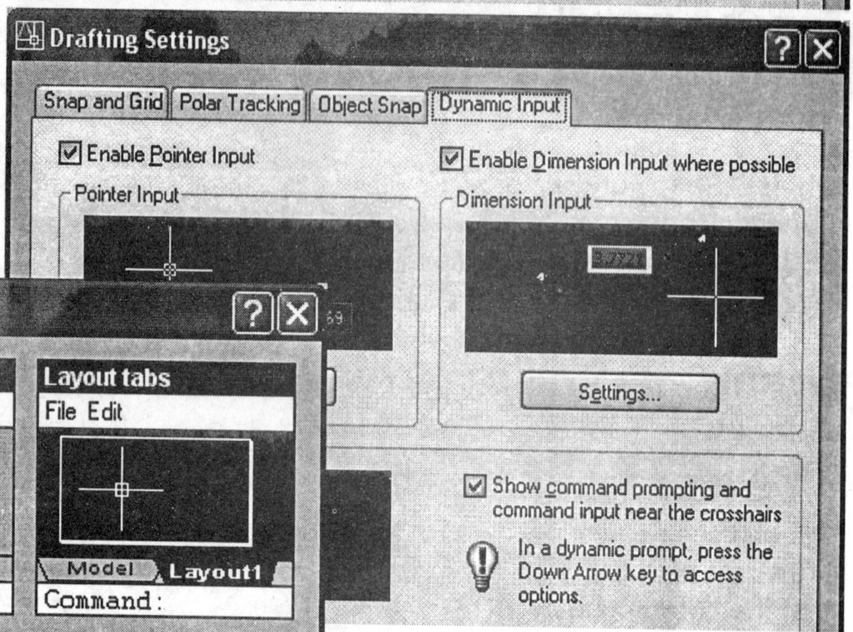

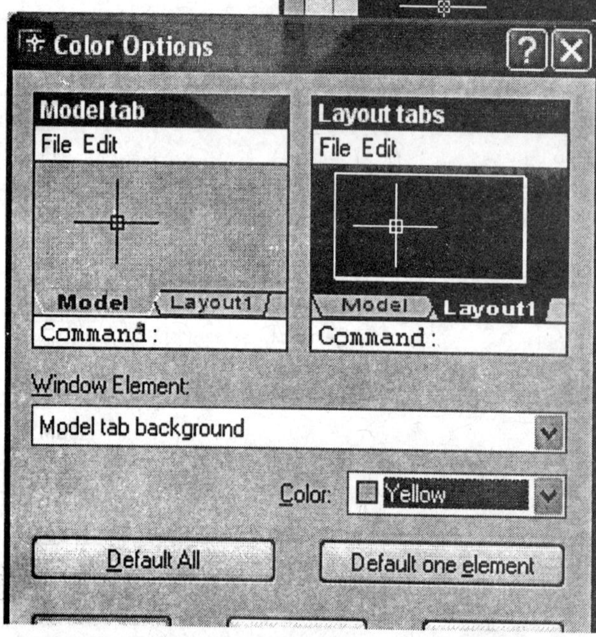

Creating Drawing using Wizards

3

Introduction

Most of the new software producers are aware of the situations in which a novice to the software could find himself while using the software. So for them AutoCAD 2006 has something called Wizards, which helps the user in creating a drawing in a snap.

Click at Wizards in the Tools menu and select Create Layout to start the Wizard. Here we give you the various options of screens which are shown on the next few pages.

These screens are self sufficient and need no other explanations.

Second Wizard

The second wizard whose working we are showing here is that of Publish to the Web. It also has a number of screens which are shown next to the screens of the first one.

Go through these screens to have an idea of the working of the wizards.

Working with Templates

Templates are ready made sample drawings which you can use to create your own similar drawing. AutoCAD 2006 has a number of them available under the New command. The list is shown after the Wizards.

A preview of the template is also shown so that you can get an idea as to how the drawing would look like.

A few samples are also shown later in the chapter.

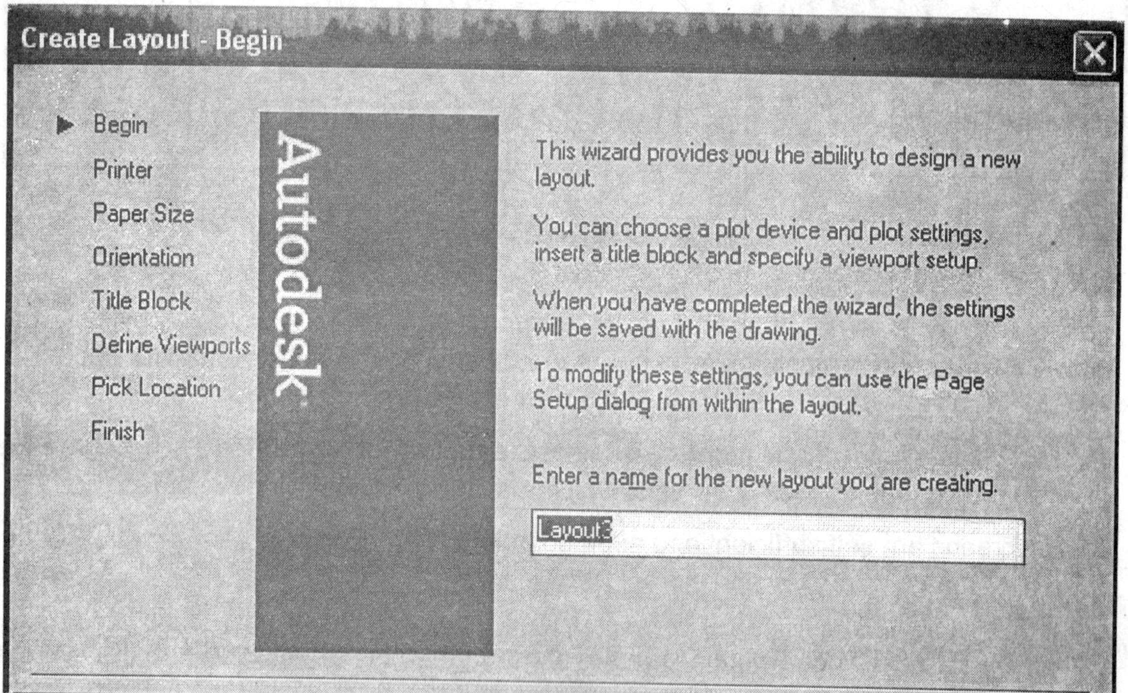
Create Layout - Begin
Begin
Printer
Paper Size
Orientation
Title Block
Define Viewports
Pick Location
Finish
Autodesk
This wizard provides you the ability to design a new layout.
You can choose a plot device and plot settings, insert a title block and specify a viewport setup.
When you have completed the wizard, the settings will be saved with the drawing.
To modify these settings, you can use the Page Setup dialog from within the layout.
Enter a name for the new layout you are creating.
Layout3

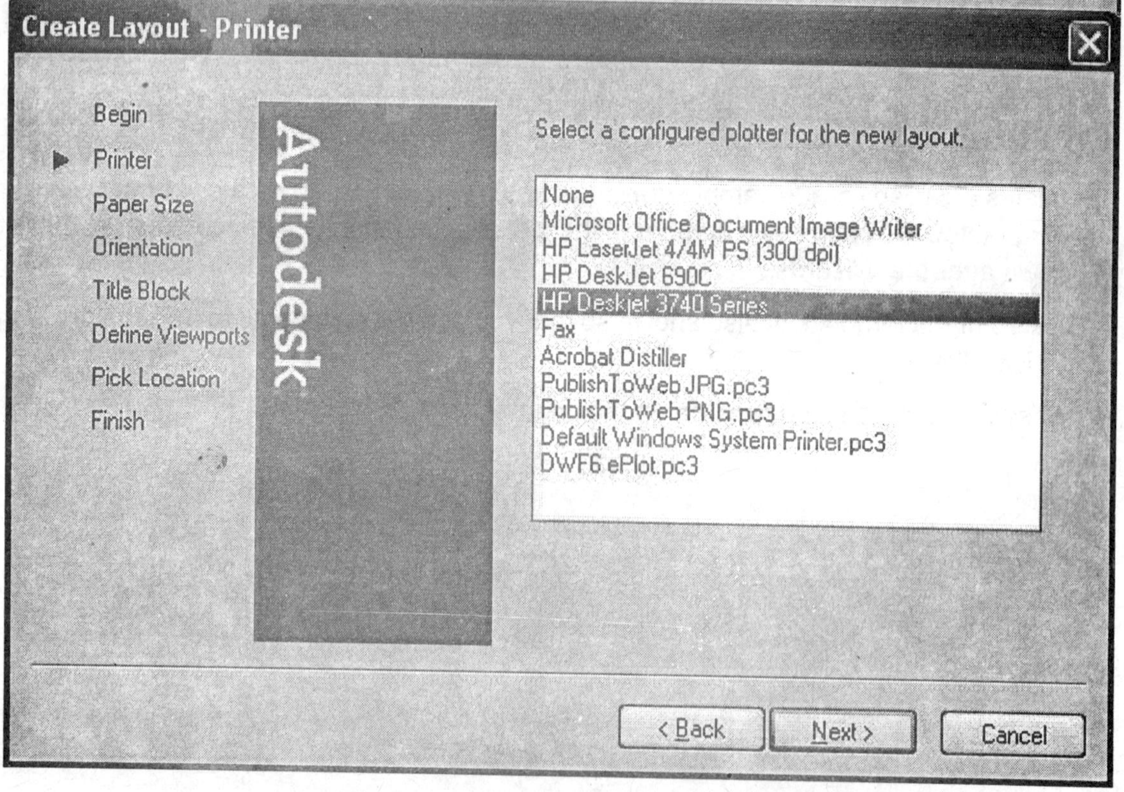
Create Layout - Printer
Begin
Printer
Paper Size
Orientation
Title Block
Define Viewports
Pick Location
Finish
Autodesk
Select a configured plotter for the new layout.
None
Microsoft Office Document Image Writer
HP LaserJet 4/4M PS (300 dpi)
HP DeskJet 690C
HP Deskjet 3740 Series
Fax
Acrobat Distiller
PublishToWeb JPG.pc3
PublishToWeb PNG.pc3
Default Windows System Printer.pc3
DWF6 ePlot.pc3
< Back
Next >
Cancel

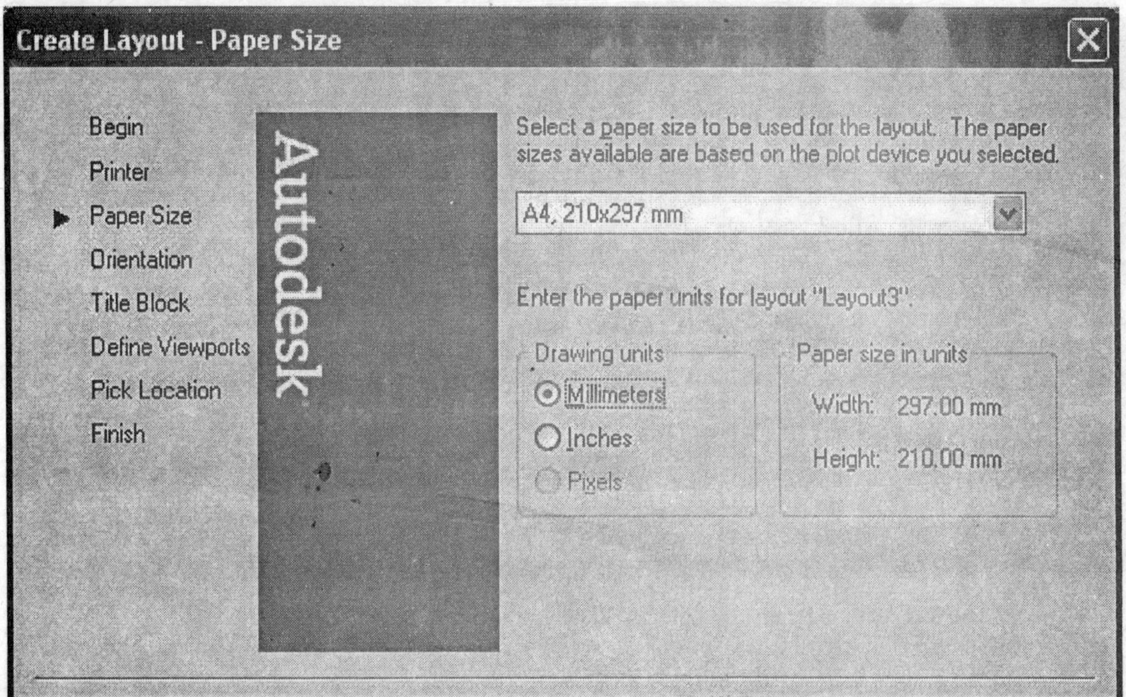
Create Layout - Paper Size
Begin
Printer
Paper Size
Orientation
Title Block
Define Viewports
Pick Location
Finish
Autodesk
Select a paper size to be used for the layout. The paper sizes available are based on the plot device you selected.
A4, 210x297 mm
Enter the paper units for layout "Layout3".
Drawing units
Millimeters
Inches
Pixels
Paper size in units
Width: 297.00 mm
Height: 210.00 mm

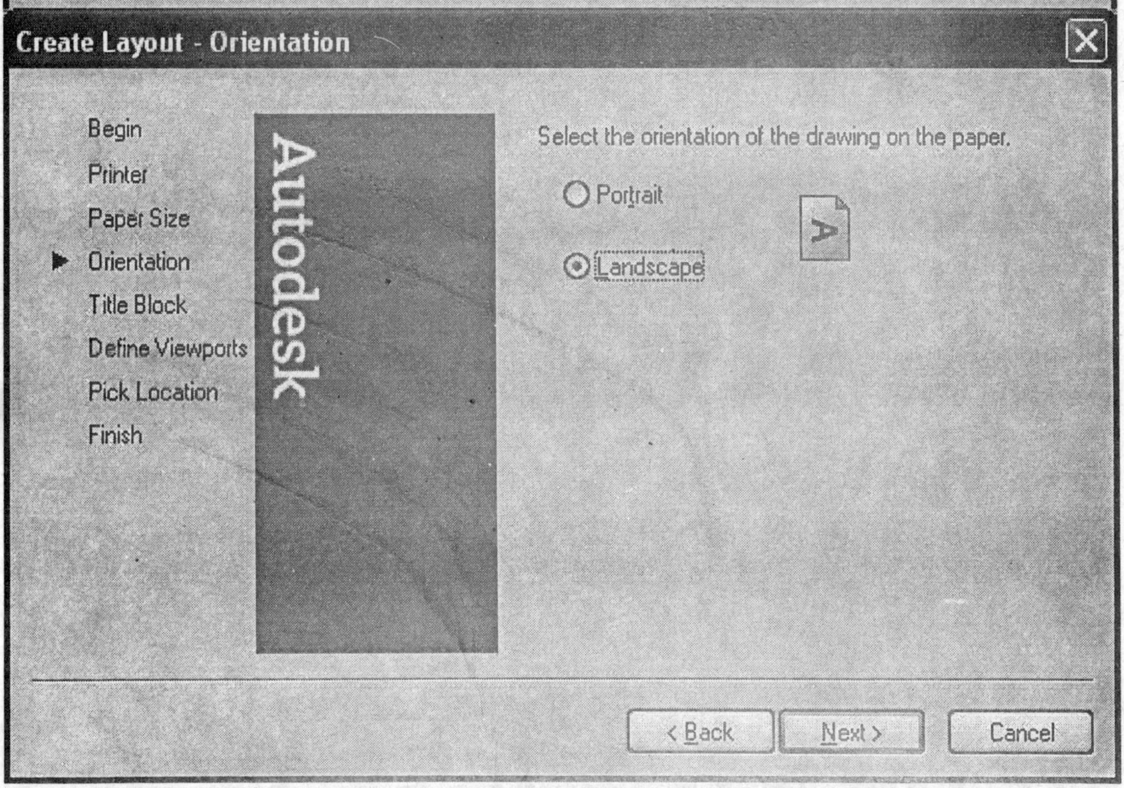
Create Layout - Orientation
Begin
Printer
Paper Size
Orientation
Title Block
Define Viewports
Pick Location
Finish
Autodesk
Select the orientation of the drawing on the paper.
Portrait
Landscape
A
< Back
Next >
Cancel

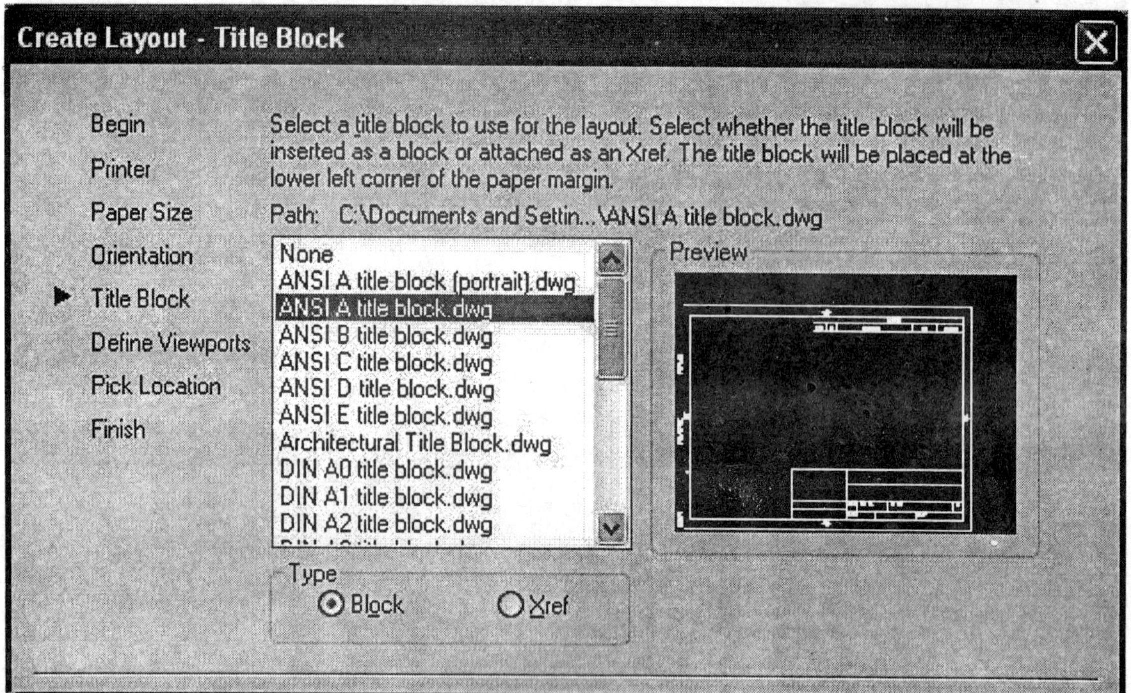
Create Layout - Title Block
Begin
Printer
Paper Size
Orientation
Title Block
Define Viewports
Pick Location
Finish
Select a title block to use for the layout. Select whether the title block will be inserted as a block or attached as an Xref. The title block will be placed at the lower left corner of the paper margin.
Path: C:\Documents and Settin...\ANSI A title block.dwg
None
ANSI A title block (portrait).dwg
ANSI A title block.dwg
ANSI B title block.dwg
ANSI C title block.dwg
ANSI D title block.dwg
ANSI E title block.dwg
Architectural Title Block.dwg
DIN A0 title block.dwg
DIN A1 title block.dwg
DIN A2 title block.dwg
Preview
Type
Block
Xref

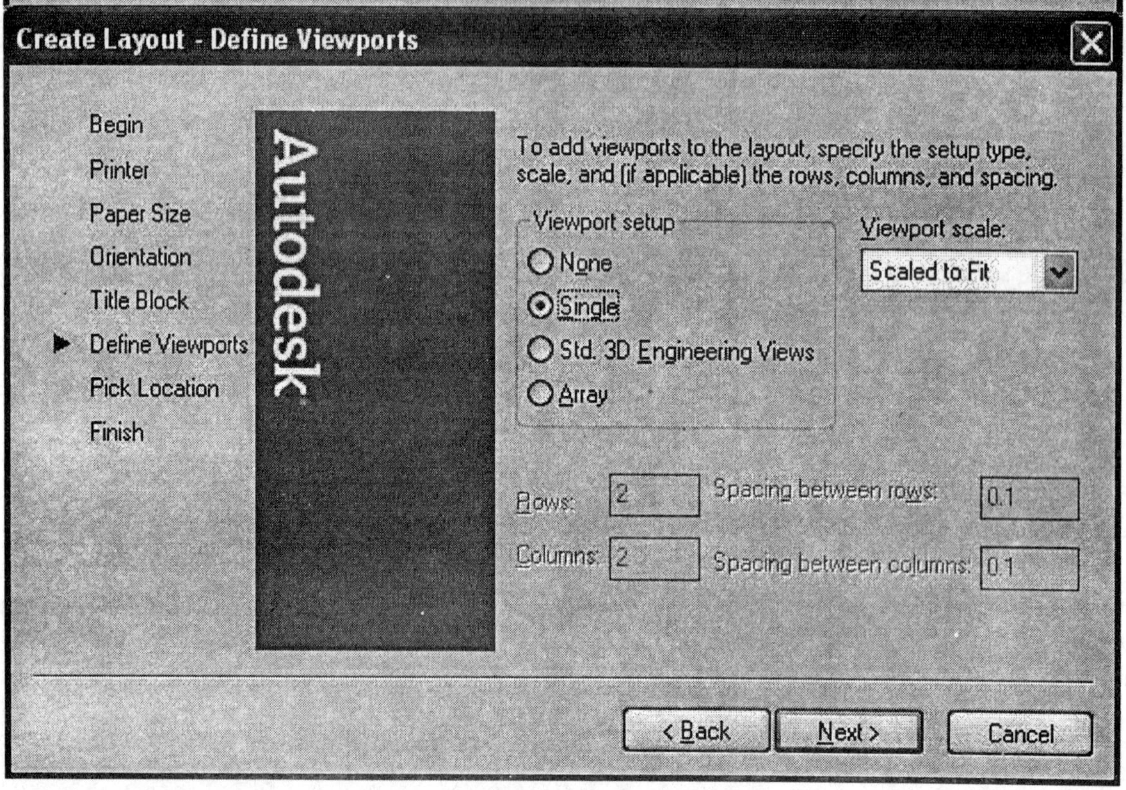
Create Layout - Define Viewports
Begin
Printer
Paper Size
Orientation
Title Block
Define Viewports
Pick Location
Finish
Autodesk
To add viewports to the layout, specify the setup type, scale, and (if applicable) the rows, columns, and spacing.
Viewport setup
None
Single
Std. 3D Engineering Views
Array
Viewport scale:
Scaled to Fit
Rows: 2
Spacing between rows: 0.1
Columns: 2
Spacing between columns: 0.1
< Back
Next >
Cancel

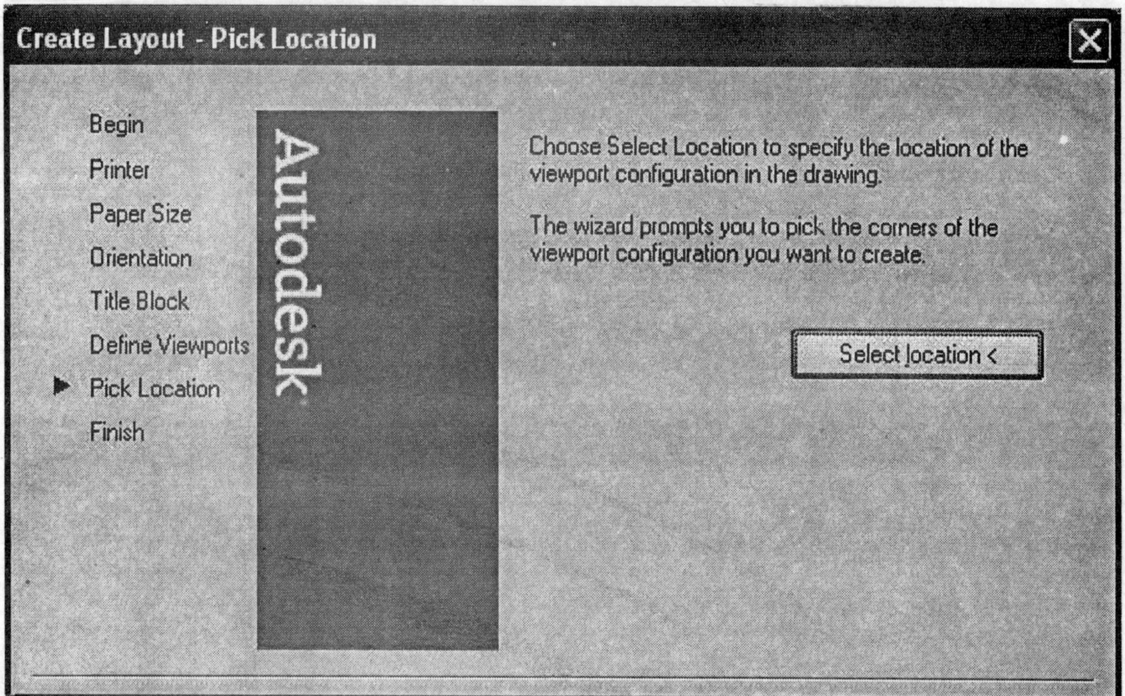
Create Layout - Pick Location
Begin
Printer
Paper Size
Orientation
Title Block
Define Viewports
Pick Location
Finish
Autodesk
Choose Select Location to specify the location of the viewport configuration in the drawing.
The wizard prompts you to pick the corners of the viewport configuration you want to create.
Select location <

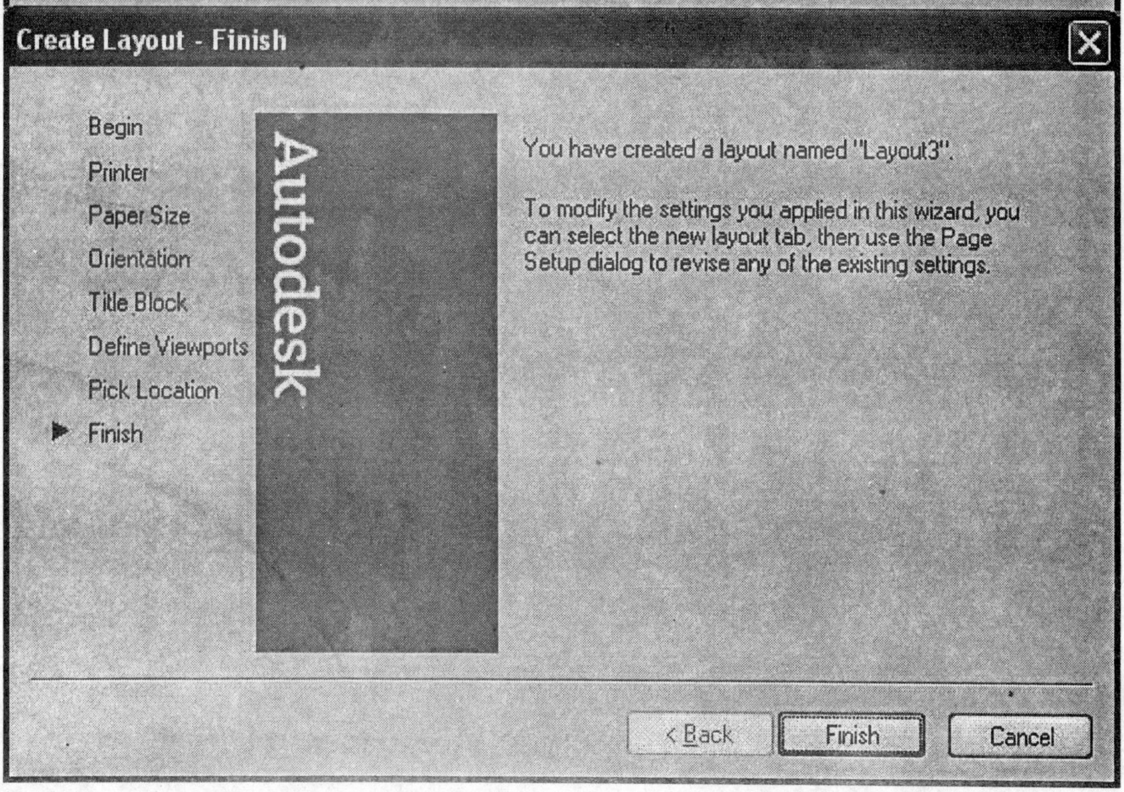
Create Layout - Finish
Begin
Printer
Paper Size
Orientation
Title Block
Define Viewports
Pick Location
Finish
Autodesk
You have created a layout named "Layout3".
To modify the settings you applied in this wizard, you can select the new layout tab, then use the Page Setup dialog to revise any of the existing settings.
< Back
Finish
Cancel

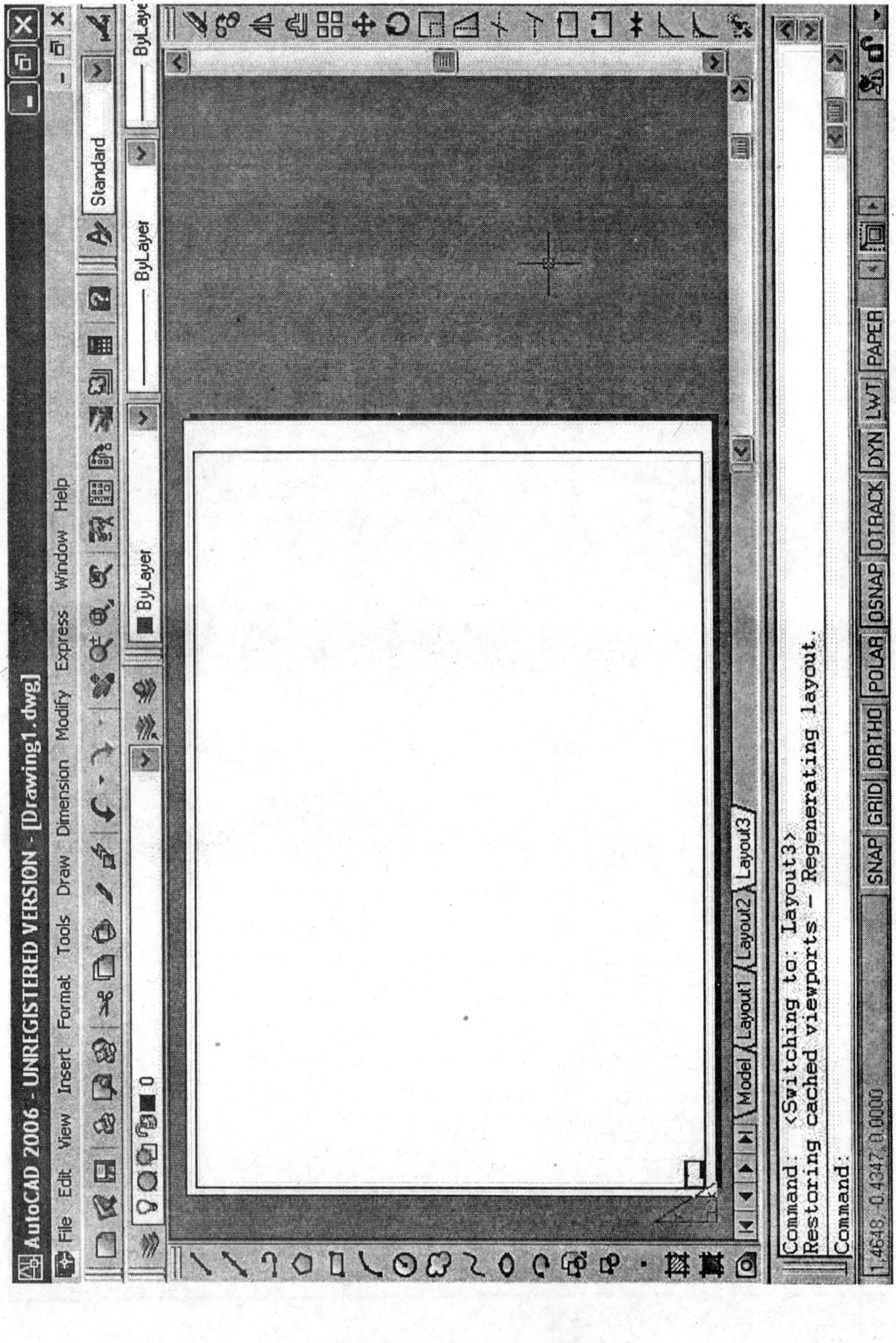
AutoCAD 2006 - UNREGISTERED VERSION - [Drawing1.dwg]
File Edit View Insert Format Tools Draw Dimension Modify Express Window Help
Standard
ByLayer
ByLayer
ByLayer
Model
Layout1
Layout2
Layout3
Command: <Switching to: Layout3>
Restoring cached viewports - Regenerating layout.
Command:
1.4648, 0.4347, 0.0000
SNAP GRID ORTHO POLAR OSNAP OTRACK DYN LWT PAPER

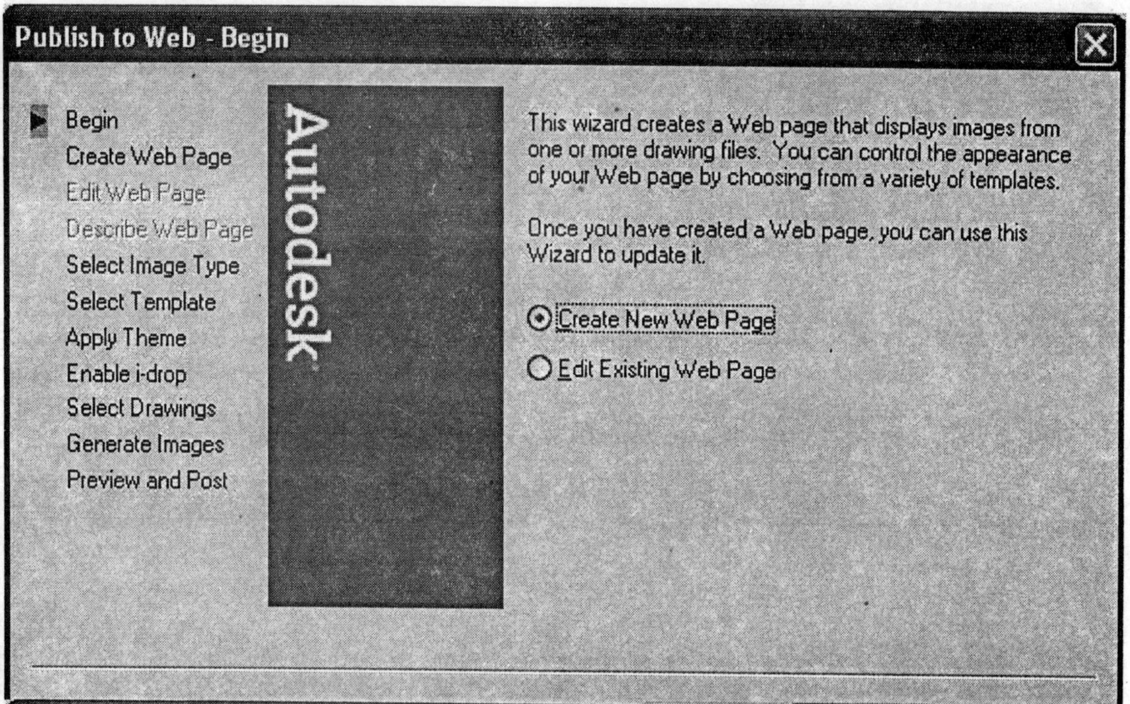
Publish to Web - Begin
Begin
Create Web Page
Edit Web Page
Describe Web Page
Select Image Type
Select Template
Apply Theme
Enable i-drop
Select Drawings
Generate Images
Preview and Post
Autodesk
This wizard creates a Web page that displays images from one or more drawing files. You can control the appearance of your Web page by choosing from a variety of templates.
Once you have created a Web page, you can use this Wizard to update it.
Create New Web Page
Edit Existing Web Page

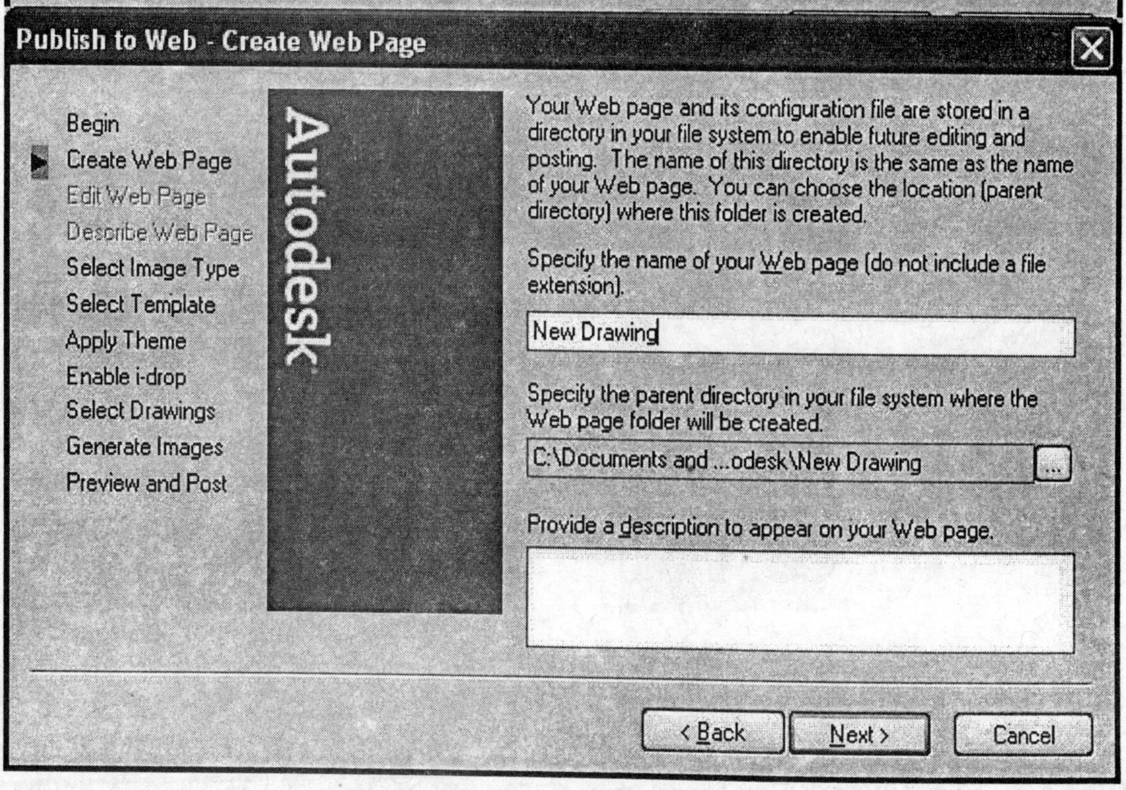
Publish to Web - Create Web Page
Begin
Create Web Page
Edit Web Page
Describe Web Page
Select Image Type
Select Template
Apply Theme
Enable i-drop
Select Drawings
Generate Images
Preview and Post
Autodesk
Your Web page and its configuration file are stored in a directory in your file system to enable future editing and posting. The name of this directory is the same as the name of your Web page. You can choose the location (parent directory) where this folder is created.
Specify the name of your Web page (do not include a file extension).
New Drawing
Specify the parent directory in your file system where the Web page folder will be created.
C:\Documents and ...odesk\New Drawing
Provide a description to appear on your Web page.
< Back
Next >
Cancel

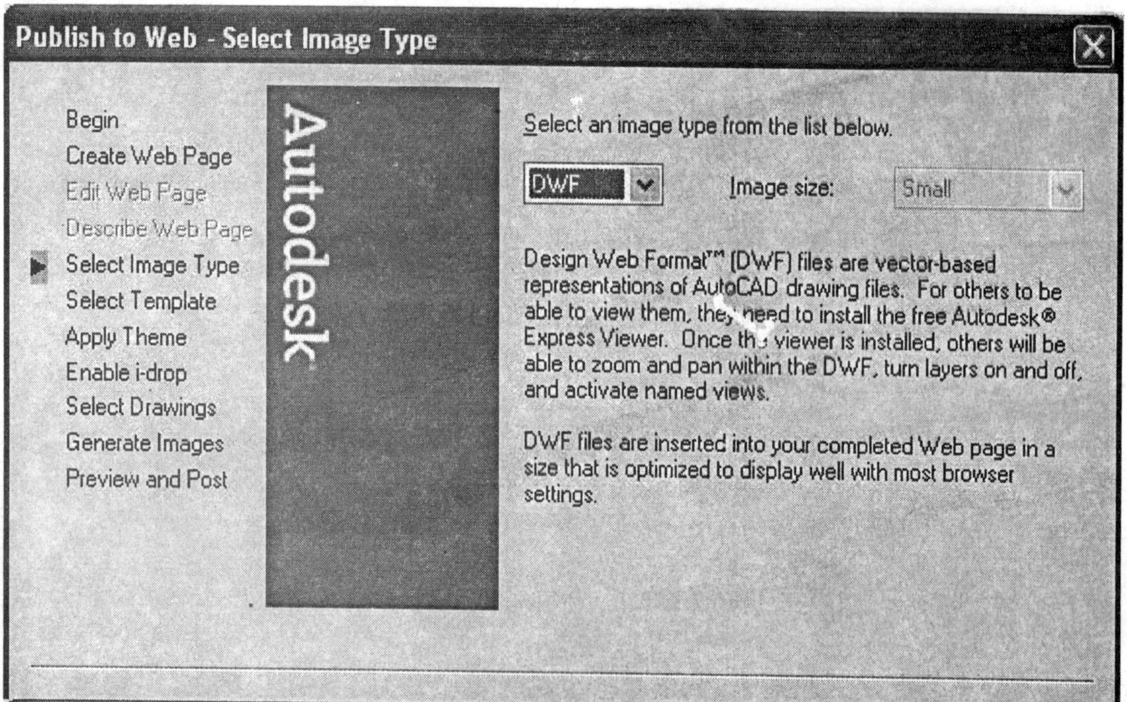
Publish to Web - Select Image Type
Begin
Create Web Page
Edit Web Page
Describe Web Page
Select Image Type
Select Template
Apply Theme
Enable i-drop
Select Drawings
Generate Images
Preview and Post
Autodesk
Select an image type from the list below.
DWF
Image size:
Small
Design Web Format™ (DWF) files are vector-based representations of AutoCAD drawing files. For others to be able to view them, they need to install the free Autodesk® Express Viewer. Once the viewer is installed, others will be able to zoom and pan within the DWF, turn layers on and off, and activate named views.
DWF files are inserted into your completed Web page in a size that is optimized to display well with most browser settings.

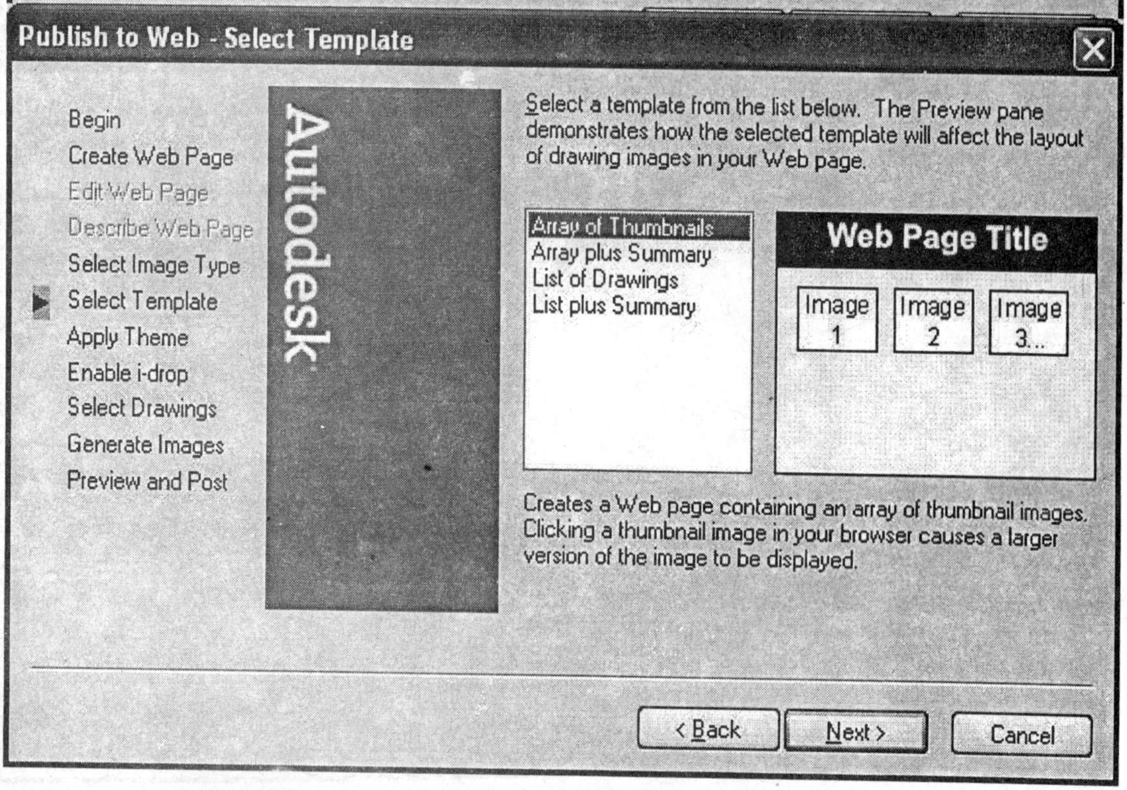
Publish to Web - Select Template
Begin
Create Web Page
Edit Web Page
Describe Web Page
Select Image Type
Select Template
Apply Theme
Enable i-drop
Select Drawings
Generate Images
Preview and Post
Autodesk
Select a template from the list below. The Preview pane demonstrates how the selected template will affect the layout of drawing images in your Web page.
Array of Thumbnails
Array plus Summary
List of Drawings
List plus Summary
Web Page Title
Image 1
Image 2
Image 3...
Creates a Web page containing an array of thumbnail images. Clicking a thumbnail image in your browser causes a larger version of the image to be displayed.
< Back
Next >
Cancel

Publish to Web - Apply Theme
Begin
Create Web Page
Edit Web Page
Describe Web Page
Select Image Type
Select Template
Apply Theme
Enable i-drop
Select Drawings
Generate Images
Preview and Post
Autodesk
Themes are preset elements that control the appearance of various elements (such as fonts and colors) of your completed Web page. Select a theme from the list below to apply to your Web page.
Autumn Fields
Web Page Title
Web Page Description
Label: Drawing 1
Description: Drawing 1
Summary Info: Field 1

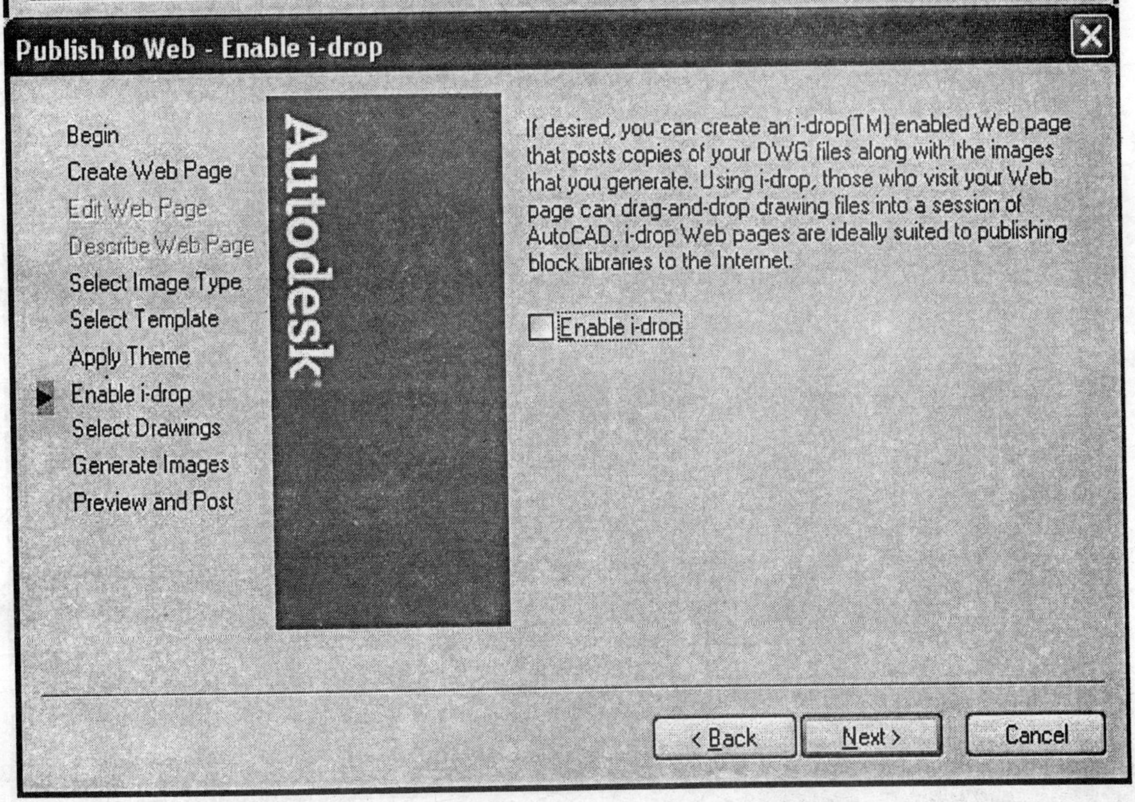
Publish to Web - Enable i-drop
Begin
Create Web Page
Edit Web Page
Describe Web Page
Select Image Type
Select Template
Apply Theme
Enable i-drop
Select Drawings
Generate Images
Preview and Post
Autodesk
If desired, you can create an i-drop(TM) enabled Web page that posts copies of your DWG files along with the images that you generate. Using i-drop, those who visit your Web page can drag-and-drop drawing files into a session of AutoCAD. i-drop Web pages are ideally suited to publishing block libraries to the Internet.
Enable i-drop
< Back
Next >
Cancel

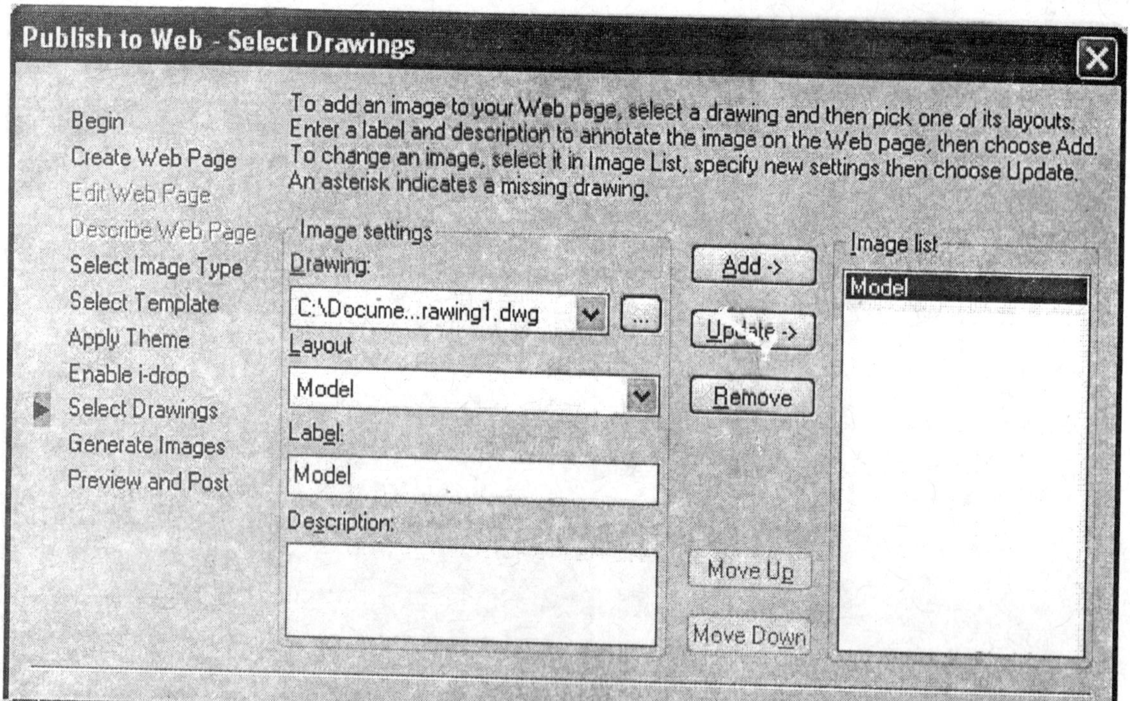
Publish to Web - Select Drawings
Begin
Create Web Page
Edit Web Page
Describe Web Page
Select Image Type
Select Template
Apply Theme
Enable i-drop
Select Drawings
Generate Images
Preview and Post
To add an image to your Web page, select a drawing and then pick one of its layouts. Enter a label and description to annotate the image on the Web page, then choose Add. To change an image, select it in Image List, specify new settings then choose Update. An asterisk indicates a missing drawing.
Image settings
Drawing:
C:\Docume...rawing1.dwg
Layout
Model
Label:
Model
Description:
Add ->
Update ->
Remove
Move Up
Move Down
Image list
Model

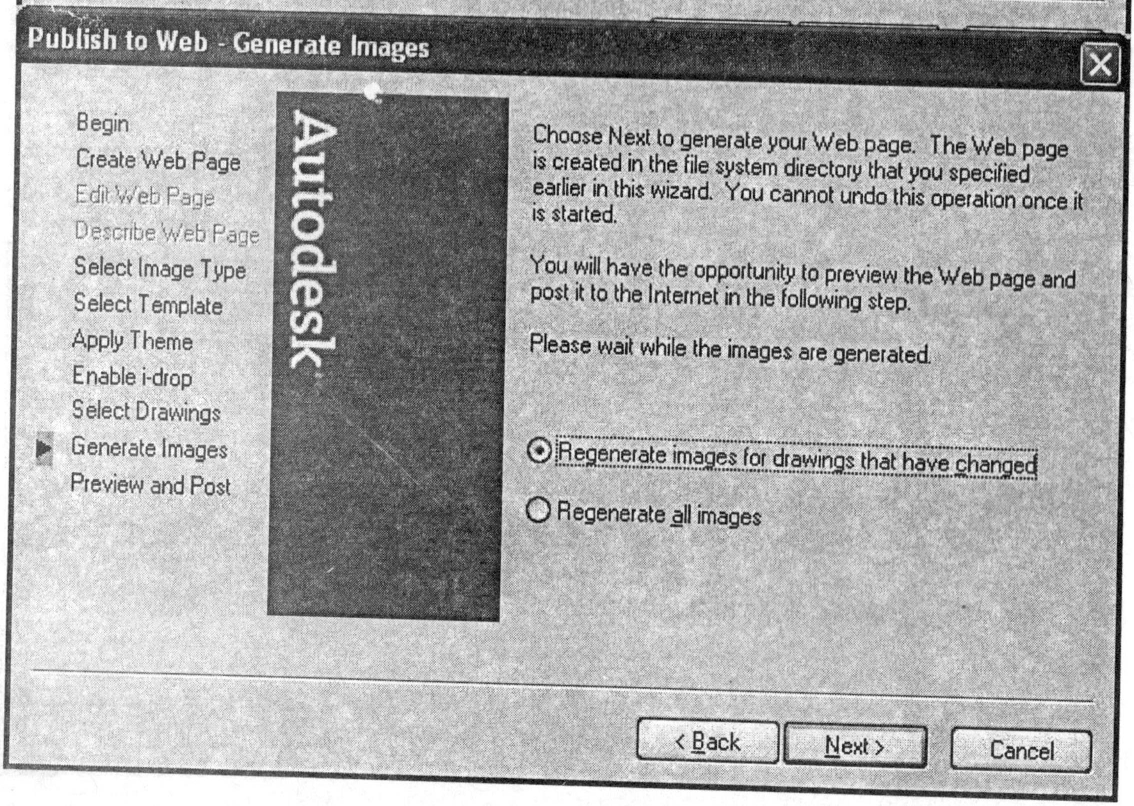
Publish to Web - Generate Images
Begin
Create Web Page
Edit Web Page
Describe Web Page
Select Image Type
Select Template
Apply Theme
Enable i-drop
Select Drawings
Generate Images
Preview and Post
Autodesk
Choose Next to generate your Web page. The Web page is created in the file system directory that you specified earlier in this wizard. You cannot undo this operation once it is started.
You will have the opportunity to preview the Web page and post it to the Internet in the following step.
Please wait while the images are generated.
Regenerate images for drawings that have changed
Regenerate all images
< Back
Next >
Cancel

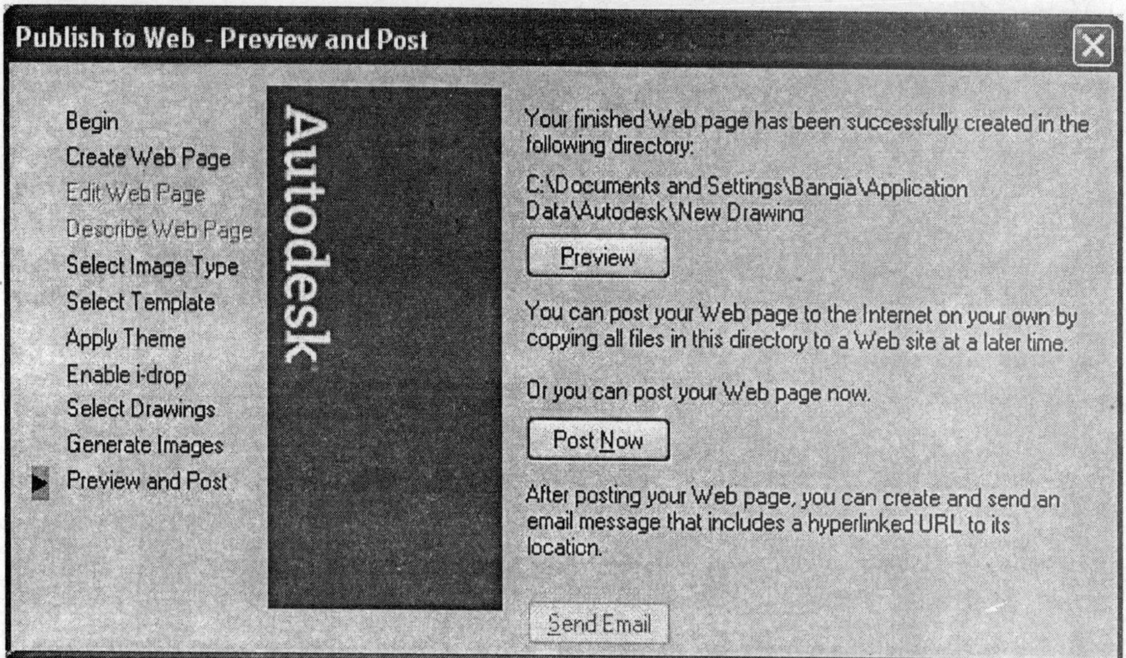
Publish to Web - Preview and Post
Begin
Create Web Page
Edit Web Page
Describe Web Page
Select Image Type
Select Template
Apply Theme
Enable i-drop
Select Drawings
Generate Images
Preview and Post
Autodesk
Your finished Web page has been successfully created in the following directory:
C:\Documents and Settings\Bangia\Application Data\Autodesk\New Drawing
Preview
You can post your Web page to the Internet on your own by copying all files in this directory to a Web site at a later time.
Or you can post your Web page now.
Post Now
After posting your Web page, you can create and send an email message that includes a hyperlinked URL to its location.
Send Email

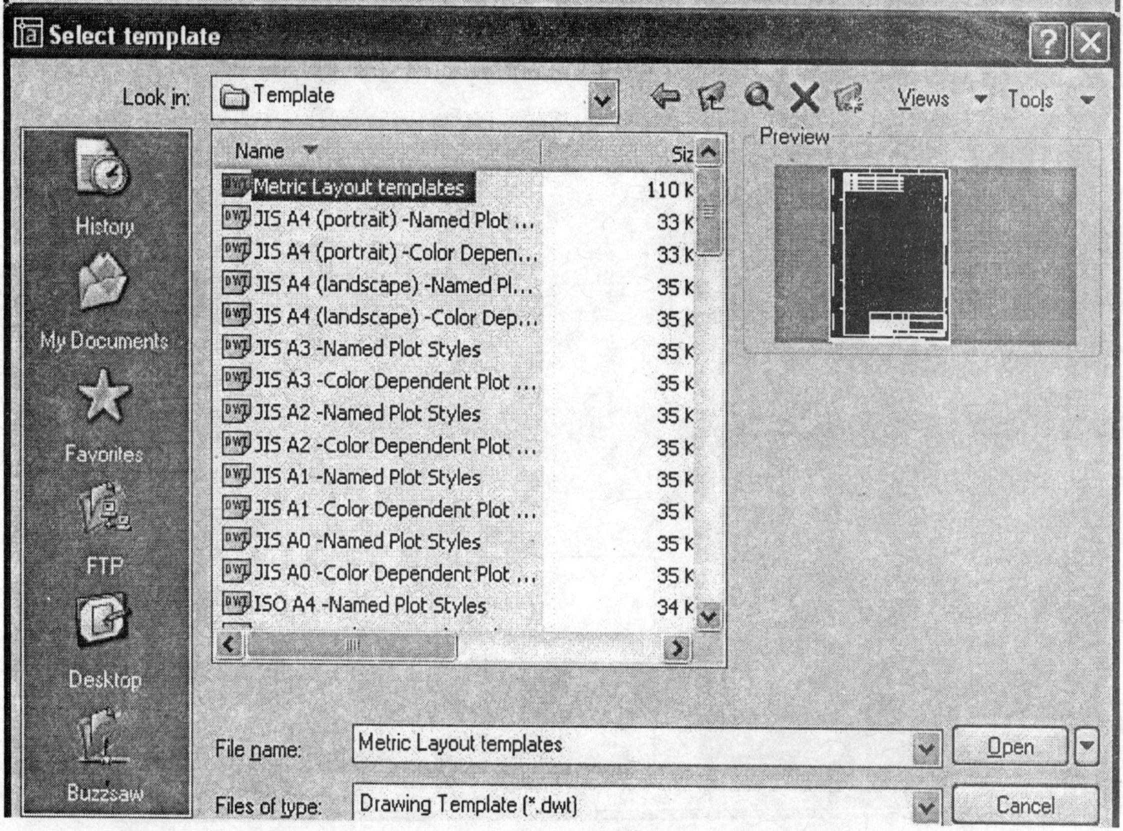
Select template
Look in:
Template
Views
Tools
Name
Siz
Preview
Metric Layout templates 110 K
JIS A4 (portrait) -Named Plot ... 33 K
JIS A4 (portrait) -Color Depen... 33 K
JIS A4 (landscape) -Named Pl... 35 K
JIS A4 (landscape) -Color Dep... 35 K
JIS A3 -Named Plot Styles 35 K
JIS A3 -Color Dependent Plot ... 35 K
JIS A2 -Named Plot Styles 35 K
JIS A2 -Color Dependent Plot ... 35 K
JIS A1 -Named Plot Styles 35 K
JIS A1 -Color Dependent Plot ... 35 K
JIS A0 -Named Plot Styles 35 K
JIS A0 -Color Dependent Plot ... 35 K
ISO A4 -Named Plot Styles 34 K
History
My Documents
Favorites
FTP
Desktop
Buzzsaw
File name:
Metric Layout templates
Open
Files of type:
Drawing Template (*.dwt)
Cancel

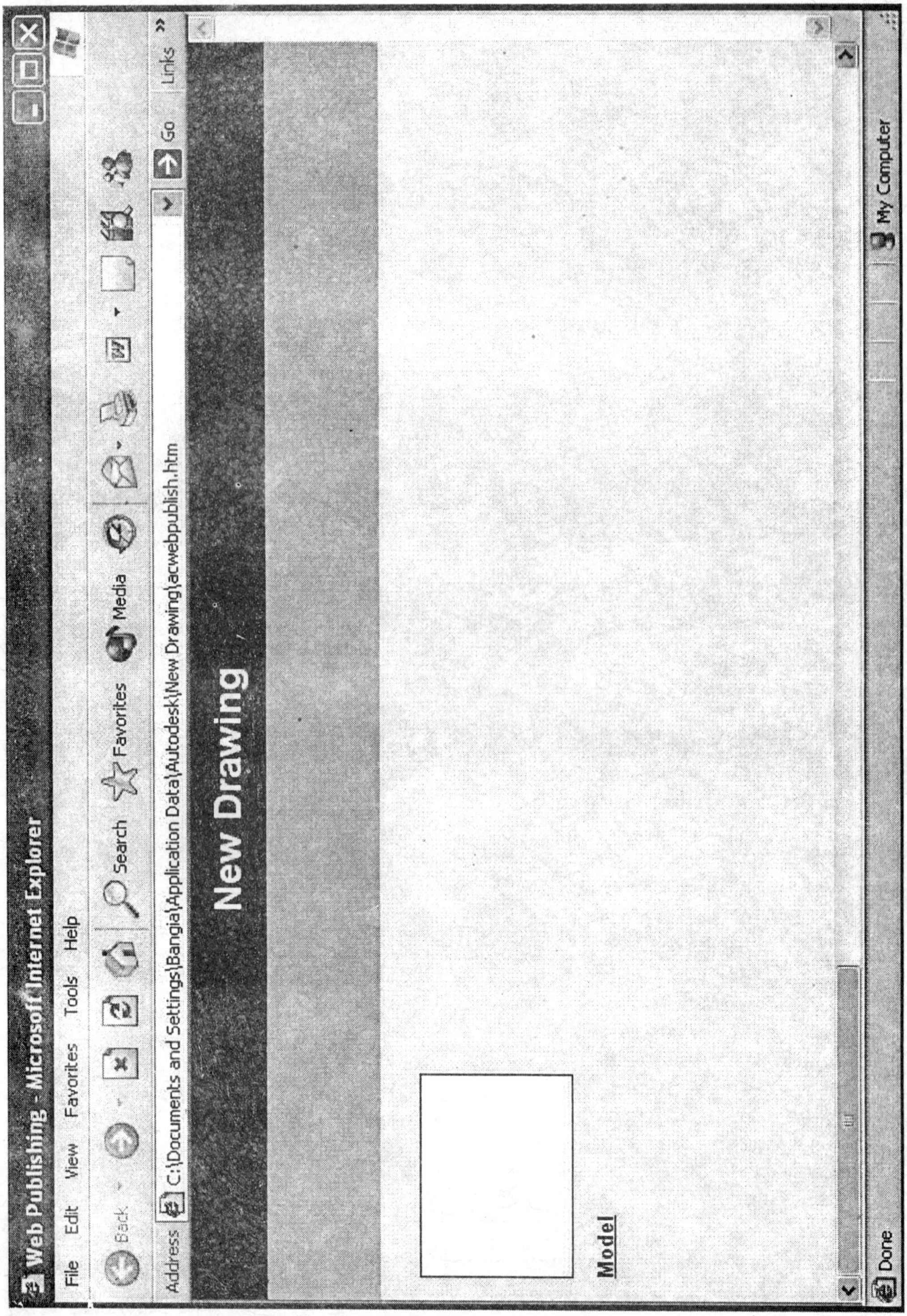
Web Publishing - Microsoft Internet Explorer
File Edit View Favorites Tools Help
Back Search Favorites Media
Address C:\Documents and Settings\Bangia\Application Data\Autodesk\New Drawing\acwebpublish.htm
Go Links
New Drawing
Model
Done
My Computer

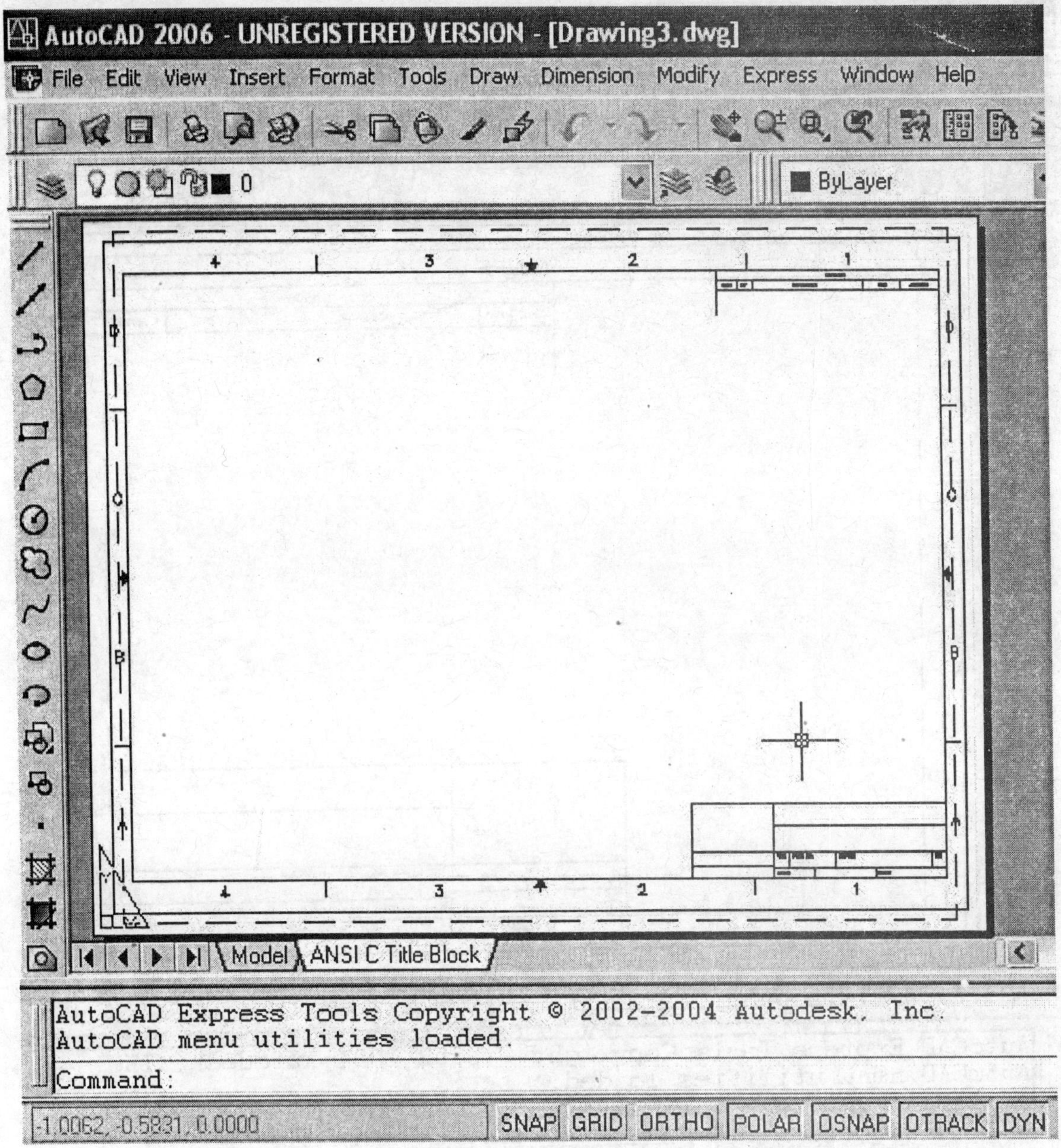
AutoCAD 2006 - UNREGISTERED VERSION - [Drawing3.dwg]
File Edit View Insert Format Tools Draw Dimension Modify Express Window Help
ByLayer
Model
ANSI C Title Block
AutoCAD Express Tools Copyright © 2002-2004 Autodesk, Inc.
AutoCAD menu utilities loaded.
Command:
-1.0062, -0.5831, 0.0000
SNAP GRID ORTHO POLAR OSNAP OTRACK DYN

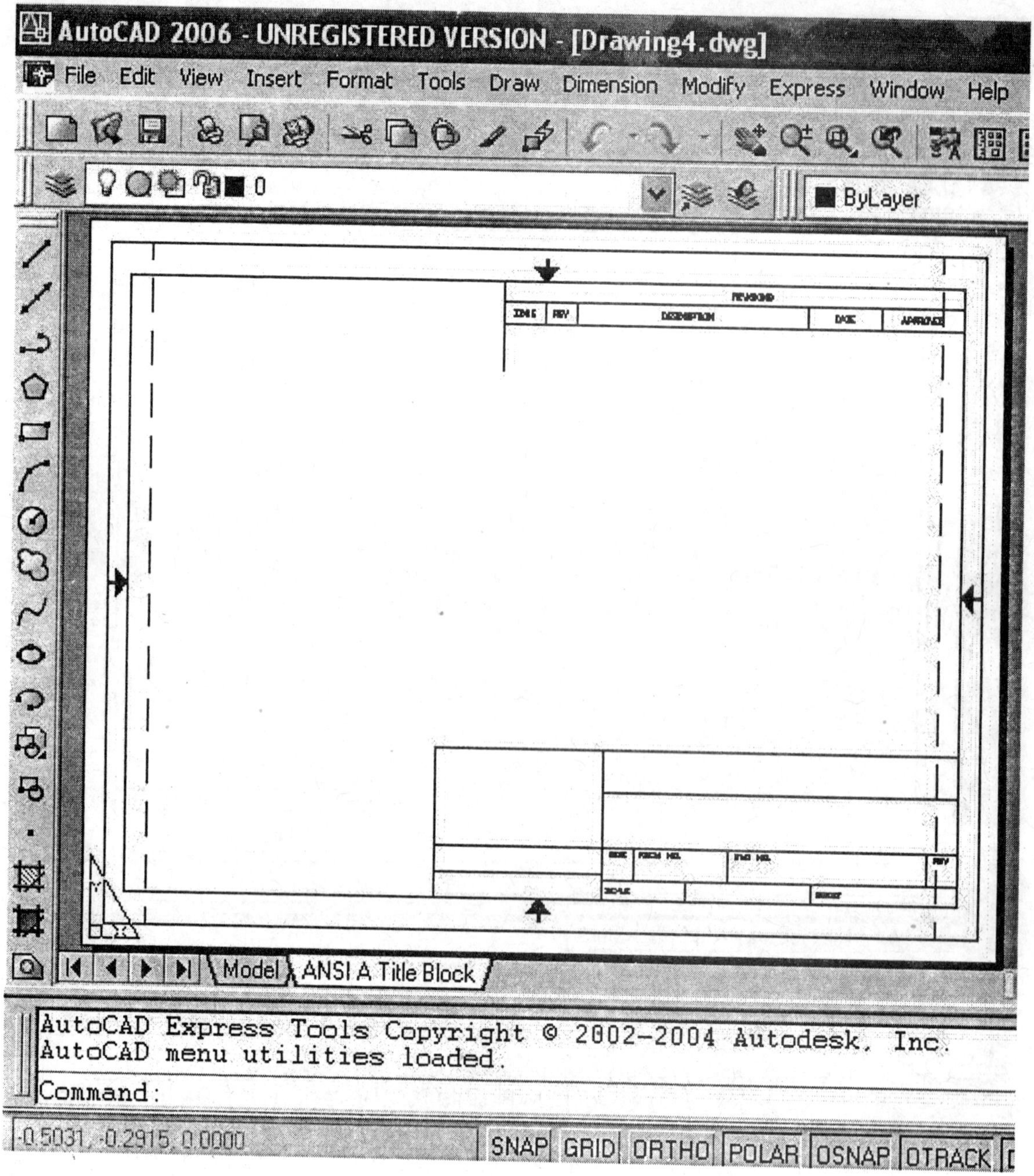

AutoCAD 2006 - UNREGISTERED VERSION - [Drawing4.dwg]
File Edit View Insert Format Tools Draw Dimension Modify Express Window Help
ByLayer
Model
ANSI A Title Block
AutoCAD Express Tools Copyright © 2002-2004 Autodesk, Inc.
AutoCAD menu utilities loaded.
Command:
-0.5031, -0.2915, 0.0000
SNAP GRID ORTHO POLAR OSNAP OTRACK

Using Tools of AutoCAD 2006

4

Two Dimensional Tools

Tools are there to help you work smoothly. They are there in AutoCAD 2006 too. There are various tools under various toolbars. Each one of them is there to do some specific job. In this chapter we would learn about some of these tools.

They are:

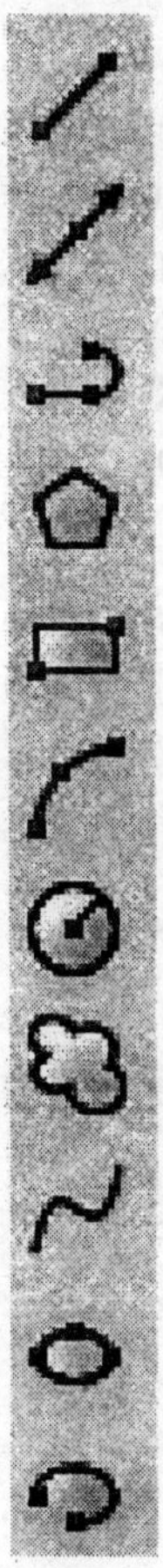

Line tool

Construction line tool

Polyline tool

Polygon tool

Rectangle tool

Arc tool

Circle tool

Revcloud tool

Spline tool

Ellipse tool

Ellipse Arc tool

Insert Block tool

Make Block tool

Point tool

Hatch tool

Region tool

Table tool

Multiline Text tool

There are 5 basic five tools: Line, Polyline, Multiline, Circle and Arc. Drawings in AutoCAD 2006 in two ways: 2D, i.e., two dimensional with x, y coordinate and 3D, i.e., three dimensional with x, y, z coordinates. X is measured horizontally, Y vertically and Z perpendicularly. So if I write 90,40 it means that a line is drawn 90 units horizontally and 40 units vertically. Similar would be a 3D figure with the dimensions of 90,40,20. Effectively if 2D drawings, the third dimension, Z is 0.

You can in fact use these units in Command window for drawing or make use of the mouse to draw. Let us first draw few figures in 2D mode.

Line Tool

This is the first tool in the list as seen earlier. Let us use it to draw something on the screen using the command window.

Give the following command answers to the various questions and you would be able to draw a figure as shown on the next page on the screen.

Command	*Answer*
Command	line <Enter>
Specify next point or [Undo]:	20,200 <Enter>
Specify next point or [Undo]:	200,40 <Enter>
Specify next point or [Undo]:	40,100 <Enter>

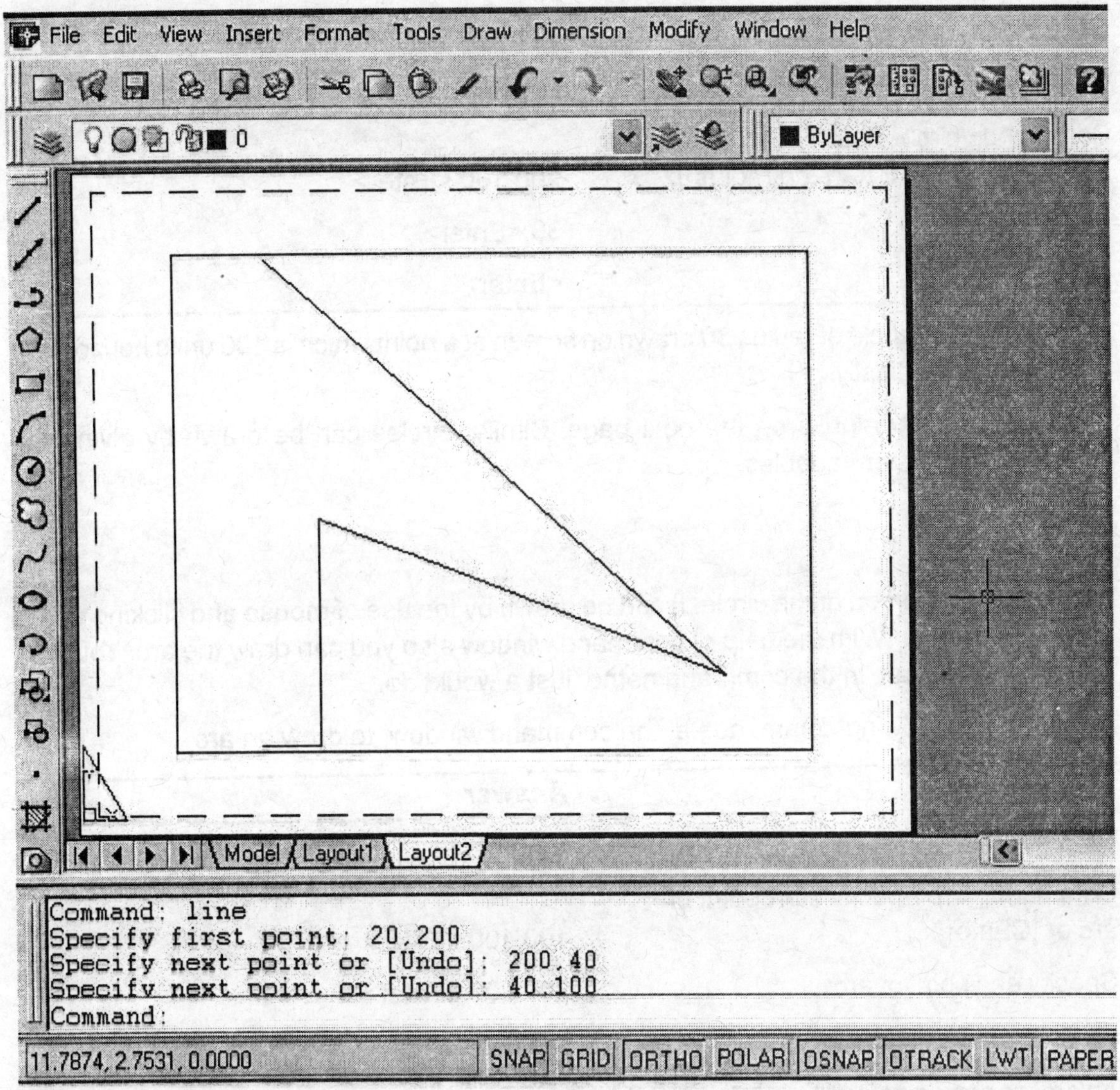

Circle Tool

This tool will help you draw a circle on the screen. Of course you can draw a circle with the mouse, but it is better to do it with the help of the command window.

Here you can easily define the place where you want the circle to be drawn and the exact size of the circle to be drawn.

At the command window give the following instructions/answers.

Command	*Answer*
Command	circle <Enter>
Command:_circle Specify center point for circle or [3P/2P/Ttr (tan tan radius)]:	100,100 <Enter>
Specify radius:	30 <Enter>
Command:	<Enter>

This will end in a circle of radius 30 drawn on screen at a point which is 100 units horizontally and 100 units vertically.

See how the figure looks on the next page. Similar circles can be drawn by giving the command with other variables.

Arc Tool

It is basically a portion of the circle. It can be drawn by the use of mouse and clicking at Arc in the Draw menu. With the help of command window also you can draw the arc. You may not enter the full arc in the command name, just a would do.

Just give the following commands at the command window, to draw an arc.

Command	*Answer*
Command	a <Enter>
Command:_arc Specify start point of arc or [CEnter]:	100,100 <Enter>
Specify end point of arc:	200,200 <Enter>
Command:	<Enter>

An arc, as shown next will be drawn like this. Of course, you can try this with other variables.

Polyline Tool

It can be drawn by the use of mouse by clicking at Polyline in the Draw menu. With the help of command window also you can draw the polyline. You may not enter the full polyline in the command name, just pl would do.

Just give the following commands at the command window, to draw a polyline.

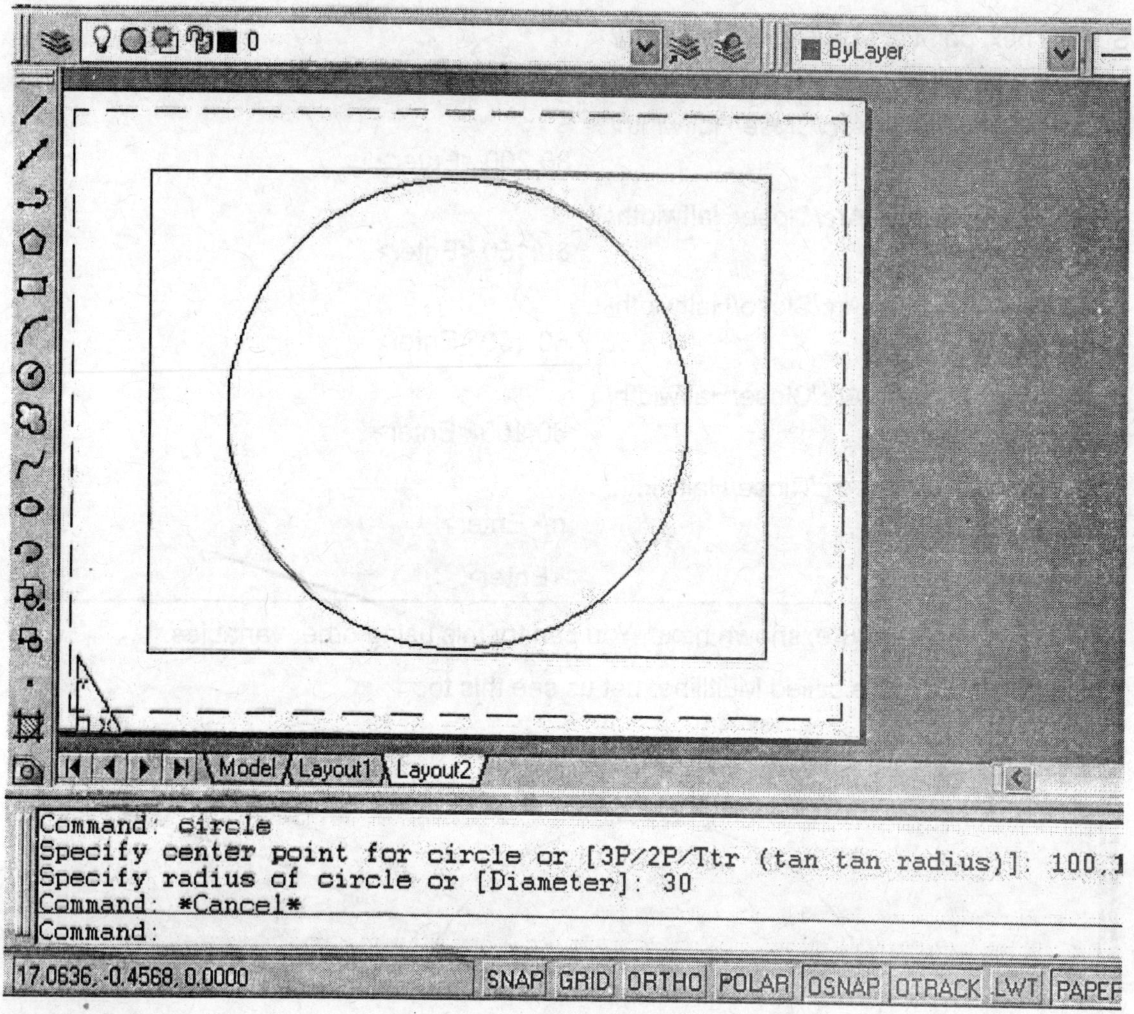

Command	***Answer***
Command	pl <Enter>
Specify start point:	30,200 <Enter>
Current line width is 0.000	<Enter>
Specify next point or [Arc/Close/Halfwidth/ Length/Undo/Width]:	30,300 <Enter>
Specify next point or [Arc/Close/Halfwidth/ Length/Undo/Width]:	100,300 <Enter>

Specify next point or [Arc/Close/Halfwidth/Length/Undo/Width]:	100,200 <Enter>
Specify next point or [Arc/Close/Halfwidth/Length/Undo/Width]:	80,200 <Enter>
Specify next point or [Arc/Close/Halfwidth/Length/Undo/Width]:	80,150 <Enter>
Specify next point or [Arc/Close/Halfwidth/Length/Undo/Width]:	60,150 <Enter>
Specify next point or [Arc/Close/Halfwidth/Length/Undo/Width]:	60,100 <Enter>
Specify next point or [Arc/Close/Halfwidth/Length/Undo/Width]:	c <Enter>
Command:	<Enter>

This will result in a figure, shown next. You can try this using other variables.

Similar to this is mline called Multiline. Let us see this too.

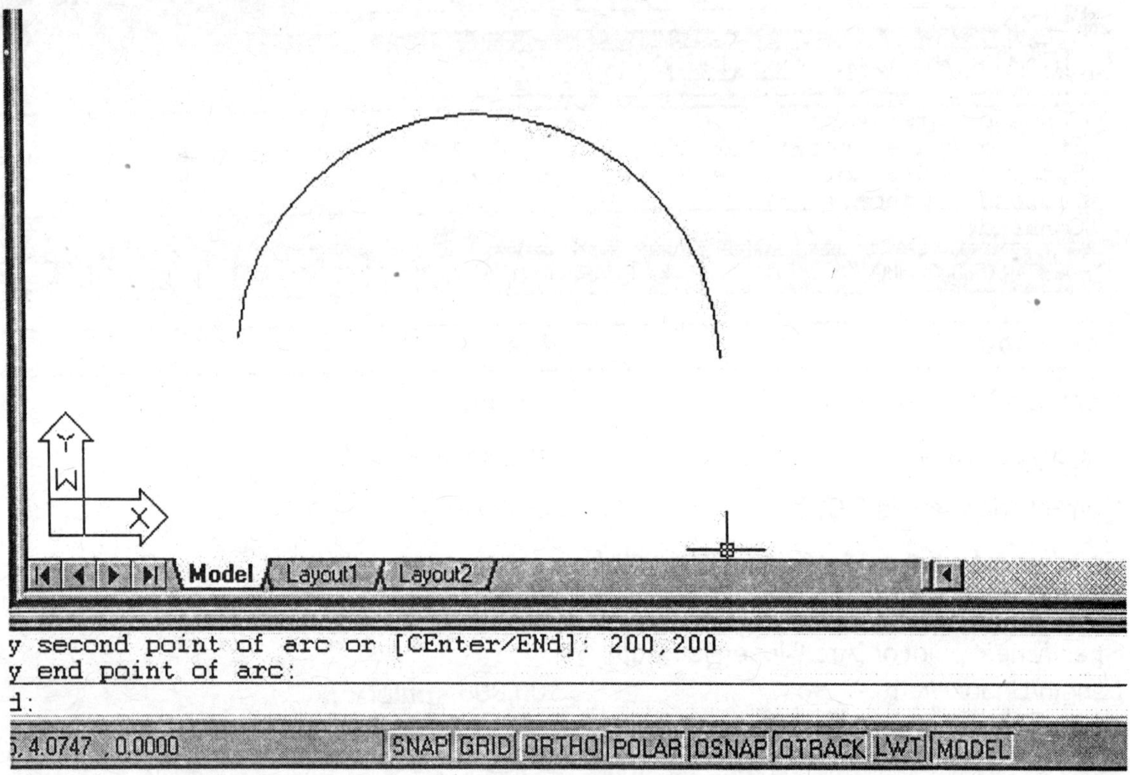

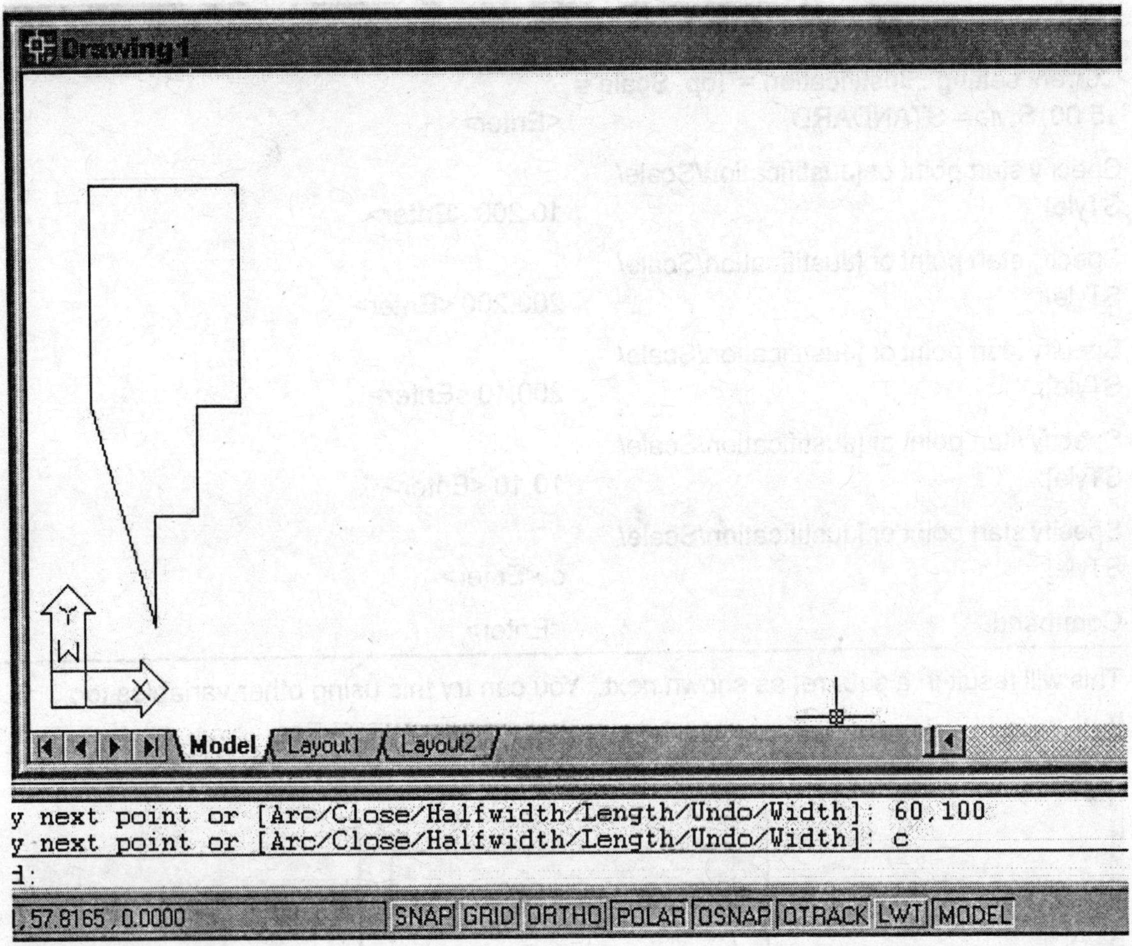

Multiline Tool

It can be drawn by the use of mouse by clicking at Multiline in the Draw menu. With the help of command window also you can draw the multiline. You may not enter the full multiline in the command name, just ml would do.

Give the following commands at the command window, to draw a multiline.

Command	***Answer***
Command	mline <Enter>
Current setting: Justification = Top, Scale = 20.00, Style = STANDARD	<Enter>
Specify start point or [Justification/Scale/STyle]:	s <Enter>

Enter mline scale <20.00>	15 <Enter>
Current setting : Justification = Top, Scale = 15.00, Style = STANDARD	<Enter>
Specify start point or [Justification/Scale/STyle]:	10,200 <Enter>
Specify start point or [Justification/Scale/STyle]:	200,200 <Enter>
Specify start point or [Justification/Scale/STyle]:	200,10 <Enter>
Specify start point or [Justification/Scale/STyle]:	10,10 <Enter>
Specify start point or [Justification/Scale/STyle]:	c <Enter>
Command:	<Enter>

This will result in a square, as shown next. You can try this using other variables too.

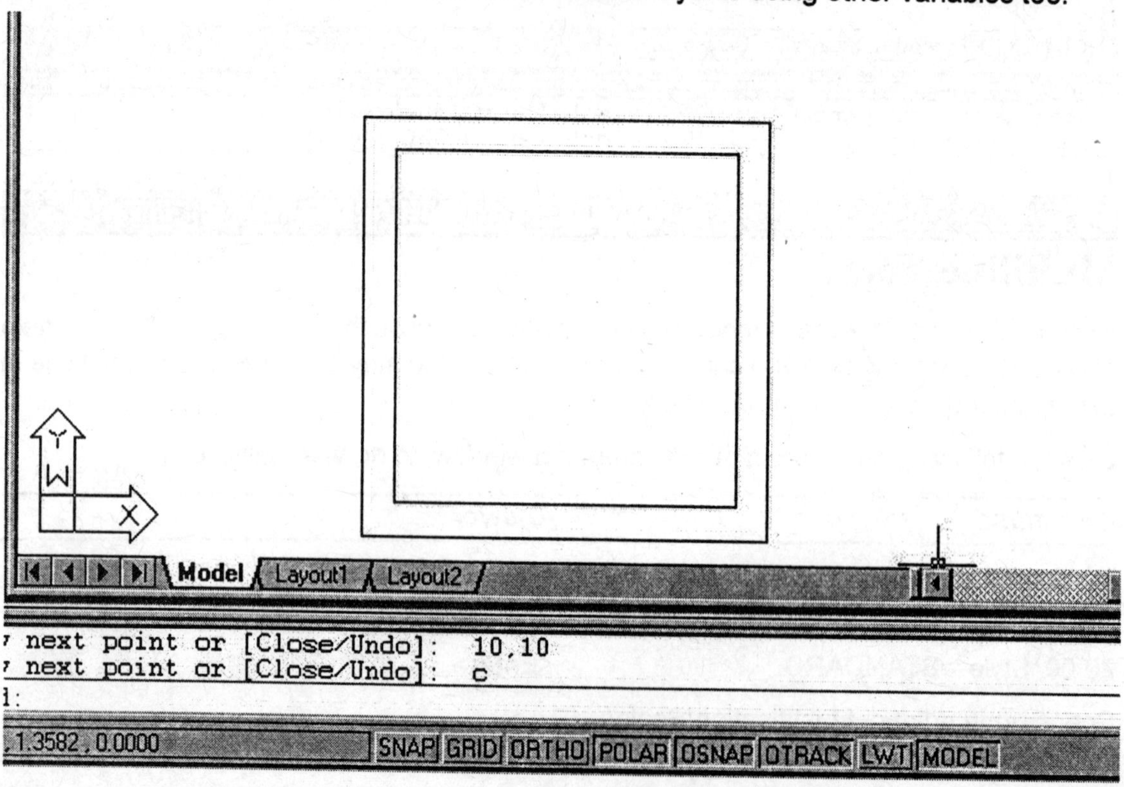

This is not that you can draw a rectangle only. You can use this to make a triangle too. For this you will have to use the option of Justification = Zero. Let us see how this is done.

Command	***Answer***
Command	mline <Enter>
Current setting: Justification = Top, Scale = 20.00, Style = STANDARD	<Enter>
Specify start point or [Justification/Scale/STyle]:	j <Enter>
Specify start point or [Justification/Scale/STyle]:	j <Enter>
Enter Justification type [Top/Zero/Bottom]:	zero <Enter>
Current Setting : Justification = Zero, Scale = 15.00, Style = STANDARD	<Enter>
Specify start point or [Justification/Scale/STyle]:	280,260 <Enter>
Specify start point or [Justification/Scale/STyle]:	430,260 <Enter>
Specify start point or [Justification/Scale/STyle]:	430,110 <Enter>
Specify start point or [Justification/Scale/STyle]:	c <Enter>
Command:	<Enter>

This would result in the figure shown on the next page.

Polygon Tool

It can be drawn by the use of mouse by clicking at Polygon in the Draw menu. With the help of command window also you can draw the polygon. You may not enter the full polygon in the command name, just pol would do.

Give the following commands at the command window, to draw a polygon.

Command	***Answer***
Command	polyline <Enter>

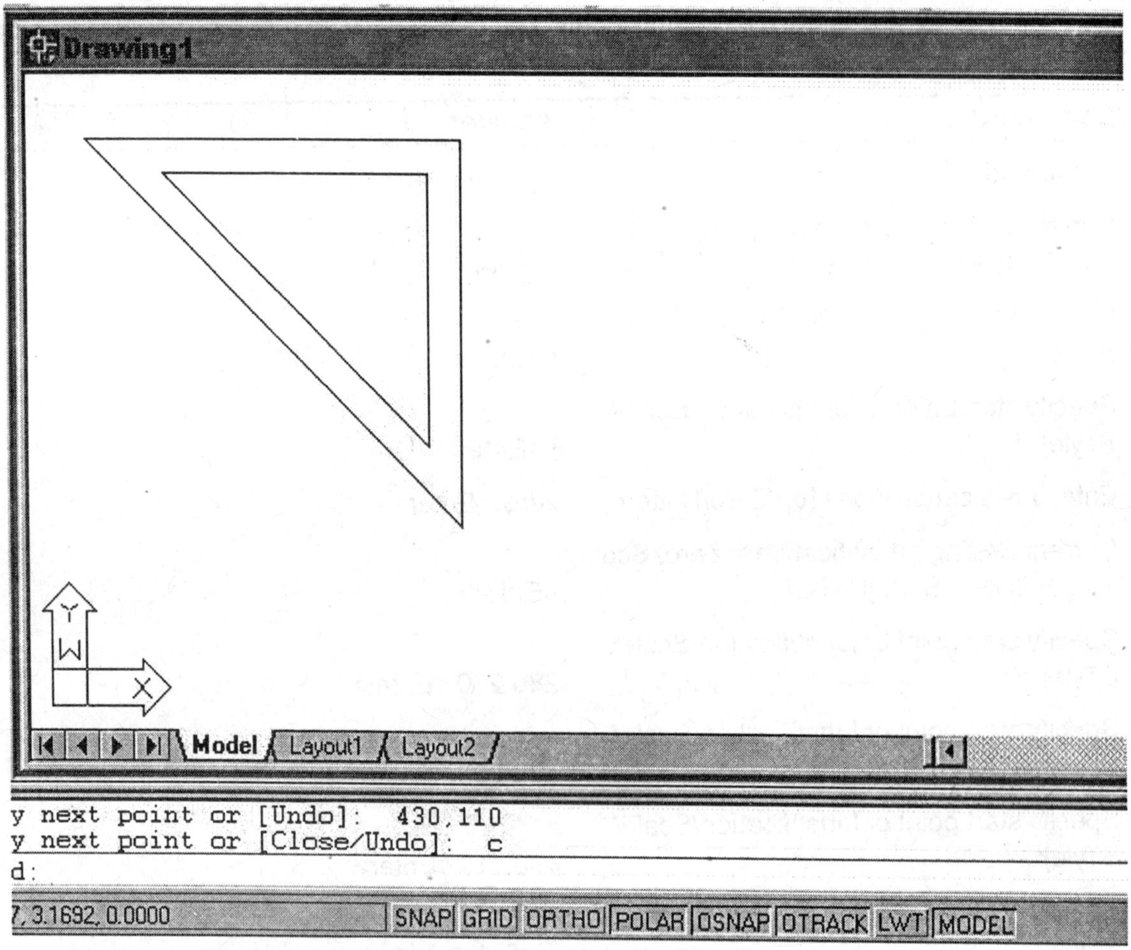

Enter number sides	8 <Enter>
Specify center of polygon or [Edge]:	40,200 <Enter>
Enter an option [Inscribed in circle/Cirumscribed about circle] <I>	<Enter>
Specify radius of circle:	50 <Enter>
Command:	<Enter>

This will result in a polygon, as shown next. You can try this using other variables too.

Rectangle Tool

It can be drawn by the use of mouse by clicking at Rectangle in the Draw menu. With the help of command window also you can draw the rectangle.

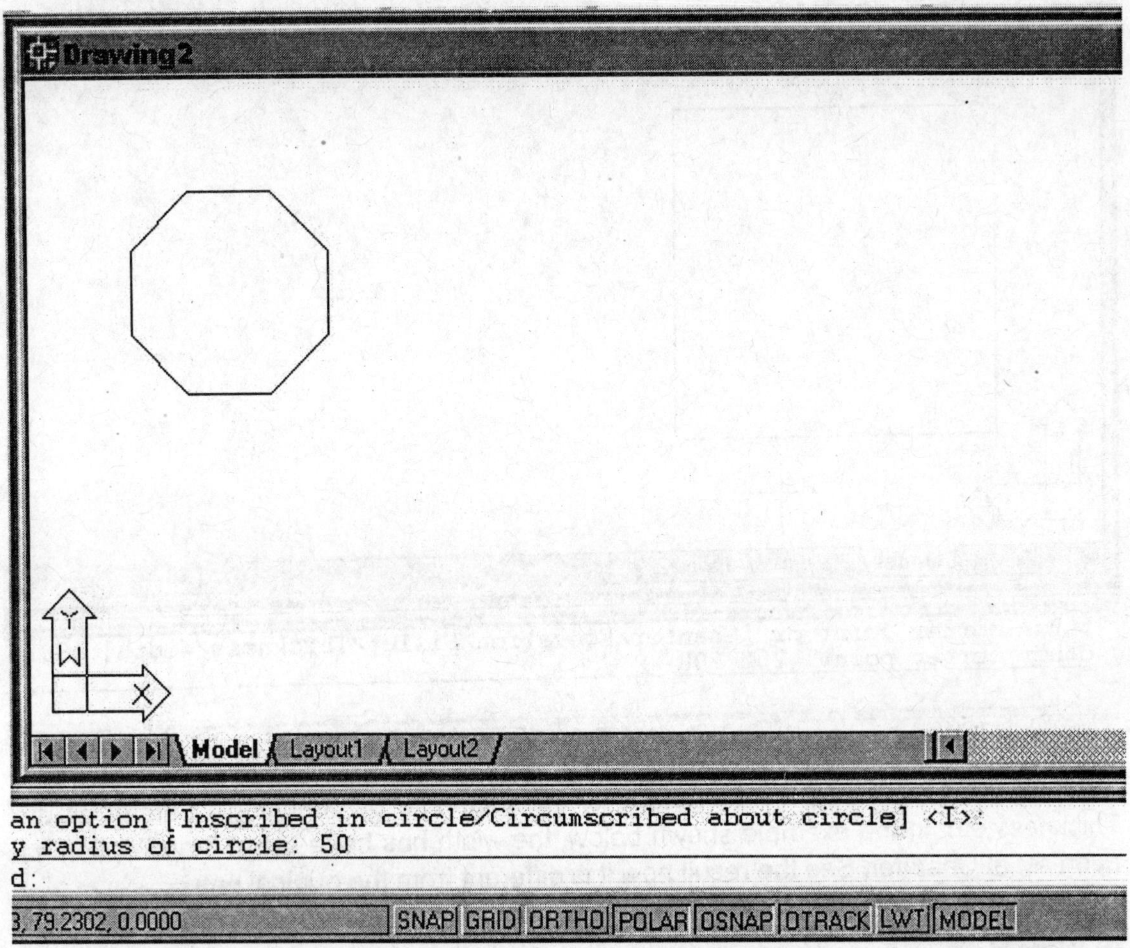

You may not enter the full rectangle in the command name, just rec would do.

Give the following commands at the command window, to draw a rectangle.

Command	***Answer***
Command	rectangle <Enter>
Specify first corner point or [Chamfer/ Elevation/Fillet/Thickness/Width] <I>	50,50 <Enter>
Specify other point	200,200 <Enter>
Command:	<Enter>

This will result in a rectangle, as shown next. You can try this using other variables too.

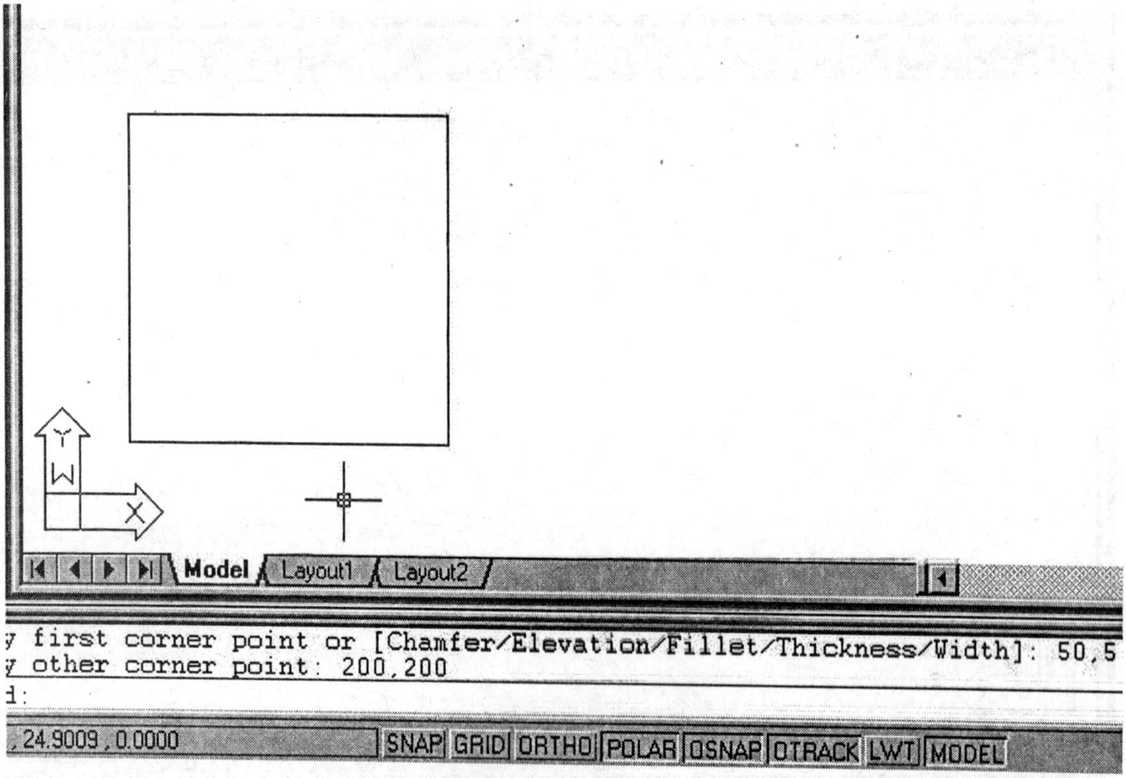

If you want you can change the shape of the rectangle by changing Chamfer, Width, Thickness etc. In the example shown below, the width has been set at 3 and option has been set at Chamfer. See the result how it is different from the original one.

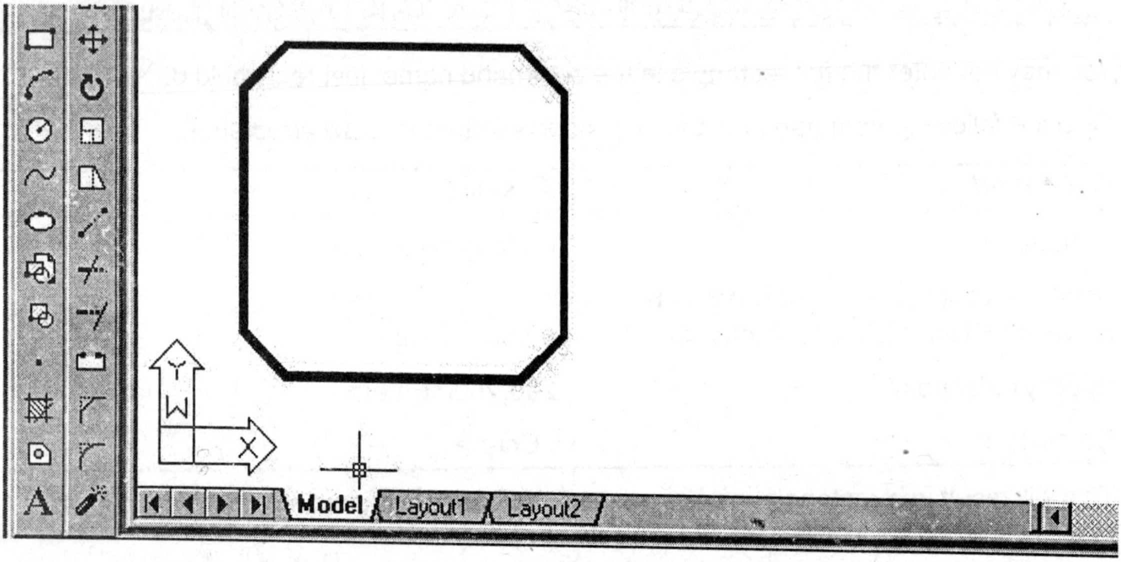

Spline Tool

It can be drawn by the use of mouse by clicking at Spline in the Draw menu. With the help of command window also you can use spline.

You may not enter the full spline in the command name, just spl would do.

Give the following commands at the command window, to draw a spline.

Command	*Answer*
Command	spline <Enter>
Specify first point or [Object]	50,150 <Enter>
Specify next point	150,250 <Enter>
Specify next point or [close/Fit tolerance] <start tangent>	300,320 <Enter>
Specify next point or [close/Fit tolerance] <start tangent>	320,250 <Enter>
Specify next point or [close/Fit tolerance] <start tangent>	<Enter>
Specify start tangent	<Enter>
Specify end tangent	<Enter>
Command:	<Enter>

This will result in a figure, as shown next. You can try this using other variables too.

In the above example at the point where we have finished with the variables and just pressed <Enter>, you can opt for Close by typing c and then pressing <Enter> to give rise to a closed figure, as shown on the next page.

Ellipse Tool

It can be drawn by the use of mouse by clicking at Ellipse in the Draw menu. With the help of command window also you can draw ellipse. You may not enter the full ellipse in the command name, just el would do.

Give the following commands at the command window, to draw an ellipse.

Command	*Answer*
Command	el <Enter>

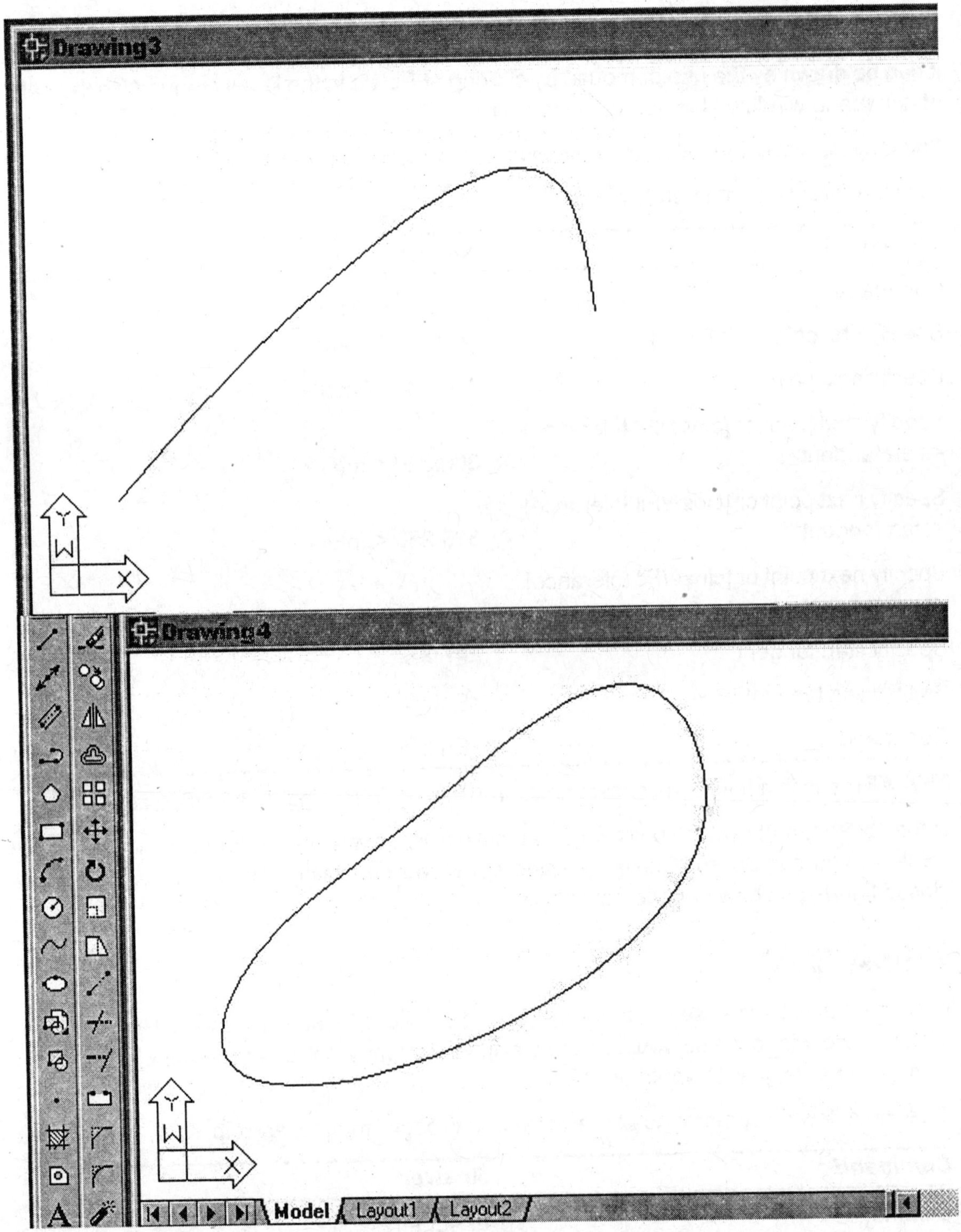
Drawing3
Drawing4
Model
Layout1
Layout2

Specify axis endpoint of ellipse or [Arc/Center]:	50,200 <Enter>
Specify other endpoint of axis	150,190 <Enter>
Specify distance to other axis or [Rotation]:	50 <Enter>
Command:	<Enter>

This will result in a figure, as shown below. You can try this using other variables too.

In the above example you can opt for case of Center and Rotation and see the results.

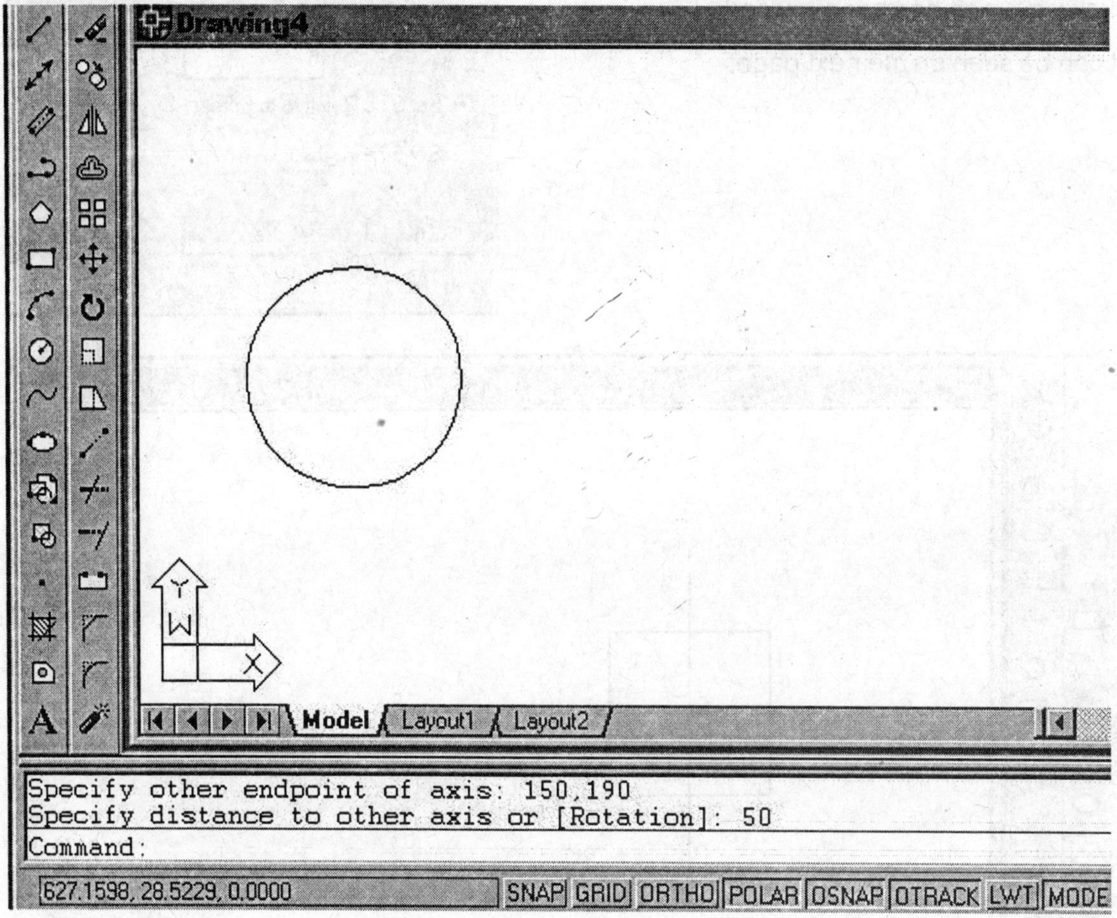

Point Tool

Before you call this tool choose a point style from the Point Style dialog box, which can be called by selecting Point Style from the Format menu. You can select any of the point tool style from here.

Just click at the screen and draw the figure with the help of the point tool, as shown, below.

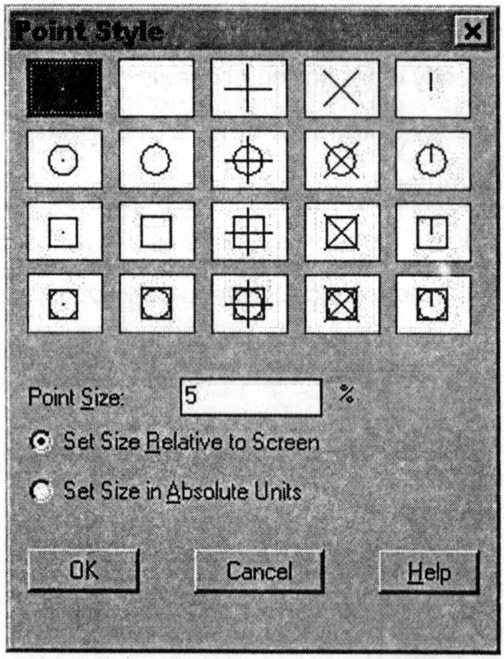

Revcloud Tool

This tool is used to draw revision clouds over the portions of the drawings which have been revised so as to make a note of them. Just click at the screen and draw the cloud over the portion of the drawing which has been revised.

It can be seen on the next page.

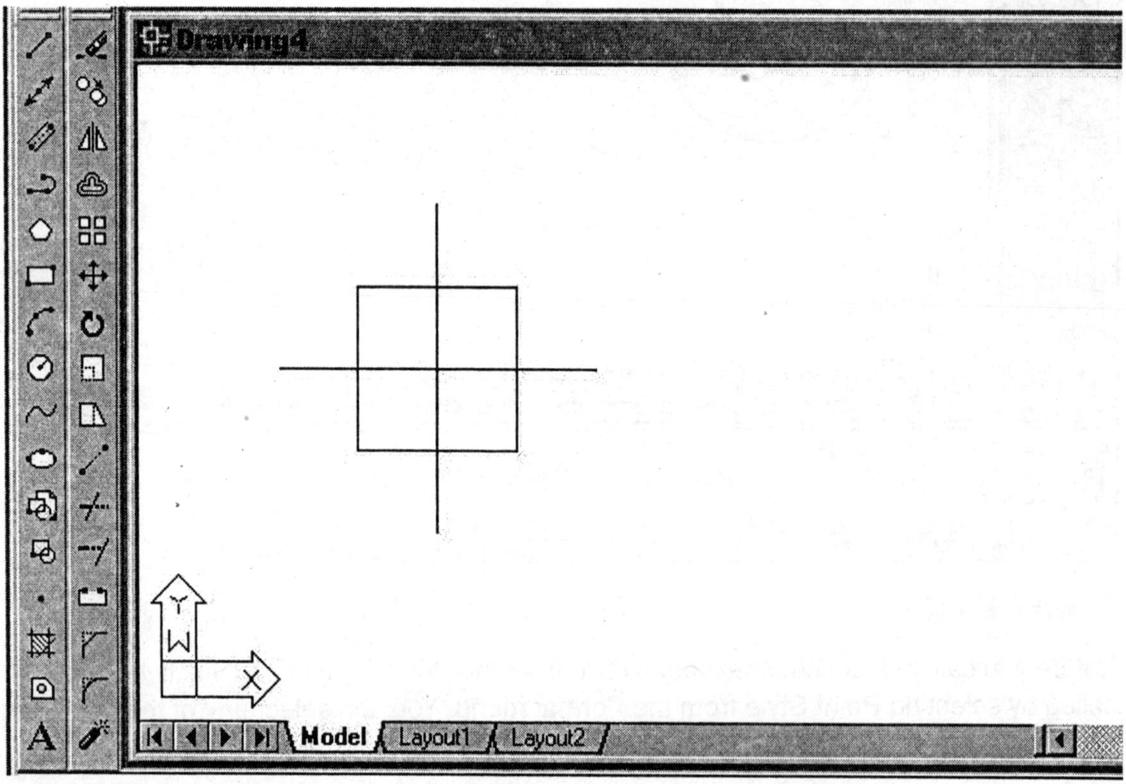

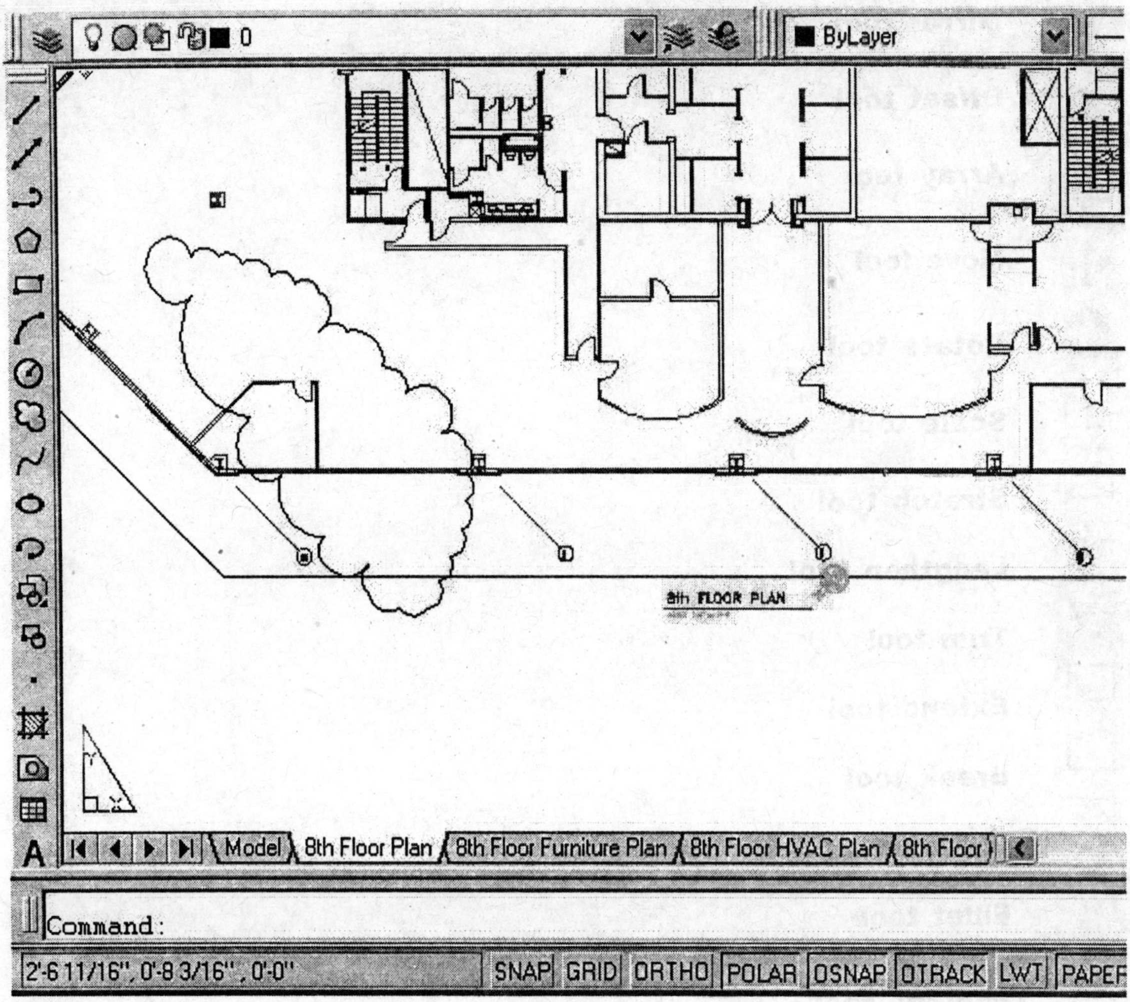

Table Tool

This tool is used to draw table in the drawing. When you select the tool, a dialog box is given to you to select the table specifications. After selecting press ok to have the table on the screen within the drawing. Fill the data and headings required to complete the job.

Now we come to other set of tools called Modify Tools. Various tools under this are:

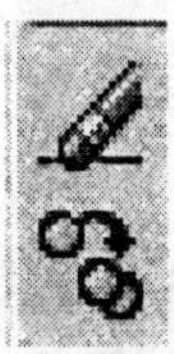

Erase tool

Copy Object tool

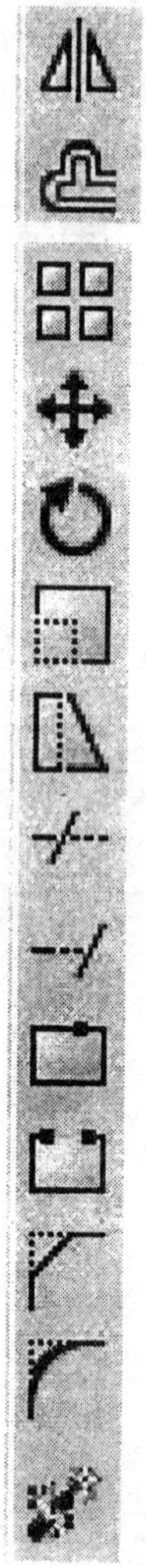

- **Mirror tool**
- **Offset tool**
- **Array tool**
- **Move tool**
- **Rotate tool**
- **Scale tool**
- **Stretch tool**
- **Lengthen tool**
- **Trim tool**
- **Extend tool**
- **Break tool**
- **Chamfer tool**
- **Fillet tool**
- **Explode tool**

Erase Tool

As the name sounds, it is used to rub off any error made by the operator in drawing on the screen. There are 3 main methods by which erasing can be carried out:

1. Erasing single objects.
2. Erasing objects within a window.
3. Erasing objects crossed by a crossing window.

The Erase tool can be called by either a click on its name in the Modify menu or from its icon in the toolbar. In the command line it can be used with the name as e.

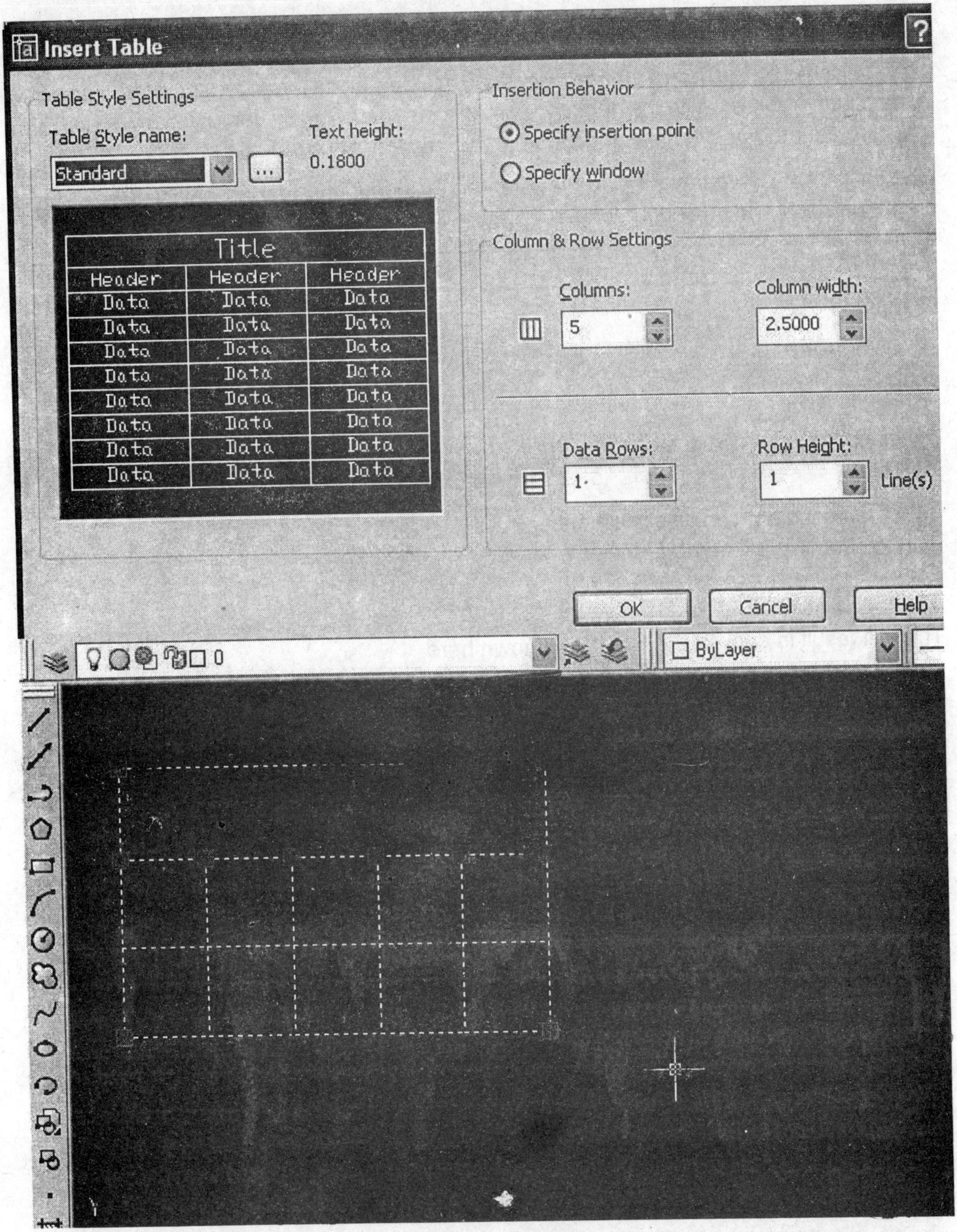
Insert Table
Table Style Settings
Table Style name:
Standard
Text height:
0.1800
Title
Header Header Header
Data Data Data
Insertion Behavior
Specify insertion point
Specify window
Column & Row Settings
Columns:
5
Column width:
2.5000
Data Rows:
1
Row Height:
1
Line(s)
OK
Cancel
Help
ByLayer

Copy Object Tool

It can be called by the use of mouse by clicking at Copy in the Modify menu or from the icon in the Modify Toolbar. With the help of command window also you can use copy object. You may not enter the copy object in the command name, just cp would do.

Give the following commands at the command window, to copy an object. Here I have created a circle and copied it.

Command	***Answer***
Command	cp <Enter>
Select objects :	1 <Enter>
Select objects:	<Enter>
Specify base point or displacement, or [Multiple]:	<Enter>
Specify second point of displacement or <use first point of displacement>:	<Enter>
Command:	<Enter>

This will result in copy of the circle, as shown here.

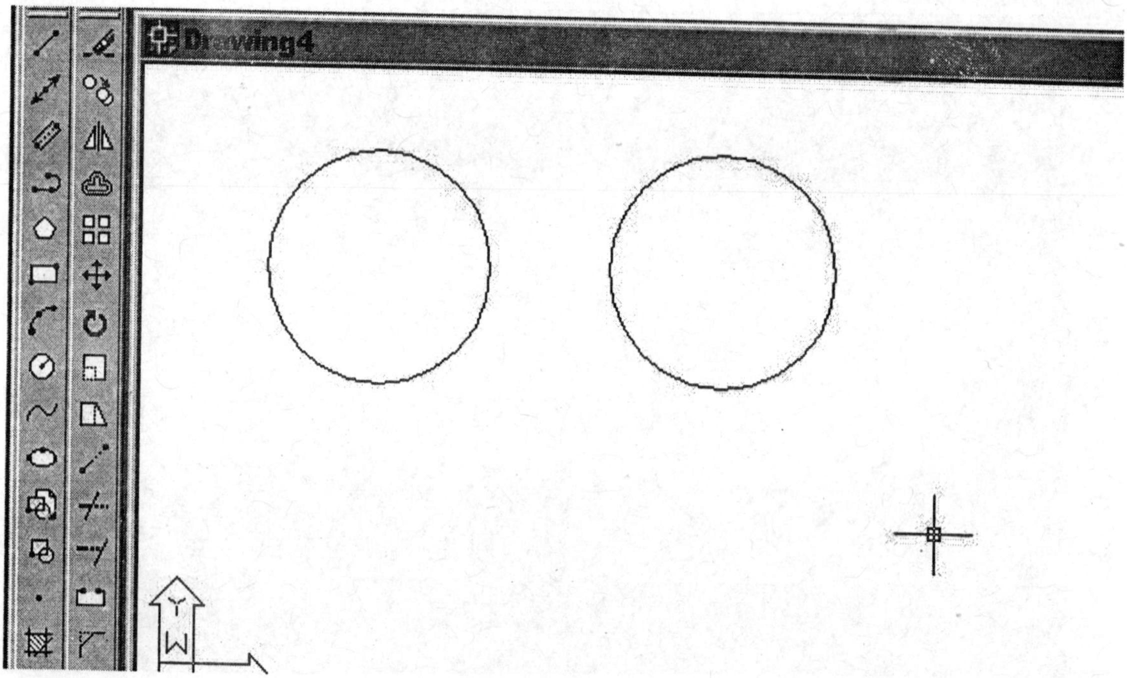

Mirror Tool

It can be called by the use of mouse by clicking at Mirror in the Modify menu or from the icon called Mirror in the Modify Toolbar. With the help of command window also you can use mirror tool. You may not enter the mirror in the command name, just mi would do.

In this case I have typed a simple text and then mirrored it.

Command	***Answer***
Command	mirror <Enter>
Select objects :	1 <Enter>
Select objects:	<Enter>
Specify first point on mirror line:	<Enter>
Specify second point on mirror line:	<Enter>
Delete source objects [Yes/No]: <N>	<Enter>
Command:	<Enter>

This will result in copy of the text but a mirror image of the same, as shown below.

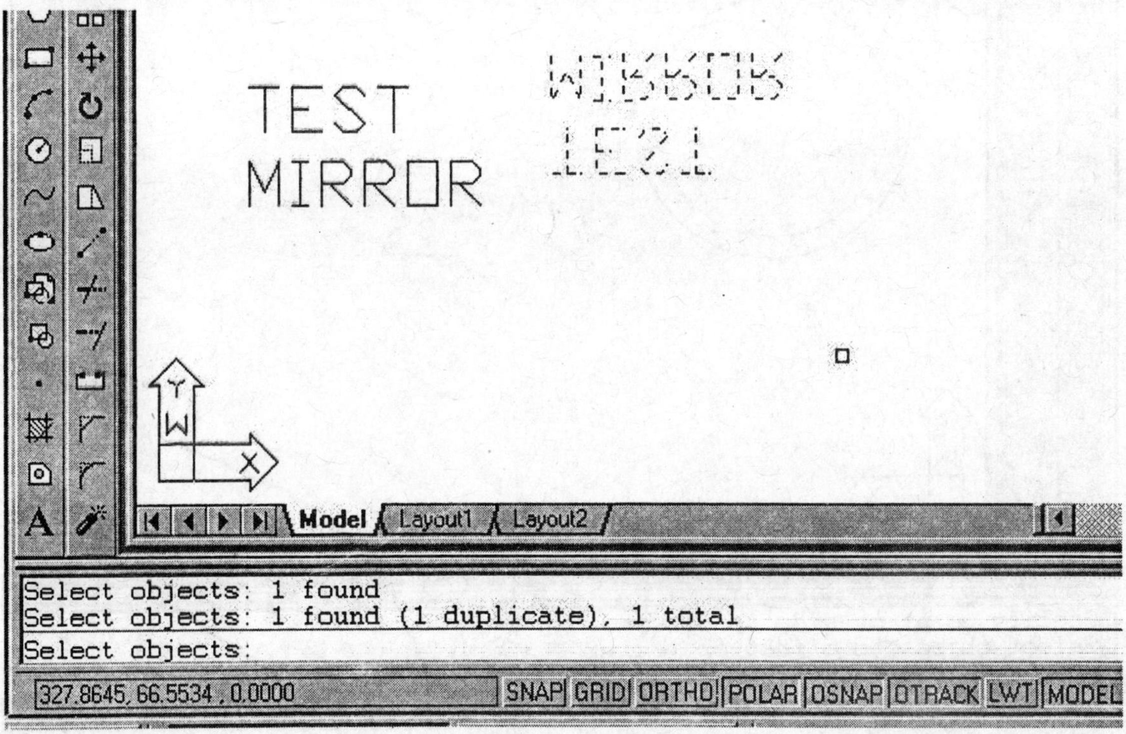

Offset Tool

It can be called by the use of mouse by clicking at Offset in the Modify menu or from the icon called Offset in the Modify Toolbar. With the help of command window also you can use offset tool. You may not enter the offset in the command name, just o would do. In this case I have drawn a circle and then I would offset it with another circle with different size.

Command	*Answer*
Command	offset <Enter>
Select objects :	1 <Enter>
Specify object to offset or <exit>:	<Enter>
Specify point on side to offset:	<Enter>
Select object to offset or <exit>:	<Enter>
Command:	<Enter>

This will result in copy of the circle offsetting it, as shown below. You can draw more figures using different variables.

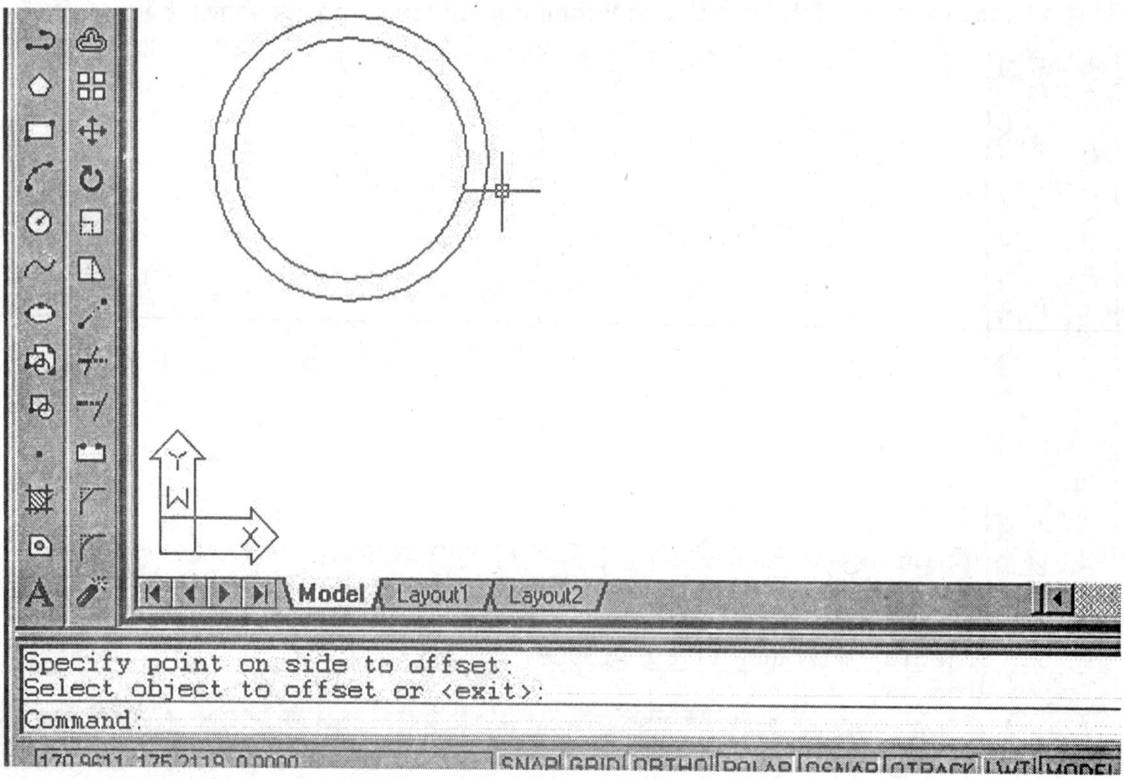

ArrayTool

It can be called by the use of mouse by clicking at Array in the Modify menu or from the icon called Array in the Modify Toolbar. With the help of command window also you can use array tool. You may not enter the array in the command name, just ar would do.

Two types of array are possible:

Rectangular Array — In which objects or groups of objects are arrayed in parallel rows and columns.

Polar Array — In which objects or groups of objects are placed in a circular or part circular array around a central point.

In this case I have drawn a polygon and then I would make an array of the same with an array of more polygons.

This is what we do for the rectangular arrays.

Command	***Answer***
Command	array <Enter>
Select objects :	*select* <Enter>
Select objects:	<Enter>
Enter the type of array [Rectangular/Polar] <R>:	<Enter>
Enter the number of rows (---) <1>:	2 <Enter>
Enter the number of columns (|||) <1>:	3 <Enter>
Enter the distance between rows or specify unit cell (---)	-100 <Enter>
Specify the distance between columns (| | |)	100 <Enter>
Command:	<Enter>

This will see that the polygon has been copied in 2 rows and 3 columns as desired. They have been distanced by 100 both horizontally and vertically. The net figure is shown on the next page. You can draw more figures using different variables.

Let us now do the polar array.

Command	***Answer***
Command	array <Enter>

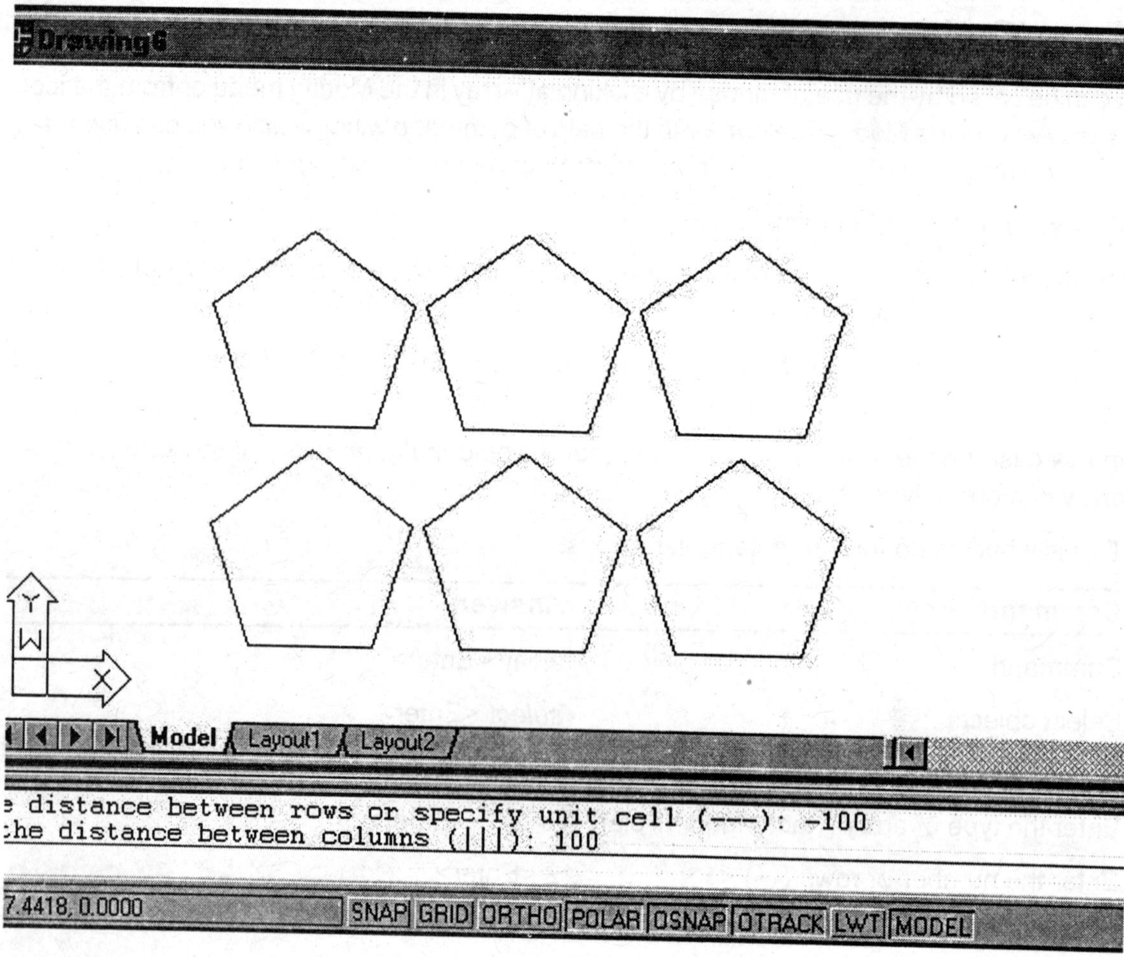

Prompt	Response
Select objects :	*select* <Enter>
Select objects:	<Enter>
Enter the type of array [Rectangular/Polar] <R>:	P <Enter>
Specify center point of array:	<Enter>
Enter the number of items in the array:	6 <Enter>
Specify the angle to fill (+=cs, –=ccw) <360>:	<Enter>
Rotate arrayed objects ? [Yes/No] <Y>	<Enter>
Command:	<Enter>

This would result in an array of polygens arranged in a polarized manner with 6 figures merged in a circular way. You can see the output next.

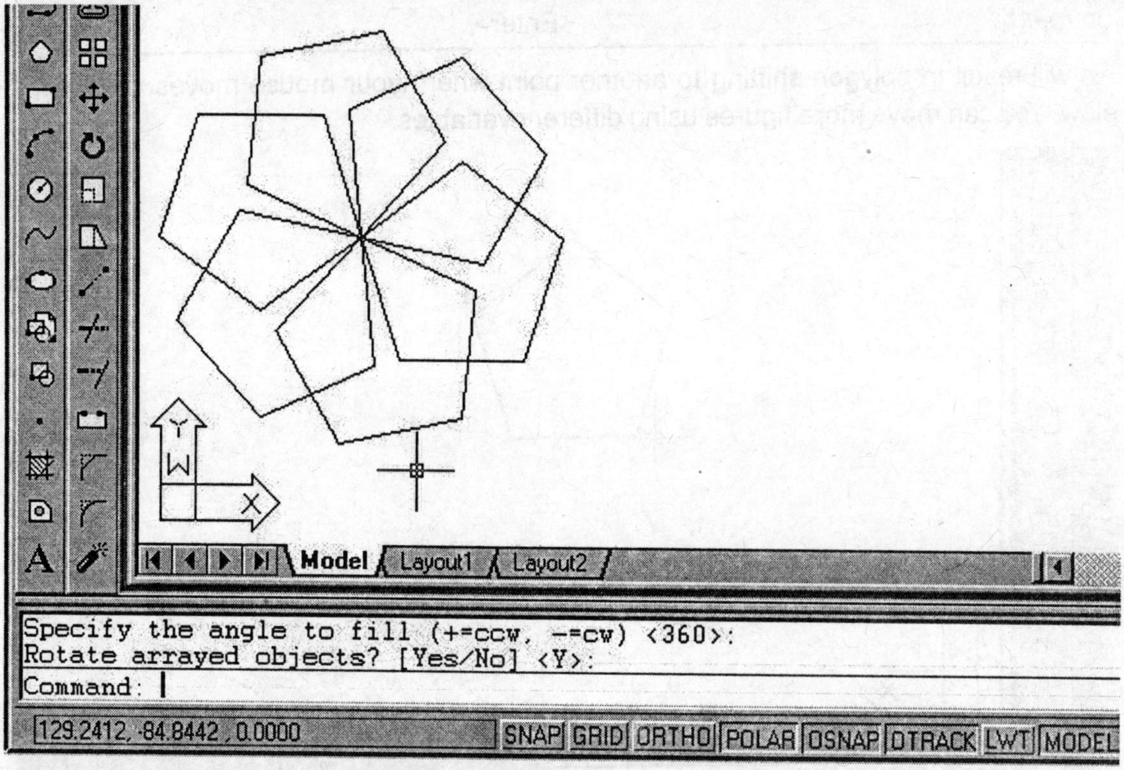

Move Tool

It can be called by the use of mouse by clicking at Move in the Modify menu or from the icon called Move in the Modify Toolbar. With the help of command window also you can use move tool. You may not enter the move in the command name, just m would do.

In this case the same polygon would be shifted to another place on the screen. Let us see how the commands are given.

Command	***Answer***
Command	move <Enter>
Select objects :	*select* <Enter>
Select objects:	<Enter>
Specify base point or displacement:	<Enter>

Specify second point of displacement or <use first point as displacement:	<Enter>
Command:	<Enter>

This will result in polygon shifting to another point where your mouse moves, as shown below. You can move more figures using different variables.

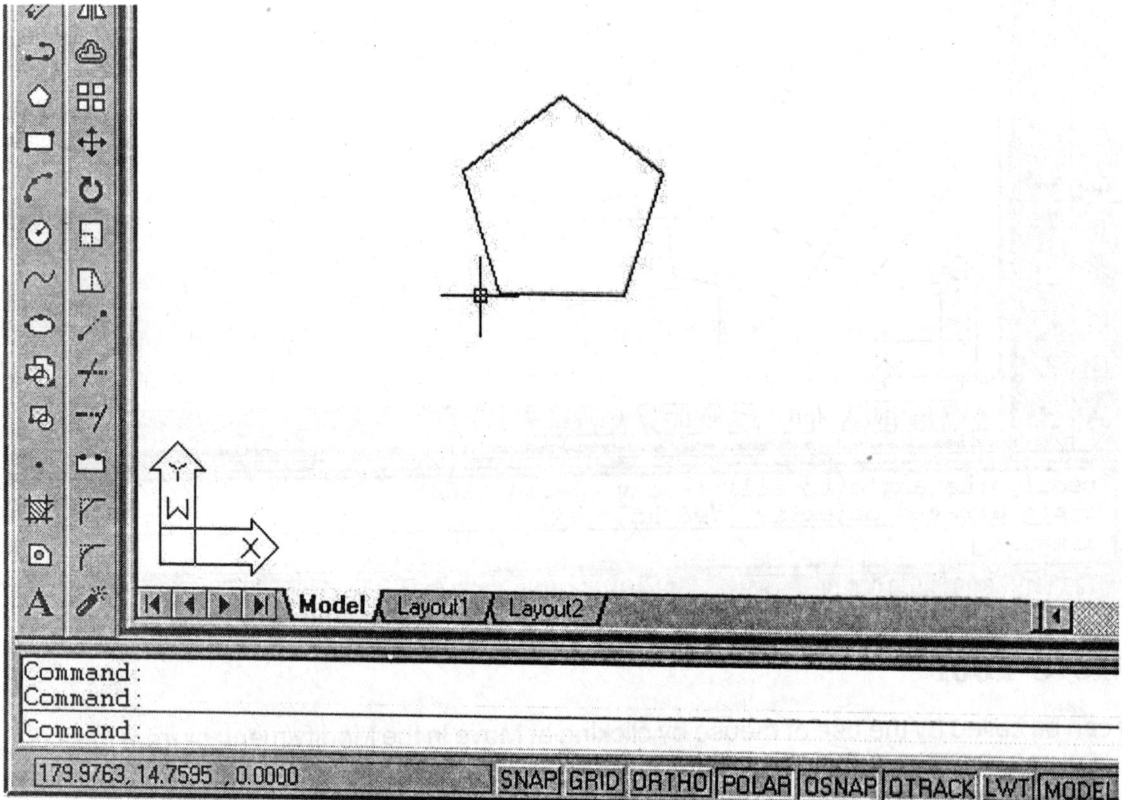

Rotate Tool

It can be called by the use of mouse by clicking at Rotate in the Modify menu or from the icon called Rotate in the Modify Toolbar. With the help of command window also you can use rotate tool. You may not enter the move in the command name, just ro would do.

In this case a triangle would be rotated to another angle on the screen. You would see the same triangle in different angles here. Let us see how the commands are given.

Command	***Answer***
Command	rotate <Enter>

Current positive angle in UCS: ANGDIR= counterclockwise ANGBASE=0	<Enter>
Select objects :	*select* <Enter>
Select objects:	<Enter>
Specify rotation angle or [Rotation]:	80 <Enter>
Command:	<Enter>

This will result in triangle rotating to angle of 80^0, as shown below. For convenience both before and after are shown. You can rotate more figures using different variables.

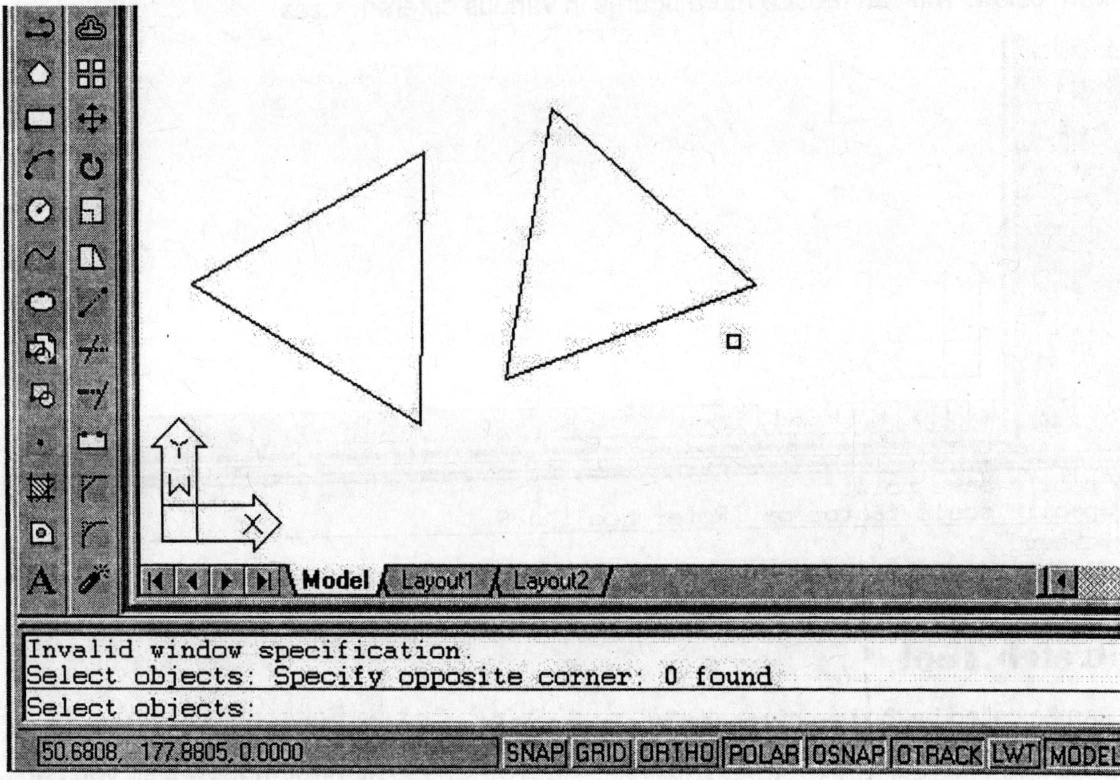

Scale Tool

It can be called by the use of mouse by clicking at Scale in the Modify menu or from the icon called Scale in the Modify Toolbar. With the help of command window also you can use scale tool. You may not enter the move in the command name, just sc would do.

Notice the size of the triangle in the example above. By scaling we would reduce it to half its size. For actual comparison do keep the above triangle in mind.

Command	*Answer*
Command	scale <Enter>
Select objects :	*select* <Enter>
Select objects:	<Enter>
Specify base point	<Enter>
Specify scale factor or [Reference]:	0.5 <Enter>
Command:	<Enter>

0.5 as we all know is ½. So this has resulted in the triangle being reduced to its half size, as shown below. You can reduce more figures in various different sizes.

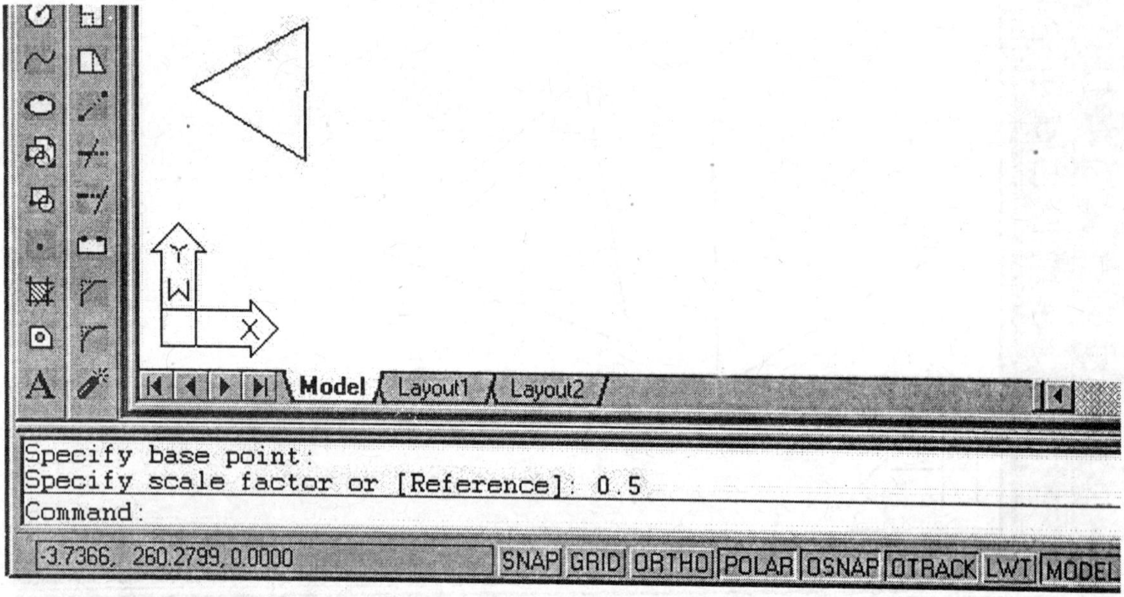

Stretch Tool

It can be called by the use of mouse by clicking at Stretch in the Modify menu or from the icon called Stretch in the Modify Toolbar. With the help of command window also you can use stretch tool. You may not enter the stretch in the command name, just s would do.

Notice the triangle in the example above. By stretching we would stretch it. Let us see what command have to be given.

Command	*Answer*
Command	stretch <Enter>

Select objects :	*select* <Enter>
Select objects:	c <Enter>
Specify first corner	*select* <Enter>
Specify opposite corner	*select* <Enter>
Select objects:	<Enter>
Specify base point or displacement:	*select* <Enter>
Specify second point of displacement	*select* <Enter>
Command:	<Enter>

This will result in the triangle being stretched to the point where you have marked at the second point, as shown below. You can stretch more figures in various different sizes.

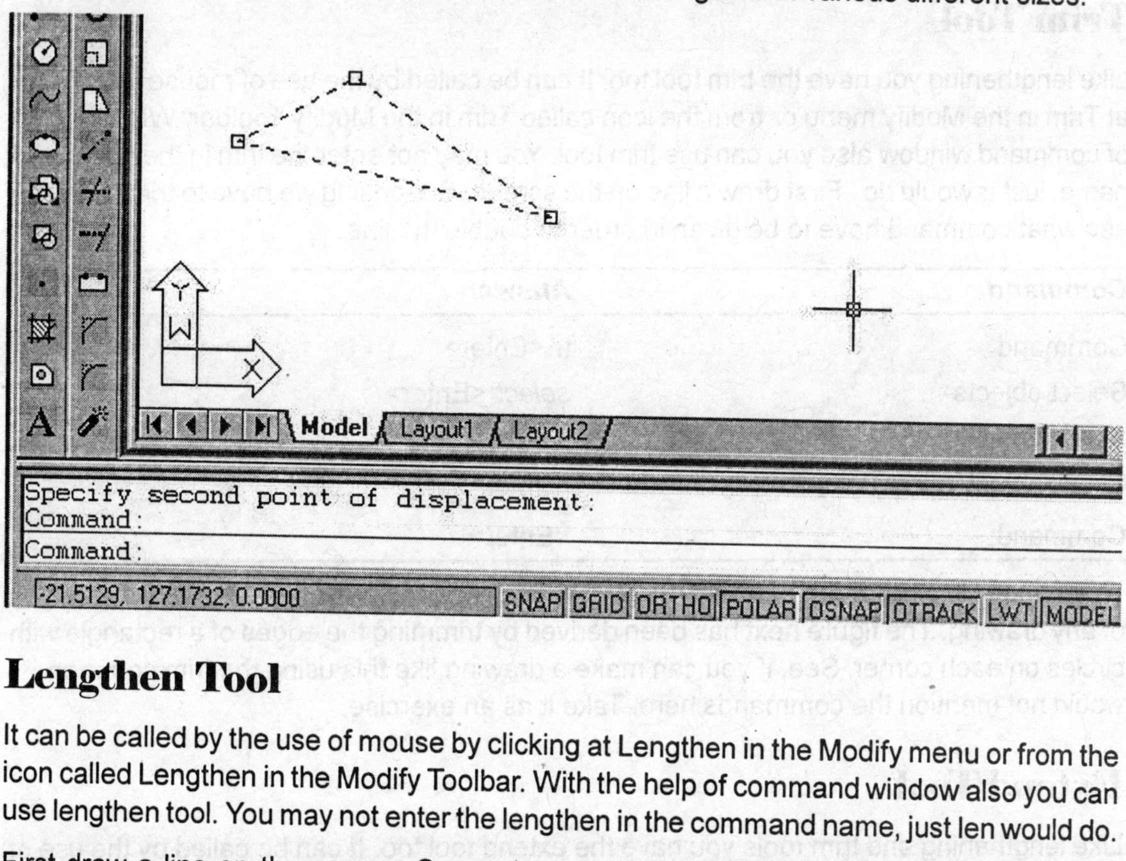

Lengthen Tool

It can be called by the use of mouse by clicking at Lengthen in the Modify menu or from the icon called Lengthen in the Modify Toolbar. With the help of command window also you can use lengthen tool. You may not enter the lengthen in the command name, just len would do. First draw a line on the screen. Supposing we have to lengthen it by 200 percent, i.e., double it. Let us see what command have to be given in order to double the line.

Command	*Answer*
Command	len <Enter>
Select objects :	*select* <Enter>
Select an object or [DElta/Percent/Total/ DYnamic]:	p <Enter>
Enter percentage length <100.000>	200 <Enter>
Specify opposite corner	*select* <Enter>
Command:	<Enter>

Click at the original line will make it double and you would see only the new lengthen line. You can lengthen more lines/figures in various different sizes.

Trim Tool

Like lengthening you have the trim tool too. It can be called by the use of mouse by clicking at Trim in the Modify menu or from the icon called Trim in the Modify Toolbar. With the help of command window also you can use trim tool. You may not enter the trim in the command name, just tr would do. First draw a line on the screen. Supposing we have to trim it . Let us see what command have to be given in order to double the line.

Command	*Answer*
Command	tr <Enter>
Select objects :	*select* <Enter>
Select objects:	<Enter>
Select object to trim [Project/Edge/Undo	<Enter>
Command:	<Enter>

Your original line has been trimmed. Similarly trim command can be used to trim the Edges of any drawing. The figure next has been derived by trimming the edges of a rectangle with circles on each corner. See, if you can make a drawing like this using the trim command. I would not mention the commands here. Take it as an exercise.

Extend Tool

Like lengthening and trim tools you have the extend tool too. It can be called by the use of mouse by clicking at Extend in the Modify menu or from the icon called Extend in the Modify

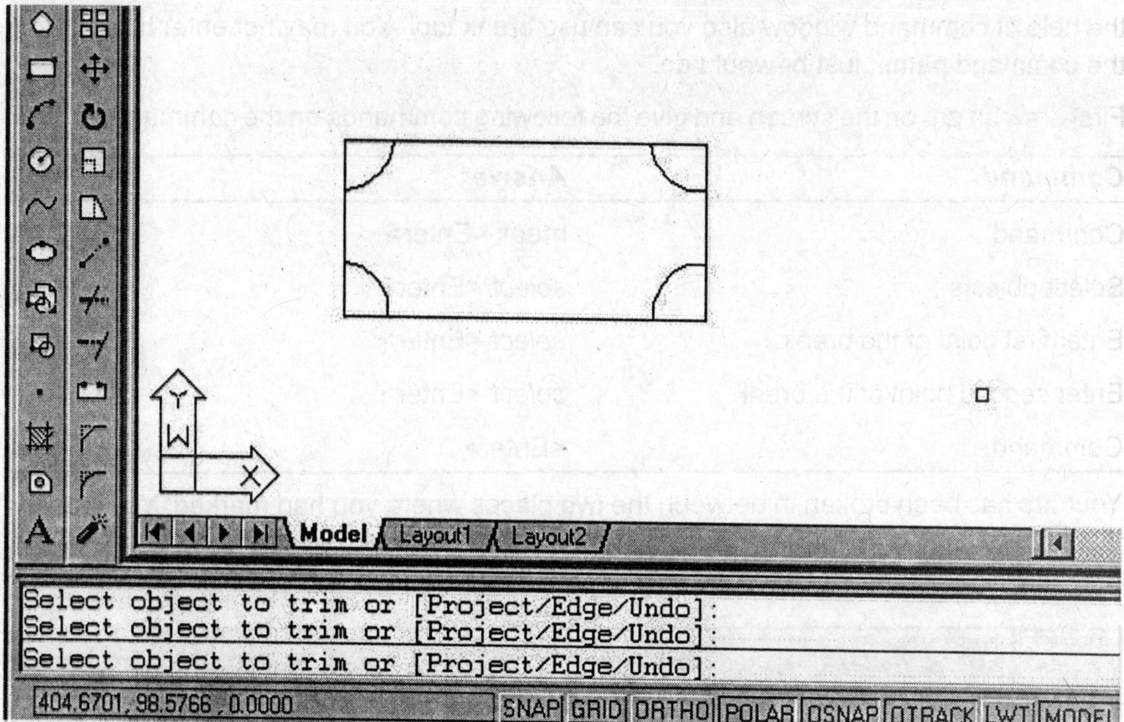

Toolbar. With the help of command window also you can use extend tool. You may not enter the extend in the command name, just ex would do.

First draw a line on the screen and give the following commands on the command window.

Command	***Answer***
Command	extend <Enter>
Select objects :	*select* <Enter>
Select objects:	<Enter>
Select object to extend [Project/Edge/Undo]:	<Enter>
Command:	<Enter>

Your original line has been extended. Similarly extend commands can be given for other objects too.

Break Tool

It is used to break the continuation of any line or arc. It can be called by the use of mouse by clicking at Break in the Modify menu or from the icon called Break in the Modify Toolbar. With the help of command window also you can use break tool. You may not enter the break in the command name, just br would do.

First draw an arc on the screen and give the following commands on the command window.

Command	***Answer***
Command	break <Enter>
Select objects :	*select* <Enter>
Enter first point of the break:	*select* <Enter>
Enter second point of the break:	*select* <Enter>
Command:	<Enter>

Your arc has been broken in between the two places where you had marked. You can see this effect in the figure shown below, where both the before and after of the arc are shown. Similarly break command can be given for other objects too.

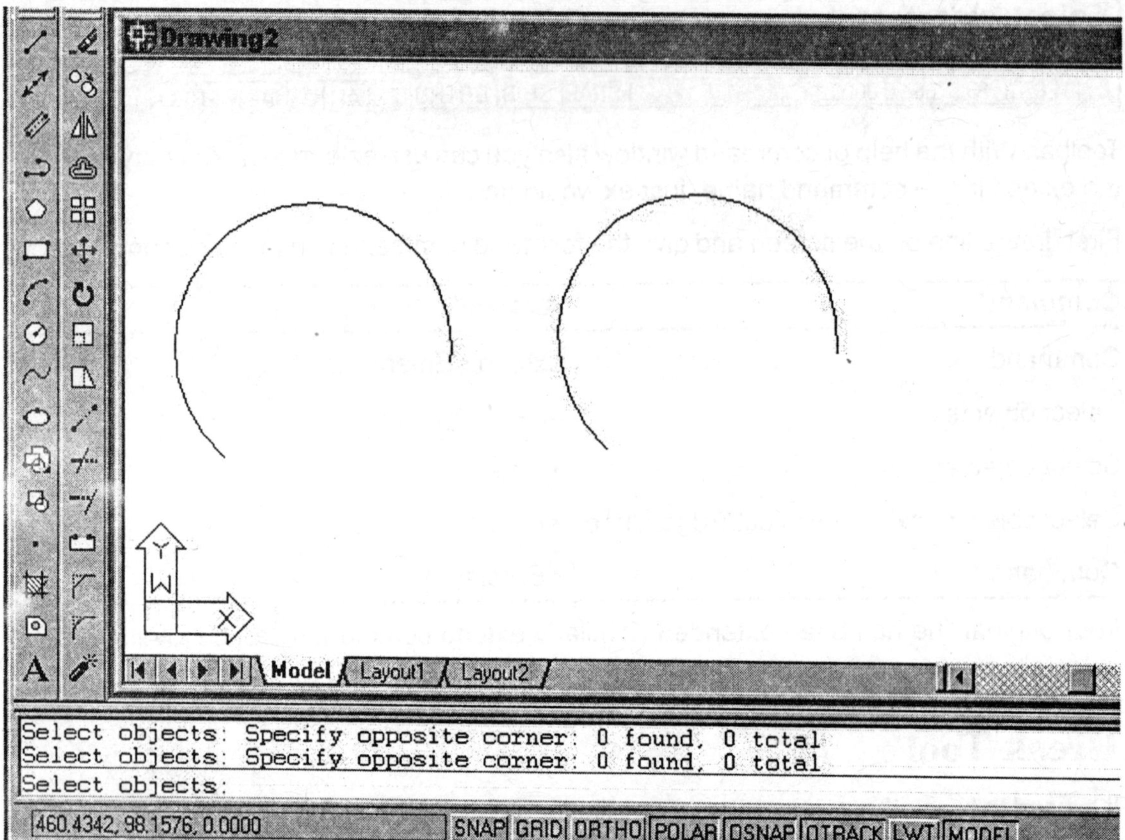

Chamfer Tool

It is used to make the rectangle or square into a chamfer shape. It can be called by the use of mouse by clicking at Chamfer in the Modify menu or from the icon called Chamfer in the Modify Toolbar. With the help of command window also you can use chamfer tool. You may not enter the break in the command name, just cha would do.

First draw a rectangle on the screen and give the following commands on the command window.

Command	***Answer***
Command	chamfer <Enter>
Select objects :	*select* <Enter>
Select first line or [Polyline/Distance/Angle/ Trim/Method:	*select* <Enter>
Select second line:	*select* <Enter>
Command:	<Enter>

Your rectangle has been camfered at the crossing of the two lines where you had marked. You can see this effect in the figure shown next, where two corners of the rectangle have been chamfered. Similarly chamfer command can be given for other objects too.

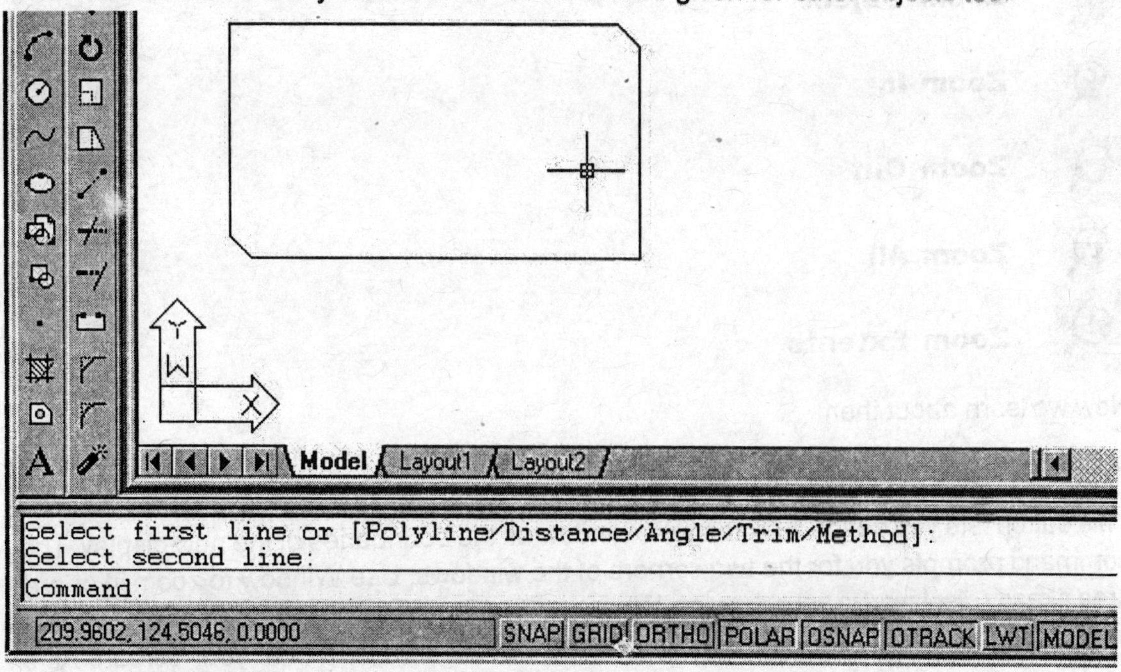

Fillet Tool

It can be called by the use of mouse by clicking at Fillet in the Modify menu or from the icon called Fillet in the Modify Toolbar. With the help of command window also you can use fillet tool. You may not enter the fillet in the command name, just f would do.

Because of similarities between using Chamfer and Fillet, I am not going into the details of this tool.

Zoom Toolbar

The following tools are available under the toolbar called Zoom.

Zoom Window

Zoom Dynamic

Zoom Scale

Zoom Center

Zoom Object

Zoom In

Zoom Out

Zoom All

Zoom Extents

Now we learn about them.

Zoom Window

This button lets you define a rectangular window as the boundaries of the new display. The command prompts you for the two corners of the windows. Use Window to zoom in or any area already displayed in your drawing. When you use Zoom Window, the command displays everything in the windows you specify but reshapes the display to fit your screen. As a result, you may see objects that were outside the specified window. You can move the mouse past the drawing area to define the window past the edge of the screen.

Zoom Dynamic

Enables you to zoom and pan in one operation.

Zoom Scale

Enter a number to scale the display relative to the drawing limits, a kind of absolute scaling. Enter a number followed by x to scale the display relative to the current view, relative scaling. Enter a number followed by xp to scale the display relative to paper space units. A number less than 1, such as 0.5, reduces the size of the objects on the screen, such as by half. A number greater than 1, such as 2, increases the size of the objects on the screen, such as by 2.

Zoom Center

Lets you specify a new center for the display, and then a new magnification/height. The current magnification/height is shown in brackets for your reference. Type a smaller number to increase the magnification, making the objects larger. Type a larger value to decrease the magnification, making the objects smaller.

Zoom Object

Lets you zoom in to selected objects. This option is new to AutoCAD 2006.

Zoom In

Uses the Scale option with a value of 2x.

Zoom Out

Uses the Scale option with a value of 0.5x.

Zoom All

Zooms the display to the greater of the drawing extents or the drawing limits.

Zoom Extents

Zooms to the outer extents of the drawing. You can also double-click the wheel of an IntelliMouse pointing device.

Surface Toolbar

By right clicking on any of the toolbars, you can get the Surface toolbar on screen. It consists of following tools:

- **2D Solid**
- **3D Face**
- **Box**
- **Wedge**
- **Pyramid**
- **Cone**
- **Sphere**
- **Dome**
- **Dish**
- **Torus**
- **Edge**
- **3D Mesh**
- **Revolved Surface**
- **Tabulated Surface**
- **Ruled Surface**
- **Edge Surface**

Let us see a few of them.

2D Solid tool

So far we have seen only the 2D tools and that too without fill. With this tool you can draw a

2D solid as shown in the following figure. You can use command window to draw this by using the command as so. You can even use the command from the Draw menu and then selecting 2D solid from the Surfaces menu.

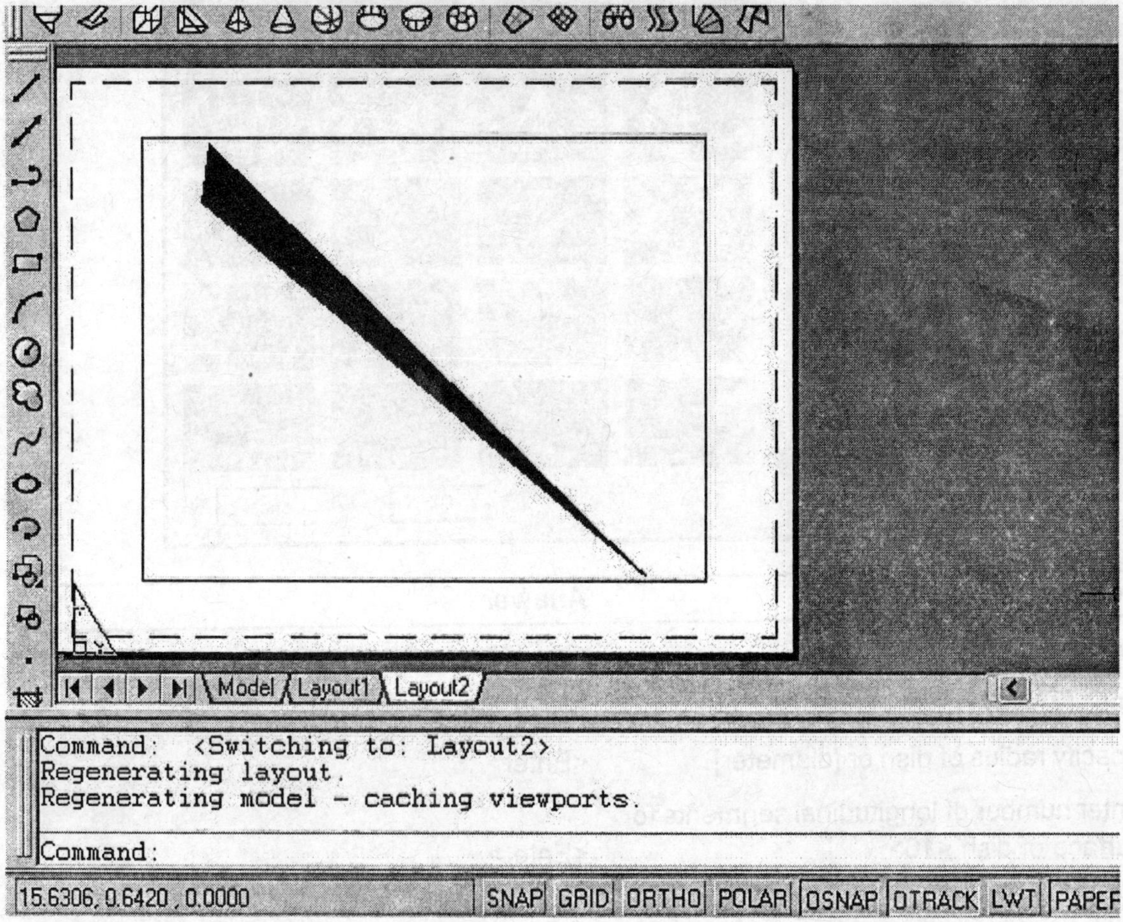

3D Objects tools

Click at 3D Surfaces in the Surfaces sub menu of Draw menu to get the following 2D Objects draw dialog box. You can select any one of them for your working.

The other figures which you can draw from here are Pyramid, Wedge, Dome, Sphere, Cone, Torus, Dish, and Mesh. Let us draw one of them from the command window.

Supposing you wish to draw a Dish, let us see how you can draw this by using the commands from the command window.

The commands to be given are:

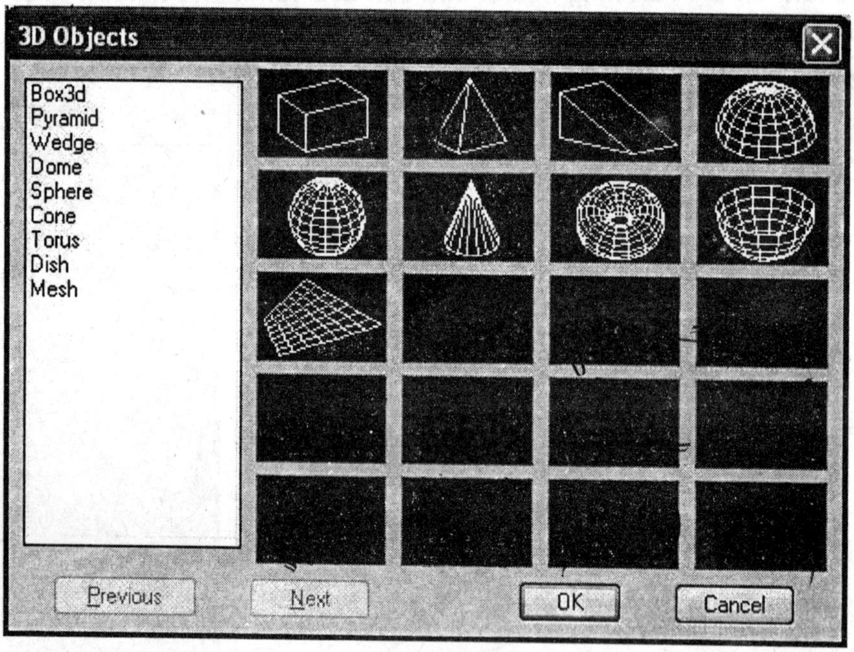

Command	***Answer***
Command	dish <Enter>
Specify centre point of the dish:	*select* <Enter>
Specify radius of dish or [diameter]	<Enter>
Enter number of longitudinal segments for surface of dish <16>	<Enter>
Enter number of latitude segments for surface of dish <8>	8 <Enter>
Command:	<Enter>

This will give you the dish as shown next. You can draw the other figures too like this.

Let us look at 3D Mesh now.

3D Mesh

It will as the name sounds will create a mesh in 3D. The command can be called from the Draw menu and Surfaces sub-menu.

However, if you wish to draw from the command menu, the commands that are to be given are as following:

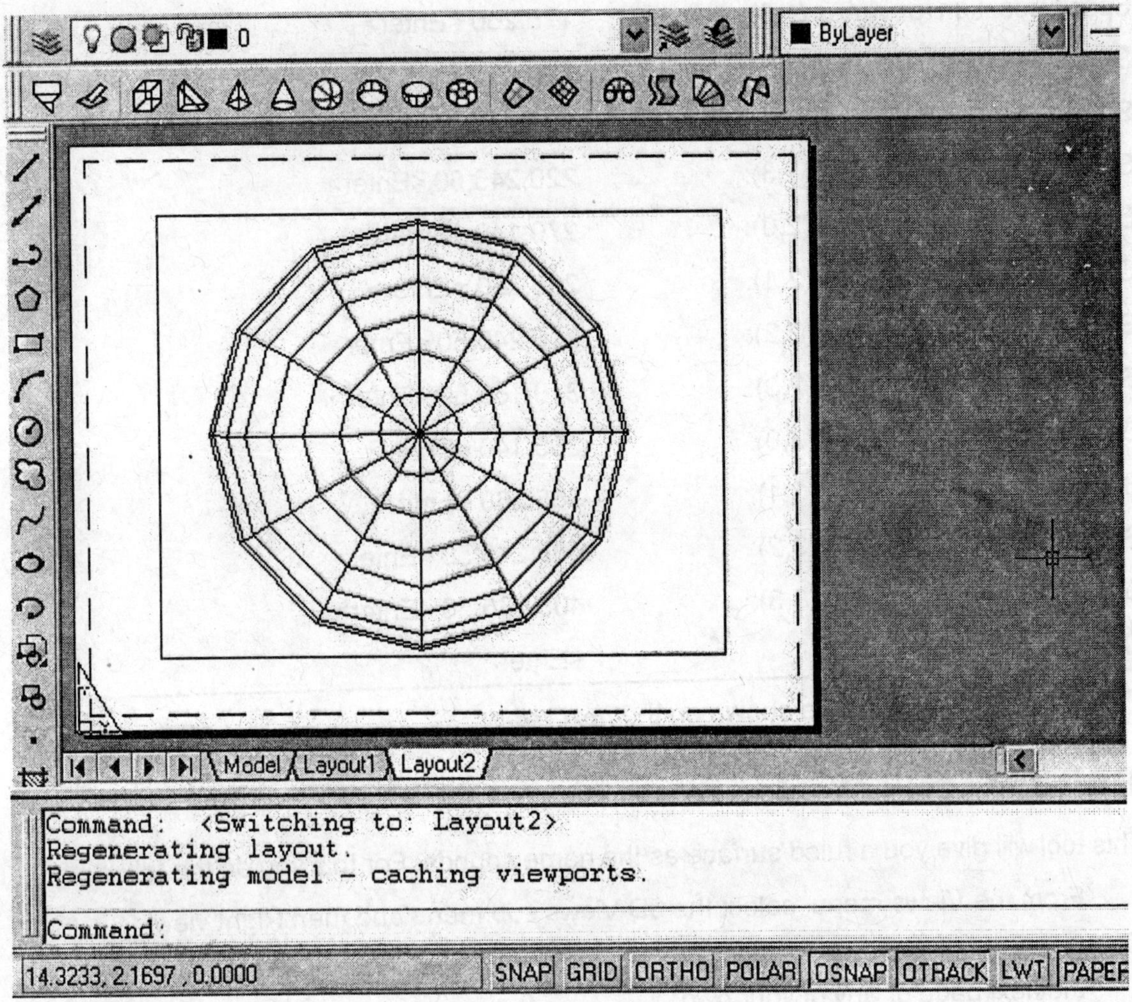

Command	*Answer*
Command	3d mesh <Enter>
Enter size of mesh in M direction:	4 <Enter>
Enter size of mesh in N direction:	4 <Enter>
Specify location for vertex (0,0):	70,260 <Enter>
Specify location for vertex (0,1):	70,140 <Enter>
Specify location for vertex (0,2):	120,165,50 <Enter>
Specify location for vertex (0,3):	120,245,50 <Enter>

Specify location for vertex (1,0):	170,260 <Enter>
Specify location for vertex (1,1):	70,140 <Enter>
Specify location for vertex (1,2):	220,245,50 <Enter>
Specify location for vertex (1,3):	220,245,50 <Enter>
Specify location for vertex (2,0):	270,140 <Enter>
Specify location for vertex (2,1):	265,260 <Enter>
Specify location for vertex (2,2):	310,245,50 <Enter>
Specify location for vertex (2,3):	310,165,50 <Enter>
Specify location for vertex (3,0):	365,140 <Enter>
Specify location for vertex (3,1):	365,260 <Enter>
Specify location for vertex (3,2):	405,245,50 <Enter>
Specify location for vertex (3,3):	405,165,50 <Enter>
Command:	<Enter>

This will result in a mesh as shown on the next page:

Ruled Surface Tool

This tool will give you a ruled surface as the name sounds. For this you do the following:

1. From the Views menu, select the 3D Views sub menu and then Right view.
2. Using the Polyline tool construct any object on the screen, similar to the one shown on the next page or any of your own.
3. Change the view to 3D Views/Top.
4. With Copy, copy the object a little to the right. The two objects should be visible on the screen, as shown on next to next page.
5. Now place the view to 3D Views/SW Isometric view.
6. Set Surftab1 to 32 by using the command set and then surftab from command window.
7. Click on the Ruled Surface tool from the Surface toolbar and give the following commands in the command window.

Command	***Answer***
Command	rulesurf <Enter>

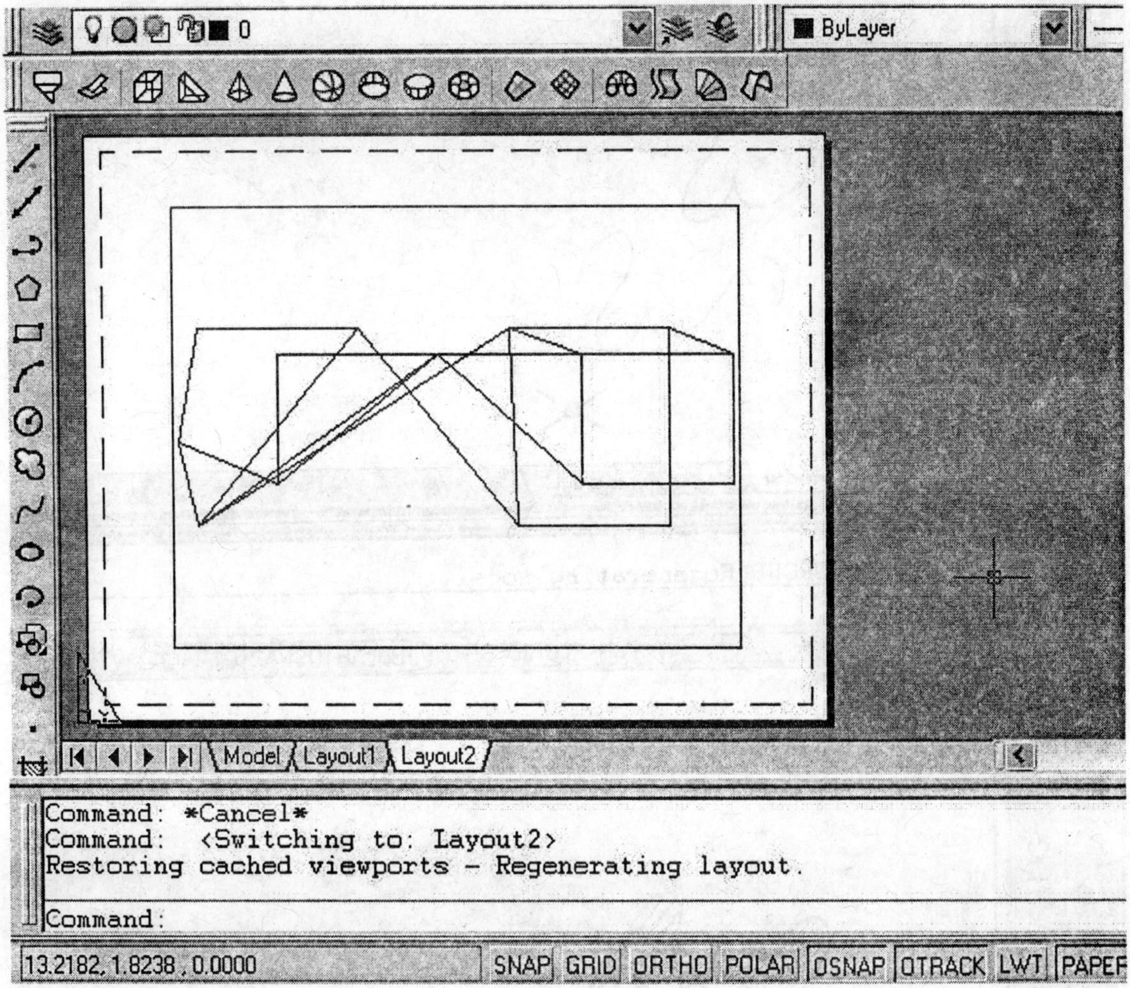

Current wire frame density:	SURFTAB1=32 <Enter>
Select first defining curve:	*select the first drawing*
Select second defining curve:	*select the second drawing*
Command:	<Enter>

This will result in a figure as shown on the next page:

Edge Surface Tool

This tool will give you a meshed surface with meshing on the edges. For this you do the following:

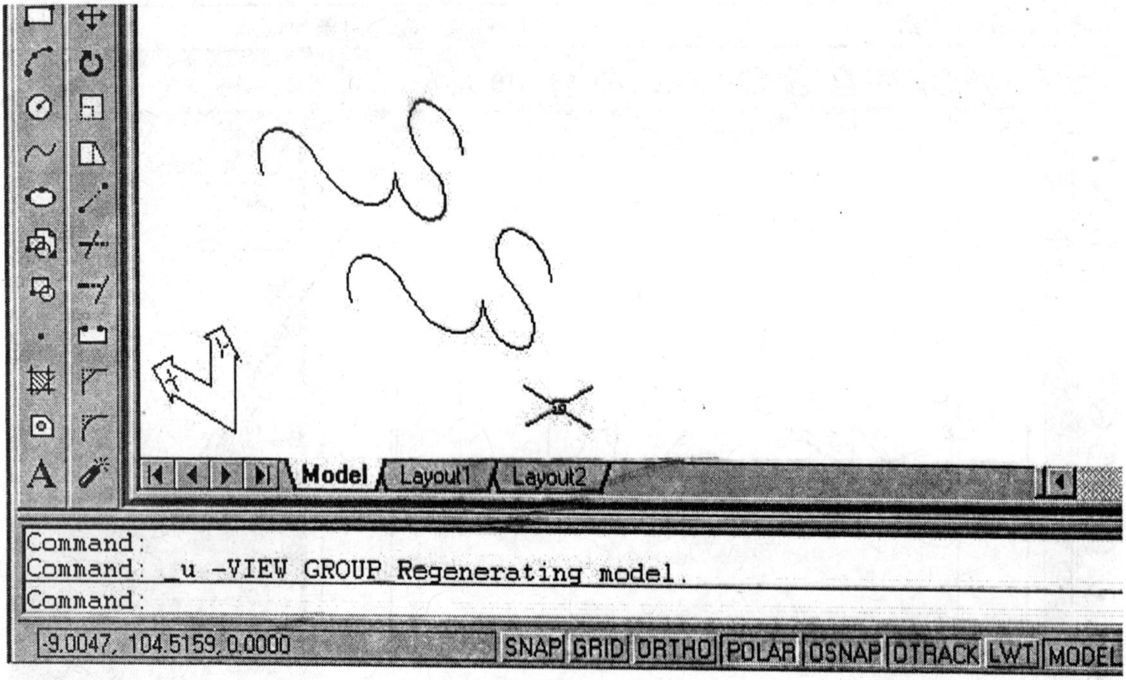
Model
Layout1
Layout2
Command:
Command: _u -VIEW GROUP Regenerating model.
Command:
-9.0047, 104.5159, 0.0000
SNAP GRID ORTHO POLAR OSNAP OTRACK LWT MODEL

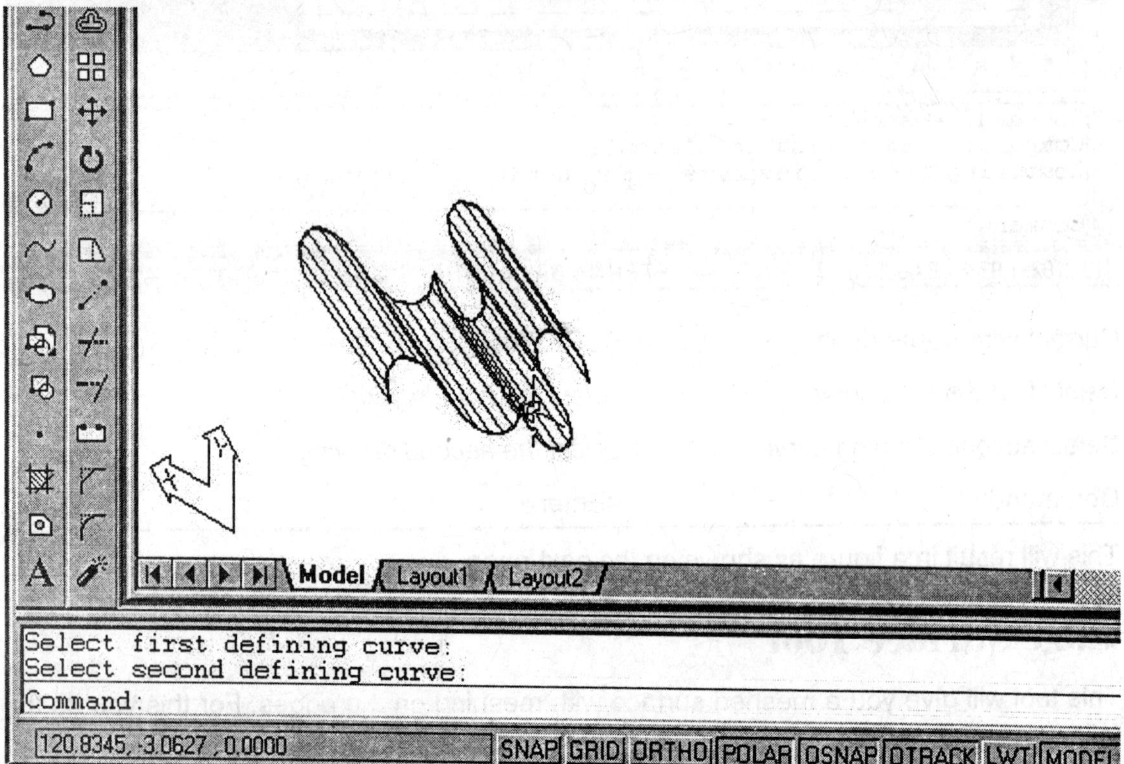
Model
Layout1
Layout2
Select first defining curve:
Select second defining curve:
Command:
120.8345, -3.0627, 0.0000
SNAP GRID ORTHO POLAR OSNAP OTRACK LWT MODEL

1. From the Views menu, select the 3D Views sub menu and then Right view.
2. Using the Polyline tool construct any object on the screen, similar to the one shown below or any of your own.

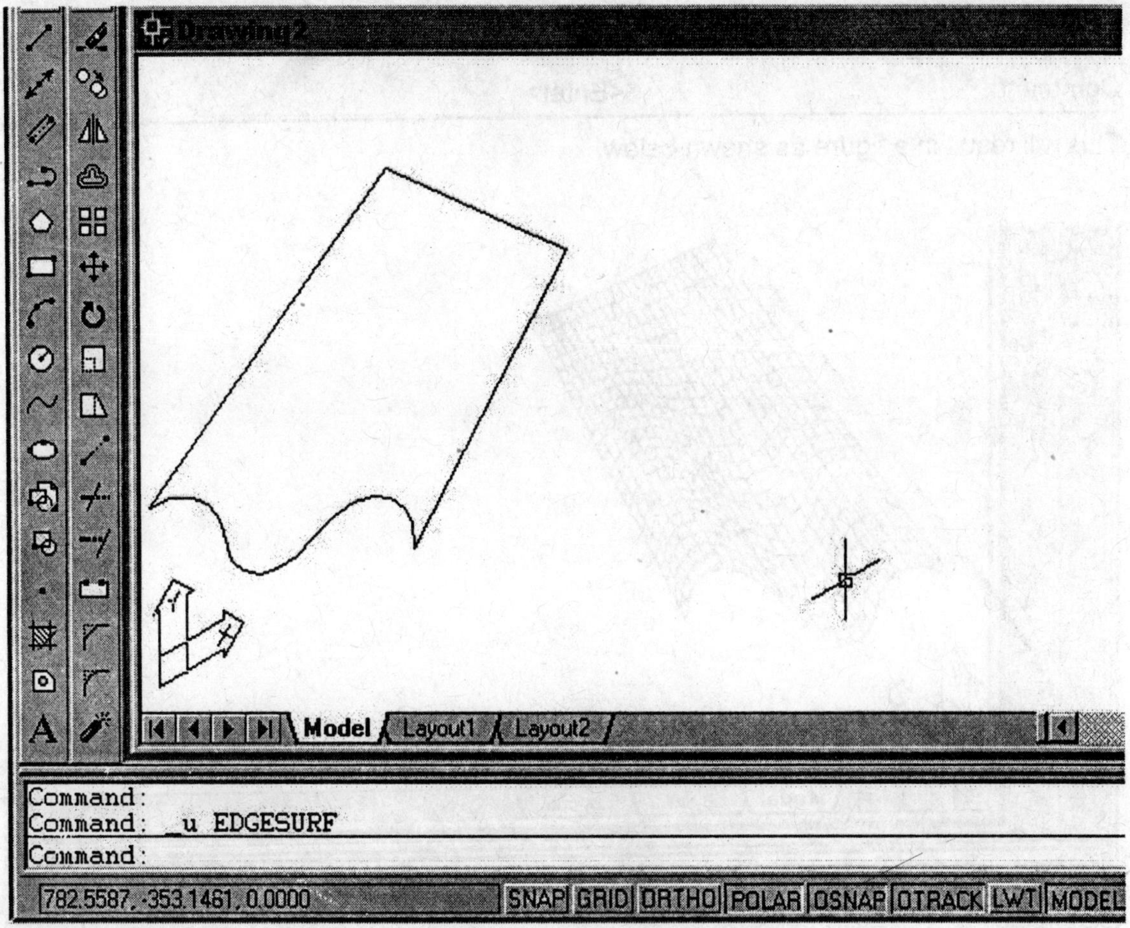

3. Change the view to 3D Views/Top.
4. Now place the view to 3D Views/SW Isometric view.
5. Set Surtab1 to 24 by using the command set and then surftab from command window.
6. Set Surfab2 to 24 by using the command set and then surftab from command window.
7. Click on the Edge Surface tool from the Surface toolbar and give the following commands in the command window.

Command	***Answer***
Command	edgesurf <Enter>

Select object 1 for surface edge: *select the first corner*

Select object 2 for surface edge: *select the second corner*

Select object 3 for surface edge: *select the third corner*

Select object 4 for surface edge: *select the fourth corner*

Command: <Enter>

This will result in a figure as shown below.

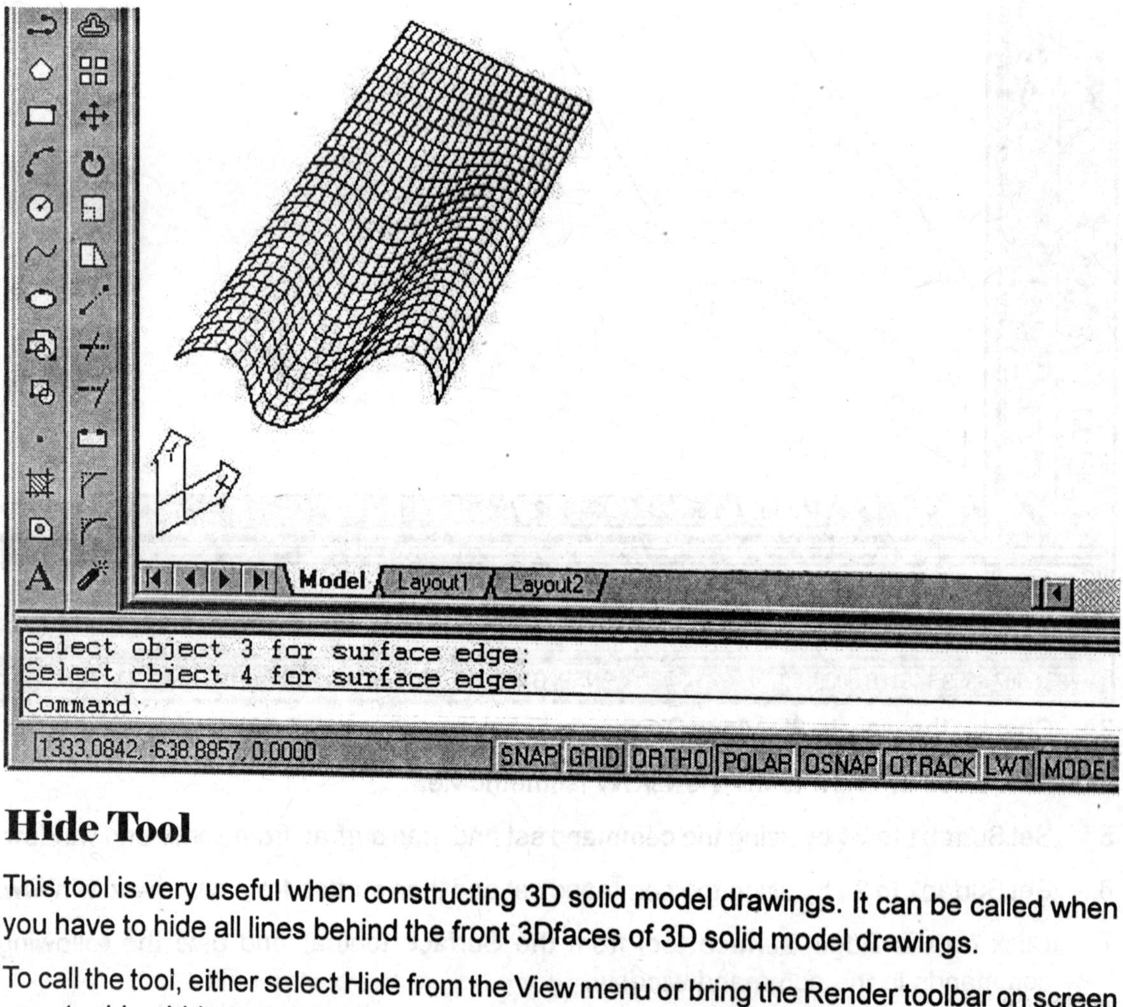

Hide Tool

This tool is very useful when constructing 3D solid model drawings. It can be called when you have to hide all lines behind the front 3Dfaces of 3D solid model drawings.

To call the tool, either select Hide from the View menu or bring the Render toolbar on screen or enter hi or hide at the Command line. All that is to call the tool.

Rendering Tools in AutoCAD 2006

Rendering is a system which produces realistic photographic like coloured images in the AutoCAD 2006 window from 3D solid drawings. The sequence involved in rendering an object has the following steps.

1. A 3D solid model drawing is constructed.
2. The model is usually placed in the WCS (see glossary of terms) to allow lights to be included for illuminating the model.
3. Either colours or materials are added to the model to give the rendering an appearance of having been made from suitable materials.
4. The model is placed in a suitable 3D Views view.
5. The model is then rendered to produce the required realism to the solid model. Backgrounds and other effects can be included with the rendering if required.

Rendering Tools

Various tools that can be used for rendering are:

Hide

Render

Scenes

Lights

Materials

Materials Library

Mapping

Background

Fog

Landscape New

Landscape Edit

Landscape Library

Render Preference

Statistics

To do rendering of a 3D model drawing, do the following.

1. Load the model to be rendered into the AutoCAD 2006 window.
2. Place the solid in a 3D Views/Top position.
3. Move the solid to a position near the upper edge of the AutoCAD 2006 window. This enables suitable lighting to be placed on screen.
4. Click on Lights tool icon in the Render toolbar. The Lights dialog box appears. In the dialog box select Point Light from the lights popup list, followed by a click on the New button. The New Point Light dialog box appears.
5. Enter a name in the Light Name:box. The AutoCAD 2006 window reappears with the position of the light held at the center of the window by a rubber band. At the Command line the following appears:

   Command: light *enter .xy* <Enter>

   of *pick a point central to the solid*

   (need Z) *enter* 300 <Enter>

   The New Point Light dialog box reappears. Click on the Ok button. The Light dialog box appears.
6. In the dialog box, select Distant Light from the popup list, followed by a click on the New button. The New Distant Light dialog box appears.
7. In the dialog box enter a name for the light and click on Modify button. The Command line sequence continues with

Enter light direction TO <current>:	*enter* .xy <Enter>
of	pick a point central to the solid
(need Z)	*enter* 50 <Enter>
Enter light direction FROM <current>	*enter* .xy <Enter>
of	*pick a suitable point*
(need Z)	*enter* 200 <Enter>

The New Distant Light dialog box reappears. Click on its Ok button.

8. Repeat item 7 for a second distant light. After finishing this sequence the Lights dialog box reappears showing the names of the lights so far added to the drawing. Click on Ok button and lighting is completed.

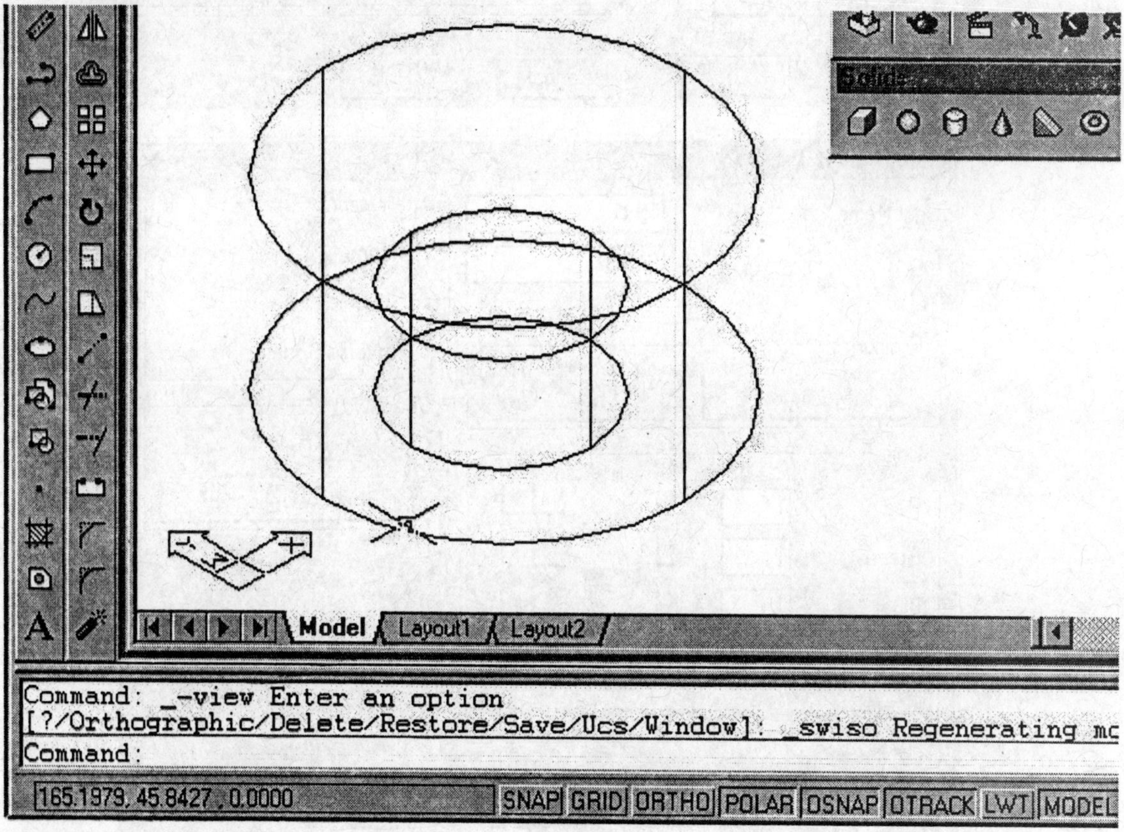

Lighting Positions

You can adjust the position of the lights according to your liking. For this do the following:

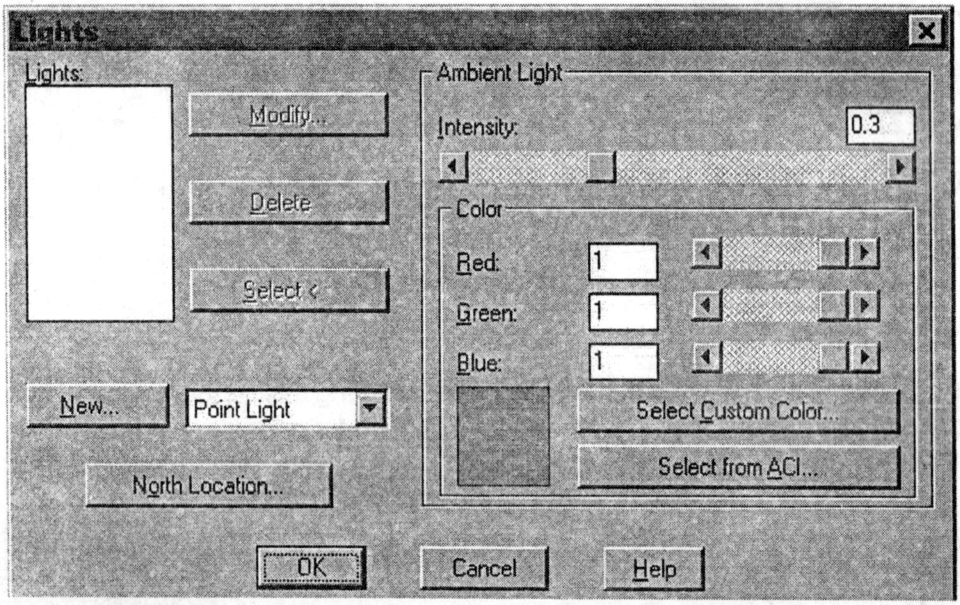
Lights
Lights:
Modify...
Delete
Select <
New...
Point Light
North Location...
Ambient Light
Intensity:
0.3
Color
Red:
1
Green:
1
Blue:
1
Select Custom Color...
Select from ACI...
OK
Cancel
Help

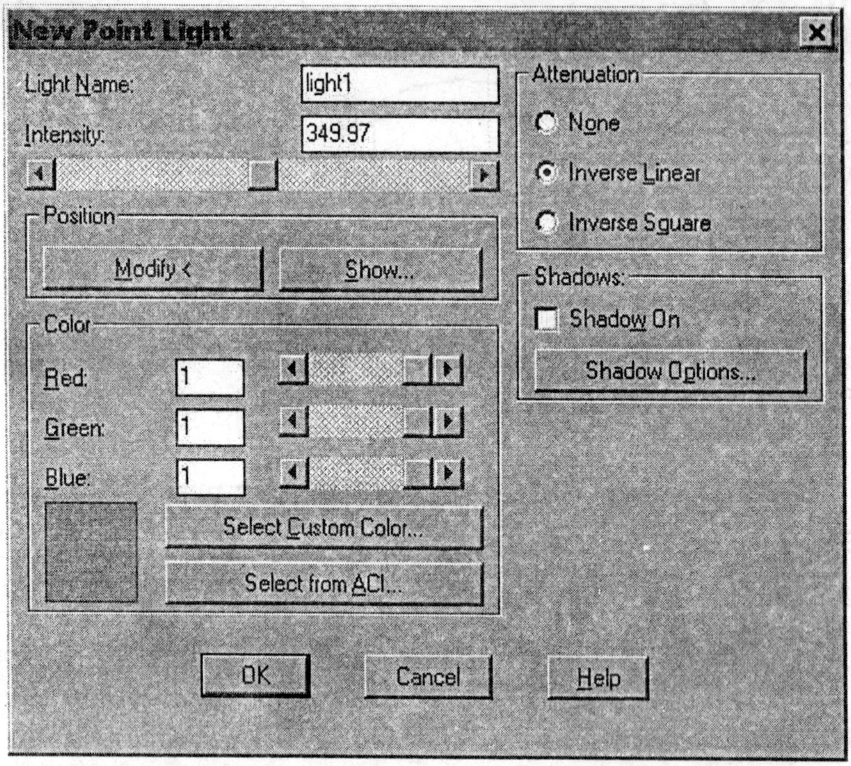
New Point Light
Light Name:
light1
Intensity:
349.97
Position
Modify <
Show...
Color
Red:
1
Green:
1
Blue:
1
Select Custom Color...
Select from ACI...
Attenuation
None
Inverse Linear
Inverse Square
Shadows:
Shadow On
Shadow Options...
OK
Cancel
Help

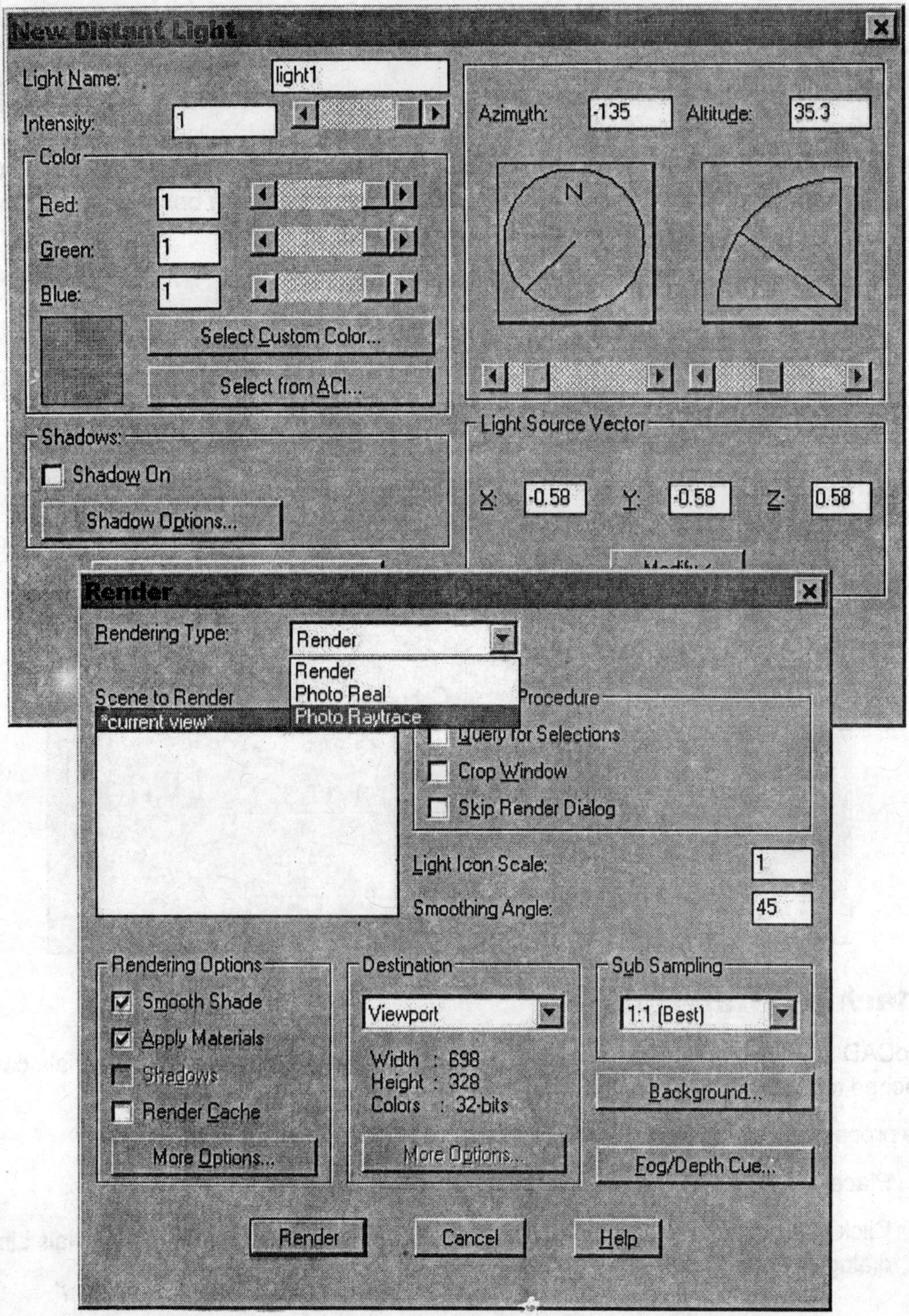
New Distant Light
Light Name: light1
Intensity: 1
Color
Red: 1
Green: 1
Blue: 1
Select Custom Color...
Select from ACI...
Azimuth: -135
Altitude: 35.3
N
Shadows:
Shadow On
Shadow Options...
Light Source Vector
X: -0.58
Y: -0.58
Z: 0.58
Render
Rendering Type: Render
Render
Photo Real
Photo Raytrace
Scene to Render
current view
Procedure
Query for Selections
Crop Window
Skip Render Dialog
Light Icon Scale: 1
Smoothing Angle: 45
Rendering Options
Smooth Shade
Apply Materials
Shadows
Render Cache
More Options...
Destination
Viewport
Width : 698
Height : 328
Colors : 32-bits
More Options...
Sub Sampling
1:1 (Best)
Background...
Fog/Depth Cue...
Render
Cancel
Help

1. Place the solid in the 3D Views/SW Isometric position. Zoom window the solid to a suitable size.
2. Select the Render tool icon from the Render toolbar. The Render dialog box appears. Select Photo Raytrace from the Rendering type popup list, followed by a click on the Options button which brings up the Photo Raytrace Render Options dialog box. Click on Ok button and on the Render button of the Render dialog box and the 3D model renders. This is after accepting the default settings.

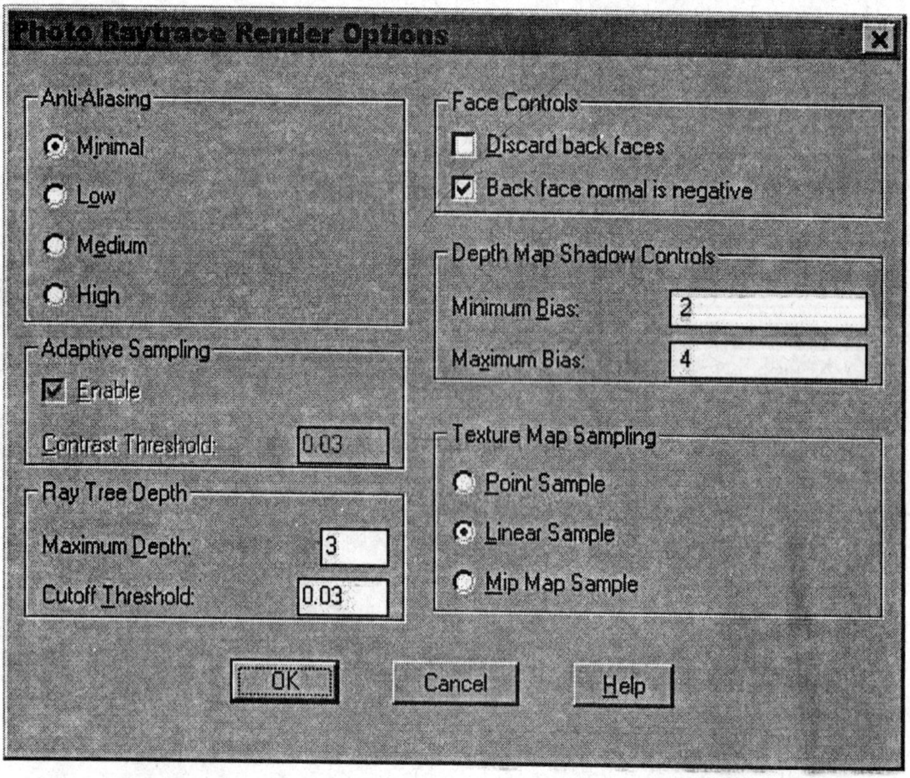

Attaching Materials

AutoCAD 2006 includes a large materials library from which a variety of materials can be attached to a 3D solid models or to their parts.

The process of attaching is as following:

1. Place the solid in the 3D Views/SW Isometric position.
2. Click on the Materials Library tool icon from the Render toolbar. The Materials Library dialog box appears.

3. From the Current Library list select the following 4 materials in turn:

   AQUA GLAZE; BEIGE MATTE; BLUE MATTE; CHICKEN TEXTURE

   As each is selected click on the Import button and the imported material name then appears in the Current Drawing list. A click on any material in either list, followed by a click on the Preview button causes the selected material to appear in the preview window showing how it will appear in a drawing when rendered.

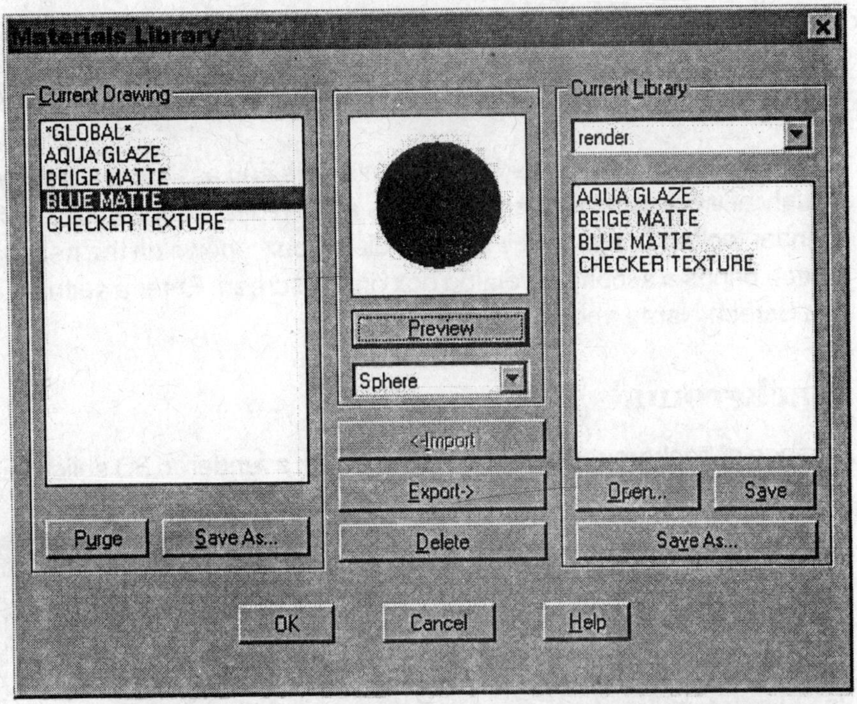

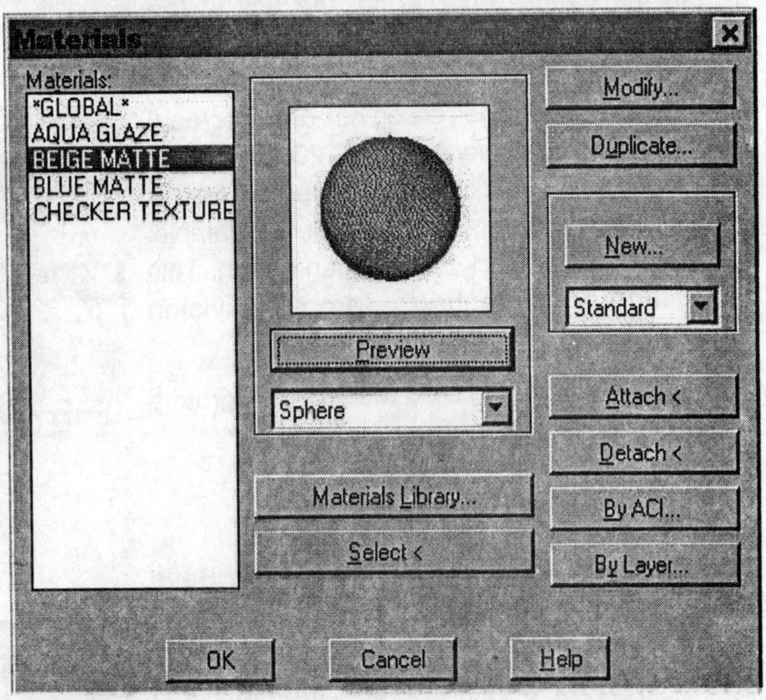

4. Click on the Materials tool icon in the Render toolbar. The Materials dialog box appears showing the 4 materials selected from the Current Library list in the Materials Library dialog box. Selecting each material name in turn, click on the Attach button.

5. Now click on the Render tool icon from the Render toolbar and render the model.

Scenes

Each 3D solid can be placed in different views and assigned a different set of materials. If a variety of views with different materials attached is required, click at Scenes tool icon in the Render toolbar brings up the Scenes dialog box, shown on the next page. A click at the New button brings a secondary dialog box on the screen. Enter a suitable name for the screen in the Screen Name and click Ok.

Background

A range of backgrounds can be included with a rendered 3D solid. The process of attaching is as following:

1. Click on background tool icon from the Render toolbar, or on the Background button in the Render dialog box. The background dialog box appears.

2. In the dialog box, cancel the tick in the AutoCAD background check box and click in the Find File button. This brings the Background Images dialog box on the screen. Select the directory AutoCAD 2006/Textures and from the File of type: box select *.tga. In the list of tga files, select 8plnt15l, for example, followed by a click in the Open button. This image corresponds to Targa Truevision Image.

3. Now render the 3D solid with this background and see the effect.

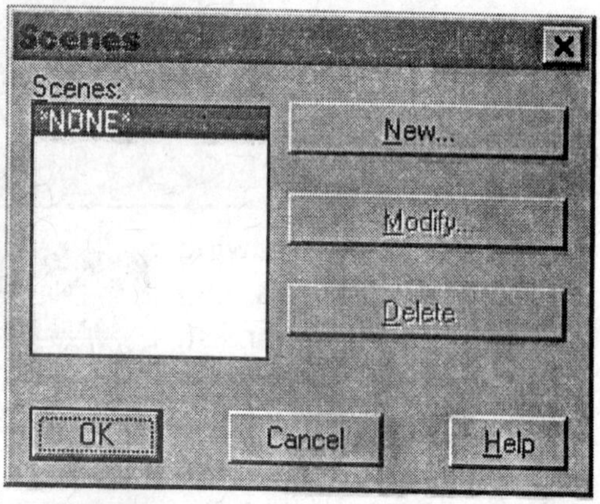

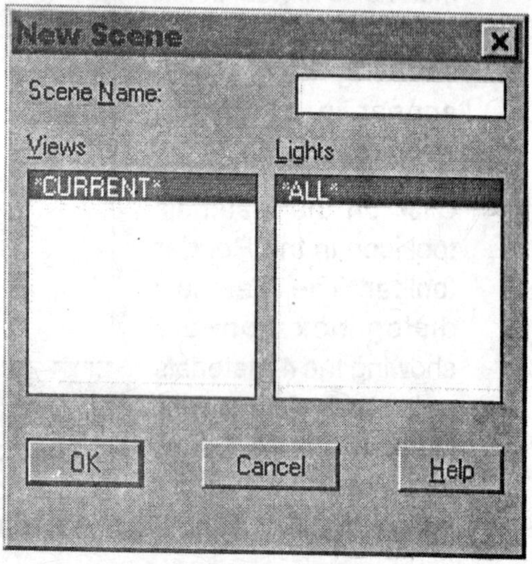

Saving the Drawing

In the File menu click at Save As. The Save Drawing As dialog box appears. In the File name box enter a name for the drawing and from the Save as Type popup list select the AutoCAD Drawing (*.dwt) option. Click on Save to save the drawing.

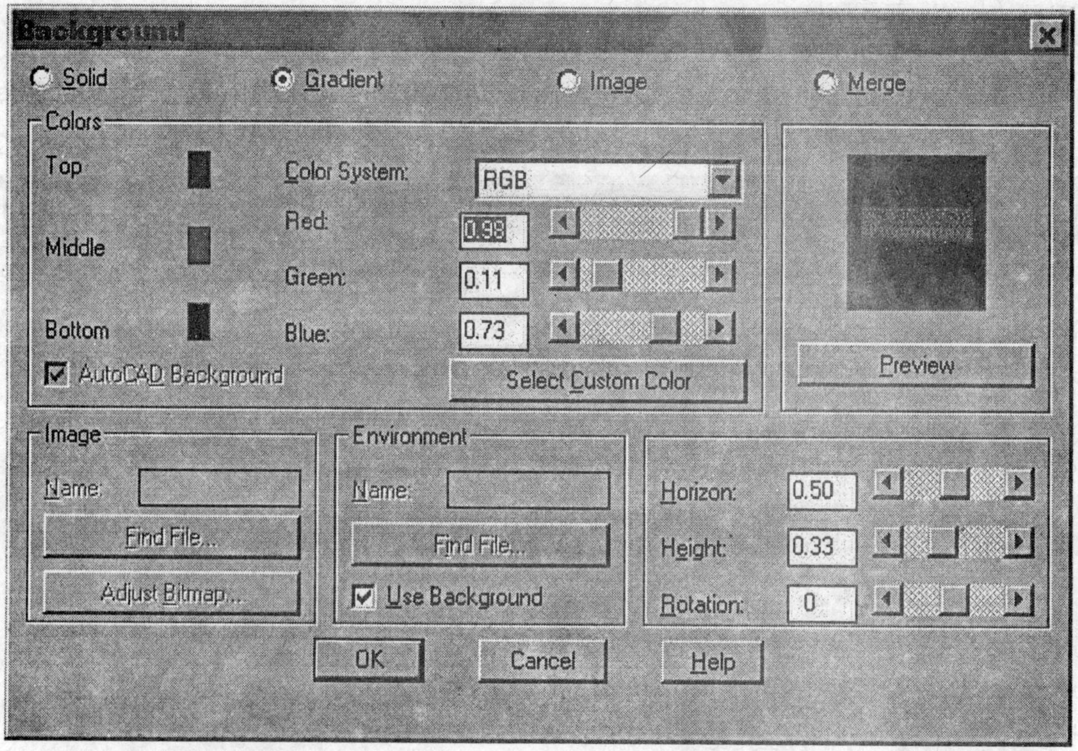
Background
Solid
Gradient
Image
Merge
Colors
Top
Middle
Bottom
Color System:
RGB
Red:
0.98
Green:
0.11
Blue:
0.73
AutoCAD Background
Select Custom Color
Preview
Image
Name:
Find File...
Adjust Bitmap...
Environment
Name:
Find File...
Use Background
Horizon:
0.50
Height:
0.33
Rotation:
0
OK
Cancel
Help

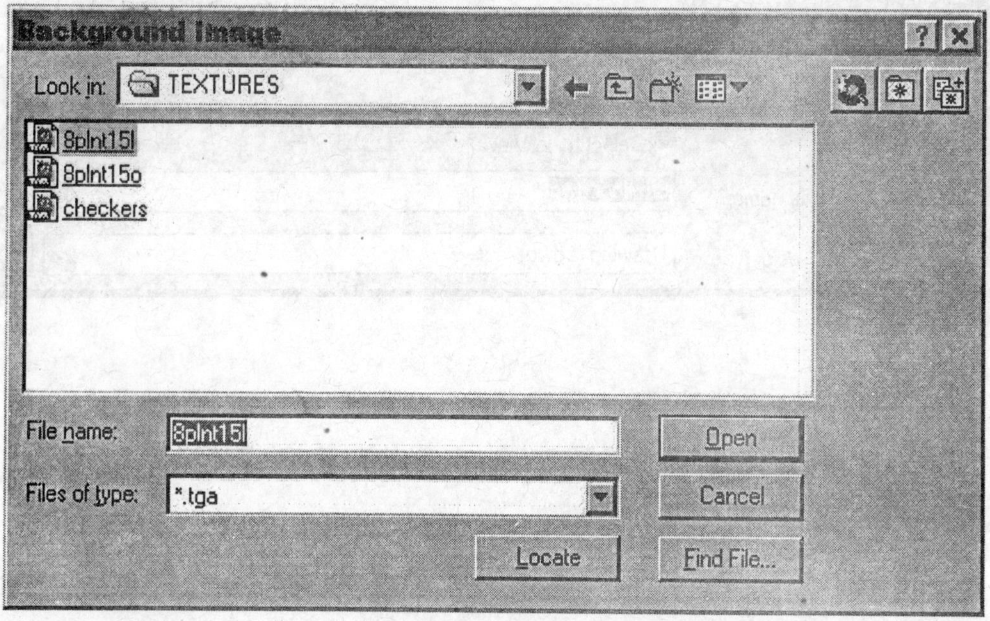
Background Image
Look in:
TEXTURES
8plnt15l
8plnt15o
checkers
File name:
8plnt15l
Files of type:
*.tga
Open
Cancel
Locate
Find File...

Open a Drawing

Similar to saving you can open a drawing in AutoCAD 2006. In the File menu, click at Open to get a Select File dialog box. From this box you can select the file to open.

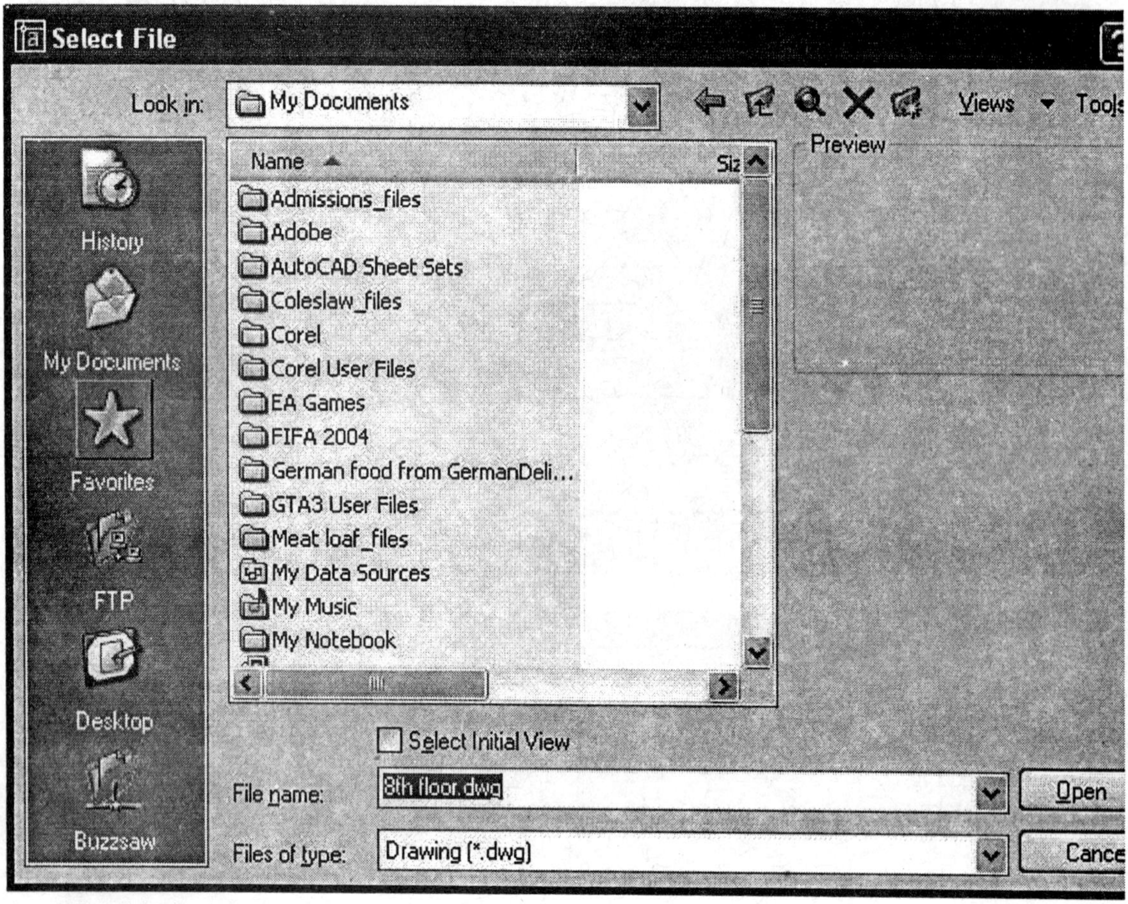

Using Drafting Tools of AutoCAD 2006 — 5

Setting Up a Work Area

Before beginning most drawings, you should set up your work area. To do this, determine the measurement system, the drawing sheet size, and the scale you want to use. the default work area is roughly16"x 9" at full scale, given a decimal measurement system in which 1 unit equals 1 inch. Metric users will find that the default area is roughly 550 mm x 300 mm, in which 1 unit equals 1 mm.

If these are appropriate settings for your drawing, you don't have to do any setting up. It is more likely, however, that you will make drawings of various sizes and scales. For example, you might want to create a drawing in a measurement system in which you can specify feet, inches, and fractions of inches at l" = 1' scale and print the drawing on an 81/2"x 11" sheet of paper.

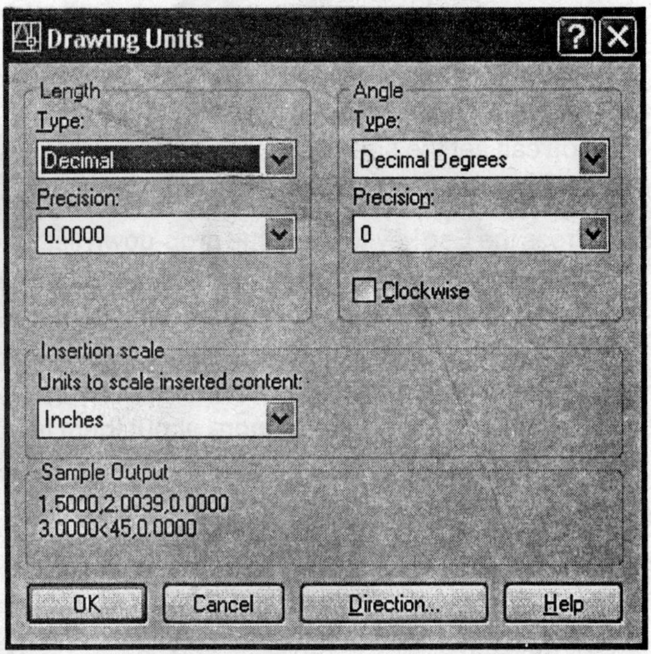

Earlier you used the Create New Drawing dialog box to set up a drawing file. The Create New Drawing Wizard is a great tool but it hides many of the drawing setup tools you'll need to know to work with AutoCad. In this section, you will learn how to set up a drawing exactly the way you want.

Specifying Units

Use these steps to create the file:

1. If you haven't done so already, start AutoCAD. If AutoCAD is already running, choose File > New.
2. In the Create New Drawing dialog box, select the Start From Scratch option, and then select metric. Imperial from the list just below the button options. Metric users can select Metric. Click OK.

3. Choose View > Zoom > All.
4. Choose File > Save As.
5. In the Save Drawing As dialog box, enter Bath for the filename.
6. Check to make sure you are saving the drawing in the Samples subfolder or in the folder you have chosen to store your exercise files, and then click Save.

The next thing you want to tell AutoCAD is the unit style you intend to use. So far, you've been using the default, which is decimal inches. In this unit style, whole units represent inches, and decimal units are decimal inches. If you want to be able to enter distances in feet, you must change the unit style to a style that accepts feet as input. You'll do this through the Drawing Units dialog box, shown here.

Follow these steps to set a unit style:

1. Choose Format > Units or type Un to open the Drawing Units dialog box.
2. Let's look at a few of the options available. Click the Type drop-down list in the Length group. Notice the unit styles in the list.
3. Click Architectural. The Sample Output section of the dialog box shows you what the architectural style looks like in AutoCAD. Metric users should keep this setting as Decimal.
4. Click the Precision drop-down list just below the Type list. Notice the options available. You can set the smallest unit AutoCAD will display in this drawing. For now, leave this setting at its default value of 1/16" . Metric users will keep the setting at 0.0000.
5. Press the Esc key to close the drop-down list, and then click the Direction button at the bottom of the dialog box to open the Direction Control dialog box, This dialog box lets you set the direction for the 0" angle and the direction for positive degrees, For now, don't change these settings-you'll read more about them in a moment

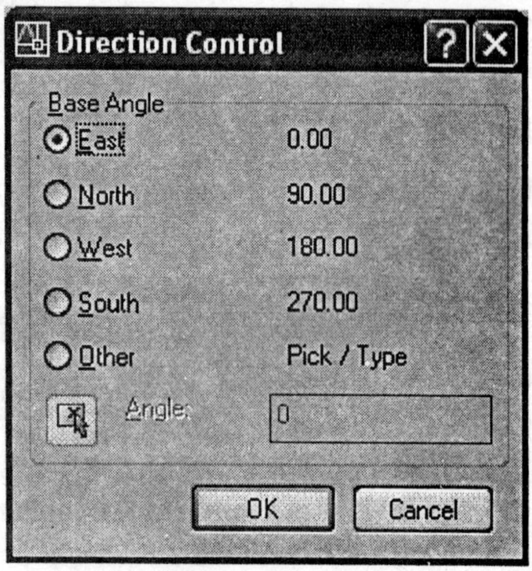

6. Click the Cancel button.
7. Now click the drop-down list in the Drag-and-Drop Scale group. The list shows various units of measure.
8. Click Inches, or if you are a metric user, choose Centimeters. This option lets you control how

AutoCAD translates drawing scales when you import drawings from outside the current drawing.

9. Click OK in the Drawing Units dialog box to return to the drawing.

Measurement System Available in AutoCAD

Measurement System	*AutoCAD'sDisplay of Measurement*
Scientific	1.55E+01 (inches or metric)
Decimal	15.5000 (inches or metric)
Engineering	1' -3.5" (input as 1'3.5")
Architectural	1'31/2" (input as 1'3-1/2")
Fractional	151/2" (input as 15-1/2")

Fine-Tuning the Measurement System

Most of the time, you will be concerned only with the units and angles settings of the Drawing Units dialog box. But as you saw from the preceding exercise, you can control many other settings related to the input and display of units.

The Precision drop-down list in the Length group lets you specify the smallest unit value that you want AutoCAD to display in the status tine and in the prompts. If you choose a measurement system that uses fractions, the Precision list includes fractional units. You can also control tins setting with the Luprec system variable.

The Angle group lets you set the style for displaying angles. You have a choice of five angle styles: decimal degrees, degrees/minutes/seconds, grads, radians, and surveyor's units. In the Angle group's Precision drop-down list, you can specify the degree of accuracy you want AutoCAD to display for angles. You can also control these settings with the Aunits and Auprec system variables.

The Direction Control dialog box lets you set the direction of the 0' base angle. The default base angle (and the one used throughout this book) is a direction from left to right. However, at times you might want to designate another direction as the 0' base angle. You can also tell AutoCAD which direction is positive, either clockwise or counterclockwise. This book uses the default, which is counterclockwlse. You can also control these settings with the Angbase and Angdir system variables.

The Drag-and-Drop Scale setting in the Drawing Units dialog box lets you control how blocks from the Tool palette or DesignCenter are scaled as they are imported into your current drawing. A block is a collection of drawing objects that form a single object. Blocks are frequently used to create standard symbols. The Drag-and-Drop Scale setting lets you compensate for drawings of different scale by offering an automatic scale translation when importing blocks from an external file. The Insunits system variable also controls the Drag-and-Drop Scale setting.

Setting Up the Drawing Limits

One of the big advantages in using AutoCAD is that you can draw at full scale; you aren't limited to the edges of a piece of paper the way you are in manual drawing. But you still have to consider what will happen when you want a printout of your drawing. When you start a new drawing, it helps to limit your drawing area to one that can be scaled down to fit on a standard sheet size. Although this is not absolutely necessary with AutoCAD, the limits give you a frame of reference between your work in AutoCAD and the final printed output.

To set up the drawing work area it helps to understand how standard sheet sizes translate into full-scale drawing sizes. The following two tables list widths and heights of drawing areas in inches, according to scales and final printout sizes. The scales are listed in the far-left column; the output sheet sizes are listed across the top.

Let's take an example. To find the area needed in AutoCAD for your bathroom drawing, look across from the scale 1" = 1' Go the column that reads 8½" x 11" at the top of the following table. You'll find the value 102 x 132. This means the drawing area needs to fit within an area 102" x 132" (8.5 feet x 11 feet) in AutoCAD in order to fit a printout of a 1" = 1'-0" scale drawing on an 8½" x 11" sheet of paper. You might want the drawing area to be oriented horizontally, so that the 11 feet will be in the X axis and the 8.5 feet will be in the axis.

Work Area in Drawing Units (inches) by Scale and Plotted Sheet Size from 81/2" x 11" to 18" x 24"

Scale	*81/2 x11"*	*11"x17"*	*17"x22"*	*18"x 24"*
3" =1'	34x44	44x68	68x88	72x96
11/2" =1'	68x88	88x136	136x176	144x192
1" =1'	102x132	132x204	204x264	216x288
¾" =1'	136x176	176x272	272x352	288x384
½" =1'	204x264	264x408	408x528	432x576
¼" =1'	408x528	528x816	816x1056	864x1152
1/8" =1'	816x1056	1056x1632	1632x2112	1728x2304
1/16" =1'	1632x2112	2112x3264	3264x4224	3456x4608
1/32" =1'	3264x4224	4224x6528	6528x8448	6912x9216
1" =10'	1020x1320	1320x2040	2040x2640	2160x2880
1" =20'	2040x2640	2640x4080	4080x5280	4320x5760

1" =30'	3060x3960	3960x6120	6120x7920	6480x8640
1" =40'	4080x5280	5280x8160	8160x10560	8640x11520
1" =50'	5100x660	660x10200	10200x13200	10800x14400
1" =60'	6120x7920	7920x12240	12240x15840	12960x17280

Work Area in Drawing Units (Inches) by Scale and Plotted Sheet Size from 22"x34" to 36" x48"

Scale	*22"x34"*	*24"x36"*	*30"x42"*	*36"x48"*
3" =1'	88x136	96x144	120x168	144x192
11/2" =1'	176x272	192x288	240x336	288x384
1" =1'	264x408	288x432	360x504	432x576
¾" =1'	352x544	384x576	480x672	576x768
½" =1'	528x816	576x864	720x1008	864x1152
¼" =1'	1056x1632	1152x1728	1440x2016	1728x2304
1/8" =1'	2112x3264	2304x3456	2880x4032	3456x4608
1/16" =1'	4224x6528	4608x6912	5760x8064	6912x9216
1/32" =1'	8448x13056	9216x13824	11520x16128	13824x18432
1" =10'	2640x4080	2880x4320	3600x5040	4320x5760
1" =20'	5280x8160	5760x8640	7200x10080	8640x11520
1" =30'	7920x12240	8640x12960	10800x15120	12960x17280
1" =40'	10560x16320	11520x17280	14400x20160	17280x23040
1" =50'	13200x20400	1440x21600	1800x25200	21600x28800
1" =60'	15840x24480	17280x25920	21600x30240	25920x34560

If you're a metric user, you'll be drawing the bathroom at a scale of 1 to 10. this scale is close to the 1" = 1'-0" scale used for the Imperial measurements in the exercises. So for an A4 sheet, your work area should be 297 cm x 210 cm. This is the equivalent of an A4 sheet (210 mmx297 mm) enlarged by a factor of 10.

Now that you know the area you need, you can use the Limits command to set up the area:

1. Choose Format > Drawing Limits.
2. At the Specify lower left corner or [ON/OFF] <0' -0" ,0' -0">: prompt, specify the lower-left corner of your work area. Press to accept the default.
3. At the specify upper right corner or <1'0" ,0'9">: prompt, specify the upper-right corner of your work area. (The default is shown in brackets.) Enter 132,102. Or if you prefer, you can enter 11' ,86, because you've set up your drawing for architectural units. Metric users should enter 297,210.

4. Next, choose View > Zoom > All. You can also select the Zoom All tool from the Zoom Window flyout on the Standard toolbar, or type Z A. Although it appears that nothing has changed, your drawing area is now set to a size that will enable you to draw your bathroom at full scale.

5. Move the cursor to the upper-right corner of the drawing area and watch the coordinate read-out, Notice that now the upper-right corner has a Y coordinate of approximately 8'-6", or 300 for metric users. The X coordinate depends on the proportion of your AutoCAD window. The coordinate readout also displays distances in feet and inches.

In step 5, the coordinate readout shows you that your drawing area is larger than before but no visual clues tell you where you are or what distances you are dealing with. To help you get your bearings, you can turn on the Grid mode, which you will learn about shortly The Grid mode displays an array of dots that help you visualize distances and the limits of your drawing before you get to grids, let's take a closer look at scale factors and how they work.

Understanding Scale Factors

When you draft manually, you work on the final drawing directly with pen and ink or pencil. With a CAD program, you are a few steps removed from the actual finished product. Because of this, you need a deeper understanding of your drawing scale and how it is derived, In particular, you need to understand scale factors. For example, one of the more common uses of scale factors is in translating text size in your CAD drawing to the final plotted text size. When you draw manually, you simply draw your notes at the size you want. In a CAD drawing, you need to translate the desired final text size to the drawing scale.

When you start adding text to your drawing (see Chapter 10), you have to specify a text height. The scale factor helps you determine the appropriate text height for a particular drawing scale. For example, you might want your text to appear 1/2" high in your final plot. But if you draw your text to 1/8" in your drawing, it appears as a dot when plotted. The text has to be scaled UP to a size that, when scaled back down at plot time, appears 1/8" high. So, for a ¼" scale drawing, you multiply the 1/8" text height by a scale factor of 48 to get 6". Your text should be 6" high in the CAD drawing in order to appear l/8" high in the final plot. So where did the number 48 come from?

The scale factor for fractional inch scales is derived by multiplying the denominator of the scale by 12 and then dividing by the numerator For example, the scale factor for ¼" 1'-0" is (4 x 12)/1, or 48/1. For 3/16" = 1'-0" scale, the operation is (16 x 12)/3, or 64 For whole-foot scales such as 1" = 10', multiply the feet side of the equation by 12. Metric scales require simple decimal conversions.

All the drawing sizes in the earlier tables were derived by using scale factors. The next table shows scale factors as they relate to standard drawing scales. These scale factors are the values by which you multiply the desired final printout size to get the equivalent full-scale size for a ¼" –scale drawing, you multiply the sheet measurements by 48. In this way, 11" becomes 528" (48"x11"), and 17" becomes 816" (48"x17"). Your work area must be 528"x816" if you intend to have a final output of 11"x17" at ¼" =1'. You can divide these inch measurements by 12" to get 44'x68'.

Scale Conversion Factors

Scale Factors For Engineering Drawing Scales

1" =n	10'	20'	30'	40'	50'	60'	100'	200'
Scale	120	240	360	480	600	720	1200	2400

Scale Factors for Architectural Drawing Scales

n = 1' -0"	1/16"	1/8"	¼"	½"	¾"	1"	11/2"	3"
Scale factor	192	96	48	24	16	12	8	4

If you are using the metric system, you can use the drawing scale directly as the scale factor. For example, a drawing scale of 1:10 has a scale factor of 10; a drawing scale of 1:50 has a scale factor of 50; and so on. The following table shows drawing areas based on scale and sheet size. The sheet sizes are shown across the top, and the scales are shown in the column to the far left.

Work Area in Metric Units (Centimeters) by Scale and Plotted Sheet Size.

Multiply Work Area Sizes by 10 for Millimeter Equivalents.

Scale	**A0 OR 841MM x1189MM (33.11" x 46.81")**
1:5	420 cm x 594 cm
1:10	841 cm x 1189 cm
1:20	1682 cm x 2378 cm
1:25	2102.5 cm x 2972.5 cm
1:331/3	2803 cm x 3962 cm
1:40	3369 cm x 4756 cm
1:50	4200 cm x 5940 cm
1:75	6307 cm x 5940 cm
1:100	8410 cm x 11890 cm

1:125	10512 cm x 14863 cm
Scale	**A or D 594mm x 841 (23.39" x 33.11")**
1:5	297 cm x 420 cm
1:10	594 cm x 841 cm
1:20	1188 cm x 1682 cm
1:25	1485 cm x 2102.5 cm
1:331/3	1980 cm x 2803 cm
1:40	2376 cm x 3360 cm
1:50	2970 cm x 4200 cm
1:75	4455 cm x 6307 cm
1:100	5940 cm x 8410 cm
1:125	7425 cm x 10512 cm
Scale	**A2 or C 420mm x 594mm (16.54" x 23.39")**
1:5	210 cm x 297 cm
1:10	420 cm x 594 cm
1:20	840 cm x 1188 cm
1:25	1050 cm x 1485 cm
1:331/3	1399 cm x 1980 cm
Scale	**A0 OR 841MM x 1189MM (33.11" x46.81")**
1:40	1680 cm x 2376 cm
1:50	2100 cm x 2970 cm
1:75	3150 cm x 4455 cm
1:100	4200 cm x 5940 cm
1:125	5250 cm x 7425 cm
Scale	**A3 or B 297mm x 420mm (11.70" x 16.54")**
1:5	148 cm x 210 cm
1:10	297 cm x 420 cm

1:20	594 cm x 840cm
1:25	742.5 cm x 1050 cm
1:331/3	990 cm x 1399 cm
1:40	1188 cm x 1680 cm
1:50	1480 cm x 2100 cm
1:75	2227 cm x 3150 cm
1:100	2970 cm x 5250 cm
1:125	3712 cm x 5250 cm
Scale	**A4 or A 210mm x 297 mm (8.27" x 11.70")**
1:5	105 cm x 148 cm
1:10	210 cm x 297 cm
1:20	420 cm x 594 cm
1:25	5250 cm x 742.5 cm
1:331/3	700 cm x 990 cm
1:40	840 cm x 1188 cm
1:50	1050 cm x 1480 cm
Scale	**A0 OR 841MM x 1189MM (33.11" x 46.81")**
1:75	1575 cm x 2227 cm
1:100	2100 cm x 2970 cm
1:125	2625 cm x 3712 cm

You will use scale factors to specify text height and dimension settings, so understanding them now will pay off later.

Using the AutoCAD Modes as Drafting Tools

After you set up your work area, you can begin the plan of a typical bathroom in your studio. You will use this example to learn about some of AutoCAD's drawing aids. These tools might be compared to a background grid (Grid mode), scale (Coordinate Readout mode), and a T-square and triangle (Object Snap Tracking mode and Polar Tracking mode). These drawing modes can be indispensable tools when used properly, The Drafting Settings dialog box helps you visualize the modes in an organized manner and simplifies their management.

Using the Grid Mode as a Background Grid

Using the Grid mode is like having a grid under your drawing to help you with layout, In AutoCAD, the Grid mode lets you see the limits of your drawing because the grid is displayed only within the limits setting of your drawing. The Grid mode also helps you visually determine the distances you are working with in any given view.

In the following exercise, you'll set the grid spacing and display the grid:

1. Choose Tools > Drafting Settings, or type Ds to open the Drafting Settings dialog box, showing all the mode settings.
2. Click the Snap And Grid tab. You see four groups: Snap, Grid, Polar Spacing, and Snap Type & Style.
3. Let's start with the Grid group. Notice that the Grid X Spacing text box contains a value of ½". Metric users see a value of 10.

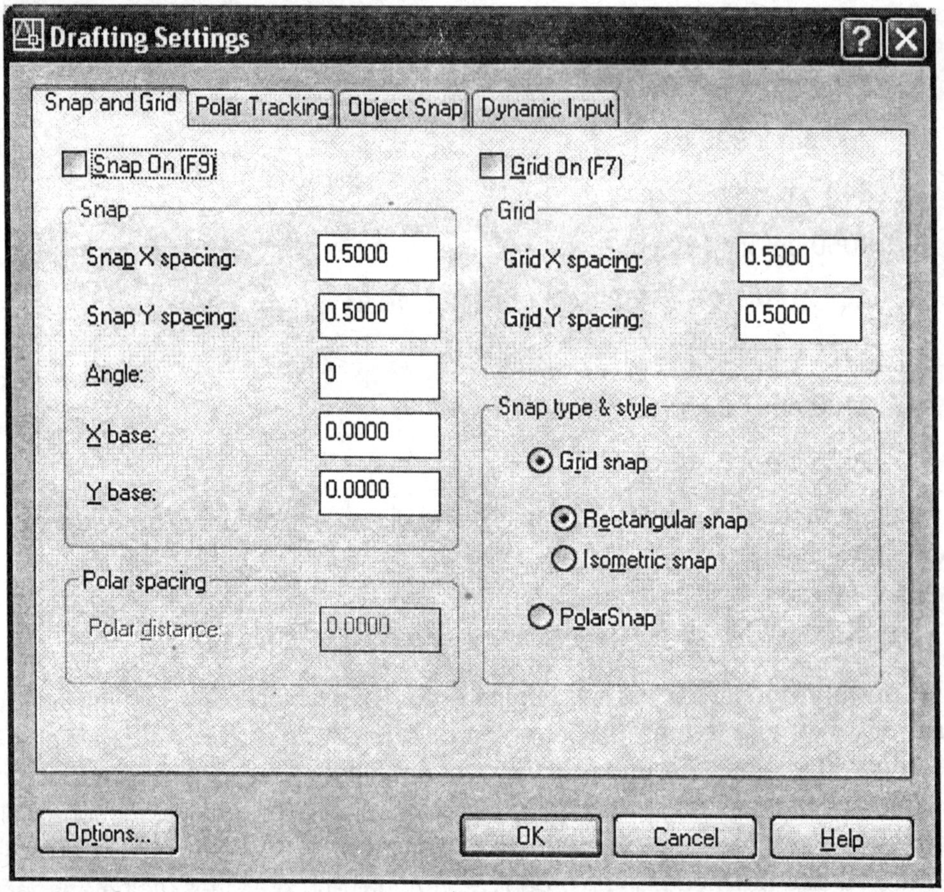

4. Double-click the Grid X Spacing text box to highlight the entry. You can now type a new value for this setting.
5. Type 12 for 12", and then press Tab to move to the Grid y Spacing text box. Metric users should type 30 and then press Tab. Notice that the Grid Y Spacing text box automatically changes to the same value as the X spacing value you just entered. In the case of the Imperial measurement, the value also changes from 12 to 1'. AutoCAD assumes you want the X and Y grid spacing to be the same, unless you specifically ask for a different Y setting.
6. Click the Grid On check box to make the grid visible. Notice the F7 in parentheses. This tells you that the F7 function key also controls the Grid On/Off function.
7. Click OK. The grid now appears as an array of dots with 12" spacing in your drawing area (30 cm if you axe following the metric version of this tutorial), The grid dots will not print or plot with your drawing. With this spacing, you can see your work area more clearly. It also gives you a visual reference for your drawing. You can see what a 1-foot (or 30-cm) distance looks like in your drawing. Because the grid appears only within the drawing limits, you are better able to see your work area.
8. Press F7, or click Grid in the status bar. (You can also hold down the Ctrl key and press G.) The grid disappears.
9. Press F7, again to turn the grid back on.

In this exercise, you set the grid spacing equal to the scale factor of your drawing. This makes the grid spacing equivalent to 1" intervals of the final plotted drawing. For example, if your drawing is ¼" = 1'-0" scale, you can set your grid spacing to 48. The grid spacing then reflects the 1-inch spacing for a ¼" scale drawing, If you're a metric user, you can keep the grid spacing at I0 to display the equivalent distance of 10 cm. This exercise used 30 for the metric grid spacing simply to match the display of the Imperial version.

Using the Snap Modes

The Snap mode forces the cursor to move in steps of a specific distance. Snap mode is useful when you want to select points on the screen at a fixed interval. Actually, two snap modes are available in AutoCAD: Grid Snap and Polar Snap. Let's start by looking at the Grid Snap mode. The F9 key toggles the Grid Snap mode on and off, or you can click the Snap button in the status bar. Follow these steps to access the Grid Snap mode:

1. Choose Tools > Drafting Settings, or type Ds to open the Drafting Settings dialog box.
2. In the Snap group of the dialog box, double-click the Snap X Spacing text box and type 4- (Metric users should enter 10.) Then press the Tab key to move to the next option.

As with the grid setting, AutoCAD assumes you want the X and Y snap spacing to be the same, unless you specifically ask for a different Y setting.

3. Click the Snap On check box to turn it on.

4. Click OK and start moving the cursor around. Notice how the cursor seems to move in "steps' rather than in a smooth motion. Also notice that the Snap button in the status bar appears pressed, indicating that the Snap mode is on.

5. Press F9 or click Snap in the status bar (you can also hold down the Ctrl key and press B); then move the cursor slowly around the drawing area. The Snap mode is now off.

6. Press F9 again to turn the Snap mode back on.

Take a moment to look at the Drafting Settings dialog box. The other options in the Snap group enable you to set the snap origin point (X Base and Y Base), rotate the cursor to an angle other than its current 0-90 (Angle), and set the horizontal snap spacing to a value different from the vertical spacing (Snap X Spacing and Snap Y Spacing).

In the Snap Type & Style group, you can change the snap and grid configuration to aid in creating isometric drawings by choosing the Isometric Snap radio button. The PolarSnap option enables you to set a snap distance for the Polar Snap feature. When you click the PolarSnap radio button, the Polar Distance option at the lower left of the dialog box changes from gray to black-and-white to allow you to enter a Polar Snap distance.

Using Grid and Snap Modes Together

You can set the grid spacing to be tile same as the snap setting, enabling you to see every snap point. Let's take a look at how Grid and Snap modes work together:

I. Open the Drafting Settings dialog box.

2. Make sure the Snap And Grid tab is selected; then double-click the Grid X Spacing text box in the Grid group and type 0.

3. Click OK. Now the grid spacing has changed to reflect the 4" (or I0 cm) snap spacing. Move the cursor and watch it snap to the grid points.

4. Open the Drafting Settings dialog box again.

5. Double-click the Snap X Spacing text box in the Snap group, and type 1 (3 for metric users).

6. Click OK. The grid automatically changes to conform to the new snap setting. However, at this density, the gild is overwhelming.

7. Open the Drafting Settings dialog box again.
8. Double-click the Grid X Spacing text box in the Grid group, and type 12 (30 for metric users).
9. Click OK. The grid spacing is now at 12 (or 30) again, which is a more reasonable spacing for the current drawing scale.

With the snap spacing set to 1 (3 for metric users), it is difficult to tell whether the Snap mode is turned on based on the behavior of the cursor, but the coordinate readout in the status bar gives you a clue, As you move your cursor, the coordinates appear as whole numbers with no fractional distances. Metric users will notice the coordinate readout displaying values that are multiples of 3.

As you move the cursor over the drawing area, the coordinate readout in the lower-left comer of the AutoCAD window dynamically displays the cursor's position in absolute Cartesian coordinates. This enables you to find a position on your drawing by locating it in reference to the drawing origin— 0,0—that is in the lower-left corner of the drawing.

You can also set the coordinate readout to display relative coordinates by clicking the readout itself or by pressing the F6 key, Throughout these exercises, coordinates will be provided to enable you to select points by using the dynamic coordinate readout.

Using Polar Tracking and Snap as Your Scale, T-Square, and Triangle

In this section, you will draw the first item in the bathroom: the toilet. It is composed of a rectangle representing the tank and a truncated ellipse representing the seat, To construct the toilet, you'll use the Polar Tracking and Polar Snap tools to learn about them firsthand. Polar Tracking helps you align your cursor to exact horizontal and vertical angles, much like a T-square and triangle. Polar Snap is similar to Grid Snap in that it forces the cursor to move in exact increments. The main difference is that Polar Snap snaps to distances from a previously selected point rather than to a fixed grid. Polar snap also works only in conjunction with Polar Tracking.

Start by setting up Polar Snap:

1. Open the Drafting Settings dialog box again.
2. Make sure the Snap And Grid tab is selected; then click the Polar Snap radio button in the Snap Type & Style group.
3. Double-click the Polar Distance setting, and type .5 for a 12-inch Snap setting. Metric users should type I for a 1 cm Polar Snap setting.
4. Click OK to close the Drafting Settings dialog box.

You've just set the Polar Snap setting to .5 or one-half (1 cm for metric users). As you move the cursor over the drawing area, notice that the Snap mode seems to be nil When Polar Snap is active, you'll have the snap in effect only when you are actually drawing an object. You can, however, switch between Grid Snap and Polar Snap on the fly. Follow these steps to see how this is done:

1. Make sure the Dynamic input display is turned off by checking the DYN button in the stains bar. It should appear to be in the up position. By turning off the Dynamic input display, you can concentrate on the behavior of the Polar Snap and Tracking.
2. Click the Line tool on the Draw toolbar or type L. You can also choose Draw > Line from the menu bar.
3. Right-dick the Snap button in the status bar.
4. Choose Grid Snap On from the shortcut menu to turn on Grid Snap mode,
5. Press F6 until you see the X,Y coordinates dynamically update as you move the cursor. You can also directly click the coordinate readout to cycle through the static, dynamic, and polar displays.

Notice that as you move your cursor, the coordinate readout shows the cursor moving in increments that you set for the Grid Snap. Next you'll see how Polar Tracking can be used to draw lines.

1. Start your line at the coordinate 5'-7", 6'-3" by enteting5'7"6'3". Metric users should enter 171,189 as the starting coordinate. This starting point is somewhat arbitrary, but by entering a specific starting location, you are coordinated with the figures and instructions.
2. Right-click the Snap button again, and then choose Polar Snap from the shortcut menu.
3. Make sure that Polar Tracking is on (the Polar button in the status bar should be in the on position), and then move the cursor directly to the right. The Polar Tracking cursor appears, along with the Polar Tracking readout. Notice that the readout shows distances in ½" increments (or l-unit increments for metric users). It also shows you the angle in the standard AutoCAD distance and angle format. Even though the Grid Snap is set to 1 (3 for metric users), the snap distance changes to the value you set for Polar Snap when Polar Tracking is active and Polar Snap is on.
4. Move the cursor until the Polar Snap readout lists 1'-10" < 0 and pick this point. Metric users should use a Polar Tracking readout of 56.0000 < 0. When you move the cursor around, the rubber-banding line follows it at any angle.

5. Move the cursor downward until the coordinate readout lists 0'-9" < 270 and click this point. Metric users should use a readout of 23.0000 < 270.

6. Continue drawing the other two sides of the rectangle by using the Polar Tracking readout After you've completed the rectangle, press .d or the Esc key to exit the Line tool.

As you can see from the exercise, you can use Polar Tracking to restrain your cursor to horizontal and vertical positions, just like a T-square and triangle. In some situations, you might find that you do not want Polar Tracking on. You can turn it off clicking the Polar button in the status bar. You can also press the FI0 function key to turn Polar Tracking on or off.

By using the Snap modes in conjunction with the coordinate readout and Polar Tracking, you can locate coordinates and measure distances as you draw lives. This is similar to the way you draw when using a scale. The smallest distance registered by the coordinate readout and Polar Tracking readout depends on the area you have displayed on your screen. For example, if you are displaying an area the size of a football field, the smallest distance you can indicate with your cursor might be 6" or 15 cm. On the other hand, if your view is enlarged to show an area of only one square inch or centimeter, you can indicate distances as small as 1/1000 of an inch or centimeter by using your cursor.

Setting the Polar Tracking Angle

You've seen how Polar Tracking lets you draw exact vertical and horizontal lines. You can also set Polar Tracking to draw lines at other angles, such as 30' or 45'. To change the angle Polar Tracking uses, you use the Polar Tracking tab in the Drafting Settings dialog box.

Right-click the Polar button in the status bar and then choose Settings from the shortcut menu to open the Drafting Settings dialog box. Or you can choose Tools > Drafting Settings from the menu bar and then click the Polar Tracking tab.

To change the Polar Tracking angle, enter an angle in the Increment Angle text box, or select a predefined angle from the drop-down list. You can do this while drawing a series of line segments, for example, so that you can set angles on the fly.

Numerous other settings are available on the Polar Tracking tab, Here is a listing of their functions, for your reference:

Additional Angles: This setting lets you enter a specific angle for Polar Tracking. For example, if you want Polar Tracking to snap to 12 degrees, click the New button next to the Additional Angle list box and enter 12, The value you enter appears in the list box, and when the Additional Angles check box is selected, Polar Tracking snaps to 12 degrees. To delete a value from the list box, highlight it and click the Delete button. The Additional Angles option

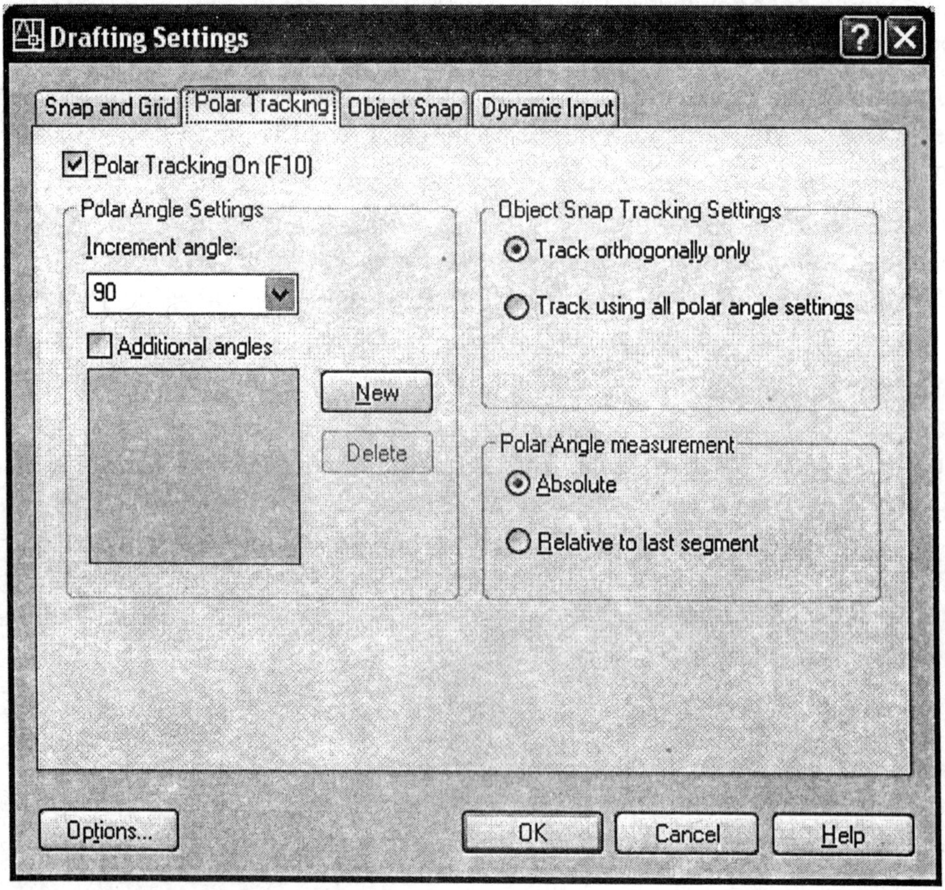

differs from the Increment Angle setting in that the Increment Angle setting causes Polar Tracking to snap to every increment of its setting, whereas Additional Angles snaps only to the angle specified. You can enter as many angles as you want in the Additional Angles list box.

Object Snap Tracking Settings: These settings let you control whether Object Snap Tracking uses strictly orthogonal directions (0 ', 90', 180', and 270') or the angles set In the Polar Angle settings group this dialog box.

Polar Angle Measurement: These radio buttons let you determine the zero angle on which Polar Tracking bases its incremental angles. The Absolute option uses the current AutoCAD setting for the 0' angle. The Relative To Last Segment option uses the last drawn object as the 0' angle. For example, if you draw a line at a 10' angle and the Relative To Last Segment option is selected with the Increment Angle set in 90', Polar Tracking snaps to 10', 100', 190', and 280' degrees, relative to the actual 0 ' direction.

Planning and Laying Out a Drawing

For the next object, the bathtub, you will use some new commands to lay out parts of the drawing. This will help you get a feel for the kind of planning you must do to use AutoCAD effectively. You'll begin the bathtub by using the Line command to draw a rectangle 2'-8" x 5'-0" (81 cm x 152 cm for metric users) on the left side of the drawing area. For a change this time, you'll use a couple of short-cut methods built into AutoCAD: the Line command's keyboard shortcut and the Direct Distance method for specifying distance and direction.

First, though, you'll go back to the previous view of your drawing and arrange some more room to work, Follow these steps:

1. Return to your previous view. A quick way to do this is to click the Zoom Previous tool on the Standard toolbar, or choose View > Zoom > Previous. Your view returns to the one you had before the last Zoom command.
2. Turn on the Grid Snap mode by right-clicking the Snap button on the status bar and chasing Grid Snap from the shortcut menu.
3. Type L and pick the coordinate location 0'-9", 0'-10" at the Specify first point: prompt. Metric users use the coordinate 24.0000, 27.0000. You can either use the cursor in conjunction with the coordinate readout or enter the coordinate from the keyboard, (Metric users can leave off the zero decimal values while entering coordinates through the keyboard.)
4. Place your cursor to the right of the last point selected so that the rubber-banding line is pointing directly to the right and type 2'8"; then press for the first side of the tub. Metric users should enter 81. Notice that the rubber-banding line is now fixed at the length you typed.
5. Now point the rubber-banding line upward toward the top of the screen and type 5'; then press for the next side. Metric users should enter 152
6. Point the rubber-banding line directly to the left of the last point and type 2'8" (81 for metric users); then press for the next side.
7. Type C to close the rectangle and exit the Line command.

   Now you have the outline of the tub. Notice that when you enter feet and inches from the keyboard, you must avoid hyphens or spaces. Thus, 2 feet 8 inches is typed as 2'8". Also notice that you didn't have to enter the at sign (@) or angle specification. Instead, you used the Direct Distance method for specifying direction mad distance.

   You can use this method for drawing lines or moving and copying objects at right angles. The Direct Distance method is less effective if you want to specify exact angles other than right angles. Some of the keyboard shortcuts for tools or commands you've used in this chapter are CO [Copy), E (Erase), EL (Ellipse), F (Fillet), M (Move), O (Offset), and TR (Trim).

Remember that you can enter keyboard shortcuts, such as keyboard commands, only when the Command prompt is visible in the Command window.

Making a Preliminary Sketch

In this section, you'll see how planning ahead will make your use of AutoCAD more efficient. When drawing a complex object, you will often have to do some layout before you do the actual drawing, This is similar to drawing an accurate pencil sketch using construction lines that you later trace over in produce a finished drawing. The advantage of doing this in AutoCAD is that your drawing doesn't lose any accuracy between the sketch and the final product. Also, AutoCAD enables you to use the geometry of your sketch to aid you in drawing. While planning your drawing, think about what you want to draw and then decide which drawing elements will help you create that object.

You will use the Offset command to establish reference lines to help you draw the Inside of the tub. This is where the Osnap overrides are quite useful. You can use the Offset tool on the Modify toolbar to make parallel copies of a set of objects, such as the lines forming the outside of your tub, Offset is different from the Copy command; Offset allows only one object to be copied at a time, but it can remember the distance you specify. The Offset option does not work with all types of objects. Only lines, arcs, circles, and 2D polylines can be offset.

Standard lines are best suited for the layout of tile bathtub in this situation. In this exercise, you will use standard lines:

8. Click the Offset tool in the Modify toolbar or type O. You can also choose Modify > Offset from the drop-down menu.

9. At the Specify offset distance or [Through/Erase/Layer] <Through>: prompt, enter 3. This specifies the distance of 3" as the offset distance. Metric users should enter 7 for 7 cm, which is roughly equivalent to 3 Inches.

10. At the Select object to offset or [Exit/Undo] <exit>: prompt, click the bottom line of the rectangle you just drew.

11. At the Specify point on side to Offset: prompt, pick a point inside the rectangle. A copy of the line appears. You don't have to be exact about where you pick the side to offset; AutoCAD wants in know only on which side of the line you want to make the offset copy.

12. The prompt Select object to offset or <exit>: appears again. Click another side to offset; then click again on a point inside the rectangle.

13. Continue to offset the other two sides; then offset these four new lines inside the rectangle toward the center.

14. When you are done, exit the Offset command by pressing.

Using the Layout

Now you will begin to draw the inside of the tub, starting with the narrow end. You will use your offset lines as references to construct the arcs that make up the tub. Also in this exercise, you'll set up some of the Osnap tools to be available automatically whenever AutoCAD expects a point selection. Here are the steps:

1. Choose Tools> Drafting Settings and then click the Object Snap tab. You can also type Ds, or tight<lick the Osnap button on the status bar and then choose Settings from the shortcut menu.

2. Click the Clear All button to turn off any options that might be selected.

3. Click the Endpoint, Midpoint, and Intersection check boxes so that a checkmark appears in the boxes, and make sure the Object Snap On option is selected; then click OK. You've just set up the Endpoint, Midpoint, and Intersection Osnaps to be on by default. This is called a Running (3snap; AutoCAD automatically selects the nearest Osnap point without your intervention. Now let's see how a Running Osnap works:

4. In the Draw toolbar, click the Arc tool or type a. Arc options available from the drop-down menu.

5. For the first point of the arc, move the cursor inward the intersection of the two lines as indicated in the left image. Notice that the intersection Osnap marker appears on the intersection.

6. With the intersection Osnap marker on the desired intersection, click the left mouse button.

7. Now move the cursor to the midpoint of the second horizontal line near the top. When the Midpoint Osnap marker appears at the midpoint of the line, click the left mouse button.

8. Finally, use the Intersection Osnap marker to locate and select the intersection of the two lines at the upper-left side of the bathtub.

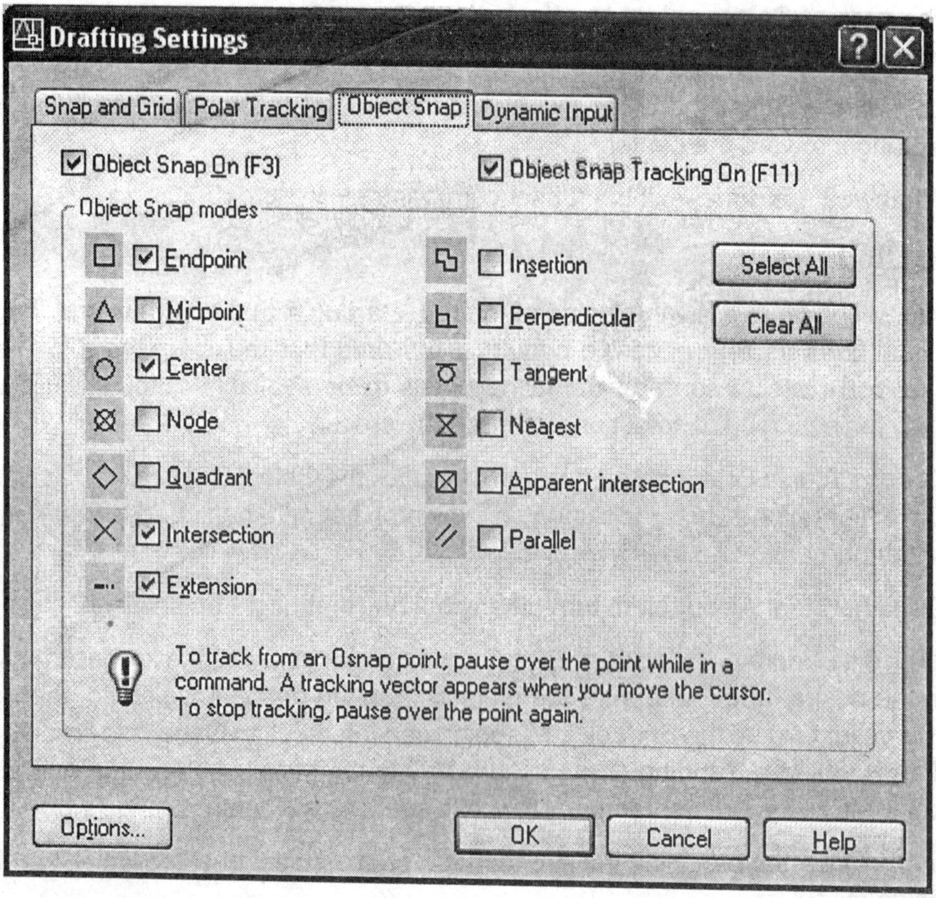

Aligning Objects by Using Object Snap Tracking

You saw how to use lines to construct an object such as the bathtub. In many situations using these construction lines is the most efficient way to draw, but they can also be a bit cumbersome. AutoCAD 2006 offers another tool that helps you align locations in your drawing to existing objects without having to draw intermediate construction lines. The tool is called Object Snap Tracking or Osnap Tracking.

Osnap Tracking is like an extension of Object Snaps that enables you to align a point to the geometry of an object instead of just selecting a point on an object. For example, with Osnap Tracking, you can select a point that is exactly at the center of a rectangle. In the following exercises, you will draw a Plan view of a bathroom sink as an introduction to the Osnap Tracking feature.

First, as a review, you'll open a new file by using the Create New Drawing Wizard. Because this drawing will be used as a symbol for insertion in other CAD drawings, don't worry about setting it up to conform to a sheet size. Chances are, you won't be printing individual symbols. Here are the steps:

1. Choose File > New to create a new drawing for your bathroom sink.
2. Click the Use A Wizard button in the Create New Drawing dialog box, select Quick Setup from the list that appears below the buttons, and then click OK.
3. In the Units screen, choose Architectural; then click Next, Metric users can use the Decimal option. This option performs the same operation as the Drawing Units dialog box you saw earlier in this chapter.
4. In the Area screen, enter 48 for the width and 36 for the length. Metric users should enter 122 for the width and 92 for the length. Then click Finish. This option performs the same operation as choosing Format > Drawing Limits from the menu bar.
5. Click the Grid button in the status bar, and then choose View > Zoom > All from the menu bar. This enables you in see your entire work area.
6. Choose File > Save As to save the file under the name Sink.

As you saw in steps 3 and 4, the Create New Drawing Wizard simplifies the drawing setup process by limiting the options you need to work with.

Drawing the Sink

Now you're ready to draw the sink, First, you'll draw the sink countertop. Then you'll make sure Running Osnaps and Osnap Tracking are turned on. Finally, you'll draw the bowl of the sink. Here are the steps for drawing the outline of the sink countertop:

1. Click the Grid button in the status bar to turn off the grid. It was helpful to let you see the work area, but you don't need it now.
2. Click the Rectangle tool in the Draw toolbar or type rec.
3. At the prompt Specify first corner point or [Chamfer/Elevation/Fillet/Thickness/Width]: enter 0,0. This places one comer of the rectangle in the origin of the drawing.
4. At the Specify other corner point or [Area/Dimensions/Rotation]: prompt, enter @2'4,1'6. Metric users should' enter @71,46. 2his makes the rectangle 2'-4" wide by 1'-6" deep, or 71 cm by 46 cm for metric users. The rectangle appears in the lower half of the drawing area.
5. Choose View > Zoom > Extents to enlarge the view of the sink outline. Then use the Zoom Realtime tool in the Standard toolbar to adjust your view.

When you draw the howl of the sink, the howl will be represented by an ellipse. You'll want to place the center of the ellipse at the center of the rectangle you've just drawn. To do this, you will use the midpoint of two adjoining sides of the rectangle as alignment locations. This is where the Osnap Tracking tool will be useful.

Useful ways of working in AutoCAD 2006 6

Introduction

In this chapter I give few hints for working in a better way in AutoCAD 2006.

To select a single object

At the Select Objects prompt of any command, move the rectangular pickbox cursor so that it touches the object that you want to select.

Click the object.

The object you selected is highlighted.

Press ENTER to end object selection.

To change the size of the pickbox cursor

From the Tools menu, choose Options. Then choose the Selection tab.

Under Pickbox Size, move the pickbox size slider until the pickbox is the size you want to use.

Choose OK.

To cycle through objects for selection

At the Select Objects prompt, hold down CTRL and click as near as possible to the object you want.

Keep clicking until the object you want is highlighted.

Press ENTER to select the object.

To remove selection from objects

Hold down SHIFT and click the objects that you want removed from the selection set.

To see a list of options at the Select Objects prompt

Enter ? at the Select Objects prompt.

To select objects within an irregularly shaped area

At the Select Objects prompt, enter wp (Window Polygon).

Specify points that define an area entirely enclosing the objects you want to select.

Press ENTER to close the polygon selection area and complete the selection.

To select objects crossing an irregularly shaped area

At the Select Objects prompt, enter cp (Crossing Polygon).

Specify points that define an area that encloses or crosses the objects you want to select.

Press ENTER to close the polygon selection area and complete the selection.

To select objects with a fence

At the Select Objects prompt, enter f (Fence).

Specify points to create a fence that passes through the objects you want to select.

Press ENTER to complete the selection.

To remove several objects from the selection set

After selecting objects, at the Select Objects prompt, enter r (Remove).

Enter any selection option such as cp (Crossing Polygon) or f (Fence), and select the objects to be removed from the selection set.

To return to adding objects to the selection set, enter a (Add).

To lock or unlock a layer

On the Layers toolbar, click the Layer Properties Manager button.

In the Layer Properties Manager, click the padlock for the layers that you want to lock.

Click OK.

If the padlock is closed, the layer is locked and objects on that layer cannot be selected.

To create a selection set using Quick Select

In the following example, you use Quick Select to select the red objects in a drawing.

From the Tools menu, choose Quick Select.

In the Quick Select dialog box under Apply To, select Entire Drawing.

Under Object Type, select Multiple.

Under Properties, select Color.

Under Operator, select Equals.

Under Value, select Red.

Under How to Apply, select Include in New Selection Set.

Choose OK.

AutoCAD selects all red objects in the drawing and closes the Quick Select dialog box. Objects that are set to BYLAYER and are red because the layer color is red are not included in the selection set.

To exclude objects from the selection set

You can exclude objects from the current selection set by using the Exclude from New Selection Set option. In the following example, you exclude all circles with a radius greater than 1 from a set of objects already selected.

With several objects selected, from the Tools menu, choose Quick Select.

In the Quick Select dialog box under Apply To, select Current Selection.

Under Object Type, select Circle.

Under Properties, select Radius.

Under Operator, select Greater Than.

Under Value, enter 1.

Under How to Apply, select Exclude from New Selection Set.

Choose OK.

To append objects to the selection set

You can use Quick Select to append objects to a current selection set. In the following example, you keep the current selection set and append all objects in the drawing that contain hyperlinks whose names begin with bld1_.

From the Tools menu, choose Quick Select.

In the Quick Select dialog box, select Append to Current Selection Set.

In the Object Type box, select Multiple.

Under Properties, select Hyperlink.

Under Operator, select Wildcard Match.

Under Value, enter bld1_*.

Under How to Apply, select Include in New Selection Set.

Choose OK.

To name and save a filtered list

At the Command prompt, enter filter.

In the Object Selection Filters dialog box under Select Filter, select a filter such as Line.

Choose Add to List.

Under Save As, enter a filter name such as Linefilter.

Choose Save As.

Choose Apply.

AutoCAD applies the filter so you can select, in this case, only lines in the drawing. If you select objects with a selection, AutoCAD applies the filter to all objects in the selection area.

To use a named filter

At the Select Object prompt, enter 'filter. (The apostrophe makes it a transparent command.)

In the Object Selection Filters dialog box under Select Filter, select the filter you want to use. Then choose Apply.

Use a crossing window to specify objects for selection.

Only the objects selected by the crossing window that match the filter criteria are selected.

To change the size of the pickbox cursor

From the Tools menu, choose Options. Then choose the Selection tab.

Under Pickbox Size, move the slider until the pickbox is the size you want to use.

Choose OK.

To change object selection settings

On the Tools menu, click Options. Then click the Selection tab.

Make changes to selection methods and pickbox size.

To ensure that overlapping objects are selected according to the order in which they were created, click the User Preferences tab, and then, in the Object Sorting Methods area, select Object Selection.

Click OK.

To create an unnamed group

Select the objects to associate into a group.

From the Tools menu, choose Group.

The selected objects are grouped together into an unnamed group, which is assigned a default name such as *A1. Unnamed groups are not displayed in the Group Manager unless Include Unnamed Groups is selected.

To create a named group

From the Tools menu, choose Group Manager.

Select the objects to associate into a group.

In the Group Manager, click the Create Group button.

Under Group, enter a group name and press ENTER.

The selected objects are grouped together into a named group.

Click in the description area and enter a description of the group (optional).

To toggle group selection for all groups

On the Group toolbar, click Group Selection On/Off.

AutoCAD displays the status of the PICKSTYLE system variable on the command line. When PICKSTYLE is set to 1 or 3, all groups are selectable.

To toggle group selection for specified groups

From the Tools menu, choose Group Manager.

In the Group Manager, select a group.

Under Selectable, click the lightbulb to switch between gray and yellow.

To select groups by name

From the Tools menu, choose Group Manager.

In the Group Manager under Group, select the names of the groups you want to select.

Click the Select Group button.

All of the objects in the selected groups are highlighted with grips.

To identify which groups an object belongs to

In the graphics area, select an object.

From the Tools menu, choose Group Manager.

With the cursor over any group name, right-click and choose Clear All.

With the cursor over any group name, right-click and choose Show Groups for Selected Objects.

The objects are highlighted in the Group column.

To remove a group

Select the group you want to remove.

From the Tools menu, choose Ungroup.

To add objects to a group

On the Tools menu, click Group Manager.

In the Group Manager, select the group name from the list of groups.

Select the objects to add to the group.

Click the Add to Group button.

The objects are added to the selected group.

To remove objects from a group

From the Tools menu, choose Group Manager.

In the Group Manager under Group, select the group you want to change.

To turn off individual selection for that group, under Selectable, click the lightbulb to make it gray.

Select the objects you want to remove from the group.

In the Group Manager, click the Remove from Group button.

The objects are removed from the selected group.

To draw a circumscribed polygon

From the Draw menu, choose Polygon.

On the command line, enter the number of sides.

Specify the center of the polygon (1).

Enter c to specify a polygon circumscribed about a circle.

Enter the radius length (2).

To draw a polygon by specifying one edge

From the Draw menu, choose Polygon.

On the command line, enter the number of sides.

Enter e (Edge).

Specify the start point for one polygon segment.

Specify the endpoint of the polygon segment.

To draw an inscribed polygon

From the Draw menu, choose Polygon.

On the command line, enter the number of sides.

Specify the center of the polygon.

Enter i to specify a polygon inscribed within a circle of specified points.

Enter the radius length.

To draw a rectangle

From the Draw menu, choose Rectangle.

Specify the first corner of the rectangle.

Specify the other corner of the rectangle.

To draw an arc by specifying three points

From the Draw menu, choose Arc 3 Points.

Specify the start point.

Specify a point on the arc.

Specify the endpoint.

To draw an arc using a start point, a center point, and an endpoint

From the Draw menu, choose Arc Start, Center, End.

Specify a start point.

Specify the center point.

Specify the endpoint.

To continue an arc with a tangential line

Complete the arc.

From the Draw menu, choose Line.

Press ENTER at the first prompt.

Enter the length of the line and press ENTER.

To continue an arc with a tangential arc

Complete the arc.

From the Draw menu, choose Arc Continue.

Specify the second endpoint of the tangent arc.

To create a rectangular array

From the Modify menu, choose Array.

In the Array dialog box, choose Rectangular Array.

Choose Select Objects

The Array dialog box closes and AutoCAD prompts for object selection.

Select the objects to be arrayed and press ENTER.

In the Rows and Columns boxes, enter the number of rows and columns in the array. Specify the horizontal and vertical spacing (offsets) between objects by using one of the following methods:

In the Row Offset and Column Offset boxes, enter the distance between rows and between columns. Adding a plus sign (+) or a minus sign (-) determines direction.

Click the Pick Both Offsets button to use the pointing device to specify the diagonal corners of a cell in the array. The cell determines the vertical and horizontal spacing of the rows and columns.

Click the Pick Row Offset or Pick Column Offset button to use the pointing device to specify the horizontal and vertical spacing.

To change the rotation angle of the array, enter the new angle next to Angle of Array.

The default angle 0 direction setting can also be changed in UNITS.

Choose OK to create the array.

To create a polar array

From the Modify menu, choose Array.

In the Array dialog box, choose Polar Array. Next to Center Point, do one of the following:

Enter an X value and a Y value for the center point of the polar array.

Click the Pick Center Point button. The Array dialog box closes and AutoCAD 2006 prompts for object selection. Use the pointing device to specify the center point of the polar array.

Choose Select Objects. The Array dialog box closes and AutoCAD 2006 prompts for object selection. Select the objects to be arrayed.

In the Method box, select one of the following methods:

Total Number of Items & Angle to Fill

Total Number of Items & Angle Between Items

Angle to Fill & Angle Between Items

Enter the number of items (including the original object), if available.

Use one of the following methods:

Enter the angle to fill and angle between items, if available. Angle to Fill specifies the distance to fill around the circumference of the array. Angle Between Items specifies the distance between each item.

Click the Pick Angle to Fill button and the Pick Angle Between Items button and use the pointing device to specify the angle to fill and the angle between items.

The example box displays the result.

You can set any of the following options:

To rotate the objects as they are arrayed, select Rotate Items As Copied. The example area displays the result.

To specify the X,Y base point, choose More, clear the Set to Object's Default option and enter values in the X and Y boxes, or click the Pick Base Point button and use the pointing device to specify the point.

Choose OK to create the array.

To calculate an area you define

From the Tools menu, choose Inquiry. Then choose Area.

Specify points in a sequence that defines the perimeter of the area to be measured. Then press ENTER.

AutoCAD 2006 connects the first and last points to form a closed area and displays the area and perimeter measurements using the settings specified with UNITS.

To calculate the area of an object

From the Tools menu, choose Inquiry. Then choose Area.

On the command line, enter o (Object).

Select an object.

AutoCAD 2006 displays the area and perimeter of the selected object.

To add areas as you calculate

From the Tools menu, choose Inquiry. Then choose Area.

Enter a (Add).

Use one of the following methods:

Specify points to define the area you want to add and press ENTER.

Enter o (Object) and select the objects you want to add.

AutoCAD 2006 displays the measurements of each new area and a running total of all areas.

Press ENTER twice to end the command.

To subtract areas from a calculation

While a combined area is displayed, enter s (Subtract).

Use one of the following methods:

Specify points to define the area you want to subtract and press ENTER.

Enter o (Object) and select the objects you want to subtract.

AutoCAD 2006 updates the running total as you define new areas.

Press ENTER to end the command.

To draw a circle by specifying a center point and radius or diameter

From the Draw menu, choose Circle Center, Radius or Center, Diameter.

Specify the center point.

Specify the radius or diameter.

To create a circle tangent to two objects

From the Draw menu, choose Circle Tan, Tan, Radius.

AutoCAD 2006 starts Tangent object snap mode.

Select the first object to draw the circle tangent to.

Select the second object to draw the circle tangent to.

Specify the radius of the circle.

To copy an object

From the Modify menu, choose Copy.

Select the objects to copy.

Specify the base point.

Specify the second point of displacement.

To copy an object multiple times

From the Modify menu, choose Copy.

Select the objects to copy.

Enter m (Multiple).

Specify the base point.

Specify the second point of displacement.

Specify the next point of displacement. Continue inserting copies, or press ENTER to end the command.

To turn the display of fill on or off

From the Tools menu, choose Options.

In the Options dialog box, select the Display tab.

Under Display Performance, choose Apply Solid Fill.

A check mark indicates that Fill mode is on.

Choose OK.

To display your changes, choose Regen from the View menu.

To turn the display of text on or off

From the Tools menu, choose Options.

In the Options dialog box, choose the Display tab.

Under Display Performance, choose Show Text Boundary Frame Only.

The check mark indicates that text is displayed as a rectangular frame.

Choose OK.

To display your changes, choose Regen from the View menu.

To turn lineweights on or off

From the Format menu, choose Lineweight.

In the Lineweight Settings dialog box, clear Display Lineweight.

Choose OK to exit.

Start a Drawing from Scratch

A quick way to begin a new drawing is to start from scratch, which starts a drawing that uses settings from a default drawing template file.

You can start from scratch from the Create New Drawing dialog box, from the Select Template dialog box, or without using a dialog box at all. In each case, you use either the NEW command or the QNEW command.

Use the Create New Drawing Dialog Box

The Create New Drawing dialog box is displayed under the following conditions:

You set the STARTUP system variable to 1 (on).

You set the FILEDIA system variable to 1 (on).

You click New on the File menu or Qnew on the Standard toolbar when no drawing template file is specified in the Options dialog box.

The Create New Drawing dialog box provides several methods for starting a new drawing.

When you use Start from Scratch, you can specify either imperial or metric units for the new drawing. The setting you select determines default values used for many system variables controlling text, dimensions, grid, snap, and the default linetype and hatch pattern file.

Imperial. Creates a new drawing based on the imperial measurement system. The drawing uses internal default values, and the default drawing boundary, called the drawing limits, is 12 × 9 inches.

Metric. Creates a new drawing based on the metric measurement system. The drawing uses internal default values, and the default drawing boundary is 429 × 297 millimeters.

Use the Select Template Dialog Box

The Select Template dialog box is displayed under the following conditions:

You set the STARTUP system variable to 0 (off).

You set the FILEDIA system variable to 1 (on).

You click New on the File menu or, by default, Qnew on the Standard toobar.

At the bottom-right corner of the Select Template dialog box, there is an Open button with an arrow button next to it. If you click the arrow button, you can choose between two internal default drawing templates, metric or imperial.

Use a Default Drawing Template File

The fastest way to begin working on a new drawing is to start automatically with a default drawing template file. No dialog box is displayed with this method:

You set the STARTUP system variable to 0 (off).

You set the FILEDIA system variable to 1 (on).

You specify a default drawing template file in the Options dialog box on the Files tab. Click the node labeled "Drawing Template Settings" and specify a path and drawing template file.

You click Qnew on the Standard toolbar.

From now on, a new drawing is immediately created that is based on the specified default drawing template file.

If no template file is specified in the Options dialog box, QNEW displays the Select Template dialog box.

Creating Drawing using Wizards

A setup wizard establishes basic drawing settings step by step. You have two wizard options to help you set up a drawing:

Quick Setup Wizard. Sets units of measurement, precision of displayed units, and grid limits.

Advanced Setup Wizard. Sets units of measurement, precision of displayed units, and grid limits. Also establishes angle settings such as units of measurement style, precision, direction, and orientation.

These wizards are available in the Create New Drawing dialog box.

Creating Drawing using Template

A drawing template file contains standard settings. Select one of the template files supplied, or create your own template files. Drawing template files have a .dwt file extension.

When you create a new drawing based on an existing template file and make changes, the changes in the new drawing do not affect the template file. You can use one of the template files supplied with AutoCAD, or you can create your own template files.

Create a Drawing Template File

When you need to create several drawings that use the same conventions and default settings, you can save time by creating or customizing a template file instead of specifying the conventions and default settings each time you start. Conventions and settings commonly stored in template files include

Unit type and precision

Title blocks, borders, and logos

Layer names

Snap, Grid, and Ortho settings

Drawing (grid) limits

Dimension styles

Text styles

Linetypes

By default, drawing template files are stored in the template folder, where they are easily accessible.

Recover the Default Drawing Template File

If the settings in the AutoCAD drawing template files aclt.dwt or acltiso.dwt have been changed from the original defaults, you can reset them by using Start from Scratch in the Create New Drawing dialog box and then saving the drawing as a drawing template file, replacing aclt.dwt or acltiso.dwt.

Saving Your Drawings

You save drawing files for later use just as you do with other Windows applications. AutoCAD also provides automatic saving, backup files, and other options for saving. When you are working on a drawing, you should save it frequently. Saving protects you from losing work in the event of a power failure or other unexpected event. If you want to create a new version of a drawing without affecting the original drawing, you can save it under another name. The file extension for AutoCAD 2006 drawing files is .dwg, and unless you change the default file format in which drawings are saved, drawings are saved in the AutoCAD 2006 2006 drawing-file format. This format is optimized for file compression and for use on a network.

Save Your Drawing Automatically

If you turn on the automatic saving option, AutoCAD saves your drawing at specified time intervals. By default, files saved automatically are temporarily assigned the name filename_a_b_nnnn.sv$. The file name is the current drawing name, a is the number of open instances of the same drawing file in the same AutoCAD 2006 session, b is the number of open instances of the same drawing in different sessions of AutoCAD 2006, and nnnn is a random number generated by AutoCAD 2006. Files that are automatically saved are deleted when AutoCAD 2006 closes a drawing in the normal way. Saved files remain in the event of a crash or power failure. To recover a previous version of your drawing from the automatically saved file, rename the file using a .dwg extension.

Use Backup Files

If you turn on automatic backups, AutoCAD 2006 saves the previous version of your drawing files to a file with the same name and a .bak file extension. To recover the previous version of your drawing from a backup file, rename the file using a .dwg extension.

Save Part of a Drawing File

If you want to create a new drawing file from part of an existing drawing, you can use BLOCK or WBLOCK. With either command, you can select objects or specify a block definition in your current drawing and save them in a new drawing file. You can also save a description along with the new drawing.

Save to a Different Type of Drawing File

You can save a drawing to an earlier version of the DWG or DXF format or save a drawing as a template file. Choose the format from Files of Type in the Save Drawing As dialog box.

Reduce the Time Required to Save a Drawing File

You can reduce the time required to save a drawing file if you specify incremental saves rather than full saves. An incremental save updates only those portions of the saved drawing file that you changed. When you use incremental saves, drawing files will contain a percentage of potentially wasted space. This percentage increases after each incremental save until it reaches a specified maximum, at which time a full save is performed instead. You can set the incremental save percentage in the Open and Save tab of the Options dialog box or by setting the value of the system variable ISAVEPERCENT. If you set the value of ISAVEPERCENT to 0, all saves are full saves. To reduce the size of drawing files, it is recommended that you perform a full save (with IPERCENTSAVE set to 0) before transmitting or archiving a drawing.

Open an Existing Drawing

To open an existing AutoCAD 2006 drawing, you can choose Open from the File menu to display the Select File dialog box. You can also open drawings by dragging them from Windows Explorer into AutoCAD 2006. If you drop one or more drawings anywhere outside the drawing area—for example, the command line or the blank space next to the toolbars—AutoCAD 2006 opens the drawings. However, if you drag a single drawing into the drawing area of an open drawing, the new drawing is not opened but inserted as a block reference. You can double-click a drawing in Windows Explorer to launch AutoCAD 2006 and open the drawing. If AutoCAD 2006 is already running, the drawing opens in the current session rather than in a second session.

Check Drawing Authenticity

If the DWGCHECK system variable is set to On (1), AutoCAD 2006 checks the DWG file format and displays an alert box if

> The drawing file format is AutoCAD 2006 97 or later or AutoCAD Release 14 or later AND

> The file was last saved by a program other than AutoCAD 2006 97 or later or AutoCAD Release 14 or later

To avoid checking for file authenticity each time you open drawings, clear the Always Show This Dialog Box option when the alert is displayed. Alternatively, you can set DWGCHECK to Off (0).

Change the Default Drawing Folder

Each time you start AutoCAD 2006, the last used paths in each particular standard file selection dialog box are remembered across AutoCAD 2006 sessions. Alternatively, you can configure AutoCAD 2006 to always default to a particular path by changing the default drawing folder.

Finding a Drawing File

You can use the Find dialog box to search for drawings using name, location, and date filters. For example, you could search a specific network location for linetype (LIN) files updated within the last ten days. The Find dialog box for AutoCADesignCenter™ provides further options. You can search for Windows file properties you added to drawings, for example, title or keyword. The Select File dialog box displays drawing file previews. When the RASTERPREVIEW system variable is on, AutoCAD 2006 automatically generates a raster preview image that is stored with the drawing when you save it.

Specifying Path Names

The Files tab of the Options dialog box is where you set the search path AutoCAD 2006 uses to find support files such as text fonts, drawings, linetypes, and hatch patterns. The MYDOCUMENTSPREFIX system variable stores the location of the My Documents folder for the current user. You also can specify the location of temporary files on the Files tab. AutoCAD 2006 creates temporary files on disk, and then deletes them when you exit AutoCAD 2006. AutoCAD 2006 sets the temporary directory to the location that Microsoft Windows uses.

If you plan to run AutoCAD 2006 from a write-protected directory (for example, if you work on a network or open files on a CD), specify a different location for your temporary files. The directory you specify must not be write-protected, and the drive containing the directory should have sufficient disk space for the temporary files. If you want to use a custom menu, specify it in the Menu, Help, and Miscellaneous File Names box. The default menu is aclt.mnu.

Working with Multiple Files

You can open more than one drawing in a single AutoCAD 2006 session. When multiple drawings are open, simply click anywhere in a drawing to make it active. You can also use CTRL+F6 or CTRL+TAB to switch between open drawings. However, you cannot switch between drawings during certain long operations such as regenerating the drawing.

Use the Window menu to control the display of multiple drawings in an AutoCAD 2006 session. You can cascade open drawings or tile them vertically or horizontally. When you have a number of drawings minimized, you can use Arrange Icons to clean up the display of the minimized drawing icons in the AutoCAD 2006 window. You can also select a drawing from the list of open drawings at the bottom of this menu. You can quickly reference other drawings, copy and paste between drawings, or drag selected objects from one drawing to another with the right button on your pointing device. You can also use Match Properties (MATCHPROP) to copy properties from objects in one drawing to objects in another drawing. You can use AutoCAD 2006 object snaps, the Copy with Basepoint (COPYBASE) command, and the Paste to Original Coordinates (PASTEORIG) command to ensure accurate placement, especially when copying objects from one drawing to another.

Adding Information to Drawings

You can track your drawings more easily by assigning properties to them in the Drawing Properties dialog box. Drawing properties are details that help you identify the drawing, including title, author, subject, keywords that identify the model, or other important information. You can store hyperlink addresses or directory paths and ten custom properties with your drawings. The Drawing Properties dialog box contains the following drawing information.

General tab. Displays the drawing type, location, size, and other information. The information is derived from the operating system. All fields are read-only. However, you can access and change these file properties through Windows Explorer.

Summary tab. Specifies properties such as author, title, and subject.

Statistics tab. Displays data such as file size and the dates files were created and last modified. You can search for all files created at a certain time, for example, after March 3, 1998, or for files you modified yesterday.

Custom tab. Specifies custom file properties, including any value you assign.

Recovering a Damaged File

Computer hardware problems, power surges, user mistakes, or software problems can cause errors that prevent you from editing or plotting the drawing. By saving your work frequently, you can ensure a minimum of lost data if your system fails. If AutoCAD 2006 encounters a problem and closes unexpectedly, you can send an error report to help Autodesk diagnose problems with the software. The error report includes information about the state of your system at the time the error occurred, and you can add other information, such as what you were doing at the time of the error. The REPORTERROR system variable controls whether the error reporting feature is available. When an error occurs, AutoCAD 2006 tries to record diagnostic information in the aclt.err file, which you can use to report a problem. AutoCAD 2006 marks a drawing as damaged if it detects corrupted data, or if you request that the drawing be saved after a system failure. If the damage is minor, you sometimes can repair the drawing simply by opening it. You can use RECOVER to perform an audit on, and attempt to open, any file you select. Use AUDIT to find and correct errors in an open file.

Displaying 3D view

You can display parallel and perspective views with several commands to facilitate constructing and visualizing 3D models. When working in 3D, you'll often want to display several different views so that you can easily verify the 3D effects of your editing.

One of these viewpoints is often an isometric view to reduce the number of visually overlapping objects. From a selected viewpoint, you can create new objects, edit existing objects, or generate a hidden-line or shaded view.

Several commands are available for viewing in 3D. You can

View parallel projections of your model by choosing standard 3D preset views, by entering the coordinate of your viewing location, or by specifying a 3D view dynamically.

View a parallel projection of your model based on the XY plane of the current UCS.

View in perspective from any angle and distance.

Overviewing of Viewing Parallel Projections in 3D

To determine the point or angle in model space, you can

Choose a preset 3D view from a toolbar.

Enter a coordinate or angles that represent your viewing location in 3D.

Change to a view of the XY plane of the current UCS, a saved UCS, or the WCS.

Change the 3D view dynamically with your pointing device.

Set front and back clipping planes to limit the objects being displayed.

Viewing in 3D is available only in model space. If you are working in paper space, you cannot use VPOINT, DVIEW, or PLAN to define paper space views. The view in paper space is always a plan view.

Choosing the Preset 3D View

A quick way to set a view is to choose one of the predefined 3D views. You can select predefined standard orthographic and isometric views by name or description. These views represent commonly used options: Top, Bottom, Front, Left, Right, and Back. In addition, you can set views from isometric options: SW (southwest) Isometric, SE (southeast) Isometric, NE (northeast) Isometric, and NW (northwest) Isometric.

To understand how the isometric views work, imagine you are looking down at the top of a box. If you move toward the lower-left corner of the box, you are viewing the box from the SW Isometric View. If you move toward the upper-right corner of the box, you are viewing it from NE Isometric View.

Define a 3D View with Coordinate Value or Angles

You can define a viewing direction by entering the coordinate values of a point or the measures of two angles of rotation. This point represents your position in 3D space as you view the model while looking toward the origin (0,0,0). Viewpoint coordinate values are relative to the world coordinate system unless you change the WORLDVIEW system variable.

The conventions for defining standard views differ between architectural (AEC) and mechanical design. In AEC design, the perpendicular view of the XY plane is the top or plan view; in mechanical design, the perpendicular view of the XY plane is the front view. You can rotate a view using DDVPOINT. The following illustration shows a view defined by two angles relative to the X axis and the XY plane of the WCS.

Changing to a View of the XY Plane

In AutoCAD 2006, a plan view is a view aimed toward the origin (0,0,0) from a point on the positive Z axis. This results in a view of the XY plane. You can restore the view and coordinate system that is the default for most AutoCAD 2006 drawings by setting the UCS orientation to World and then setting the 3D view to Plan View.

Changing to 3D View Dynamically

With dynamic viewing, you can display the effects of changing your viewpoint as you make the changes. Using this method, you can also simplify your view temporarily by choosing only the objects that you need to determine the view. Alternatively, if you press ENTER without selecting any objects, 3D Dynamic View displays a model of a small house instead of your actual drawing. You can use this house to define the viewing angle and distance. When your adjustments are complete, and you exit the command, AutoCAD 2006 applies the changes to the entire 3D model in the current view.

System and Dimension Variables of AutoCAD 2006

6

Introduction

System variables let you fine-tune your AutoCAD environment. You set a system variable by entering the variable name at the command prompt. If you are in the middle of a command, you can set a system variable by entering the variable name preceded by an apostrophy. Following is the complete list of system variables.

Variable Name	*Associated Command*	*Where Saved*	*Use*
Acadlspasdoc	Options	Registry	Controls the loading of the Acad.lsp file when present:0 = load only into first drawing (initial value); 1 = into every opened drawing.
Acadprefix	Options	NA	Indicates the AutoCAD environment setting.
Acadver	NA	NA	Indicates the AutoCAD version number.
Acisoutver	Acisout	With drawing	Controls ACIS version of SAT files.
Adcstate (read-only)	NA	Registry	Indicates the current display state of the AutoCAD DesignCenter: 0=closed;1 = opened
Aflags	Units	NA	Controls attribute mode settings: 1 = invisible; 2 = constant; 4 = verify; 8 = preset.
Angbase	Units	With drawing	Controls direction of 0 degree angle relative to the current UCS.
Angdir	Units	With drawing	Controls positive direction of angles: 0 = counterclockwise; 1 = clockwise.
Apbox	Draw, Edit	Registry	Displays AutoSnap aperture box when AutoSnape is activated: 0 = off; 1 = on.
Aperture	Draw, Edit	Registry	Sets size of Osnap cursor in pixels.
Area (read-only)	Area	NA	Displays last area calculation; use with Setvar or AutoLISP's Getvar function.
Assistate*	Quick Help	NA	Controls the display of the Informátion palette Quick Help:0 = off; 1 = on.
Attdia	Insert/Attribute	With drawing	Controls attribute dialog box: 0 = no dialog box; 1 = dialog box.

Variable Name	Associated Command	Where Saved	Use
Attmode	Attdisp	With drawing	Controls attribute display mode: 0 = off; 1 = normal; 2 = on.
Attreq	Insert	With drawing	Controls the prompt for attributes: 0 = no prompt or dialog box for attributes (attributes use default values); 1 = normal prompt or dialog box upon attribute insertion.
Audictl	Config	Registry	Controls whether an audit file is created: 0 = disable; 1 = enable creation of ADT file.
Aunits	Units	With drawing	Controls angular units: 0 = decimal degrees; 1 = degrees – minutes – seconds; 2 = grads; 3 = radians; 4 = surveyor's units.
Auprec	Units	With drawing	Controls the precision of angular units determined by decimal place.
Autosnap	Draw, Edit	Registry	Controls AutoSnap display and fetures: 0 = everything off; 1 = marker on; 2 = Snaptip on; 4 = magnet on.
Backgroundplot*	Plot, Publish	Registry	Controls the background plot feature: 0 = off; 1 = background for plot but not Publish; 2 = background for Publish but not Plot;4 = background for both Plot and Publish
Backz	Dview	With drawing	Displays distance from Dview target to back clipping plane.
Bactioncolor**	Bedit	Registry	Controls the color of Actions in the Block Editor. Values can be index colors from 1 to 255 or RGB colors specified as RGB:CCC, CCC, CCC; CCC is a value from 1 to 255.
Bdependancyhighlight**	Bedit	Registry	Controls the highlighting of dependent objects when Actions or parameters are selected; 1 = highlight on; 0 = highlight off.
Bgripobjcolor**	Bedit	Registry	Sets the colors of grips in the Block Editor. See Bactioncolor for settings.
Bgropobjsize**	Bedit	Registry	Sets the display size of grips. Values can be from 1 to 255.
Bindtype	Xref	NA	Controls the way Xref names are handled when bound to a file: 0 = maintain Xref filename prefix (initial value); 1 = remove Xref filename prefix.
Btipmode	NA	With drawing	Controls appearance of blips: = off; 1 = on.

Variable Name	*Associated Command*	*Where Saved*	*Use*
Blockeditlock**	Bedit	Registry	Locks the Block Editor from use; 0 = not locked; 1 = locked.
Blockeditor**	Bedit	NA	Indicates if the Block Editor is open; 0 =not open; 1 = open.
Parametercolor**	Bedit	Retistry	Controls the fonts used for parameters. TrueType or AutoCAD SHX fonts can be specified. Include the SHX file extension for SHX fonts.
Bparametersize**	Bedit	Registry	Controls the parameter text sizes relative to the screen. Accepts intigers from 1 to 255.
BtMarkdisplay**	Bedit	Registry	Controls the display of values set markers; 0 = not displayed; 1 = displayed.
Bvmode**	Bedit	NA	Controls how "invisible" objects are displayed; o =– not visible; 1 = grayed out.
Calcinput**	Dialog box Input Boxes	Registry	Controls whether mathematical expressions are evaluated when entered in input boxes; 0 = not evaluated; 1 = evaluated by pressing the END key.
Cdate (read-only)	Time	NA	Displays calendar date/time read from system date (YYYY MMDD.HHMMSSMSEC).
Cecolor	Color	With drawing	Controls current default color assigned to new objects.
Celtscale	NA	With drawing	Controls current linetype scale for individual objects.
Celtype	Linetype	With drawing	Controls current default linetype assigned to new objects.
Centermt**	Mtext	User settings	Controls how the Mtext bounding box behaves; 0 = one corner remains stationary while other corner moves; 1 = center remains stationary while both corners move.
Celweight	Lineweight	With drawing	Controls the default lineweight for new objects: -1=Bylayr; -2 = Byblock; -3=default as set by Lwdefault. Specific lineweight values can also be entered in millimeters.
Chamfera	Chamfer	With drawing	Controls first chamfer distance.
Chamferb	Chamfer	With drawing	Controls second chamfer distance.
Chamferc	Chamfer	With drawing	Controls chamfer distance for Angle option.
Chamferd	Chamfer	With drawing	Controls chamfer angle for Angle option.
Chammode	Chamfer	NA	Controls method of chamfer: 0 = use two distances; 1 = use distance and angle.

Variable Name	*Associated Command*	*Where Saved*	*Use*
Circlerad	Circle	NA	Controls the default circle radius: 0 = no default.
Clayer	Layer	With drawing	Sets the current layer.
Clistate**	Command window	NA	Indicates whether the command window is hidden or displayed; 0 = hidden; 1 = displayed.
Cmdactive	NA	NA	Displays whether a command, script or dialog box is active: 1 = command active; 2 = transparent command active; 4 = script active; 8 = dialog box active (values are cumulative, so 3 = command and transparent command are active).
Cmddia	NA	Registry	Controls use of dialog boxes for some commands: 0 = don't use dialog box; 1 = use dialog box.
Cmdecho	Autolisp	NA	With AutoLISP, controls display of prompts from embedded AutoCAD commands: 0 = no display of prompt; 1 = display prompts.
Cmdhistoryinputmax**		NA	Registry Sets the maximum number of command input values stored for later retrieval from the shortcut menu.
Cmdname	NA	NA	Displays the English name of the currently active command.
Cmljust	Mline	With drawing	Sets method of justification for multilines: 0 = top; 1 = middle; 2 = bottom.
Cmlscale	Mline	With drawing	Sets scale factor for multilane widths: a 0 value collapses the multilane to a single line; a negative value reverses the justification.
Cmlstyle	Mline	With drawing	Displays current multilane style by name.
Compass	3dorbit	NA	Controls the display of the 3D compass: 0 = off (initial value); 1 = on.
Cords	F6, Ctrl + D	With drawing	Controls coordinate readout: 0 = coordinates displayed only when points are picked; 1 = absolute coordinates dynamically displayed as cursor moves; 2 = distance and angle displayed during commands that accept relative distance input.
Cplotstyle	Plot, Pagesetup	With drawing	Controls the default plot style for new objects; Startup values are Bylayer, Byblock, Normal and User Defined.
Cprofile	Options	Registry	Displays the current profile name.

Variable Name	*Associated Command*	*Where Saved*	*Use*
Crossingareacolor**	Object Selection	Registry	Sets the color for the crossing window. Use the AutoCAD color numbers. Selectionarea must be on for this system variable to work.
Ctab	(tabs)	With drawing	Displays the name of the current tab.
Ctablestyle*	Table	With drawing	Controls the name of the current table style.
Cursorsize	NA	Registry	Determines size f crosshairs as a percentage of the screen size 91-100).
Cvport	Vports	With drawing	Displays ID number of current viewport.
Date	Time	NA	Displays date and time in Julian format.
Dbmox	NA	NA	Displays drawing modification status: 1 = object database modified; 2 = symbol table modified; 4 = dataset variable modified; 8 = window modified; 16 = view modified.
Dbstate	DbConnect	With drawing	Read-only. Displays the display state of the dbConnect Manager dialog box: 0 = closed; 1 = opened.
Dctcust	Spell	Registry	Sets default custom spelling dictionary filename including path.
Dctmain	Spell	Registry	Sets default plot style for new layers.
Deflplstyle	Plotstyle	With drawing	Sets the default plot style for new layers.
Defplstyle	Plotstyle	Registry	Sets the default plot style for new objects.
Delobj	NA	With drawing	Controls whether source objects used to create new objects are retained: 0 = delete objects; 1 = retain objects.
Demandload	NA	Registry	Controls loading of third-party applications required for custom objects in drawing (0-3).
Diastat	NA	NA	Displays how last dialog box was exited: 0 = Cancel; 1 = OK.
Dispsilh	All curved solids	With drawing	Controls silhouette display of curved 3D solids: 0 = no silhouette; 1 = silhouette curved solids.
Distance	Dist	NA	Displays last distance calculated by Dist command.
Donutid	Donut	NA	Controls default outside diameter of a donut.
Dragmode	NA	With drawing	Controls dragging: 0 = no dragging; 1 = if requested; 2 = automatic drag.
Dragp1	NA	With drawing	Controls regeneration drag input sampling rate.
Dragp2	NA	Registry	Controls t\fast – drag input sampling rate.

Variable Name	Associated Command	Where Saved	Use
Drawordertl*	Draworder	With drawing	Controls the level of functionality offered by the Draworder command: 0 = regen required to display draw order; 1 = draw order display is immediate; 2 = adds inheritance to objects with draw order; 3 = full Draworder functionality (1 and 2 combined).
Drstate**	NA	NA	Indicates whether the Drawing Recovery window is open; 0 = not open; 1 = open.
Dtexted**	Dtext	Registry	Controls Dtext behavior; 0 = in place editing; 1 = opens dialog box for editing as in previous versions of AutoCAD.
Dwgcheck	NA	Registry	Controls the display of a warning dialog bo xindicating that a drawing was last edited in a program other than AutoCAD: 0 = suppress dialog box; 1 = display dialog box when needed.
Dwgcodepage	NA	With drawing	Displays code page of drawing.
Gname	Open	NA	Displays drawing name and drive/folder, if specified by user.
Dwgprefix	NA	NA	Displays drive and folder of current file.
Dwgtitled	NA	NA	Displays whether a drawing has been named: 0 = untitled; 1 = named by user.
Dyndigrip**	Dynamic Input	Registry	Controls how dimensions are displayed while grip editing. Values can be the sum of the following for combined settings: 0 = none; 1 = resulting dimension; 2 = change in dimension; 4 = absolute angle; 8 = change in angle; 16= arc radius; 31 = all settings on.
Dyndivis**	Dynamic Input	User settings	Controls the number of dimensions that are visible while grip editing; 0 = first two dimensions; 2 = all dimensions allowed by the Dyndigrip setting.
Dynmode**	Dynamic Input	User settings	Controls the overall behavior of Dynamic Input; 0 = off; 1 = prompt input only; 2 = dimensions only; 3 = both prompt and dimension input. Negative values can be used and toggled on or off using he F12 key.
Dynpicoords**	Dynamic Input	User settings	Controls whether dynamic Input uses relative or absolute coordinates; 0 = relative; 1 = absolute.
Dyinformat**	Dynamic Input	User settings	Controls whether Dynamic Input uses polar or Cartesian coordinates; 0 = polar; 1 = Cartesian.
Dynpivis**	Dynamic Input	User settings	Controls when keyboard input is displayed; 0 = when

Variable Name	*Associated Command*	*Where Saved*	*Use*
			you type; 1 = automatically when prompted for input; 2 = always.
Dynprompt**	Dynamic Input	User settings	Controls the display of prompts; 0 = no display;; 1 = display.
Dynotoolstips**	Dynamic Input	User settings	Controls the extent of tooltip display; 0 = Dynamic Input fields only; 1 = all tooltips.
Edgemode	Trim, Extend	Registry	Controls how trim and extend boundaries are determined: 0 = boundaries defined by object only; 1 = boundaries defined by objects and their extensions.
Enterprisemenu**	Custom User Interfact (CUI)	Registry	Displays the CUI filename and path.
Elevation	Elev	With drawing	Controls current 3D elevation relative to current UCS.
Expert	NA	NA	Controls prompts, depending on level of user's expertise: 0 = normal prompts; 1 = suppresses About to regen and Really want to turn the \current layer off prompts;2 = suppresses Block already defined and A drawing with this name already exists prompts for Block command;3= suppresses An item with this name already exists prompt for the Linetype command; 4 = suppresses An item with this name already exists prompt for the UCS/Save and Vports/Save options; 5 = suppresses An item with this name already exists prompt for Dim/ Save and Dim/Override commands.
Explmode	Explode	With drawing	Controls whether blocks inserted with different x, y and z values are exploded: 0 = blocks are not exploded; 1 = blocks are exploded.
Extmax	Zoom	With drawing	Displays upper-right corner coordinate of Extents view.
Extmin	Zoom	With drawing	Displays lower-left corner coordinate of Extents view.
Extnames	Options	With drawing	Controls the length of names for named objects in AutoCAD: 0 = limit names to 31 characters; 1 = allow up to 255 characters.
Facetratio	Shade, Hide	NA	Controls aspects ratio of faceting of curved 3D surfaces. Value is 0 or 1; 1 increases the density of the mesh.
Facetres	Shade, Hide	With drawing	Controls appearance of smooth, curved, 3D surfaces when shaded or hidden. Value can be between 0.01 and 10. The higher the number, the more faceted (and smoother) the curved surface and the longer the time needed for shade and hidden – line removal.

Variable Name	*Associated Command*	*Where Saved*	*Use*
Fielddisplay*	Field	Registry	Controls the gray, non – plotting background of fields: 0 = no background; 1 = background.
Fieldeval**	Field	With drawing	Controls the way fields are updated. Values can be added for combined features: 0 = no update; 1 = on open; 2 = on save; 4 = on plot; 8 = on use of Transmit; 16 = on regen.
Filedia	Dialog box	Registry	Specifies whether a file dialog box is used by default: 0 = don't use unless requested with a ~ (a tilde); 1 = use whenever possible.
Filletrad	Fillet	With drawing	Controls fillet radius.
Fillmode	FILL	With drawing	Controls fill status: 0 = off; 1 = on.
Fontalt	Open, Dxfin, other File – Import options	Registry	Lets you specify an alternative font when AutoCAD cannot find the font associated with a file. If no font is specified for Fontalt, AutoCAD displays a warning message and a dialog box in which you manually select a font.
Fontmap		Registry	Similar to Fontalt, but lets you designate a set of font substitutions through a font-mapint file. Example line from mapping file: romans: C:\WINDOWS\FONTS\Times.ttf. This substitutes Romans font with Times TrueType font. Font-mapping file can be any name, with extension .fmp.
Frontz	Dview	With drawing	Controls front clipping plane for current viewport; use with Viewmode system variable.
Fullopen	Open	NA	Displays whether the current drawing is fully or partially opened.
Fullplotpath**	Plot Spool	Registry	Controls whether the full plot path is sent to the plot spooler; 0 = send only the drawing filename; 1 = send full path.
Gfang	Bhatch	With drawing	Controls the gradient fill angle.
Gfclr1	Bhatch	With drawing	Controls the gradient fill color #1. Values can be index colors from 1 to 255 or RGB colors specified as RGB: CCC,CCC,CCC;CCC is a value from 1 to 255.
Gfclr2	Bhatch	With drawing	Controls the gradient fill color #2. See Gfclr1 for settings
Gfclrlum	Bhatch	With drawing	In single - color gradients, controls the shade of hte noncolor end of the gradient.

Variable Name	*Associated Command*	*Where Saved*	*Use*
Gfclrstate	Bhatch	With drawing	Controls whether gradient is one or two color. 0 = two color; 1 = single color.
Gfname	Bhatch	With drawing	Controls the gradient pattern. Values are from 1 to 7. See gradient tab of Hatch And Gradient dialog box for the patterns. Patterns are numbered from top to bottom, left to right starting with 1.
Gfshift	Bhatch	Not saved	Controls whether gradient fills are centered: 0 = centered; 1 = shifted up and to the left.
Gridmode	Grid	With drawing	Controls grid: 0 = off; 1 = on.
Gridunit	Grid	With drawing	Controls grid spacing.
Gripblock	Grips	Registry	Controls display of grips in blocks: 0 = show insertion point grip only; 1 = show grips of all objects in block.
Gripcolor	Grips	Registry	Controls color of unselected grips. Choices are integers from 1 to 255; default is 5.
Griphot	Grips	Registry	Controls color of hot grips. Choices are integers from 1 to 255; default is 1.
Griphover	Grips	Registry	Controls the color of a grip when the cursor hovers over the grip. Values are index colors from 1 to 255; default is 3.
Gripobjlimit	Grips	Registry	Controls the display of grips based on the number of objects selected. If set to 1, grips are not displayed if more than one object is selected. Range is from 1 to 32,767; default is 100.
Grips	Grips	Registry	Controls use of grips: 0 = grips disabled; 1 = grips enabled (default).
Gripsize	Grips	Registry	Controls grip size (in pixels), from 1 to 255; default is 3.
Griptips	Grips	Registry	Controls the display of grip tips for custom objects: 0 = no grip tips, 1 = grip tips; default is 1.
Handles	NA	With drawing	Displays status of object handles: 0 = off; 1 = on.
Hideprecision	Hide, Shade, HIsettings	NA	Controls the Hide/Shade precision accuracy: 0 = single precision; 1 = double precision.
Highlight	Select	NA	Controls whether objects are highlighted when selected: 0 = none; 1 = highlighting.
Hpang	Hatch	NA	Sets default hatch pattern angle.

Variable Name	*Associated Command*	*Where Saved*	*Use*
Hpassoc	Hatch	Registry	Controls associative property of hatch pattern: 0 = not associative; 1 = associative; default = 1.
Hpbound	Hatch	Registry	Controls type of object created by Hatch and Boundary commands: 0 = region; 1 = polyline.
Hpdouble	Hatch	NA	Sets default hatch doubligh for user-defined hatch pattern: 0 = no doubling; 1 = doubling at 90 degree.
Hpdraworder*	Hatch	NA	Controls the draw order of hatches: 0 = no draw order; 1 = send hatch to back of all objects; 2 = bring to front of all objects; 3 = behind boundary; 4 = in front of boundary.
Hpgaptol*	Hatch	Registry	Controls the gap tolerance for hatch boundaries. values are from 0 to 5000. When the value is 0, the hatch requires a completely closed outline with no gaps.Hpinherit** Hatch With drawing Controls how the hatch origin is determined when using the Inherit Properties option; 0 = hporigin; 1 = origin of source hatch pattern.
Hpname	Hatch	NA	Sets default hatch pattern name; use a period (.) to set to no default.
Hpobjwarning**	Hatch	Registry	Sets the maximum number of boundary objects that are selected before a warning is issued.
Hporitin**	Hatch	Drawing	Controls the hatch origin point.
Hporiginmode**	Hatch	Registry	Controls how the hatch origin is determined; 0 = Hporigin; 1 = 5 = use extent of rectangular boundary of hatch; 1 is the bottom left, 2 is bottom right, 3 is top left, 4 is top right and 5 is center.
Hpscale	Hatch	Registry NA	Sets default scale for hatch patterns; cannot be 0.
Hpseparate**	Hatch		Controls whether separate hatch objects are created when separate areas are selected. 0 = single hatch object; 1 = one hatch object per boundary area.
Hpspace	Hatch	NA	Sets default line spacing for user-defined hatch pattern; cannot be 0.
Hyperlinkbase	Hyperlink	With drawing	Sets the base location for hyperlink addresses. If belt blank, the drawing path is used.
Imagehlt	Options	Registry	Controls highlighting of raster imates: 0 = frame only; 1 = entire image.

Variable Name	*Associated Command*	*Where Saved*	*Use*
Indexctl	NA	With drawing	Controls whether Layer and Spatial indexes are created and saved in drawings: 0 = no index; 1 = Layer index; 2 = Spatial index; 3 = both.
Intlocation	Browser	Registry	Sres the Internet location used by the Browser comand.
Inputhistorymode**	Input History	Registry	Controls the display of the input history; 0 = none; 1 = displayed in command line or Dynamic Input through Up and Down arrow keys; 2 = through shortcut menu for all commands; 4 = through shortcut menu for current command; 8 = display markers for recent input of points.
Insbase	Base	With drawing	Controls insertion base point of current drawing.
Insname	Insert	NA	Sets default block of filename for Insert command; enter a period (.) to set to no default.
Insunits	Units	With drawing	Sets the units value for the Design Center insert: 0 = initless; 1 = inches; 2 = feet; 3 = miles; 4 = millimeters; 5 = crentimeters; 6 = meters; 7 = kilometers; 8 = microinches; 9 = mils; 10 = yards; 11 = angstorms; 12 = nanometers; 13 = microns; 14 = decimeters; 15 = decameters; 16 =hactometers; 17 = gigameters; 18 = astronomical units; 19 = light years; 20 = parsecs.
Insunitsdefsource	Units	Registry	Sets the default source units. Values are the same as for Insunits.
Insunitsdeftarget	Units	Registry	Sets the default target units. Values are the same as for Insunits.
Intelligentupdate**	Display	Registry	Controls the display refresh rate in frames per second. Affects scripts and AutoLISP graphic routines.
Intersectioncolor	Hide	With drawing	Controls the color of the intersection of 3D surfaces when Hide or Hidden Shademode are used. the interesting surfaces are used. The interesting surfaces are displayed by "intersection plylines." 0 = Byblock; 256 = Bylayer; 257 = entity color; 1 through 255 = AutoCAD index color. Intersection color is value only when the Intersectiondispaly system variable is set to 1; default = 257.
Intersectiondisplay	Hide	With drawing	Controls whether the intersection of 3D surfaces are dispalyed with a line, called an intersection polyline: 0 = no intersection polyline; 1 = display itersetion polyline; default = 0.

Variable Name	*Associated Command*	*Where Saved*	*Use*
Isavebak	Save	Registry	Controls the creation of BAK ffiles: 0 = no BAK file created; 1 = BAK file created.
Isavepercent	Save	Registry	Determines whether to do a full or an intcremental save based on the amount of wasted space tolerated in a drawing file: (0 - 100).
Isolines	Curved solids	With drawing	Specifies the number lines on a solid's surface to help visualize its shape.
Lastangle	Arc	NA	Displays ending angle for last arc drawn.
Lastpoint	NA	NA	Sets or displays coordinate normally referenced by @
Lastprompt	NA	NA	Saves last string echoed to the command line.
Layerfilteralert**	Layer	Registry	Deletes layer filters when they become too numerous. 0 = off; 1 = delete when layer Manager is opened without warning; 2 = display a warning and offer options when drawing is opened.
Layoutregenctl	Options	Registry	Controls the way regens occur when switching between Model/Layout tabs: 0 = regen at each tab selection; 1 = no regen for Model tab or last used Layout tab; 2 = after initial opening of tabs, no regens while switching between tabs.
Lenslength	Dview	With drawing	Displays focal length of lens used for perspective display.
Limcheck	Limits	With drawing	Controls limit checking: 0 = no checking; 1 = checking.
Limmax	Limits	With drawing	Controls coordinate of drawing's upper-right limit.
Limmin	Limits	With drawing	Controls coordinate of drawing's lower-left limit.
Lispinit	Load	Registry	Preserves AutoLISP-defined functions and variables beyond current drawing session: 0 = AutoLISP variables preserved; 1 = AutoLISP functions valid for current session only.
Local	NA	NA	Displays ISO language code used by your version of AutoCAD.
Localrootprefix	Options	Registry	Displays file path for support and custom files. If entered at the command prompt through AutoLISP [as in (getvar "localrootprefix")], the full path is displayed.
Locui**	AutoCAD Window	Registry	Locks location and size of toolbars and other windows. 0 = not locked; 1 = docked toolbars are locked; 2 =

Variable Name	*Associated Command*	*Where Saved*	*Use*
			docked windows are locked; 4 = floating toolbars are locked; 8 = floating windows are locked.
Logfilemode	NA	Registry	Determines whether log file is recorded: 0 = log file off; 1 = log file on.
Logfilename	NA	Registry	Specifies name/path of log file
Logfilepath	Options	Registry	Sets the path for the log file.
Loginname	NA	NA	Displays user's login name
Ltscale	Ltscale	With drawing	Controls the global linetype scale fator.
Lunits	Units	With drawing	Control unit styles: 1 = seientific; 2 = decimal; 3 = engineering; 4 = architectural; 5 = fractional
Intersectiondisplay	Hide	With drawing	Controls whether the intersection of 3D surfaces are displayed with a line, called an intersection polyline: 0 = no intersection polyline; 1 = display intersection polyline; default = 0.
Isavebak	Save	Registry	Controls the creation of BAK files: 0 = BAK file created; 1 = BAK file created
Isavepercent	Save	Registry	Determines whether to do a full or an incremental save based on the amount of wasted space tolerated in a drawing file: (0 – 10).
Isolines	Curved solids	With drawing	Specifies the number of lines on a solid's surface to help visualize its shape.
Lastangl	Arc	NA	Displays ending angle for last arc drawn.
Lastpoint	NA	NA	Sets or displays coordinate normally referenced by @.
Lastprompt	NA	NA	Saves last string echoed to the command line.
Layerfilteralert**	Layer	Registry	Deletes layer filters when they become too numerous. 0 = off; 1 = delete when Layer Manager is opened without warning; 2 = display a warning and offer options when Layer Manager is opened; 3 = display a warning and offer options when drawing is opened.
Layoutregentcl	Options	Registry	Controls they way regens occur when switching between Model/Layout tabs: 0 = regen at each tab selection; 1 = no regen for model tab or last used Layout tab; 2 = after initial opening of tabs, no regens while switching between tabs.
Lenslength	Divew	With drawing	Displays focal length of lens used for perspective display.

Variable Name	Associated Command	Where Saved	Use
Limcheck	Limits	With drawing	Controls limit checking: 0 = no checking; 1 = checking.
Limmax	Limits	With drawing	Controls coordinate of drawing's upper-right limit
Limmin	Limits	With drawing	Controls coordinate of drawing's lower-left limit.
Lispinit	Load	Registry	Preserves AutoLISP defined functions and variables beyond current drawing session: 0 = AutoLISP variables preserved; 1 = AutoLISP functions valid for current session only.
Locale	NA	NA	Displays ISO language code used by your version of AutoCAD.
Localrootprefix	Options	Registry	Displays file path for support and custom files. If entered at the Command prompt through AutoLISP [as in (getvar "localrootprefix")], the full path is displayed.
Luprec	Units	With drawing	Controls unit accuracy by decimal place or size of denominator.
Lwdefault	Lineweight	Registry	Sets the default lineweight. Values are specified in millimeters (25 = 0.25mm).
Lwdisplay	Lineweight	With drawing	Determines whether lineweights are displayed: 0 =not displayed; 1 = displayed.
Lwscale	Lineweight	With drawing	Determines whether lineweights are scaled with plotter scale settings or are absolute values: 0 =scaled with plot; 1 = absolute value.
Lwunits	Lineweight	Registry	Sets the display of lineweight units: 0 =inches; 1 = millimeters.
Maxactvp	Viewports, Vports	With drawing	Controls maximum number of viewports to regenerate at one time.
Maxobjmem	NA	NA	Specifies the amount of virtual memory that can be used before AutoCAD starts paging a drawing out to disk.
Maxsort	NA	Registry	Controls maximum number of items to be sorted when a command displays a list.
Mbuttonpan	Options	Registry	Determines the behavior of the pointing device's wheel or third button: 0 =behavior determined by menu file; 1 = click-and-drag panning.
Measureinit	Open	Registry	Sets the unit style for new drawings. Determines whether metric or Imperial template file should be used. Determines which default linetype and hatch pattern files should be used: 0 =Imperial; 1 = metric.

Variable Name	*Associated Command*	*Where Saved*	*Use*
Measurement	Bhatch, Linetype	With drawing	Sets drawing units as Imperial or metric: 0 =Imperial; 1 = metric.
Menuctl	NA	Registry	Controls whether side menu changes in response to a command name entered from the keyboard: 0 = no response; 1 = menu response.
Menuecho	NA	NA	Controls messages and Command prompt display from commands embedded in menu: 0 =display all messages; 1 = suppress menu item name; 2 = suppress Command prompts; 4 = disable toggle of menu echo; 8 = debugging aid for Diesel expressions.
Menuname	Menu	With drawing	Displays name of current menu file.
Mirrtext	Mirror	With drawing	Controls mirroring of text: 0 =disabled; 1 = enabled.
Modemacro	NA	NA	Controls display of user-defined text in status line.
Msolescale*	OLE	With drawing	Sets the scale of OLE objects that include text. If the value is 0, scale is set by the Dimscale value.
Mtexted	Mtext	Registry	Controls name of program used for editing Mtext objects.
Mtextfixed	Mtext	Registry	Controls how text in the Multiline Text Editor is displayed: 0 =AutoCAD attempts to display the text as closely as possible to the actual size and appearance in the drawing; 1 = text is displayed in a fixed size and location based on the last size and position.
Mtjigstring	Mtext	Registry	Controls the display of the sample text that is displayed when placing the text boundary for Mtext. The default is abc, but can be set to anything up to 10 characters. Enter a period (.) for no display.
MMydocuments-prefix *	Options	Registry	Displays the full path for the current user's My Documents folder.
Nfwstate*	New Feature Workshop	Registry	Turns the New Feature Workshop on or off: 0 = off and not displayed in Help; 1 = on and displayed in Help.
Nodename	NA	Registry	Controls the filename extension for AutoCAD temporary files.
Nomutt	NA	NA	Suppresses message display (muttering): 0 = normal display; 1 = suppress messages.
Obscuredcolor	Hide, Shade, Hlsettings	With drawing	Controls the color of obscured lines in hidden or shaded views: 0 and 256 = object color; 1

Variable Name	Associated Command	Where Saved	Use
			through 255 = AutoCAD color index. This feature is disabled when Obscuredltype is set to 0.
Obscuredltype	Hide, Shade, Hlsettings	With drawing	Controls the linetype of obscured lines in hidden or shaded 3D views: 0 = obscured lines are not displayed (default); 1 = solid line; 2 through 11 = various dashed and dotted lines.
Offsetdist	Offset	NA	Controls default offset distance.
Offsetgaptype	Offset	Registry	Controls how polyline line segments are joined when offset; 0 = extend line segments to join ends; 1 = keep line segments the same length and join endpoints with arcs; 2 = keep line segments the same length and join endpoints with lines.
Oleframe*	OLE	With drawing	Controls the display of the frame around OLE objects: 0 =no frame; 1 = frame displays and plots; 2 = frame displays but does not plot.
Olehide	NA	Registry	Controls display of OLE objects.
Olequality	Options	Registry	Controls the quality of OLE objects: 0 = line art; 1 = text; 2 = graphics; 3 = photograph; 4 = high-quality photograph.
Olestartup	Options	With drawing	Determines whether the source application of an OLE object is loaded when the OLE object is plotted: 0 = no load; 1 = load.
Opmstate (read-only)	Properties	Registry	Displays the current state of the Properties palette: 0 =not open; 1 = open.
Orthomode	F8, Ortho	With Drawing	Controls Ortho mode: 0 = off; 1 = on.
Osmode	Osnap	With drawing	Sets current default Osnap mode: 0 = none; 1 = endpoint; 2 = midpoint; 4 = center; 8 = node; 16 = quadrant; 32 = intersection; 64 = insert; 128 = perpendicular; 256 = nearest; 512 = quick. If more than one mode is required, enter the sum of those modes.
Osnapcoord	Osnap	Registry	Controls whether coordinates entered at the command line use running object snaps: 0 = Running Osnaps settings override; 1 = keyboard entry overrides; 2 = keyboard entry overrides, except in scripts.
Osnaphatch*	Hatch, Osnap	With drawing	Controls how osnap behaves with hatches: 0 = osnap ignores hatches; 1 = osnap does not ignore hatches.

Variable Name	*Associated Command*	*Where Saved*	*Use*
Osnapnodelegacy**	Mtext, Osnap	With drawing	Controls how osnaps behave with Mtext bounding box grips: 0 = osnap recognizes Mtext grips; 1 = osnap ignores Mtext grips.
Osnapz**	Osnaps	NA	Controls the Z value of osnap selections; 0 = use Z of selected point; 1 = use current Z of current UCS.
Paletteopaque*	Toolpalettes	Registry	Controls the transparency of palettes that offer transparency. Availability of transparency depends on the operating system and whether hardware accelerators are in use. 0 = turned on by user; 1 = off by user; 2 = on by user but unavailable; 3 = off by user but unavailable.
Paperupdate	Plot	Registry	Controls the display of paper size warning message: 0 = display warning if the paper size in a Paper Space layout is not supported by the specified plotter; 1 = adjust paper size to conform with plotter configuration.
Pdmode	Ddptype	With drawing	Controls type of symbol used as a point during Point command.
Pdsize	Point	With drawing	Controls size of symbol set by Pdmode.
Peditaccept	Pedit	Registry	Controls the display of the Object selected is not a polyline prompt when selecting nonpolyline object with the Pedit command: 0 = prompt; 1 = no prompt.
Pellipse	Ellipse	With drawing	Controls type of object created with Ellipse command: 0 = true NURBS ellipse; 1 = polyline representation of ellipse.
Perimeter	Area, List	NA	Displays last perimeter value derived from Area and List commands.
Pfacevmax	Pface	NA	Displays maximum number of vertices per face. (PFaces are 3D surfaces designed for use by third-party software producers and are not designed for end-users.)
Pickadd	Select	Registry	Determines how items are added to a selection set: 0 ; only most recently selected item(s) become selection set (to accumulate objects in a selection set, hold down Shift while selecting); 1 ; selected objects accumulate in a selection set as you select them (hold down Shift while selecting items to remove those items from the selection set).

Variable Name	Associated Command	Where Saved	Use
Pickauto	Select	Registry	Controls automatic window at Select objects: prompt: 0 = window is disabled; 1 = window is enabled.
Pickbox	Select	Registry	Controls size of object-selection pickbox (in pixels).
Pickdrag	Select	Registry	Controls how selection windows are used: 0 = click each comer of the window; 1 = Shift+ click and hold on first comerand then drag and release for the second corner.
Pickfirst	Select	Registry	Controls whether you can pick object(s) before you select a command: 0 = disabled; 1 = enabled.
Pickstyle	Group, Hatch	With drawing	Controls whether groups and/ or associative hatches are selectable: 0 = neither are selectable; 1 = groups only; 2 = associative hatches only; 3 = both groups and associative hatches.
Platform	NA	NA	Identifies the version of AutoCAD being used.
Plinegen	Pline, Pedit	With drawing	Controls how polylines generate linetypes around vertices: 0 = linetype pattern begins and ends at vertices; 1 = linetype patterns ignore vertices and begin and end at polyline beginning and ending.
Plinetype	Pline	Registry	Controls whether AutoCAD creates optimized 20 polylines and/or converts existing polylines to optimized polylines: 0 = polylines in existing drawings are not converted and new polylines are not optimized; 1 = polylines in existing drawings are not converted, but new polylines are optimized; 2 = polylines in existing drawings are not convertedand new polylines are optimized.
Plinewid	Pline	With drawing	Controls default polyline width.
Plotoffset	Plot	Registry	Controls whether the plot offset is relative to the edge of paper or printable area: 0 = printable area; 1 = edge of paper.
Plotrotmode	Plot	Registry	Controls orientation of your plotter output.
Plquiet	NA	Registry	Controls the display of dialog boxes for batch plotting and scripts: 0 = display dialog boxes; 1 = do not display dialog boxes.
Polaraddang	Dsettings	Registry	Sets the value of the Additional Angle setting of the Polar Snap tab of the Drafting Settings dialog box. You can enter as many as 10 angles of 25 characters each separated by semicolons.

Variable Name	*Associated Command*	*Where Saved*	*Use*
Polarang	Dsettings	Registry	Sets the Increment Angle setting of the Polar Snap tab of the Drafting Settings dialog box.
Polardist	Dsettings	Registry	Sets the Polar Snap distance.
Polarmode	Dsettings, Options	With drawing	Sets Polar and Object Snap Tracking settings. The value is the sum of four pairs of codes as follows. Polar angle measurement: 0 = absolute; 1 = relative. Object Snap Tracking: 0 = orthogonal only; 2 = use Polar Tracking settings. Use additional Polar Tracking angles: 0 = no ; 4 = yes. Acquire Object Snap Tracking points (Options dialog box): 0 = automatically; 8 = Shift to acquire.
Polysides	Polygon	NA	Controls the default number of sides for a polygon.
Popups	NA	NA	Displays whether the current system supports drop-down menus: 0 = no; 1 = yes.
Previeweffect**	Object Selection	Registry	Controls the visual effect of hovering over objects (preview selection). 0 = dashed lines; 1 = thickened lines; 2 = dashed and thickened lines
Previewfilter**	Object Selection	Registry	Controls the type of object that is highlighted when the cursor hovers over it; 0 = no exclusion; 1 = excluded locked layers; 2 = excludes x refs; 4 = excludes tables; 8 = excludes mtext; 16 = excludes hatches; 32 = excludes groups.
Product	AutoCAD	NA	Displays product name.
Projectname	Options	Registry	Assigns a project name to a drawing. The project name can be associated with one or more folders.
Projmode	Trim, Extend	Registry	Controls how the Trim and Extend commands affect objects in 3D: 0 = objects must be coplanar; 1 = trims/ extends based on a plane parallel to the current UCS; 2 = trims/ extends based on a plane parallel to the current view plane.
Proxygraphics	NA	With drawing	Controls whether images of proxy objects are stored in a drawing: 0 = images not stored; 1 = images saved.
Proxynotice	NA	Registry	Issues a warning to the user when a proxy object is created, i.e., when user opens a drawing containing custom objects created using an application that is not loaded: 0 = no warning; 1 = warning displayed.
Proxyshow	NA	Registry	Specifies whether and how proxy objects are displayed:

Variable Name	Associated Command	Where Saved	Use
			0 = no display; 1 = graphic display of all proxy objects; 2 = only bounding box shown.
Proxywebsearch	Options	Registry	Controls whether AutoCAD searches the Web for Object Enablers: 0 = prevent search; 1 = search Web for Object Enablers if there is an Internet connection; 2 = specify the number of attempts to find Object Enablers.
Psltscale	Pspace	With drawing	Controls Paper Space linetype scaling.
Psquality	Psin	Registry	Controls how images are generated in AutoCAD with the Psin command. Value is an integer: 0 = only bounding box is drawn; >0 = number of pixels per AutoCAD drawing unit; <0 = outline with no fillsand absolute value of setting determines pixels per drawing units.
Pstylemode	Options	Drawing	Determines the type of plot styles used in new or imported drawings: 0 = color plot styles; 1 = named plot styles.
Pstylepolicy	NA	Registry	Determines whether object colors are associated with its plot style: 0 = no association; 1 = association.
Psvpscale	Vports	NA	Sets the default view scale factor for new viewports in paper space. The value is a ratio between the model space scale and the paper space scale. Values must be positive real: 0 = scale to fit.
Pucsbase	Ucsman	With drawing	Stores the name of a UCS that you want to use as the base for orthographic UCS settings. Paper Space only.
Qcstate**	QuickCalc	NA	Indicates whether QuickCalc is active; 0 = not active; 1 = active.
Qtextmode	Qtext	With drawing	Controls the quick text mode: 0 = off; 1 = on.
Rasterdpi*	Plot	Registry	Controls the conversion from millimeters or inches to dots per inch when working with dimensionless output such as the raster plotter option. Acceptable value range is 100 to 32.767dpi.
Rasterpreview	Save	Registry	Controls whether raster preview images are saved with the drawing and sets the format type: 0 = no preview image created; 1 = BMP preview image.
Recoverymode**	Drawing Recovery	Registry	Controls how the Drawing Recovery feature behaves after a system failure; 0 = recovery information is not

Variable Name	*Associated Command*	*Where Saved*	*Use*
			recorded; 1 = recovery information is recorded but the recovery window is not displayed; 2 = recovery information is recorded and recovery window is displayed at startup.
Refeditname	Refedit	NA	Displays the current reference-editing state of a drawing.
Regenmode	Regenauto	With drawing	Controls Regenauto mode: 0 = off; 1 = on.
Re-init	Reinit	NA	Reinitializes 1/0 ports, digitizers, display, plotterand ACAD .PG P: 1 = digitizer port; 2 = plotter port; 4 = digitizer; 8 = display; 16 = POP file reload.
Rememberfolders	NA	Registry	Controls the default folder displayed in file dialog boxes. 0 = use Start In Path specification from AutoCAD icon; 1 = last used path.
Reporterror	NA	Registry	Controls whether errors can be reported to Autodesk as they occur; 0 = no error report; 1 = error report message is displayed with option to send error report to Autodesk.
Roamablerootprefix	NA	Registry	Displays the full path name for customizable support files for roaming profiles.
Rtdisplay	Rtpan, Rtzoom	Registry	Controls display of raster images during real. time Pan and Zoom.
Pucsbase	Ucsman	With drawing	Stores the name of a UCS that you want to use as the base for orthographic UCS settings. Paper Space only.
Savefile	Autosave	Registry	Displays filename that is autosaved.
Savefilepath	NA	Registry	Specifies the folder location for automatic save files.
Savename	Save	NA	Displays user filename under which file is saved.
Savetime	Autosave	Registry	Controls time interval between automatic saves, in minutes: 0 = disable automatic save.
Screenboxes	Menu	Registry	Displays number of slots or boxes available in side menu.
Screenmode	NA	Registry	Displays current display mode: 0 = text; 1 = graphics; 2 = dual screen.
Screensize	NA	NA	Displays current viewport size in pixels.
SDI	NA	Registry	Determines whether AutoCAD allows multiple documents or limits user to single document editing: 0 = multiple documents; 1 = single document; 2 =

Variable Name	Associated Command	Where Saved	Use
			single documents because loaded third-party application does not support multiple documents (read-only); 3 = same as 2 with SDI set to 1 by user.
Selectionarea**	Object Selection	Registry	Controls whether a shaded area is displayed with selection windows, including crossing and polygon windows. 0 = off; 1 = on
Selectionareaopacity**	Object Selection	Registry	Controls the opacity of the shaded area of a selection window. Range is from o to 100 with low values being more transparent.
Selectionpreview**	Object Selection	Registry	Controls object's selection preview when the cursor hovers over an object; 0 = off; 1 = preview when no command is active; 2 = preview when Command prompts to select object.
Shadedge	Shade	With drawing	Controls how drawing is shaded: 0 = faces shaded, no edge highlighting; 1 = faces shaded, edge highlighting; 2 = faces not fined, edges in object color; 3 = faces in object color, edges in background color.
Shadedif	Shade	With drawing	Sets difference between diffuse reflective and ambient light. Value represents percentage of diffuse reflective light.
Shortcutmenu	Right-click	Registry	Controls the Default, Editand Command mode shortcut menus. For multiple options, use the sum of option values: 0 = restore R14 behavior; 1 = Default mode shortcut enabled; 2 = Edit mode shortcut enabled; 4 = Command mode shortcut enabled; 8 = Command mode shortcut enabled only when options are shown in command line.
Showlayerusage**	Layer	Registry	Controls the display of the Layer Usage icon in the Layer Properties Manager. This icon indicates whether a layer is in use; 0 =off; l=On.
Shpname	Shape	NA	Controls default shape name.
Sigwam	Sigvalidate	Registry	Controls whether the digital signature waming message is displayed when a file containing a digital signature is opened: 0 =warning appears only if a digital signature is present and is not valid; 1 = warning appears if digital signature is present.
Sketchinc	Sketch	With drawing	Controls sketch record increment.

Variable Name	*Associated Command*	*Where Saved*	*Use*
Skpoly	Sketch	With drawing	Controls whether the Sketch command uses regular lines or polylines: 0 = line; 1 = polyline.
Snapang	Snap	With drawing	Controls snap and grid angle.
Snapbase	Snap	With drawing	Controls snap, gridand hatch pattern origin.
Snapisopair	Snap	With drawing	Controls isometric plane: 0 =left; 1 = top; 2 = right.
Snapmode	F9, Snap	With drawing	Controls snap toggle: 0 =off; 1 = on.
Snapstyl	Snap	With drawing	Controls snap style: 0 =standard; 1 = isometric.
Snaptype	Snap	Registry	Controls whether polar or grid snap is current: 0 =grid snap; 1 = polar snap.
Snapunit	Snap	With drawing	Controls snap spacing given in x and y values.
Solidcheck	Solidedit	NA	Controls solid validation for 3D solids in current session: 0 =off; 1 = on.
Sortents	NA	Registry	Controls whether objects are sorted based on their order in database: 0 =disabled; 1 = sort for object selection; 2 = sort for object snap; 4 = sort for redraws; 8 = sort for Mslide; 16 = sort for regen; 32 = sort for plot; 64 = sort for Psout.
Splframe		With drawing	Controls display of spline vertices, defining mesh of a surface-fit meshand display of "invisible" edges of 3D Faces: 0 =no display of spline vertices, display only fit surface of a smoothed 3D Meshand no display of "invisible" edges of 3D Face; 1 = spline vertices are displayed, only defining mesh of a smoothed 3D Mesh is displayed, "invisible" edges of 3D Face are displayed.
Splinesegs	Pline, Pedit	With drawing	Controls number of line segments used for each spline patch.
Splinetype	Pline, Pedit	With drawing	Controls type of spline curve generated by Pedit spline: 5 = quadratic B-spline; 6 = cubic B-spline.
Ssfound*	Sheet Set Manager	NA	Displays the location of a sheet set after a search for sheet sets.
Sslocate*	Sheet Set Manager	User settings	Controls whether sheet sets are automatically located and opened when a drawing associated with a sheet set is opened: 0 =do not open sheet set; 1 = open sheet set. Ssmautoopen must also be set to 1.
Ssmautoopen*	Sheet Set Manager	User settings	Controls whether the Sheet Set Manager

Variable Name	Associated Command	Where Saved	Use
			is opened when a drawing associated with a sheet set is opened: 0 =do not open sheet set; 1 = open sheet set. Sslocate must also be set to 1.
Ssmstate*	Sheet Set Manager	NA	Shows whether the Sheet Set Manager is open: 0 =not open; 1 = open.
Standardsviolations	Standards	Registry	Controls whether user is notified when a file contains standards violations: 0 =no notification; 1 = notification when standards violations occur; 2 = notification via icon in status bar.
Startup	New/Qnew	Registry	Controls whether the Startup dialog box appears when AutoCAD is first opened. Also controls whether the Create New Drawing dialog box appears when a new document is created by choosing File - New. 0 =displays Select Template dialog box for File - New, opens AutoCAD with no Startup dialog box; 1 = displays Create New Drawing or Startup dialog box.
Surftabl		With drawing	Controls number of facets in the m direction of meshes.
Surftab2	ERevsurf, Edgesurf	With drawing	Controls number of facets in the n direction of meshes.
Surftype	Pedit	With drawing	Controls type ofsurfacentting used by the Pedit command's Smooth option: 5 = quadratic B-spline surface; 6 = cubic B- spline surface; 8 = Bezier surface.
Surfu	3Dmesh	With drawing	Controls surface density in the m direction.
Surfv	3Dmesh	With drawing	Controls surface density in the n direction.
Syscodepage	NA	NA	Displays system code page specified in Acad.xmx.
Tableindicator**	Tables	User settings	Controls the display of row numbers and column letters when editing table entries; 0 = off; 1 = on.
Tabmode	Tablet	NA	Controls tablet mode: 0 =off; 1 = on.
Targe	Dview	With drawing	Displays coordinate of perspective target point.
Tbcustomize*	Customize	Registry	Controls whether toolbars can be customized: 0 = customize disabled for toolbars; 1 = customize enabled.
Tdcreate	Time	With drawing	Displays time and date of file creation in Julian format.
Tdindwg	Time	With drawing	Displays total editing time in days and decimal days.
Tducreate	Time	With drawing	Displays the time and date that a drawing was created.

Variable Name	*Associated Command*	*Where Saved*	*Use*
Tdupdat	Time	With drawing	Displays time and date of last file update in Julian format.
Tdusrtimer	Time	With drawing	Displays user-controlled elapsed time in days and decimal days.
Tduupdate	Time	With drawing	Displays the time and date of last update or save.
Tempoverrides**	Drafting Settings	Registry	Controls the drafting settings' temporary override key function; 0 =off; 1 = on.
Tempprefix	NA	NA	Displays location for temporary files.
Texteval	NA	NA	Controls interpretation of text input: 0 =AutoCAD takes all text input literally; 1 = AutoCAD interprets "(" and "!" as part of an AutoLISP expression, unless either the Text or Dtext command is active.
Textfill	Text	Registry	Controls display of Bitstream, TrueTypeand PostScript Type 1 fonts: 0 =outlines; 1 = filled.
Textqlty	Text	With drawing	Controls resolution of Bitstream, TrueTypeand PostScript Type 1 fonts: values from 1.0 to 100.0. The lower the value, the lower the output resolution. Higher resolutions improve font quality but decrease display and plot speeds.
Textsize	Text, Dtext	With drawing	Controls default text height.
Textstyle	Text, Dtext	With drawing	Controls default text style.
Thickness	Elev	With drawing	Controls default 3D thickness of object being drawn.
Tilemode	Mspace, Pspace	With drawing	Controls Paper Space and viewport access: 0 =Paper Space and viewport objects enabled; 1 = strictly Model Space.
Tooltips	Icon tool palettes	Registry	Controls display of tool tips: 0 =off; 1 = on.
Tpstate	Toolpalettes	NA	Tells whether the Tool Palettes window is active. 0 =not active, 1 = active
Tracewid	Trace	With drawing	Controls trace width.
Trackpath	Options	Registry	Controls the display of the tracking vector: 0 = full screen; 1 = only between alignment points; 2 = no Polar Tracking vector; 3 = no Polar or Object Snap Tracking vector.
Trayicons	NA	Registry	Controls the display of the AutoCAD tray icons in the lower-right comer of the AutoCAD window: 0; no display; 1; display.

Variable Name	Associated Command	Where Saved	Use
Traynotify	NA	Registry	Controls the display of service notifications in the AutoCAD tray: 0 =no notification; 1 = notification.
Traytimeout	NA	Registry	Controls how long tray notifications are displayed. Values from 0 to 10 are valid.
Treedepth	Treestat	With drawing	Controls depth of tree-structured Spatial index affecting speed of AutoCAD database search. First two digits are for Model Space nodes; second two digits are for Paper Space nodes. Use positive integers for 3D drawings and negative integers for 2D drawings. Negative values can improve speed Of2D operation.
Treemax	Regen, Treedepth	Registry	Limits memory use during regens by limiting maximum number of nodes in Spatial index created with the Treedepth command.
Trimmode	Chamfer, Fillet	Registry	Controls whether lines are trimmed during the Chamfer and Fillet commands: 0 =no trim; 1 = trim (as with pre-Release-13 versions of AutoCAD).
Tspacefac	Mtext	NA	Sets multiline text line spacing as a percentage of text height.Valid range is between 0.25 and 4.0.
Tspacetype	Mtext	NA	Controls multiline text line spacing quality: 1 = use tallest letter for basis of line spacing; 2 = use text height specification as basis of line spacing.
Tstackalign	Mtext	With drawing	Controls text alignment for stacked text: 0 =bottom; 1 = center; 2 = top.
Tstacksize	Mtext	With drawing	Sets stacked fraction text height as percent of normal text height. Valid range is 1 to 127.
Ucsaxisang	Ucs	Registry	Sets the default rotation angle for X, Y or Z axis option of UCS command.
Ucsbase	Ucs	With drawing	Sets the name of the UCS used as a basis for orthographic UCS options.
Ucsfollow	Ucs	With drawing	Controls whether AutoCAD automatically changes to Plan view of UCS while in Model Space: 0 =UCS change does not affect view; 1 = UCS change causes view to change with UCS.
Ucsicon	Ucsicon	With drawing	Controls UCS icon: 1 = on; 2 = UCS icon appears at origin.
Ucsname	Ucs	With drawing	Displays name of current UCS.

Variable Name	*Associated Command*	*Where Saved*	*Use*
Ucsorg	Ucs	With drawing	Displays origin coordinate for current UCS relative to World Coordinate System.
Ucsortho	Ucs	With drawing	Controls whether the UCS follows orthographic views: 0 =does not follow; 1 = follows orthographic view.
Ucsview	View	With drawing	Controls whether a UCS is saved with a named view: 0 =not saved; 1 = saved.
Ucsvp	Vport	With drawing	Controls whether the UCS follows the orientation of a new viewport: 0 =current UCS; 1 = follow orientation of viewport view.
Ucsxdir	Ucs	With drawing	Displays x direction of current UCS relative to World Coordinate System.
Ucsydir	Ucs	With drawing	Displays y direction of current UCS relative to World Coordinate System.
Undoctl	Undo	NA	Displays current state of Undo feature: 1 = Undo enabled; 2 = only one command can be undone; 4 = Autogroup mode enabled; 8 = group is currently active.
Undomarks	Undo	NA	Displays number of marks placed by Undo command
Unitmode	Units	With drawing	Controls how AutoCAD displays fractional, foot-and-inch and surveyor's angles; 0 = industry standard; 1 = AutoCAD input format.
Updatethumbnail*	Sheet Set Manager	With drawing	Controls the display of the Sheet Set Manager preview thumbnail: 0 =no updates; 1 = update model view thumbnail; 2 = update sheet view thumbnail; 4 = update sheet thumbnail; 8 = update thumbnails when sheets are edited or created; 16 = update when drawing is saved.
Useri1-Useri5	Autolisp, Diesel	With drawing	Indicates five user variables capable of storing integer values.
Userr1-Userr5	Autolisp, Diesel	With drawing	Indicates five user variables capable of storing real values.
Users1-Users5	Autolisp, Diesel	With drawing	Indicates five user variables capable of storing string values.
Viewctr	NA	With drawing	Displays center of current view in coordinates.
Viewdir	Dview	With drawing	Displays camera-viewing direction in coordinates.
Viewmode	Dview	With drawing	Displays view-related settings for current viewport: 1 = perspective on; 2 = front clipping on; 4 = back clipping

Variable Name	Associated Command	Where Saved	Use
			on; 8 = UCS follow on; 16 = front clip not at a point directly in front of the viewer's eye.
Viewsize	NA	With drawing	Displays height of current view in drawing units.
Viewtwist	Dview	With drawing	Displays twist angle for current viewport.
Visretain	Layer	With drawing	Controls whether layer setting for X refs is retained: 0 =current layer color, linetypeand visibility settings retained when drawing is closed; 1 = layer settings of X ref drawing always renewed when file is opened.
UVpmaximizedstate*	Vpmax	NA	Indicates whether a viewport is maximized: 0 = not maximized; 1 = maximized.
Vsmax	NA	With drawing	Displays coordinates of upper-right corner of virtual screen.
Vsmin	NA	With drawing	Displays coordinates of lower-left comer of virtual screen.
Vtduration**	Zoom and Pan	Registry	Controls the duration of Zoom or pan transitions. Range is from 0 to 5000 milliseconds.
Vtenable**	Zoom and Pan	Registry	Controls the View Transition feature for pan/ zoom, rotationand scripts. Values from 0 to 7 are valid. 0 = off; 1 = pan/zoom only; 2 = rotation only; 3 = pan/ zoom and rotation; 4 = scripts only; 5 pan/ zoom and scripts; 6 = rotation and scripts; 7 = all.
Vtfps**	Zoom and Pan	Registry	Controls the view transition smoothness in frames per second, from 1 to 30.
Whiparc	NA	Registry	Controls the tessellation of circles and arcs: 0 =tessellated; 1 = not tessellated.
Windowareacolor**	Window Selection	Registry	Controls the color for window selection with a range of 1 to 255. Selectionarea must be on.
Wmfbkgnd	Export, Cut	NA	Sets the way backgrounds and borders are generated in exported Windows metafiles: 0 = transparent backgrounds, no borders; 1 = background same as AutoCAD background, border is reverse color of background.
Wmfforeground	Options	NA	Controls the appearance of Windows metafile export from AutoCAD: 0 =ensures foreground color is darker than background; 1 = ensures background color is darker than foreground. This feature takes effect only if Wmfgkgmd is set to 0.

Variable Name	*Associated Command*	*Where Saved*	*Use*
Worlducs	UCS	NA	Displays status of WCS: 0 =current UCS is not WCS; 1 = current UCS is WCS.
Worldview	Dview,Vpoint	With drawing	Controls whether the Dview and V point commands operate relative to UCS or WCS: 0 =current UCS is used; 1 = WCS is used.
Writestat	NA	NA	Displays the current drawing's read/write status: 0 =read-only; 1 = drawing can be written to.
Wscurrent**	Workspace	NA	Indicates the current workspace name.
Xclipframe	Xref	With drawing	Controls visibility of X ref clipping boundaries: o : clipping boundary is not visible; 1 : boundary is visible.
Xedit	Options	With drawing	Controls Refedit availability of current drawing: 0 =not available for in-place X ref editing; 1 = available for in-place X ref editing.
Xfadectl	Options	NA	Controls fading intensity in percent value for objects not selected while using Refedit (in- place X ref editing). Valid range is o to 90.
Xloadctl	Xref, Xclip	Registry	Controls X ref demand loading and creation of copies of original X ref: 0 = no demand loading allowed, entire X ref drawing is loaded; 1 = demand loading allowed and original X ref file is kept open; 2 = demand loading allowed, using a copy of X ref file stored in AutoCAD temp files folder.
Xloadpath	Xref	Registry	Creates a path for storing temporary copies of demand-loaded X ref files.
Xrefctl	Xref	Registry	Controls whether Xreflog files are written: 0 =no log files; 1 = log files written.
Xrefnotify	Xref	Registry	Determines whether notification appears in the AutoCAD tray for updated or missing X refs: 0 = no notification; 1 = notification that current drawing contains X refs (if X refs are missing, a yellow alert icon is displayed); 2 = same as 1 notification and includes a balloon message.
Xreftype*	Time	Registry	Controls whether the default X ref type is Attach or Overlay: 0 = Attach; 1 = Overlay.
Zoomfactor	Mouse wheel	Registry	Controls the amount of Zoom applied to a drawing when the moUSe wheel is turned. Valid range is between 3 and 100. Default is 10.

Setting Dimension Variables

This section provides further information about the dimension variables. For starters, Table C.2 lists each variable, its default statusand a brief description of what it does. You can get a similar listing by entering –Dimstyle enter at the Command prompt and then typing ST to select the Status option. Alternatively, you can use the AutoCAD Help system. This section also discusses a few system variables that do not appear in the Dimension Style dialog box.

General Dimension Controls

Dimension Variable	*Default Setting*	*Description*
Dimaso	On	Turns partial associative dimension on and off (obsolete).
Dimassoc	2	Turns true associative dimension on and off: 0 = exploded dimension; 1 = pre-2002 associative dimensions; 2 = fully associative dimensions.
Dimsho	On	Updates dimensions dynamically while dragging.
Dimstyle	Standard	Indicates name of current dimension style.
Dimtmove	0	Sets the way dimension text behaves when moved: 0 =move dimension line with text; 1 = add leader and move text freely; 2 = no leader and move text freely.
Dimupt	Off	Controls user positioning of text during dimension input: 0 = automatic text positioning; 1 = user-defined text positioning allowed.

Scale

Dimasz	0.18 (approx. 3/16")	Indicates arrow size.
Dimcen	0.09 (approx. 3/32")	Indicates center mark size.
Dimlfac	1.0000	Multiplies measured distance by a specified scale factor.
Dimscale	1.0000	Indicates overall scale factor of dimensions.
Dtmtsz	0"	Indicates tick size.
Dimtxt	0.18 (approx. 3/16")	Indicates text height.

Offsets

Dimdle	0"	Indicates the amount the dimension line extends beyond the extension line.
Dimdli	0.38 (approx. 3/8")	Indicates the dimension line offset for continuation or base.
Dimexe	0.18 (approx. 3/16")	Indicates the amount the extension line extends beyond the dimension line.
Dimexo	0.0625 or 1/16"	Indicates extension line origin offset.

Tolerances

Dimalttz	0	Controls zero suppression of tolerance values: 0 = leave out zero feet and inches; 1 = include zero feet and inches; 2 = include zero feet; 3 = include zero inches; 4 = suppress leading zeros in decimal dimensions; 8 = suppress leading zeros in decimal dimensions.
Dimdec	4	Sets decimal place for primary tolerance values.
Dimlim	Off	When on, shows dimension limits.
Dimtdec	4	Sets decimal place for tolerance values.
Dimtm	0"	Indicates minus tolerance.
Dimtol	Off	When on, shows dimension tolerances.
Dimtolj	1	Controls vertical location of tolerance values relative to nominal dimension: 0 = bottom; 1 = middle; 2 = top.
Dimtp	0"	Indicates plus tolerance.
Dimtzin	0	Controls zero suppression in tolerance values: 0 = leave out zero feet and inches; 1 = include zero feet and inches; 2 c include zero feet; 3 = include zero inches; 4 = suppress leading zeros in decimal dimensions; 8 = suppress leading zeros in decimal dimensions; 12 = suppress leading and trailing zeros in decimal dimensions.

Rounding

Dimazin	0	Controls zero suppression for angular dimensions: 0 = display all zeros; 1 = suppress leading zeros; 2 suppress trailing zeros; 3 = suppress all zeros.
Dimrnd	0"	Indicates a rounding value.
Dimzin	0	Controls zero suppression dimension text: 0 = leave out zero feet and inches; 1 = include zero feet and inches; 2 = include zero feet; 3 = include zero inches; 4 = suppress leading zeros in decimal dimensions; 8 = suppress leading zeros in decimal dimensions; 12 = suppress leading and trailing zeros in decimal dimensions.

Dimension Arrow & Text Control

Dimadec	-1	Controls the number of decimal places shown for angular dimension text: 1 = uses the value set by Dmdec dimension variable; 0-8 = specifies the actual number of decimal places to be shown.
Dimatfit	3	Controls the way text and arrows are placed when there is not enough room to fit both within extension lines: 0 = place both outside extension lines; 1 = move arrows first; 2 =

		move text first; 3 = move either text or arrows, whichever is best fit.
Dmaunit	0	Controls angle format for angular dimensions; settings are the same as for Aunits system variable.
Dimblk	""	Predefined or user-defined arrow block name. You can enter a user-defined block name or one of the following: _DOT, _DOTSMALL, _DOTBLANK, _ORIGIN, _ORIGIN2, _OPEN, _OPEN9O, _OPEN30, _CLOSED, _SMALL, _OBLIQUE, _BOXFILLED, _BOXBLANK, _CLOSEDBLANK, _DATUMFILLED, _DATUMBLANK, _INTEGRAL, ARCHTICK.
Dimblkl	""	Predefined or user-defined arrow block name for first end of dimension line used with Dimsah. See Dimblk for valid options.
Dimblk2	""	Predefined or user-defined arrow block name for second end of dimension line used with Dimsah. See Dimblk for valid options.
Dimdsep	.(period)	User-defined separator for decimals when dimension units are set to decimal.
Dimfit	3	Controls location of text and arrows for extension lines, if space is not available for both: 0; text and arrows placed outside; 1; text has priority, arrows are placed outside extension lines; 2 = arrows have priority; 3 = AutoCAD chooses between text and arrows, based on best fit; 4 = a leader is drawn from dimension line to dimension text when space for text not available; 5 = no leader.
Dimfrac	0	Sets the fraction format for architectural and fractional formats: 0 =vertical; 1 = diagonal; 2 = not stacked.
Dimgap	1/16" or 0.09"	Controls distance between dimension text and dimension line.
Dimjust	0	Controls horizontal dimension text position: 0 = centered between extension lines; 1 = next to first extension line; 2 = next to second extension line; 3 = above and aligned with the first extension line; 4 = above and aligned with second extension line.
Dimldrblk	0	Sets the arrow type for leaders: 0 = standard closed filled arrow; (period) = no arrow. See Dimblk for valid options.
Dimlunit	Off	Sets unit style for all dimension types except angular: 1 = Scientific; 2 = Decimal; 3 = Engineering; 4 = Architectural; 5 = Fractional; 6 = Windows Desktop.

Dimsah	Off	Allows use of two different arrowheads on a dimension line. See Dimblkl and Dimblk2.
Dimtfac	1.0"	Controls scale factor for dimension tolerance text.
Dimtad	0	When on, places text above the dimension line.
Dimtih	On	When on, text inside extensions is horizontal.
Dimtix	Off	Forces text between extensions.
Dimtoh	On	When on, text outside extensions is horizontal.
Dimtvp	0	Controls text's vertical position based on numeric value.
Dimtxsty	Standard	Controls text style for dimension text.
Dimunit	2	Controls unit style for all dimension style groups except angular Settings are same as for Lunit system variable.

Dimension & Extension Line Control

Dimsd1	Off	When on, suppresses the first dimension line.
Dimsd2	Off	When on, suppresses the second dimension line.
Dimse1	Off	When on, suppresses the first extension line.
Dimse2	Off	When on, suppresses the second extension line.
Dimsoxd	Off	When on, suppresses dimension lines outside extension lines.
Dimtofl	Off	When on, forces a dimension line between extension lines.

Alternate Dimension Options

Dimalt	Off	When on, alternate units selected are shown.
Dimaltd	2	Indicates alternate unit decimal places.
Dimaltf	25-4000	Indicates alternate unit scale factor.
Dimalttd	2	Indicates alternate unit tolerance decimal places.
Dimaltu	2	Indicates alternate unit style. See Lunits system variable for values.
Dimaltz	0	Controls the suppression of zeros for alternate dimension values.
Dimapost	""	Adds suffix to alternmension text.
Dimpost	""	Adds suffix to dimension text.

Colors and Lineweights

imclrd	0 or By Block	Controls color of dimension lines and arrows.
Dimclre	0 or By Block	Controls color of dimension extension lines.
Dimclrt	0 or By Block	Controls color of dimension text.
Dimlwd	ByBlock	Controls the lineweight of dimension lines. Valid values are ByLayer, ByBlock or integer representing 100th millimeter.
Dimlwe	ByBlock	Controls the lineweight of extension lines. Valid values are ByLayer, ByBllock or integer representing 100th millimeter.

Questions 8

Answer the Following Questions

Chapter 1 — Introduction to AutoCAD 2006

1. Describe the various commands on different menus of AutoCAD 2006.

Chapter 2 — Customizing AutoCAD 2006

1. How would you customize different menus?
2. How would you customize toolbars?
3. How would you customize tool palette?
4. Describe the various options which you can set.
5. How would you set the limits?
6. Describe the process of setting Units.
7. Describe the process of setting Grid and Snap.
8. Describe the process of setting Screen Colours.

Chapter 3 — Creating Drawings using Wizards in AutoCAD 2006

1. Describe the process of creating drawing using Wizard.
2. What are templates and how are they used?

Chapter 4 — Using Tools of AutoCAD 2006

1. Describe the working of following tools:

Line Tool	Circle Tool
Arc Tool	Polyline Tool
Multiline Tool	Polygon Tool
Rectangle Tool	Spline Tool

Ellipse Tool
Point Tool
Erase Tool
Copy Object Tool
Mirror Tool
Offset Tool
ArrayTool
Move Tool
Rotate Tool
Scale Tool
Stretch Tool
Lengthen Tool
Trim Tool
Extend Tool
Break Tool
Chamfer Tool
Fillet Tool

2. Describe the various surface tools of AutoCAD 2006.
3. Describe the various rendering tools of AutoCAD 2006.
4. Describe the method of adding materials to the drawing.
5. Describe the method of setting the background images in AutoCAD 2006.
6. Describe the method of setting scenes in AutoCAD 2006.
7. Describe the various Zoom tools.

Chapter 5 — Using Drafting Tools in AutoCAD 2006

1. How would you set up the work area in AutoCAD 2006?
2. How would you set up the Drawing Limits?
3. What do you understand by Scale Factors?
4. How are modes used?
5. How would you plan and layout a drawing?
6. How would you set up the Polar Tracking Angle?